MW00795849

Nation as Grand Narrative

Rochester Studies in African History and the Diaspora

Toyin Falola, Series Editor

The Jacob and Frances Sanger Mossiker Chair in the
Humanities and University Distinguished Teaching Professor

University of Texas at Austin

Recent Titles

Blood on the Tides: "The Ozidi Saga" and Oral Epic Narratology
Isidore Okpewho

The Politics of Chieftaincy: Authority and Property in Colonial Ghana, 1920–1950
Naaborko Sackeyfio-Lenoch

Nigerian Pentecostalism
Nimi Wariboko

*Building a Peaceful Nation: Julius Nyerere and the
Establishment of Sovereignty in Tanzania, 1960–1964*
Paul Bjerk

*Kingdoms and Chiefdoms of Southeastern Africa:
Oral Traditions and History, 1400–1830*
Elizabeth A. Eldredge

Manners Make a Nation: Racial Etiquette in Southern Rhodesia, 1910–1963
Allison K. Shutt

*Guardians of the Tradition:
Historians and Historical Writing in Ethiopia and Eritrea*
James De Lorenzi

Ira Aldridge: The Last Years, 1855–1867
Bernth Lindfors

Population, Tradition, and Environmental Control in Colonial Kenya
Martin S. Shanguhyia

Humor, Silence, and Civil Society in Nigeria
Ebenezer Obadare

A complete list of titles in the Rochester Studies in African History and
the Diaspora series may be found on our website, www.urpress.com.

Nation as Grand Narrative

The Nigerian Press and the
Politics of Meaning

Wale Adebanwi

UNIVERSITY OF ROCHESTER PRESS

First published 2016

University of Rochester Press
668 Mt. Hope Avenue, Rochester, NY 14620, USA
www.urpress.com
and Boydell & Brewer Limited
PO Box 9, Woodbridge, Suffolk IP12 3DF, UK
www.boydellandbrewer.com

ISBN-13: 978-1-58046-555-7
ISSN: 1092-5228

Library of Congress Cataloging-in-Publication Data

Names: Adebanwi, Wale, author.
Title: Nation as grand narrative : the Nigerian press and the politics of
    meaning / Wale Adebanwi.
Other titles: Rochester studies in African history and the diaspora ; v. 70.
    1092-5228
Description: Rochester, NY : University of Rochester Press, 2016. | Series:
    Rochester studies in African history and the diaspora, ISSN 1092-5228 ;
    v. 70 | Includes bibliographical references and index.
Identifiers: LCCN 2015049856 | ISBN 9781580465557 (hardcover : alk.
    paper)
Subjects: LCSH: Press and politics—Nigeria. | Government and the
    press—Nigeria. | Nigeria—Politics and government—Press coverage. |
    Nationalism—Press coverage—Nigeria.
Classification: LCC PN5499.N5 A334 2016 | DDC 079.669—dc23 LC
    record available at http://lccn.loc.gov/2015049856

A catalogue record for this title is available from the British Library.

This publication is printed on acid-free paper.
Printed in the United States of America.

For my son, Demilade Jayden,
and in fond memory of my dad, Paul Ojuade,
whose sermons about the afterlife first alerted me to the
Borgesian imagination of paradise as "a kind of library."

Contents

List of Illustrations ix

Acknowledgments xi

Part 1: Contextual and Conceptual Perspectives

1 Nation as Grand Narrative 3

2 Interpretive Theory, Narrative, and the
Politics of Meaning 30

Part 2: Colonial Agency and Counterhegemonic Struggles

3 In Search of a Grand Narrative: The Press and the
Ethno-Regional Struggle for Political Independence 47

4 Hegemony and Ethno-Spatial Politics: "Nationalizing"
the Capital City in the Late-Colonial Era 83

Part 3: Inclusion, Exclusion, and Democratic Contestations

5 Paper Soldiers: Narratives of Nationhood and
Federalism in Pre–Civil War Nigeria 107

6 Representing the Nation: Electoral Crisis and the
Collapse of the Third Republic 146

7 The "Fought" Republic: The Press, Ethno-Religious
Conflicts, and Democratic Ethos 190

**Part 4: Domination and Resistance in
Majority-Minority Relations**

8 Narratives, Territoriality, and Majority-Minority
Ethnic Violence 227

9   Narratives, Oil, and the Spatial Politics of
     Marginal Identities   258

     Conclusion: Beyond Grand Narratives   281

     Notes   293

     Bibliography   335

     Index   363

Illustrations

Figures

6.1 Cover of *TheNEWS*, July 20, 1998, with the
photograph of Moshood Abiola   148

8.1 *TheNEWS* cover story (February 22, 1993) on the
Kataf-Hausa crisis   251

9.1 *Newswatch* cover story on the minorities in
oil-producing areas of Nigeria   260

Acknowledgments

Given this book's long gestation, my debt of gratitude is extensive and heartfelt. After years of working as a journalist, I was interested in studying Nigeria through the stories that are told about the country in the press. The intellectual nurturing of Adigun Agbaje in the political science department at Ibadan, complemented by scholarly pestering, fired my imagination and enabled me to write the earliest drafts of this book.

In the years of adversity when I wavered between singularity and solidarity, so many friends and colleagues made life more livable, offering kind words, kind countenances, and much more. I thank Muyiwa Adekeye, Kunle Ajibade, Dele Momodu, Olu Daramola, Femi Ojudu, Odia Ofeimun, Bayo Onanuga, Folu Olamiti, Nosa Osaigbovo, Demola Oyinlola, Chris Uroh (late), Waziri Adio, Laolu and Olawunmi Akande, Remi Oyeyemi, Festus Adedayo, Adeolu Akande, Rotimi Akande, Adebisi Bola Agbaje, Segun and Oyinlola Olatunji, Chiedu Ezeanah, Fati Asibelua (née Ezeanah), Adegboyega and Karen Somide, Abu Satar Ahmed, Muyiwa Apara, Dejo Olatoye, Agboola Sanni, Wale Ademowo, and Yemi Olowolabi. *Oba* Dokun Abolarin, the affable Orangun of Oke-Ila, has been wonderful over the years. I thank him. I acknowledge the kindness of the master satirist Olatunji Dare, who read parts of the manuscript.

"Our hands," writes Derek Walcott in "White Egrets," "like ants, keep building libraries, storing leaves." Ebenezer Obadare reminds me constantly of Walcott's assertion, particularly the poet's more solemn reminder that "our books are tombstones." Whenever I have serious doubts about the order, the other, and the "under" of things, Ebenezer displays the most unaffected proficiency for clearing conceptual and practical puzzles. For his friendship and endless intellectual dialogues, I owe him much more than he should be willing to collect!

In seeking a mooring place in my scholarly journey, particularly in the early years when this work took shape, the following persons helped in different ways: Eghosa Osaghae, Olufemi Vaughan,

Iris Marion Young (late), Ebere Onwudiwe, Niyi Osundare, Willy Fawole, Kunle Amuwo (late), Rotimi Suberu, Maria Grosz-Ngate, Elzbieta Matynia, Mahua Sakar, Abu Bakkar Bah, Paul Nkwi, Alex Gboyega, Fred Onyeoziri, Yahaya Hashim, Judith Walker, Chris Ikporukpo, O. B. C. Nwolise, Nikolai Genov, and Ina Breuer. At Davis, Moradewun Adejunmobi has been very supportive. For important perspectives on Nigeria and other personal and social interventions over the years, I thank the late Uncle Bola Ige, Ambassador Ibrahim Agboola Gambari, Chief Olu Onagoruwa, and Chief Harry Akande.

I recognize the institutions that supported my research, including the Program in Federal and Ethnic Studies (PEFS), University of Ibadan, the Transregional Center for Democratic Studies (TCDS), New School for Social Research, New York, and the International Social Science Council (ISSC) and UNESCO for the International Summer School Comparative Research in the Social Sciences, Sofia, Bulgaria, from which I benefitted immensely. The librarians in the following libraries deserve my immense gratitude: in Nigeria—Kenneth Dike Library, University of Ibadan, National Archives, Ibadan, Nigerian Tribune library, Daily Times library, TheNEWS library, TELL library, Arewa House Archives, Kaduna; in the United Kingdom—Cambridge University Library, Jerwood Library, Trinity Hall, Cambridge; and in the United States—The New School Library, New York, and Peter J. Shields Library, University of California–Davis.

I thank the anonymous reviewers for their very useful suggestions. At the University of Rochester Press, I worked with an earnest but cordial editor, Sonia Kane. She has my gratitude. I thank her assistant, Julia Cook, too. The support and kindness of the series editor, Toyin Falola, made this book possible.

Earlier versions of chapters 4 and 8 were published as "The City, Hegemony and Ethno-Spatial Politics: The Press and the Struggle for Lagos in Colonial Nigeria," *Nationalism and Ethnic Politics* 9 (2004): 25–51; and "Territoriality and the Discourse of Ethnic Groups' Clashes," *Nationalism and Ethnic Politics* 13 (2007): 213–43, respectively. I thank Taylor & Francis (http://www.tandfonline.com/) for their kind permission to reproduce both here. I thank Sage Publications for their kind permission to reproduce chapter 9, an earlier version of which was published as "The Press and the Politics of Marginal Voices: Narratives of the Experiences of the Ogoni of Nigeria," *Media, Culture & Society* 26, no. 6 (2004): 763–83. I thank Palgrave

Macmillan for permission to reproduce chapter 7, an earlier version of which appeared as "The Press and the Democratic Question: Narrating Ethno-Religious Identities and Conflicts in Nigeria," in *State, Economy, and Society in Post-military Nigeria*, edited by Said Adejumobi (New York: Palgrave Macmillan, 2011), 23–48.

I owe no greater debt than to my wife, Temitope. She and our daughter, Liberty, and son, D. J., constitute the sunshine of my life. This book is dedicated to my late father, Paul Ojuade Adebanwi, and my son. What Jorge Luis Borges said of his father is most appropriate for mine: "My father's library was the capital event in my life. The truth is that I have never left it." It is a cardinal wish of my life that Demilade will be able to echo that too—someday.

Wale Adebanwi, Davis, August 2015.

Part 1

Contextual and Conceptual Perspectives

1

Nation as Grand Narrative

In 1953 a political crisis threatened to break up colonial Nigeria and terminate the possibility of common political independence for the country. This crisis was partly instigated, elaborately reported, and, ultimately, profoundly shaped by newspaper narratives. Anthony Enahoro, the anticolonial activist and leading member of the Action Group, one of the major political parties in late colonial Nigeria, whose motion at the federal parliament provoked this crisis, had been a journalist most of his adult life. Enahoro became the editor of the *Southern Nigerian Defender* at age twenty-one in 1944. He was later the editor of *Comet,* associate editor of *West African Pilot,* and editor in chief of *Morning Star.* Indeed, Enahoro left his position at the *Morning Star* to become a member of the federal parliament in late colonial Nigeria. Therefore he was a product of the struggle by the radical—or what was called "nationalist"—press to end colonial rule in Nigeria.

On March 31, 1953, the Honorable Anthony Enahoro submitted a motion in the House of Representatives for a resolution "as [a] primary political objective" that Nigeria achieve self-government in 1956.[1] Enahoro added that any other proposal short of full political independence for Nigeria "has ceased to be a progressive view, because Nigerian nationalism has moved forward from that position." In a response that showed the fault lines of Nigerian nationalism in the late colonial era—and since then—Sir Ahmadu Bello, leader of the Northern People's Congress (NPC), introduced a dilatory motion substituting the phrasing "as soon as practicable" for the year "1956" proposed by Enahoro.[2] A "bitter and tempestuous" debate ensued, as Bello insisted that Enahoro's motion "merely serve[s] to destroy inter-regional unity which the [Richards] Constitution is building."[3]

As if to remind Enahoro and the other proindependence leaders of the southern political parties of the artificiality of the "Nigerian nationalism" that Enahoro was glorifying, Bello added that "sixty years ago, there was no Nigeria but merely a collection of communities very different in outlook and mode of life."[4] An independent, united Nigeria almost ended with this debate and the consequent recriminations. The northern region, which made up more than half of the land space of colonial Nigeria, threatened to leave the union. In February 1950, the *Nigerian Tribune*, the voice of Nigeria's western region, had editorialized that British colonialism, which forced together the different ethnic groups and regions constituting Nigeria, had "failed to fulfil the mission for which it set out," the "UNITY of the North, East and West they [had] promised us. They have achieved, to our horror, DISUNITY."[5] About a year later, a northern newspaper, *Nigerian Citizen*, editorialized that the new telephone line linking Kaduna, the capital of the northern region, with Lagos and Enugu, the major cities of the two southern regions, signified the "gaining [of] momentum towards bringing the people of Nigeria closer together," thus urging Nigerians to "sink regional prejudices as much as possible for a wider patriotism" because "*Nigeria must come first.*"[6] Thus *Citizen* dismissed the "Southern polemics"[7] expressed by the *Tribune* as demonstrative of the "extremism" of the southern newspapers and of southerners in general. In response, *West African Pilot* also derided *Citizen* (which was used as a metonym for the northerner) as a "very patient imperialist pet," while expressing hope that in the end "the Northerner will soon come to realise that we must grow homogeneously as one nation."[8] The *Pilot* elaborated that "from the days of Lord [Frederick] Lugard [the first governor-general of amalgamated Nigeria], every effort has been made to keep the North and South poles apart in all matters, social, political, educational and otherwise. . . . [But] thanks to NCNC and Action Group heroes, militant nationalism has come into the North and will stay until freedom is won."[9]

The *Pilot* added that the "alliance of imperialism and feudalism," that is, the colonial government and the northern region, "will henceforth be fought" by "the holy crusaders of the nationalist army as they enter the first phase of psychological warfare."[10] However, when the *Tribune* and *Pilot*'s patron (southern) political parties, the Action Group and the National Council of Nigeria and the Cameroons (NCNC; later, National Council of Nigerian

Citizens), respectively, disagreed on the political architecture best suited to ensure that Nigeria become a "nation," the *Pilot* urged the NCNC to "relentlessly continue to pilot the nation along [the] . . . road to the beautiful sunny meadows where an independent Nigeria will thrive."[11]

As the narrative of this crisis regarding the date of Nigeria's independence in the newspaper press shows, narratives of what constitutes a nation and how to understand and relate to the idea and practices of such a "nation" in the context of the challenges of nation-building in multiethnic states are central to understanding such states. As the following chapters illustrate, despite the constant divisive narratives that present, defend, and contest the diverse and sometimes contradictory interests of Nigeria's many ethno-regional, ethnic nationalist, or ethno-religious groups, there is constant gesturing toward a nation of aspiration, a Nigerian grand nation that, it is assumed, surpasses or subsumes the many nations forced to live together within the Nigerian federation. It is this grand nation that this book captures as a narrative in itself, a grand narrative. A grand narrative constitutes, or in fact attempts to establish, an overarching interpretive lens through which past, present, and future events and identities in society and state are encountered and analyzed. A grand narrative compels or obliges antagonistic relations and identities as well as competing accounts of events over the *longue durée* to be reconciled or else denied or expunged.[12] A *Daily Times* editorial spoke to this in the context of the ethno-regional acrimonies preceding independence, when it declared: "Nigeria must be a nation. If present day leaders fail to make that possible, a new generation will rise to break the foundations of tribal hate to build a great nation"[13]

This book argues that in the practical amalgamation of the two protectorates and the symbolic "invention" of Nigeria, including the contention over these events, the narratives in the press are not tangential but critical. And by critical I mean that the narratives are fundamental or indispensable and even potentially dangerous. Therefore, in conceiving of the possibility of Nigeria as a polity, particularly as a viable and durable polity, we must examine one of the most important ideological apparatuses for ensuring or contesting this viability and durability. Understanding Nigeria involves understanding the print media, which represent the most critical and powerful contending forces in the polity seeking to dominate—or fight against the domination of—the political, economic, and social orders that compose and constitute Nigeria. Any account of what Nigeria is (notionally as well as practically) has been (the experience in time) or ought to or might be (nation as aspiration) remains inadequate without examining the narratives in the press. As Phillip L. Hammack and Andrew Pelecki have argued, "our political existence is fundamentally storied," thus narratives constitute a principal way by which people come to terms with "what it means to inhabit a particular political entity."[14]

Most political scientists writing on African states in general, and Nigeria in particular, have focused on interests, institutions, and political formations while paying little attention to, or totally ignoring, narratives. In so doing, their accounts not only lose "the color, the passion and the drama of real politics" but they also miss "the best clues about why people act as they do," because narratives "are particularly central for the core problem of politics"—that is, the problem of collective identity, which constitutes the basis for collective action.[15]

Although the narratives in the Nigerian press do not represent the totality of what is, has been, or might be, they constitute cardinal perspectives in accounting for the political formation that is called Nigeria and the struggle for collective identity. Therefore, at the vortex of the century-old political struggle that articulates and acknowledges the challenging diversities of colonial and postcolonial Nigeria—as it wrestles with the opportunities and possibilities for unity and cohesion—are the newspaper narratives that reflect, construct, deconstruct, and reconstruct the struggle as well as the diversities, opportunities, and possibilities of single or multiple nationhoods in Nigeria.

How does the press construct, deconstruct, and reconstruct the idea of the "grand nation" and "national unity" in a typical multinational, postcolonial state? How do the competing narratives of the multiple nations within the grand nation clash and contend with one another? How is meaning mobilized to sustain or contain the relations of power and domination within the grand narrative? How are different narratives constructed and elaborated in the struggles and tensions over single nationhood? What implications do these narratives have for relations among the ethnic nationalities (constructed as nations) within contemporary postcolonial polities?

In attempting to answer the foregoing questions, this book contributes to the growing body of literature on the intersection of the media and the nation or nationalism or nation-building in general, and the printed news media in Africa specifically. There is a noticeable paucity of monographs on the print media in Africa, especially those that address the role of the print media in society in the *longue durée* of African politics. Beyond this, the book analyzes the interface of the nation and the media in Africa's most populous country by engaging in comparison across time. It also raises important conceptual and practical questions in terms of how the media-nation interface manifests in specific political and social configurations in a typical postcolonial state, such as between space and ethnicity, minority and majority relations, democracy and democratization, and the politics of ethnicity and religion.[16]

Indeed, understanding the media-nation interface is critical to the analysis of the crisis of nationhood in postcolonial states, particularly their African variants. Even though two and a half decades ago the leading media scholar Phillip Schlesinger called for a reassessment of the relationship between media and nationhood given the existing "gratuitous assumptions about the nation-state, national culture, and national identities,"[17] only five years ago, despite the studies published since Schlesinger's call, Alex Law could still declare that "there is a paucity of studies of the nation/media problematic."[18]

Ernest Renan has famously described the nation as a "daily plebiscite."[19] Against this backdrop, Benedict Anderson argues that early print media created "an imagined community among a specific assemblage of fellow-readers."[20] In anticipating, convening, and constituting a "national audience," a newspaper, to quote Volosinov, engages "in [an] ideological colloquy of large scale: it responds to something, objects to something, affirms something, anticipates possible responses and objections, seeks support and so on."[21] Volosinov's insight is important in that it alerts us to the fact that the nation and the media are not always mutually constitutive.[22] This book demonstrates the tensions that exist at the heart of the commonality and singularity that banal nationalism assumes, as expressed through the print media.[23] Thus meaning can be mobilized in the print media not only in the service of the ideology of commonality and the singularity of nationalist aspirations within a postcolonial context; meaning can also be mobilized to challenge the idea and practices of commonality and singularity while presenting opposing or contrary commonalities or singularities along ethno-nationalist or even religious lines. *Nation as Grand Narrative* argues that narratives are central to the process of establishing and challenging the assumptions and practices of commonality and the singularity of national solidarity within multinational states in Africa. It contends that the way various ethnicities within an emerging nation imagine the nation and the contradictions of such imaginations in postcolonial states are primarily evident in narratives, particularly the narratives that alternatively affirm or challenge the postcolonial nation as a grand narrative. I use a hermeneutical framework to investigate how the interpretation of ideology in the press serves to stimulate critical reflections on the relation of power and domination in a grand narrative, in this case, an idealized and aspirational nation.

The Postcolonial "Nation" and Its Fragments

I suggest that whereas the postcolonial state in Africa is "densely corporeal," the nation in the postcolonial context is "elusively spectral."[24] The spectral elusiveness of the nation and the corporeal density of the state are demonstrated in many contexts in Africa. Thus even though the Nigerian experience possesses its own specificities, it is not peculiar. Most postcolonial states continue to face the problem of the conditions under which the various nations or ethnic nationalities have been forced to live together.[25] Two broad solutions have been expounded within this context. The first sees society as held together by the coercive power of dominant groups that maintain their interest through military force. The other emphasizes the crucial nature of a common value system that binds people in a social contract.[26] In practice, both overlap. As Doornbos argues, questions concerning state power and state capacity vis-à-vis national identity and unity largely define the debate about the nature and role of the postcolonial state.[27] These questions are also central to understanding the options for these troubled polities.[28]

Some scholars argue for deconstructing the concept of "nation" within postcolonial polities, whether as a preexisting community into which one is born or as one built from a plurality of cultures.[29] Degenaar argues that the "use of nationalist terminology is dangerous since it feeds on the myth of a collective personality and creates wrong expectations in the minds of citizens while not preparing them to accept the difficult challenge to create a democratic culture which accommodates individuality and plurality."[30] However, Degenaar's position elides the democratic uses of nationalist terminology in the struggle for plurality, a phenomenon that is not uncommon in Africa.

Before independence, many African nationalists emphasized the artificiality of colonial boundaries with the resultant push for self-determination among disparate ethnic nationalities trapped in colonial boundaries. But after independence, mostly in the 1960s and early 1970s, the emergent ruling elite insisted on the permanence of the colonial map.[31] They adopted the logic of C. J. Fredrick, who shares Rupert Emerson's view that "both nation and state are incomplete when they are not linked."[32] The Jacobin notion of "state-nation" that became prevalent among the ruling elite in postcolonial Africa assumed "that [the] Leviathan (the state) can, and is morally entitled to, forge a national identity out of diverse ethnic groups." Tamarkin adds that this notion "is as deterministic as it is dangerous . . . because it assumed that the end result of the endeavour of the state-nation is bound to be a nation-state."[33] As one of the African leaders in the late colonial and early postcolonial era, Leopold Sedar Senghor captures this sentiment with the argument that "the state is an expression of the nation, it is primarily a means to achieve a nation."[34] Yet the "nations" being forged in Africa are defined, essentially, in their boundaries and character, by the preceding colonial states.[35]

As postcolonial African states grew older, acquiring more capacities, they consolidated their influence within the arbitrary state boundaries and became *sanctified* and *sacralized*; the Organization of African Unity (now called African Union) declared the boundaries "definitive and immutable."[36] However, since independence, it has not been smooth sailing, as the states frequently bumped into discomforting realities produced by multiple crises centered on ethnic and ethno-regional as well as religious-political rivalries and competition.[37] Given the fact that state boundaries did not result from internal or local choices, the resultant problems were to be expected.[38] The fallouts of the crises in the pseudo-nations or the attempts to build nation-states[39] have brought issues of nationalism, nation, and nationhood to the forefront with a force denied them before now in many African states where centrifugal forces continue to challenge the postcolonial entities.[40] There are many examples of such entities throughout Africa.

For instance, in South Africa, the last country liberated on the continent, there is general recognition of the challenge of nation-building set against the backdrop of a history of racial domination and hatred. In acknowledging South Africans as a "deeply divided" people, the 1994 African National Congress (ANC) manifesto states that the challenge was to build "a nation . . . by developing our different cultures, beliefs and languages as a course of common strength."[41] In this context, as Charmaine McEachern posits, "newness emerged as the discourse speaking (in the sense of bringing into being) the nation."[42] Brendan Boyce argues that, given the centrality of "identity," the important question faced in postapartheid South Africa is to "reconcile the issue of identity redefinition . . . given South Africa's unique historical limitations and opportunities."[43] Reflecting on how the antiapartheid struggle determined the fundamental basis of "nation-making's impact on the emergent state,"[44] Ivor Chipkin argues that "in the hands of nationalists, democratic sovereignty refers to the sovereignty of the nation over the state . . . [and in] the name of freedom, therefore, nationalists substitute the goal of a democratic society for that of the nation." Chipkin suggests that situating the genealogy of the South African "nation" in the history of its "struggle for independence" is "potentially banal." He contends that since nationalism is a response to the general "question of the people . . . the substance of a nation must be located in the determinate history of a 'struggle for democracy' in which it was elaborated." In other words, "the postcolonial nation is imagined as a space of freedom in a context of subjection and violence."[45]

This position is illuminating in terms of how it can help to map the contours of the debates about what constitutes a nation in the postcolonial context. The argument that democracy in South Africa is not contingent on the substance of the nation but is central to it, I maintain, emphasizes the aspirational nature of the South African nation, but one that is firmly focused on the present and future possibilities of democratic nationhood founded on freedom. When Chipkin's argument travels around the continent, its essentialization of democracy and freedom holds true but with different inflections on how to constitute and understand democracy and freedom in relation to nation. In many contexts in Africa, the existing postcolonial states are not imagined as spaces of freedom but rather as spaces of domination and unfreedom, whereby subjection and violence are the only conditions by which the states continue to pretend to be nation-states, that pretense constituting a fundamental criterion of survival for the states. Against this backdrop, the "ethnic question," although considered "an anachronistic obstacle to national unity"—in some cases, even by the ethnic brokers themselves—continues to "linger beneath the surface of larger debates," given that it constitutes "a potent symbol of contemporary identity."[46] As evident in the example of Nigeria, the narratives about such a state that hopes for, or pretends to hope for, nation-state status are understandably centered on identities. However, here identity is approached by its promoters as the fundamental condition of freedom in the space of subjection and violence.

It is important to contextualize the historical backdrop to this discussion. When the mass media appeared as significant factors (and actors) in the peculiar history of the postcolonial state, they were seen as "the primary means of bringing together people who spoke different languages, had different value systems, different religious backgrounds, and different cultural histories,"[47] and also, in the African context, as "educating the citizens about their nation,"[48] whereas the existence (or coming to being) of that nation was taken for granted by African nationalists. However, in most cases, postcolonial states have failed to accomplish the task of harmoniously bringing people together. The many and varied attempts to ignore or overcome cultural factors for the sake of political unification have been largely unsuccessful.[49] Fundamental questions of political identity and political community continue to be implicated in the wider framing of the relationship of the media to the political and of ethnicities to the nation.

In modern times, states have struggled to invest in the emotional apparatus of a nation,[50] or what Anderson calls an "imagined community." Anderson argues that the news media—which he calls "print capitalism"—are pivotal to the fabrication of shared national identities.[51] Michael Billig, in his influential work *Banal Nationalism*, alerts us to how nationalism is an "endemic condition" that (particularly in "established nations") can become so routine that we overlook how it is reproduced. Indeed, although the work of nationhood, as Billig shows, remains unfinished (even in "established nations" such as Britain), the unfinished nature of the postcolonial "nation" is more regularly demonstrated and contested in the print media.[52] This is expected given the crucial roles that "print capitalism" plays "in producing nations and shaping national imaginaries."[53]

Genealogy of the Nigerian Narrative

Nigeria is a typical example of the states in Africa that face the challenges of nationhood in the context of divergent identities.[54] The idea of a Nigerian "nation" is said to have emerged in 1914 when Lord Lugard, on behalf of the British Crown, amalgamated the northern and southern protectorates to form a single political unit. Since then, much about Nigeria has been controversial.[55] The period of colonialism empowered certain nations and ethnic or ethno-regional groups and weakened others,[56] reversing or changing in some cases the hegemonic configurations organized around the slave trade and, later, commerce.[57] It also worsened the tension among competing collective identities. However, all the woes of the country cannot be blamed on colonialism, whether it is regarded as episodic or epochal in African history.[58]

Anthony Smith, a leading scholar on ethnonationalism, argues that "given the near-parity and rivalry of the three main ethnic communities, the Hausa-Fulani, the Yoruba and the Ibo, the construction of a Nigerian cultural and political identity was bound to be an arduous task."[59] This arduous task, involving the struggle to forge a nation out of an amalgam of competing nations and the insertion of the press into this struggle, which exacerbated, deepened, responded to, or resolved the crisis of nationhood is reflected in print media narratives.

The Nigerian press has been at the center of the struggle for common nationhood and the hegemonic and counterhegemonic battles of the disparate ethnic nationalities or nations. Interestingly enough, the press predates the political geography and has for many years constituted one of the most crucial sites of competing and clashing narratives on the idea and ideal of the "Nigerian nation." One significant pattern is the attempt to construct the "Nigerian nation" idea as a grand narrative that supersedes or that can impede "lesser" narratives of nations within the grand narrative, as typified by the *Daily Times* quote above.[60] As would be expected, this grand narrative has been contested and continues to be contested.

Meaning is deployed or mobilized in the press, either to establish, nourish, and sustain relations of domination (power),[61] or to counteract, subvert, or deflect the same.

At the end of November 1918, Lord Frederick John Dealtry Lugard, the British soldier and colonial administrator who had supervised the formation of the single colonial state of Nigeria in 1914, retired and sailed back to England. Prior to the formal establishment of British colonialism in what became Nigeria, Lugard commanded the West African Frontier Force, a military contingent deployed by the Royal Niger Company, a British firm, to defend its territorial claims. He later laid the foundation for British rule in what became northern Nigeria, through the force of arms and diplomacy. Lugard initially left Nigeria in 1906 as the high commissioner of the northern protectorate but returned in September 1912 to prepare the ground for the amalgamation of the northern and southern protectorates, after which he was appointed the governor-general of a "united" colony and protectorate of Nigeria on the eve of January 1, 1914.

The decision of the British to amalgamate the two different territories—which included three or four dominant ethnic nationalities (the Hausa-Fulani of the north, the Igbo of the east, and the Yoruba of the west) and about three hundred others—was not made in consultation with the British subjects of either territory.[62] Many were not even aware, or understood the implications, of the amalgamation. Such were the general differences between the two protectorates, in topography and specific ethno-cultural distinctions, that, more than a century later, Nigeria is yet to be truly united. In his scholarly critique of the Lugardian enterprise, I. F. Nicolson concludes that "easily the most remarkable thing about Lugard's 'amalgamation' of Nigeria is that it never really took place."[63] More than two decades before Nicolson, Obafemi Awolowo, one of the political leaders who negotiated Nigeria's independence from the British and was involved for all of his political life in contesting and interrogating the idea of "Nigeria," surmised that Nigeria was "a mere geographical expression."[64] In her foreword to Awolowo's important book, *Path to Nigerian Freedom,* the British historian and Lugard's biographer Margery Perham states that "the day when Nigeria from being a name written on a map by Sir George Goldie and an administrative framework put together by Lord Lugard, becomes a true federation, still more a nation, is still far away."[65]

The African educated elite of the colony of Lagos in the south, who, by the time of the amalgamation, had established a fairly modern and articulate press and a putative modern public sphere, opposed the amalgamation and were, subsequently, critical of Lugard's administration. For instance, the *Standard* had by 1909 convinced its readers about "the history of amalgamations and their disastrous results," and the *Lagos Weekly Record* added in 1913 that Lugard's rule over the soon to be amalgamated territories "is a disappointment to Southern Nigeria."[66] The preamalgamation Lagos press also compared and contrasted the "democratic, industrious and peaceful South" with the "autocratic, hectoring, rough and ready" north, whose "moral darkness" marked the region as the "place of despotism."[67] The print media continues to reflect this condescending and divisive attitude toward the northern region more than a century after it was initially articulated in the Lagos press.

On February 1, 1919, three months after Lugard's rule ended, one of the most critical and vociferous of the emergent newspapers in Lagos, the *Lagos Weekly Record*, described Lugard's administration as "enmeshed in a series of blunders and violent misrule which constituted the indelible stains of his inglorious administration." The paper hoped that Lugard's "legacy . . . will be consigned to the limbo of oblivion where, embedded in the historical strata of British imperial colonization, it will exist as the fossilized remains of an administrative experimental failure." The *Weekly Record* concluded that Lugard himself was "a huge failure," "a hopeless anachronism," and "the victim of exaggerated personality."[68]

Long before the amalgamation and shortly before the formal establishment of colonial rule in much of Southern Nigeria, Lagos and its environs (particularly Abeokuta) had hosted a vibrant modern press. The first newspaper, *Iwe Irohin fun Awon Egba ati Yoruba* (Newspaper for the Egba and Yoruba), was established in Abeokuta in 1859 by the missionary Henry Townsend. Shortly thereafter, other newspapers, largely published in English, emerged in Lagos; they debated, articulated, and contested the basis (of the cultural and administrative realities) of colonialism and explored the challenges of modern life imposed by colonial rule.[69] They first campaigned for greater involvement of African "natives" in the administration of the country and later began demanding full political independence.

However, since 1914 when the two protectorates were amalgamated, the struggle to create a truly united country, a modern (colonial and eventually postcolonial) state, and a nation commanding common allegiance remains alive, even if perennially contested. As Nigeria moved toward independence in the 1940s and 1950s, the creation of three regions—eastern, northern, and western—turned a bipartite struggle (between the old northern and southern protectorates) into a tripartite struggle (among the three regions) for domination or accommodation within the emergent nation. That the three regions were each dominated by a national majority group (the Igbo, Hausa-Fulani, and Yoruba, respectively) exacerbated the struggle among them. In light of this, prominent nationalists became symbols and synthesizers of the aspirations of their respective regions and ethnic nationalities. These nationalists often engaged in a two-pronged struggle that, on the one hand, involved winning independence for a united Nigeria and speaking to the imminent glory of such a putative African nation-state, and, on the other hand, mobilizing for or against the domination of their ethno-regional group in the emerging Nigerian political union.

The statements of three key leaders from the three regions reflected greater salience of the micro nations (ethno nations) to which these leaders belonged than to the hoped-for macro nation (Nigeria) they were fighting to make free. Dr. Nnamdi Azikiwe, an Igbo from the eastern region and a journalist, author, newspaper publisher, orator, and leader of the National Council of Nigerian Citizens (NCNC), who brought an unusual dynamism to the anticolonial movement when he returned to Nigeria after his education in the United States (and who later became the first and only ceremonial president of independent Nigeria), stated during the first meeting of the Ibo (Igbo) State Union that "it would appear that the God of Africa has specifically created the Ibo nation to lead the children of Africa from the bondage of the ages. The martial prowess of the Ibo nation at all stages of history has enabled them not only to conquer others but also to adapt themselves to the role of preserver. . . . The Ibo nation cannot shirk its responsibility."[70] Even though Azikiwe was the most vociferous among his contemporaries about Nigeria's unity and the creation of a common nationhood (which included his advocacy for a unitary system of government over the "divisive" federal system), his quote is regularly used to emphasize the differences among Nigerians and the struggle for and against domination.

Azikiwe's counterpart and lifelong political rival, Obafemi Awolowo—a journalist, author, newspaper publisher, founder of the Action Group (AG), and first premier of the western region—was similarly concerned with his Yoruba constituents. He stated that his mission was to "do all in my power to infuse solidarity into the disjointed tribes that constitute the Yoruba ethnic group, to raise their morale, to rehabilitate their self-respect, and to imbue them with the confidence that they are an important factor in the forging of the federal unity of Nigeria."[71] The primacy of the Yoruba nation for Awolowo at the start of his political career over and above a "Nigerian nation" was clear, even though it was to be, as he expressed it, within a federal Nigeria. As noted earlier, he had dismissed Nigeria as a "geographical expression."

Abubakar Tafawa Balewa, a teacher, politician, and one of the leaders of the NPC who later became the first prime minister of independent Nigeria, stated in 1948 on the floor of the federal parliament: "Many [Nigerians] deceive themselves by thinking that Nigeria is one . . . particularly the press people. . . . This is wrong. I am sorry to say that this presence of unity is artificial and it ends outside this Chamber. . . . The southern tribes who are now pouring into the North in ever increasing numbers, and more or less domiciled here do not mix with Northern people . . . and we in the north look upon them as invaders. Since 1914, the British Government has tried to make Nigeria into one country, but Nigerians themselves are historically different in their backgrounds, in their religious beliefs and customs and do not show themselves any sign of willingness to unite. . . . Nigerian unity is only a British invention in the country."[72] The narratives of the three leaders, as W. Lance Bennett and Murray Edelman argue, were "appealing because they embod[ied] the fears, hopes, and prejudices of the cultures in which their audiences live[d]."[73] They also point to the fact that, as Nikos Papastergiadis stated, "within the very notion of the 'nation' there are already other nations in contention with *the* nation."[74]

The central themes of the narratives of the leaders from Nigeria's three regions and their formulaic stories have been taken up in different ways by the political and ethno-regional partisans and intellectuals in the press over the past few decades. Such narratives are examined in episodic contexts in this book. In themselves, the perspectives of these leaders and the newspapers that represent their visions of nation(s) within Nigeria reflect the centrality of narratives in the creation, contestation, and negotiation of national identity and national unity. They emphasize that, as Joshua F. Dienstag states, we increase "the threat that history will enslave us . . . when we attempt to deny the role of narratives in politics."[75] Indeed, so strong is "the relationship between political legitimacy and narrative authenticity," as Bennett and Edelman remind us, that "political actors and journalists alike maximize their chances of gaining credibility with the mass audience by fitting new events into symbolic molds." Consequently, "the goal of narrative analysis . . . [is] an understanding of the strains that make alternative narratives inevitable and a recognition of the diversity of human frustrations, aspirations, satisfactions, and imaginative constructions" embedded in, and reflected through, narratives.[76]

Against this backdrop, narrative, as a multifaceted object of inquiry, has in the past few decades become a major focus of research in the humanities and social sciences.[77] From Aristotle, through the relatively early literary criticism on narratives, to structuralism and sociolinguistics, to contemporary developments in narrative theory, stories have come to be recognized as a "basic human strategy for coming to terms with time, process and change."[78] Consequently, Plato's remark that those who tell stories also rule the society has become a part of the conventional wisdom in the social sciences.[79] In the reemergence of storytelling as an important metaphor of political communication, Walter R. Fisher's formulation of "narrative paradigm" is considered a touchstone for the reexamination of narrative. Fisher's narrative paradigm "sees people as story-tellers."[80]

In the context of Lucaites and Condit's attempt to reconstitute narrative theory by focusing on the "interaction of *form* and *function*" critical to the role of narratives in "the formation of political and social consciousness,"[81] I suggest that a more useful theory of narrative metacode would emphasize the interaction of narrative *content* and *function* in the construction of social and political consciousness in the context of relations of domination. Such a reformulation of Lucaites and Condit's reconstruction of narrative theory connects well with Ernest G. Bormann's "symbolic convergence theory." Within the general theoretical framework that constructs human beings as narrative beings—*homo narrans*—the symbolic convergence theory attempts to explain "the appearance of a group consciousness, with its implied shared emotions, motives, and meanings, not in terms of individual daydreams and scripts but rather in terms of socially shared narrations or fantasies."[82] Bormann could be read into Lucaites and Condit by arguing that socially shared or socially shareable narrations or fantasies are products of, and reproduce, the social and political consciousness of group life, such as a nation or ethnic nationality. They are accurate and real (externally valid) to the extent that they reflect this social and political consciousness, which is in turn informed by, or reflective of, the interest and power of the group. This reading is further explicated in the three-part structure of the symbolic convergence theory.[83]

Narrative is often a challenge that invites counternarratives. This is an inescapable fact of human life. Owing to the "diversity of the human frustrations, aspirations, satisfactions and imaginative constructions," there are usually multiple narratives and counternarratives. These multiple narratives are accepted as "basic human strategy for coming to terms with time, process and change."[84] As Bennett and Edelman argue, "the seedbed of creative use and creative reception of narrative lie . . . in learning to recognize and appreciate the inevitability of contradictory stories, the multiple realities they evoke, and their links to the conditions of people's lives."[85]

This book significantly departs from common practice in the literature by using narrative not just as a process of bringing a nation into being through telling stories, but also as the nation itself. That is, the nation exists in and through its narratives; thus the nation is a grand narrative.

Studying the Postcolonial Nation

Even though the concept of "nation" lacks a generally acceptable definition, there is a consensus in extant literature on what it captures. Emerson's important definition, which establishes the crucial nature of the linkage between past and the future, thus making the present both important and transitory for a community of people, is a useful one: "A nation is a body of people who feel that they are a nation . . . a community of people who feel that they belong together in a double sense that they share deeply significant elements of a common heritage and that they have a common destiny for the future."[86]

Indeed, although Emerson's definition captures the "modular" form of nation in the Euro-American world, Partha Chatterjee offers an important critique of this idea. Even though Chatterjee's primary focus is Benedict Anderson's approach to the concept of "nation" and "nationalism," his position applies to the dominant strand of Western approaches to those concepts. He therefore challenges the assumption that the Euro-American experience with nationalism "has supplied for all subsequent nationalisms a set of modular forms from which nationalist elites in Asia and Africa had chosen the one they liked." The nation, Chatterjee argues brilliantly, has been imagined differently in Asia and Africa from the "modular . . . forms of the national society propagated by the modern west."[87] The narratives in this book reflect the conflation—in the Nigerian press—of both the modular form of "nation" inherited from colonialism, which sought to make a nation out of the myriad of nations and other identities in the colony, and the ethnic nations that were reinvented through colonial contact against the backdrop of existing ethnic affinities. Alternating between these two different notions of "nation" constitutes a crucial way in which media narratives engage with relations of domination.

Indeed, the idea of "a nation" is highly problematic in multiethnic postcolonial states where particular national (ethno-linguistic) identities were either created or ossified by the colonial experience. As Smith shows, there are central propositions of nationalist ideology that are relevant in this context. These include: (1) that the world is divided into nations, each having its own individuality, history, and destiny; (2) that the nation is and remains the source of all political and social power, and thus that loyalty to the nation overrides every other allegiance; (3) that every human being has a need to identify with a nation to be able to live a life of fulfillment and freedom; and (4) that nations must be free and secure for the world to experience peace and justice.[88] Reconciling these propositions in the existing or emergent ethno nations in the African postcolony with the colonially created nation-state (the grand nation with its attendant grand narrative) has become a perennial problem.

This book analyzes the nature and character of grand narratives, grand nations, meaning, and power as they pertain to efforts aimed at constructing a grand nation in a typical multiethnic, postcolonial state—Nigeria. It examines the salient features and character of the Nigerian grand nation and other disparate ethnic nations in the

Nigerian press relative to the theory of relations of domination. It also attempts to analyze how symbolic forms within the contexts in which they are produced, received, and understood serve to establish and sustain or contest and counteract relations of domination in a multiethnic polity.

A survey of postcolonial states reveals a succession of situations that involve "competing allegiances" to "imagined communities," showing that the intuitive bond felt by people toward "informal or unstructured subdivisions of mankind"—ethno nations—is far more profound and potent than the ties that connect them with "formal and legalistic state structures" in which they find themselves.[89] The crisis of legitimacy that has plagued many postcolonial states shows the failure of central states to attract loyalty from citizens over and above human groupings in the form of nationalities.

Since the amalgamation of 1914, the geographical political entity called "Nigeria" has grappled with the problem of attracting loyalty from citizens who are more attuned to the psychological needs of their ethno nations or ethnonationalities. Efforts to ensure the transfer of this primordial loyalty[90] to the bigger "nation" have been unsuccessful. This failure has manifested in the several crises that Nigeria has witnessed in her journey to nationhood. This book is not merely timely; the problems it grapples with have a current urgency that could provide a useful path to understanding enduring problems. In contrast to the received and orchestrated notions that concentrate struggles within the grand narrative as solely efforts at legitimizing the grand narrative, this work examines the dynamic relationship between the legitimacy of existing narratives and the legitimacy crisis of the grand narrative.

This book theoretically and empirically analyzes this crisis of nationhood as it is reflected and contested in the press. It is important to do so because the Nigerian press has influenced—both positively and negatively—the pattern of interaction among the disparate ethnic nationalities in Nigeria before and since the 1914 amalgamation. As Dr. Nnamdi Azikiwe, publisher of the *West African Pilot*, acknowledged in speaking about the "pioneers of the Nigerian press," the activities of political journalists and their newspapers are "identical with the intellectual and material [also political] developments" of Nigeria.[91] Nigeria's foremost media historian, Fred Omu, adds that "the [Nigerian] newspaper press has been a significant force in national development."[92]

The Media and Nation-Building in Africa

Around the world, studies of the link between nationalism and the media—whether they address readers as "members of the nation"[93] or highlight differences within what others assume to be a national community[94]—have become part of the larger literature on nationalism and ethnonationalism.[95] This literature, in different ways, shows how states "use the modern media to 'build' nations within their allocated territories"[96] and how the narratives or discourses of the nation through the media "are not homogenous and uniform, but rather dynamic and relational."[97]

In Africa, the interface of the press and nationalism has largely been rendered as the role of the media in "nation-building"—given the preoccupation with African countries' "ability or inability to reconcile national unity and mainstream civic institutions with the culturo-historical and ethnic diversity of the broad spectrum of society."[98] Francis Nyamnjoh, a leading media scholar in Africa, notes that despite the seeming triumph of liberal democracy and its emphasis on the autonomous individual, the media in Africa continue to promote "the struggles for recognition and representation of the various cultural, ethnic or sectarian groups with which they identify." Thus, Nyamnjoh posits, the "politics of belonging is . . . central to understanding democracy in Africa and the role of the media in promoting democratic pluralism."[99] In light of this, students of the nation-media interface study different kinds of media and cultural performances, including television, radio, newspapers, videos, music, and theater, within the context of how they construct images of the nation in Africa. Lila Abu-Lughod has studied television serials in Egypt in terms of how they construct "national interest" and "set the very rhythms of national life." Abu-Lughod concludes in her analysis that Egyptian television serials "participate in a shared discourse about nationhood and citizenship that manifests itself most directly . . . in their treatment of religion [Islam]." However, these television serials do not simply reflect or produce "the interests of the nation-state," thus reminding us "of the continuing importance of regional identities within nation-states."[100] In South Africa, "with its depictions of the dramas of everyday life," television has also provided "a compelling medium for building a normative national consciousness," writes Sarah Ives. Since its arrival in the country in the 1970s, television has "influenced [a] countrywide belief system" for sustaining apartheid while later providing "an image of South Africa that serves the government's attempts to construct a nation out of a divided past." Television is therefore central to South Africans' attempt to "construct a coherent nation" against the backdrop of "an extremely divided past [and] multiplicity of ethnicities and languages."[101]

Charmaine McEachern's *Narratives of Nation Media* (2002), is similar to the intellectual orientation of this book. She examines the "narratives of nation media" in the context of "memory and representation in the making of the new South Africa." She emphasizes the "prevalence of narrative; the pervasiveness of storytelling . . . narrating people and their encompassing identity" as key to "both a process of imagining the nation and a political issue of representation." Analyzing both the apartheid past and post-apartheid present, McEachern considers the "ways in which media operated to support the apartheid state's vision and operation of nation," and the contemporary "fundamental role [of the South African media] in telling the new narratives of nation, enacting the story of sameness and difference which was understood to characterize the new South Africa."[102]

Debra Spitulnik analyzes how "national publics" are produced in the Zambian case.[103] She argues that in Zambia radio broadcasting "plays a very powerful role in constructing the communicative spaces of nation-states."[104] In investigating mass mediation of national identity and the public sphere, she focuses on "radio's temporality and the recycling and reworking of mass-mediated state discourse within Zambian popular culture" in a context in which the repetition of the slogan "One Zambia, One Nation" on the national airwaves is a national pastime. Spitulnik concludes that "radio broadcasting is underlain by several regular processes which allow it to represent a synchronized national community and to mark its movement through time."[105]

Laura Edmondson demonstrates how theater puts the "nation on stage," that is, how it is used in the "mission of nation-building" in the context of "widespread investment in the nation-state" in postcolonial Tanzania.[106] Kelly Askew shows how the nation is "performed" through music in Tanzania. Such performance, in a country created by the political union of the mainland (Tangayika) and an island (Zanzibar)—"fraught by competing agendas, visions, and visionaries"—is used not only in the service of power, she argues, but it also "readily constitutes a means of countering and destabilizing established power structures." Even though Tanzania is one of the least conflictual polities in Africa, like most postcolonial states in Africa that are unions of contrary and contradictory identities and geographies, Tanzania's "continued existence," Askew concludes, is "open to question."[107]

The literature on the print media, covering more than one century of the existence of Nigeria, reflects tensions similar to those captured by Askew. There have been scholarly attempts to understand and analyze the centrality of the press not only in the making of the Nigerian (colonial and postcolonial) state but also in the struggles to define the age-long efforts to forge national unity and create "one and indivisible" democratic and egalitarian polity—which one of the political parties in the Second Republic described as "one nation, one destiny." From Omu's classic *Press and Politics in Nigeria, 1880–1937*, through Adigun Agbaje's *The Nigerian Press, Hegemony, and the Social Construction of Legitimacy, 1960–1983*, to Ayo Olukotun's *Repressive State and Resurgent Media under Nigeria's Military Dictatorship, 1988–1998*, such books have emphasized particular trajectories of the press in Nigeria. Omu presents the social, economic, and political contexts of the evolution of the newspaper press from the period of European contact through the earliest colonial era up to the eve of the birth of "modern" (colonial) Nigerian journalism. Agbaje uses the theory of hegemony in light of the practices of legitimacy to interrogate the role of the newspaper press in Nigeria from the period of independence through the military years (1966–79) up to the collapse of the Second Republic (1979–83). Olukotun employs a neo-Gramscian framework in documenting the resistance of the radical press as a component of a resurgent civil society in the context of a repressive militarist state in 1980s and 1990s Nigeria. It is significant that these three signal works do not make the problems and tensions of nationalism and national integration the exclusive target of their interrogation of the activities of the press.

However, several important works focus directly on the press and nationalism or the press and the struggle for national integration and unity in Nigeria. John D. Chick examines the role of the press in the struggle for national integration and disintegration. Raphael Chude Okonkwor investigates the ways in which the press in Nigeria reacted to and articulated the idea of "Nigerian nationalism" from 1859 when the first newspaper (*Iwe Irohin*) was started until 1960 when Nigeria gained independence. Samuel Okafor Idemili focuses on the central role of the *West African Pilot*, owned by Azikiwe, in the articulation of Nigerian nationalism between 1937 and 1960.[108] The *Pilot* is important because its entry into the media and the political scene in colonial Nigeria marked "the beginning of a new era," writes Omu. With its "eloquent and sensational tone" and "its pugnacious political journalism," the paper became "an effective purveyor of popular views and sentiments [and] a symbol of increased political awareness and sophistication."[109]

Despite the important insights into the interface of the press and nationalism provided by Chick, Okonkwor, and Idemili (and, to a limited and different extent, Omu, Agbaje, and Olukotun), this book differs in three important ways. First, it combines different epochs and episodes in Nigeria's struggle for nationhood and national unity. Like Okonkwor and Idemili, this book engages with the late colonial period, but unlike both, and like Agbaje and Olukotun, it goes beyond the epoch of colonialism when the grounds were prepared for the tone and tenor of Nigerian nationalism and its engagement with the challenges of the postcolonial era. Second, this book is essentially comparative. It compares and contrasts the colonial and the postcolonial eras to show the continuities and discontinues in the approaches to, contestation of, and affirmations of the idea of the "Nigerian nation" in the press. Omu, Okonkwor, and Idemili provide only the colonial background to the social construction of nationalist politics in Nigeria, whereas Agbaje and Olukotun deal with only the postcolonial milieu. Third, this book also differs in theoretical orientation. Agbaje and Olukotun use only neo-Gramscian perspectives, with a focus on the framework of hegemony (and counterhegemony) to interrogate their data. Although this book uses the Gramscian perspective in some chapters, on the whole it goes beyond this approach. Both theoretically and empirically, this work is an interrogation and elaboration of narrative theory. Also, hermeneutics or interpretive theory is used as both a theoretical and methodological framework. While approaching those writing in, and speaking through, the press as *homo narrans* (narrative beings), this book uses depth hermeneutics in elaborating ideology as meaning "in the service of power."[110] It is used to tease out and interrogate meaning(s) in the press and how meaning(s) are mobilized in the service of the construction, deconstruction, or reconstruction of the idea of "nationhood."

There is no work of this scope that examines how the grand nation and the competing ethno-linguistic nations are narrated, articulated, and disarticulated in the press in Nigeria. The mobilization of meaning in the service of power, in the context of interpretation and counterinterpretation—within a *narrativized* nation—raises stimulating theoretical questions, particularly within the ambit of a concept of "ideology" as recast by John B. Thompson in his important work *Ideology and Modern Culture*. As a case study, the analysis of the Nigerian press in this context promises a major contribution to the extant literature in ethnonationalism, in Africa in general and in media narratives in particular.

Narratives and Meaning in the Service of Power

In the struggle over nation, and related struggles over nationalism, nationhood, and nation-building, the mobilization of meaning in the service of specific interests is unavoidable. Thus scholars recognize that the idea and practice of "nation" is "a fluid battleground for meaning."[111] Print media narratives constitute one of the most powerful means of constructing, mobilizing, and contesting meaning in the service of power. Therefore, central to the idea of "nation" and "narrative" and the mobilization of meaning is the notion of power as a specific element of the relations of domination. Yet the conventional ways of conceptualizing power based on intuitive ideas or as a medley are unsatisfactory.[112] One major reason for thinking of power as intractable is that power encompasses seemingly unrelated ideas. As Robert Dahl states, power is "not a thing at all but many things."[113] Power is linked with narrative, social cognition, and social representation. The reproduction of power, therefore, presupposes or involves the reproduction of social representation and its organizing ideologies, which sustain the reproduction of power.[114] Such reproduced social representations and cognitions are expressed, described, explained, prescribed, normalized, defended, and legitimated in myriad discourses, which form the symbolic framework of power. Norman Fairclough, a leading scholar on discourse analysis, alerts us to what he calls the "discoursal nature of the power of the media."[115] As van Dijk puts it, "discourse in . . . society is the essential communicative dimension of power."[116] The discursive nature of media messages, Fairclough argues, contains three key elements:

representation, identities, and relations. In this way, discourse in the media involves "particular ways of representing the world . . . particular constructions of social identities . . . and particular constructions of social relations." Fairclough characterized this, following Foucault, as "the socially constitutive properties of discourse and text," thereby arguing that "texts are social spaces in which two fundamental social processes simultaneously occur: cognition and representation of the world, and social interaction."[117]

Central to the construction of power in the media is meaning. Thompson recasts the concept of "ideology" as referring to "ways in which meaning serves, in particular circumstances to establish and sustain relations of power, which are systematically asymmetrical"— that is, "meaning in the service of power." This position radically challenges the assumption that had long dominated the literature, which viewed ideology as a kind of "social cement" that triumphs in stabilizing societies by binding their members together in collectively shared values and norms. Analyzing relations of domination in this sense does not involve incontestable demonstration, because meaning and power are in the "realm of shifting sense and relative inequalities, of ambiguity and word-play, of different degrees of opportunity and accessibility, of deception and self-deception, of the concealment of the very process of concealment."[118]

Homi Bhabha is one of the leading modern touchbearers of the tradition of examining the nation through its narratives. In the celebrated work he edited, *Nation and Narration*, Bhabha asks: "If the ambivalent figure of the nation is a problem of its transitional history, its conceptual indeterminacy, its wavering between vocabularies, then what effect does this have on narratives and discourses that signify a sense of 'nationness'?" The study of the nation through its narratives, Bhabha argues, not only draws attention to its language and rhetoric but it also attempts to change the conceptual object itself.[119]

The power to narrate or, in the alternative, block other narratives from coming into existence is central to the notion of "nationhood" in postcolonial states.[120] To cast the nation as narration—what Foucault describes as "discursive formations"—highlights not only the centrality of myths (as explanations) in the constructions of nations but also the insistence on political power and cultural authority. Derrida describes this as the "irreducible excess of the syntactic over the semantic."[121]

In place of a nation that fits the generally acceptable conditions of nationhood in Europe, grand narratives (metanarratives, grand myths, or metafictions) have emerged in multinational postcolonial polities that seek to impose the myth of common nationhood on disparate nations. It is argued here that a nation in this context is not just a narrative, it is also a grand narrative in that it seeks to supersede other narratives, casting them as lesser and surpassable narratives. It is therefore necessary to go beyond the general trend in the literature that examines the idea of a "single nation" (in a typical multinational state) as a narrative, in order to capture it as a grand narrative in which meaning discursively defines the relations of power. This book fills this apparent vacuum in the literature by linking narratives and nation in the African postcolonial context in order to elucidate the mobilization of meaning in the service and disservice of power within a grand narrative.

Method

Data was gathered for this work mainly through archival and library sources. Major national and regional English-language newspapers and magazines were selected for their ownership, philosophy, and editorial policy, all of which impacts their coverage of events. Newspapers in the vernacular languages were not selected because they had the same content as their sister publications in English and they reflected similar positions. The national narratives—as narrated by elites—tended to be articulated in English. I ensured that newspapers and newsmagazines represented the key contending regions, ethnic groups, and political interests of the country. For the first case study, I selected *West African Pilot, Nigerian Citizen, Daily Service,* and *Nigerian Tribune and Daily Times.* For the second case study, *West African Pilot* and *Daily Service.* For the third case study, *Nigerian Citizen, West African Pilot, Daily Service, Nigerian Tribune,* and *New Nigerian.* For the fourth, *TELL, The News, The Guardian, Daily Champion,* and *New Nigerian.* For the fifth, *New Nigerian* and *TELL.* For the sixth, *Newswatch, TELL, The News, Tribune, The Guardian,* and *New Nigerian.* And for the seventh case study, *The Guardian, Post Express, TELL,* and *Weekly Trust.*

The data came from news reports, editorials, select opinion articles, and features. Editorials constitute the main narratives examined because they often address issues of nationalism. Newspaper articles, cover stories, and special reports in news magazines are next, also because of their regularity in newspapers and news magazines. These items also receive greater attention because they are more expressive of the negotiation of interests and power. The data gathered were subjected to narrative analysis, which organized around the Thompsonian typology of the mode of operation of ideology (see chapter 2). The analysis (in chapters 3–9) identifies the relations of domination evident in the intricate linkage of the network of meaning and power.

The result enriches the extant literature by reformulating the concept of "ideology." It casts ideology as "meaning in the service of power," which slant is scant, if present, in contemporary social science. Another contribution is the relevance of the relations of domination evident in the narratives in understanding the crisis of nation-building and interethnic relations in multiethnic African postcolonial polities. This book also combines literary analysis and political analysis in examining media coverage of interethnic relations within a fractious nation-state.

Scope of the Book

The scope of this book is not particularly periodic. It focuses on specific issues and controversies, even though they fall into rough periods. But they are approached as contextual issues or controversies that define the parameters of the relations of domination. There are seven case studies and the book is organized into four parts.

Part 1, "Contextual and Conceptual Perspectives," presents the background to the book and reflects on the conceptual and theoretical issues raised by narratives of the idea of the "nation" within the context of relations of domination. Part 2, "Colonial Agency and Counterhegemonic Struggles," examines the narratives of the struggle for and against hegemony among the major ethno-regional groups in colonial Nigeria. Chapter 3 focuses on the key issues that defined the late-colonial era when the major ethno-regional groups and their representative political parties challenged one another on when and how to best achieve independence for Nigeria. Chapter 4 focuses on the ethno-spatial struggles surrounding the need to "nationalize" the capital city of colonial Nigeria. Part 3, "Inclusion, Exclusion, and Democratic Contestations," explores how the struggles over inclusion and exclusion in postindependent Nigeria determined the narratives of democratic contestations about the idea and nature of the Nigeria "nation." The first case examines Nigeria under the military, the other two cases are set in the Third and Fourth Republics. Chapter 5 examines the narratives of nationhood in relation to the debates concerning the best political structure for a multinational state such as Nigeria. These debates and the realities they attempted to capture were conducted on the eve of the Nigerian civil war; the press played a central role in exacerbating the crisis. Chapter 6 focuses on how the "nation" was represented during the crisis that resulted from the annulment by the military regime of the June 12, 1993, presidential election, an annulment that almost plunged Nigeria into another civil war. Chapter 7 explores the narratives about ethno-religious crisis in Nigeria's Fourth Republic. Part 4, "Majority-Minority Relations," focuses on narratives about the minorities that "split the nation from its desire for cohesion" and "interrupt the successive seriality of the narrative of plurals and pluralism" in that they constitute "both a re-articulation of the mode of addressing the 'national community' and a revelation of the ruptures within the totalizing discourse on nationhood."[122] Chapter 8 examines the narratives of the struggle over territoriality between two ethnic groups in northern Nigeria, one a minority and the other a majority group. Chapter 9 focuses on the narratives of the struggles of a southern minority group in the oil-bearing Niger delta region against the three dominant majority ethno-regional groups and a multinational oil company.

Parts 2 through 4 examine key issues and crises in the context of how the press narrated, counternarrated, contested, or constructed them in the service of power within relations of domination. I identify the patterns and tendencies of the construction of meaning in the service of power and key national themes constructed in the press in order to adequately capture the character of the grand- and counternarratives of the Nigerian nation. The diversity of the coverage allows for cross-section comparison and the time span allows for comparison across decades. I present the narratives in their various dimensions and capture the expression and counterexpression of relations of domination.

2

Interpretive Theory, Narrative, and the Politics of Meaning

The social sciences have been concerned for many decades with fundamental questions concerning the nature of social life and its investigation. Whereas some of these concerns, and the debates they have generated, have been geared toward resolving ontological and epistemological dilemmas, others have focused on methodological challenges of the process of social enquiry.[1] This concern forms my examination of the hermeneutical analysis of social phenomenon such as the narratives about the idea and practices of the "nation." Using interpretive theory, or hermeneutics, this chapter explores how interpreting ideology as "meaning in the service of power" illuminates the analysis of media narratives in the African postcolony.

Interpretive Theory and the Hermeneutics of Political Life

Interpretive theory directly challenges the positivist approach to social and political inquiry.[2] Many interpretive theorists and philosophers whose departure point is hermeneutical, including Alfred Schütz, Husserl, Wittgenstein, Heidegger, Dilthey, Gadamer, Peter Winch, Habermas, Ricoeur, Michael Gibbons, and others, raise critical issues with the positivist approach. They argue, for example, that the positivist view demeans the relationship between social and political life and the language that is embedded in them.[3] An empiricist approach assumes that political life is not connected to the language used to appropriate it; therefore, the reality of political life exists independently of the language of the polity.[4] Contrary to this view, interpretive theorists contend that language is constituted by and expressive of the particular political life from which the language draws its essence and logic. As Charles Taylor writes, political practices "cannot be identified in abstraction from the language we use to describe them, or invoke them, or carry them out. . . . The situation we have here is one in which the vocabulary of a given social dimension is grounded in the shape of social practices in this dimension; that is, the vocabulary wouldn't make sense, couldn't be applied seriously, where the range of practices couldn't exist without the prevalence of this or some related vocabulary. . . . The language is constitutive of reality, is essential to being the kind of reality it is."[5]

Interpretive theorists argue that the empiricist approach assumes a disjuncture between political life and its language and therefore downplays, as Gibbons writes, "the internal connections between social and political life and the language that is embedded in it." Although empirical and quantitative methods are still regarded as useful, interpretive theory insists that the explanation of social and political life "is at rock bottom an interpretation." Consequently, explanation of political life, continues Gibbons, "must delve deeper in an attempt to uncover those meanings and practices of language and political form that form the social matrix against which subjective intentions are formed." What these "basic inter-subjective and common meanings and practices" require surpasses the common rules of empirical method. It requires a depth hermeneutics—as practices and meanings informed by language, they are often inchoate, tacit, and not clearly articulated. Against this background, argues Gibbons there is the need to interpret those fundamental aspects of political and social life that ordinary empirical social science cannot fully explain.[6] Following from the view of man as a self-interpreting agent, any such inquiry is of value.

From the viewpoint of analytical philosophy, from which it originated, interpretive social science claims that much of the vocabulary of the discipline comprises action concepts whose logical implications are subsequently examined.[7] Action concepts, argues Brian Fay, are geared toward describing purposive behavior, which provokes questions on its point, aim, and intent, or its goal, desire, or meaning. It is these that constitute the data that the social scientist seeks to explain. Fay strengthens this argument by stating that the use of action concepts involves more than mere observation and requires interpretation on the part of the observer. This task has been described historically as *verstehen* (explanation), a description, writes Fay, that is mired in confusion and controversy. It is sufficient here to state that such explanation has dwelled, at the level of individual actions, on showing the rationale for particular acts through contextualizing the acts within the larger context in which they are enacted. Thus, continues Fay, interpretive social science attempts to uncover the sense of given actions, practices, and constitutive meanings by pointing to the intentions and desires of particular actors and the structures and contexts that inform not only the actions and practices but also the social scientist's understanding of these actions and practices. The social scientist is able to places disparate experiences and practices into larger, more intelligible, contexts.[8] Because the desires of actors already constitute an interpretation of the world, John B. Thompson terms this process of "re-describing an act or experience" as "re-interpret[ing] a pre-interpreted domain."[9] The "knowledge" that the intentions and desires of actors are based on are pretheoretical. Therefore they need to be theorized and reinterpreted.

The works of Paul Ricoeur and Jurgen Habermas provide illuminating perspectives on the tradition of interpretive theory called "depth hermeneutics."[10] As Thompson elaborates: "The idea underlying depth hermeneutics is that, in social inquiry as in other domains, the process of interpretation can be, and indeed demand to be, mediated by a range of explanatory or 'objectifying' methods. When dealing with a domain which is constituted as much by force as by meaning, or when analysing an artefact which displays a distinctive pattern through which something is said, it is both possible and desirable to mediate the process of interpretation by employing explanatory or objectifying techniques."[11] For Habermas, "the social scientist encounters symbolically pre-structured objects; they embody structures of the pre-theoretical knowledge with the help of which speaking and acting subjects produced these objects."[12] Anthony Giddens describes this as "double hermeneutics."[13]

This perspective clarifies to actors the nature and dynamics of what they and others do, by articulating the symbolic structures within which people in specific social contexts act, and by clarifying the criteria of rationality that undergird their chosen positions and worldview.[14] As Habermas argues, because the "object domain of social inquiry is symbolically pre-structured, antecedently-constituted by the interpretive activities of its members," the social scientist can access social objects only through interpretive understanding

(*Sinnverstehen*)—whether it is of social actions, texts, traditions, or configured institutions, practices, systems, or structures.[15] My analysis of news sources uses configured institutions, existing systems, practices, and structures within the Nigerian context to provide a credible interpretation of how the press narrates the conflictual understanding of what constitutes a nation and the parameters of national unity and nation-building, within the context of relations of dominations in an archetypal African polity.

Marxist theorists have contributed to this debate on how to understand and interpret the social world with their searing critique of the ontological backdrop of the relations of domination. They criticize the bourgeois position of an unmediated empirical world as a myth that invests a process of legitimation with the status of scientific validity.[16] Mediation as a real historical process is regarded as part of the natural history of man.[17] Hegel asserts that "there is no such thing as unmediated knowledge. Unmediated knowledge is where we have no consciousness of the mediation; but even this is mediated. . . . Thought, concrete thought, understanding is mediated knowledge."[18] However, unlike others, classical Marxists argue that mediation is borne by labor, which mediates the objective nature of the world.[19] Following Marx and Engels, Franz Dröge avers that consciousness is of similar origin and is therefore also mediated, given the fact that man works with consciousness as well as creates such consciousness. Labor mediates the level of knowledge and the development of consciousness.[20] The overriding Marxist project— societal transformation expressed in historical or dialectical materialism—explains why the Marxian perspective on mediation of the world argues for some kind of interrelationship between knowledge and action. As Has Jurgen Helle argues, "action mediates between the realm of things and the realm of knowledge." The two realms are united in action—"productive activity"—in which knowledge is confirmed, maintained, and renewed.[21]

Dröge distills three social moments of knowledge from the unity present in the knowledge that mediates between individual and collective subjects, such as class, groups, and organizations. These are factual knowledge, value knowledge, and normative knowledge. According to him, factual knowledge originates "in the sphere of primary experience of individual and collective labor." Value knowledge "makes it possible for individuals, groups and the entire society to make choices between alternative ends for their actions." Ideologies and understandings of what constitutes reality are located here but "they represent the knowledge of society as a whole." Normative knowledge decides which among the alternative choices within value knowledge is right in any given context as a basis for action. Thus factual and value knowledge form a dialectical unity by being absorbed by normative knowledge. This dialectic becomes historical and, consequently, serves the domination relationship in the realm of knowledge that had hitherto been objectively given through the relations of production under capitalism. In a class-based society, therefore, mediating normative knowledge serves as a tool of domination, given that it "standardizes and naturalizes" a particular value knowledge so as to discriminate against and demean the "remaining" value knowledge that is linked to the evolution of productive forces. Social antagonism is therefore believed to produce hegemonic normative knowledge, which eventually hides its own hegemonic character and obstructs or limits the process of reflecting social totality.[22] This position, as I will discuss later, eventually produced an interesting critique of Marxian analysis of ideology.

Classical Marxism and some contemporary variants have been under attack from within and outside this intellectual tradition for insisting that mediation is borne exclusively by labor, which then mediates the objective nature of the world.[23] Yet Marxist theorists and their critics have provided important critiques of the idea of the unmediated nature of the world, which have encouraged a rich discourse captured by the idea of the "sociology of knowledge."

Ideology and the Sociology of Knowledge

Since every assertion of a "fact" about the social world touches the interest of some individual or group, one cannot even call attention to the existence of certain facts without courting the objections of those whose very raison d'être in society rests on a divergent interpretation of the factual situation.[24]

The sociology of knowledge, as articulated by Karl Mannheim, is a major intervention in the attempt to resolve the dilemma of objectivity in the process of establishing validity for knowledge.[25] First, Mannheim arrives at his conclusions through searching out the motives that underlie intellectual activity and how the thinker in society is implicated in his or her thought. Related to that, he reworks the data of intellectual history toward discovering the modes and methods of thought that dominated different social-historical epochs. Furthermore, his analysis brings to light how the interests and purposes of particular groups are implicated in particular theories, doctrines, and intellectual traditions. He argues, "In every society there are individuals whose special function is to accumulate, preserve, reformulate and disseminate the intellectual heritage of the group. The composition of this group, their social derivation and the method by which they are recruited, their organization, their class affiliation, the rewards and prestige they receive, their participation in other spheres of social life, constitute some of the more crucial questions to which the sociology of knowledge seeks answers."[26]

Though Mannheim fails to make the argument strongly, the approach of the sociology of knowledge is theoretical analysis of social phenomenon as much as methodology.[27] His perspective alerts us to the centrality of narrative in the social process of accumulating, preserving, reformulating, and disseminating the heritage of groups such as ethno-regional, ethnic, political, and religious groups in the context of the issues and events examined in the next chapters.

The principal thesis of this approach is that "there are modes of thought which cannot be adequately understood as long as their social origins are obscured."[28] As a methodology for capturing, understanding, and explaining[29] social phenomenon, the sociology of knowledge offers two important points: It comprehends thought concretely as a socio-historical phenomenon, which provides the context for individually differentiated thought; that is, men and women in group think based on and in response to the dynamics of their common environment.[30] It also links the "concretely existing modes of thought" with "the context of collective action" through which the world is discovered in an intellectual sense. Individuals within groups think, interact, and act with or against individuals in other groups. Consequently, the goal is to either maintain the world as it is if it favors the group, or change the world if it does not favor the group. The interest of the group, therefore, determines whether the world will be maintained or changed collectively. As Mannheim asserts, the "will to change or to maintain" collective activity produces the "the guiding thread" responsible for the problems and forms of thought within a group. Human beings see the world in accordance with the particular context of collective activity in which they partake.[31]

Thus knowledge is bound to group life; it is a cooperative project and process of group life, one in which every member of the group makes his or her contribution to the common font of fate, activity, and triumph over collective problems.[32] Therefore, within the context of ethnic and national group belongingness, certain forms of knowledge about social reality are connected to the project and process of group life. Whether this manifests as newspapers' support of a specific vision of such group life as evident in ethnonationalist boundaries (ethno nation), or as their support of a vision of such group life as evidenced only in state boundaries (grand nation), the emergent forms of knowledge are connected generally to such visions, projects, and processes of group life.

Central to the idea of a "collective" mode of thought—as explicated by the sociology of knowledge perspective—is ideology. The relationship between ideology and the sociology of knowledge and the reformulation of ideology, which constitutes my departure point in analyzing newspaper narratives, is also examined here with Thompson's *Ideology and Modern Culture* as a guide. Ideology has been central to social and political thought in the last two centuries, even though, asserts Thompson, its centrality has been largely captured negatively. It was originally introduced by Destutt de Tracy as a label for his proposed science of ideas—"which would be concerned with the systematic analysis of ideas and sensations, of their generation, combination and consequences." It became, however, a linguistic weapon in political battles. Given this peculiar origin, the term "ideology" was used in the social sciences in the nineteenth and twentieth centuries in different ways, writes Thompson, even while retaining its central utility in political struggles. Contemporary uses of the term carry the baggage of its particular rendering in different epochs and for different purposes.[33]

De Tracy's central argument is that things cannot be known in themselves, except through ideas that our sensations form; therefore, if we analyze our ideas and sensations systematically, we will arrive at a firm basis for all scientific knowledge and be well placed to draw inferences that have practical utility. He calls this process "ideology," or, literally, the "science of ideas," which should be "positive, useful, and susceptible of rigorous exactitude."[34]

This position became triumphant in late-seventeenth-century France. But the ascendancy of Napoleon Bonaparte produced mixed blessings. Although he used some of the ideas of de Tracy and gave de Tracy's followers key political posts, Napoleon also detested the science of ideas and its adherents, given their romance with republicanism. The fortune of these thinkers in Napoleonic France was tied to the crisis of that period. As Napoleon suffered defeat after defeat, he accused the *ideologues* of undermining the French state, and he dismissed ideology.[35] Progressively, "ideology" became a curse word imposed on all enemies of the crumbling regime. Even though de Tracy was restored to political influence after Napoleon's abdication in 1814, by then ideology had been compromised. It had entered fully into the political arena and was thrown back at the philosophers and referred to as "ideas themselves" and no longer as the "science of ideas." The ideas to which it referred were assumed to be erroneous and impractical in political life.[36]

From this period on, the meaning of the term "ideology" was split between the positive and neutral meaning and the negative and critical meaning.[37] Mannheim, however, makes a critical point that cannot be overemphasized. He argues that Napoleon's condemnation of de Tracy and other philosophers as "ideologists" has important theoretical implications in that the condemnation involved core epistemological and ontological questions. According to Mannheim, "What is depreciated is the validity of the adversary's thought because it is regarded as unrealistic." Since this period, the question of what is real and how we know reality never disappeared from intellectual and political disputations from Napoleon to Marx and the present.[38]

Although his writings on ideology are far from clear, Marx's oeuvre constitutes a crucial intervention in the history of the science of ideas. He turned the concept of "ideology" into a critical tool and made it integral to a new theoretical analysis of society. Thompson distills the different concepts of ideology in Marx into polemical, epiphenomenal, and latent conceptions. In the first, ideology is a doctrine "which fails to grasp the real conditions and characteristics of social-historical life." In the second, ideology is a "system of ideas which expresses the interests of the dominant class." In the third, ideology is a "system of representation which serves to sustain existing relations of class domination by orienting individuals towards past rather than future." The phenomenon referred to here is not mere epiphenomena of economic and class relations, notes Thompson, but symbolic constructions that are autonomous and efficacious to a certain degree. According to Thompson, "They constitute symbols and slogans, customs and traditions which move people or hold them back, propel them or constrain them, in such a way that we cannot think of these symbolic constructions as solely determined by, and fully explicable in terms of, the economic conditions of production."[39]

This is a crucial point, particularly as Thompson argues further that traditional symbols and values—such as ethnicity, nationalism, religion, etc.—rather than being swept away or transcended by capitalist relations of production, are persistent and prevalent in modern society.[40] A typical example is the African postcolonial state, where the latent conception of "ideology" is demonstrated in the resurgence and triumph of traditional values and symbols and ethno-religious identities. As I attempt to show in this book, what Marx assumes to be parts of the epiphenomenon—such as ethnic and religious identities—are, in practice, the fundamental bases of sociopolitical relations in most postcolonial states and are reflected in the press.

Before Thompson, Mannheim had argued that there were two distinct and separable meanings of ideology, the particular and the total. He posits that when we are skeptical of the ideas presented by our opponents, the particular conception is implied, whereas the ideology of an age or the ideas that make up the total structure of a concrete group or a class is implied by the total conception of ideology.[41] Mannheim's distinction between the particular and the total conception of ideology is illuminating in that, in the context of newspaper narratives examined in this book, it points to a difference between narratives that present or question conflicting views of a particular social reality and those that absolutely reject the foundational sociocultural or political standpoints or contexts determining the narratives of the opposing side. In the former, there is disagreement over the proper interpretation and meaning of what has happened in a particular context; in the latter, there is total rejection of the worldview of the other side, which dictates or informs the narratives in the press. I make this clear in the next chapters, as the narratives concerning antagonistic and competing regions, ethnicities, ethno-regional and religious groups, etc., reflect particular and total rejection of the positions expressed by all concerned.

Marxism was responsible for merging the particular and the total conception of ideology, giving due emphasis, like never before, to the role of class in thought. "Ideology" became a dominant concept, writes Thompson. After Marx, however, the concept—assumed to be negative and oppositional—was neutralized. The neutralization, particularly within Marxism, was not the result of an explicit drive toward such, but was produced by an implicit generalization of what is described by Thompson as the epiphenomenal conception of ideology.

Thompson argues that although Mannheim recognizes Marx's genius in making a transition from the particular to the total conception of ideology, he notes a limitation in Marx's analysis of the total conception. Mannheim consequently draws a distinction between Marx's special formulation of the total conception and his own general formulation. Therefore, what was once the intellectual weapon of the Communist Party became a method of research in the social sciences. Consequently, knowledge conditioned by social-historical circumstances is not vitiated, but rather it is the condition on which valid knowledge in the sphere is based. Thompson, however, points out that Mannheim's general formulation of the total conception of ideology is a "restricted conception," which ultimately regards ideology as "ideas, which are discordant with reality and unrealisable in practice." More concretely, Thompson argues that Mannheim's restricted conception thus preserves the negative slant in the conception of ideology; more important, Mannheim ignores or neglects the phenomenon of domination, which is present in Marx's conceptualization of ideology.[42] Against this backdrop, Thompson proposes what I describe as a symbolic conception of ideology.

Symbolic Conception of Ideology

Thompson recovers the phenomenon of domination lost in Mannheim's elaboration of Marx's analysis. He locates the possibility of this recovery in Marx's latent conception of ideology, which is, however, drained of all its negative features except the criterion of sustaining the relations of domination. Thompson conceives of ideology as primarily concerned with how symbolic forms conflate and conflict with relations of power; that is, the ways in which meaning is mobilized in the social world to serve the interests of individuals and groups who have power. The study of ideology is "the study of ways in which meaning serves to establish and sustain relations of domination." Thompson argues: "Ideological phenomena are meaningful symbolic phenomena insofar as they serve, in particular circumstances, to maintain relations of domination. Insofar as: it is crucial to stress that symbolic phenomena, or certain symbolic phenomena, are not ideological as such, but are ideological only insofar as they serve, in particular circumstances, to maintain relations of domination. . . . We can grasp symbolic phenomena as ideological, hence we can analyse ideology, only by situating symbolic phenomena in the socio-historical context within which these phenomena may, or may not, serve to establish and sustain relations of domination."[43]

A symbolic conception for the study of ideological texts emphasizes the need to locate our understanding and analysis of ideology at the interface of meaning and power, particularly in sociopolitical contexts. A symbolic conception overcomes the a priori assumptions of Marx and Mannhaim by insisting that what ideology does—whether it services, establishes, or sustains relations of domination—can only be discovered in specific conjectures in the social history of a people. Unlike Marx, Thompson posits that it is not essential for ideology to be false or deceitful or to mask, conceal, or obstruct social relations. These are only contingent possibilities. When we realize this, argues Thompson, and accept that ideology is not represented only in error and illusion, we relieve ideology of some of the epistemological dilemmas in which it had been trapped since Napoleon.

Therefore, what is crucial is the way in which symbolic forms serve in particular contexts to establish and sustain power. A symbolic conception is more useful than Marx's concepts because it is not trapped in class relations. Whereas Marx considers class relations the major and most crucial form of domination and subordination, the symbolic conception points to several other types of domination, each of which may be singly and jointly more salient in different contexts. These include relations of sexual domination, relations of ethnic domination, relations of regional domination, and so on.[44] A symbolic conception makes it possible to analyze relations of ethnic or ethno-regional domination—real and imagined—and resistance to domination, and the attendant conflictual politics registered and played out at the symbolic level. For instance, class relations are relatively unimportant for narratives of the struggles of minorities against majority groups (as discussed in part 4).

An additional strength of a symbolic conception is that, unlike Marx, it emphasizes how symbolic forms and the meaning they mobilize constitute social reality, thereby creating and sustaining relations of domination. Yet another strength of this conception is in what Thompson calls the "era of mass communication": it is sensitive to the deluge of symbolic forms as they define and largely determine contemporary public life.[45] This is true in the Nigerian case, where the press not only predates but is also central to political contestations.

In this reformulation of the concept of "ideology," Thompson elaborates the ways in which meaning intersects with relations of domination. His explication of the concept of "domination" is integral to the reformulation of ideology adopted here. "Domination" occurs, Thompson explains, when "established relation of power are "systematically asymmetrical," that is, when particular agents or groups of agents are endowed with power in a durable way that excludes, and to some significant degree remains inaccessible to, other agents or groups of agents, irrespective of the basis on which such exclusion is carried out."[46]

Regarding how meaning intersects with power, Thompson presents a typology that he calls general modes of operation of ideology (see table 2.1). Although it does not exhaust all the modes available, the typology is comprehensive enough to be adequate for my purposes.[47] The five general modes have thirteen typical strategies of symbolic construction inherent in, but not exclusive to, them.

Modes of Operation of Ideology

There are three qualifications that Thompson emphasizes concerning the five modes of operation of ideology: (1) They are not the only ways in which ideology operates and they do not always operate independent of one another. (2) The strategies identified with certain modes of operation of ideology are not unique to these modes, they are only typical of them. (3) The typical strategies of symbolic construction are not intrinsically ideological; their ideological nature depends on whether they serve in particular contexts to sustain or subvert, establish or undermine, relations of domination.[48]

Table 2.1. General modes and typical strategies of "meaning in the service of power"

General modes	Some typical strategies of symbolic construction
Legitimation	Rationalization Universalization Narrativization
Dissimulation	Displacement Euphemization Trope (e.g., synecdoche, metonymy, metaphor)
Unification	Standardization Symbolization of unity
Fragmentation	Differentiation Expurgation of the other
Reification	Naturalization Eternalization Normalization/passivization

Source: Thompson, *Ideology and Modern Culture*, 60.

These five modes and thirteen strategies are not exhaustive, but they constitute identifiable ways in which meaning intersects with power in political and social life, particularly when the ideas and the practices of nations, identities, ethnicities, and faiths clash and contend. The analysis in the next six chapters (3–9) shows how these modes and their attendant strategies are deployed to create meaning in the service or disservice of power.

However, some crucial points must be made regarding the criticisms this kind of methodology raises. Even though Thompson fails to constantly emphasize that both the thesis and the antithesis of relations of domination are simultaneously ongoing in symbolic construction—without producing a terminal synthesis—he notes that ideology invites its opposite. Following Thompson, I approach the study of ideological texts as the study of how meaning serves to establish or invalidate, sustain or demobilize, nourish or subvert, relations of domination. Thus, in the context of this book, ideology is meaning in the service or disservice of power.

The theoretical and methodological departure points adopted here do not admit "incontestable demonstration," which is the preoccupation of positivist science. In seeking to grasp the complex interplay of meaning and power, "we are in the realm of shifting sense and relative inequalities, of ambiguity and word-play, of different degrees of opportunity and accessibility, of deception and self-deception. Of the concealment of social relations and the concealment of the very process of concealment," writes Thompson.[49] Therefore, the analysis in this book is adequate, but not absolute, grounds for understanding how the press mobilizes meaning in the service or disservice of power. Ultimately, it should be understood in the larger context of other processes, institutions, and practices—both forcible and nonforcible—of hegemonic and counterhegemonic struggles in Nigeria.

Part 2

Colonial Agency and Counterhegemonic Struggles

3

In Search of a Grand Narrative

The Press and the Ethno-Regional
Struggle for Political Independence

In the decade leading up to Nigeria's independence, the three major ethno-regional blocs in the country, the eastern region, the northern region, and the western region, organized essentially around the three major political parties, the National Council for Nigeria and the Cameroons (NCNC) the Northern People's Congress (NPC), and the Action Group (AG), respectively. The struggle to define the character and logic of the emergent state and imagined grand nation by the many ethnic nationalities of the regions, through the leveraging of group interests within the larger context, was evident in the major newspapers that represented each of these major political parties and, by extension, their regions.

The date for the attainment of self-rule was one of the principal controversies of this era. *When* to achieve political independence and move together into an independent future with a common destiny was as important—and as challenging—as *how* to do so. On March 31, 1953, the Honorable Anthony Enahoro introduced a motion in the House of Representatives to resolve "as [a] primary political objective the attainment of self-government for Nigeria in 1956."[1] The AG member added that "the bare idea of self-government is no longer attractive, is no longer enough."[2]

Ahmadu Bello, the leader of the NPC and the Sardauna of Sokoto, aborted this effort through a dilatory motion. He introduced the adoption of an amendment substituting the words "as soon as practicable" with "1956."[3] A "bitter and tempestuous" debate ensued, during which the members of the NCNC and AG staged a walkout. Bello clarified the position of northern delegates, stating that "before we commit ourselves, we must . . . seek a mandate from our people so that when we speak we know that we are voicing their feelings. . . . [Motions like this] merely serve to destroy interregional unity which the [Richards] Constitution is building." Bello added that "sixty years ago, there was no Nigeria but merely a collection of communities very different in outlook and mode of life."[4]

The events that followed the crisis in the House almost ended the possibility of an independent and united Nigeria. After the adjournment, northern members of the House were abused by the Lagos crowd and subsequently ridiculed and criticized by the southern press for what was believed to be their opposition to independence in general, and independence in 1956 in particular. Consequently, when the northern representatives returned to their region, which was about twice as large as the two southern regions, they swore to never again endure such humiliation. They then announced an eight-point program, the implementation of which would have signaled the virtual secession of the northern region from colonial Nigeria.[5] The Sardauna who described the Lagos crowd as "bands of hooligans" stated: "The abusive language they used and their behaviour disgusted us and left us in no doubt as to the type of undemocratic tactics that were being used to attempt to frighten us Northerners."[6]

The decision by the southern parties, NCNC and AG, to send delegates to the northern region to campaign for self-government in 1956 only worsened matters; the AG delegation, led by Samuel Ladoke Akintola, provoked riots in Kano and thirty-six people reportedly died. This crisis was a manifestation of a deeper problem, which included the fear in the north of southern domination and the dissatisfaction of southerners with the 1951 constitution and the slow pace of the movement toward self-government.[7] Dr. Nnamdi Azikiwe, the leader of the NCNC, articulated the position of his party by saying that the "issue of self-government (in or before 1956) is paramount in our political programme."[8]

The newspapers, within the context of the struggles for ethno-regional validation and ascendancy and the attempts by each of the power blocs and their political representatives to become the authoritative embodiment of the grand nation, demonstrated interesting facets of the mobilization of meaning in the service of power. As mouthpieces of powerful groups, newspapapers "accumulate, reformulate and disseminate the . . . heritage of group(s)" and their interests.[9] Given that every political narrative concerns the interests of some group or individuals, they invite divergent interpretations and opposing narratives.

This chapter examines the narratives of five newspapers regarding the struggle for independence, particularly regarding when and how, the status of Lagos, and related issues. The newspapers include the *West African Pilot*, owned by Dr. Nnamdi Azikiwe, the leader of the NCNC (eastern gegion); the *Nigerian Tribune*, owned by Chief Obafemi Awolowo, leader of the AG (western region); the *Daily Service*, the official organ of the Nigerian Youth Movement (NYM); the *Daily Times*, owned by the British Mirror Group; and the *Nigerian Citizen*, owned by the northern region's colonial government. My focus is solely on the issues. Yet the controversial issues arose at a specific conjuncture in the history of the Nigerian "nation," therefore the period covered falls roughly between 1950 and 1953.

Fragments of the Grand Nation

As the imagined grand nation found its way through many roadblocks on the path to political independence, two issues attracted the greatest attention of the newspapers: the date of independence and the status of Lagos. Several other issues related to these two or, more generally, to the dynamics of the contending nations within the emerging grand nation were also narrated by the press.

In 1950, the *Nigerian Citizen*—the mouthpiece of the northern region and eventually the NPC—does not devote much attention to the heated debates on the future of Nigeria, which had been going on even before then in the southern newspapers. But there are a few narratives that directly and indirectly reflect the pattern of the struggles for power or focus on the place of the northern region in the emergent equation.

It is evident that even the newspapers saw one another as important vehicles and extensions of the struggle for the creation or negotiation of meaning in the service of power. The *Nigerian Citizen*, for instance, reports that Ladoke Akintola, the former editor of *Daily Service* and one of the leading members of AG, ridiculed Dr. Nnamdi Azikiwe (the NCNC leader, popularly called "Zik"), who had announced that he might quit politics: "Mr. Akintola wondered how it would be possible for Zik to quit politics when he retained his interests in the *West African Pilot* and the Ibo State Union, two political organisations."[10] The obvious position here is that anyone who is involved in narrating the relations of domination, such as a newspaper editor, cannot pretend to have withdrawn from politics.

The *Citizen* was also concerned with indices of development that are tied to political power. When Sokoto province set a target in 1951 of ten thousand new literates per year, the paper describes it as "giving a lead to the rest of [the eleven provinces] in the North." Yet the paper is unhappy about this, given the implications for the interests of the region in relation to the other two more education-ally advanced regions (eastern and western) of colonial Nigeria "in this year of great constitutional changes and elections." First, the *Citizen* camouflages the reason for the "pity," stating that literacy is "only the beginning of the emancipation of the people of Nigeria." Its real concern is to follow later, when the paper states: "Without mass literacy, the prospect of the true development of the North in politics, commerce, agriculture and industry, are remote indeed."[11] Even without this statement, the reference to the "year of great constitutional changes and elections" indicates the political impli-cations of literacy for the northern region in relation to the other two regions. It is understandable, therefore, that even in matters of scholarship, the political implications of the procedure of applica-tion is raised in a letter to the editor. For instance, the *Citizen* writes: "When the British Council announced in the *Citizen* that applicants from Kabba and Ilorin Provinces for scholarship should apply to the Western Provinces it seems that it was forgotten that under the new Constitution these two provinces are to remain in the North. The majority of the people of these provinces want to stay in the North— then let us deal exclusively with the North on all matters."[12]

These provinces of the northern region, Kabba and Ilorin, were historically Yoruba areas that were lost to the Fulani and were incorporated into the Sokoto caliphate following the jihad starting in 1804, which took advantage of the power struggle in the Yor-uba empire of Oyo. The colonialists accepted the incorporation of these areas into the caliphate, thus making them territorially and administratively parts of the northern region. A major struggle in this era was the attempt by the Yoruba west to reintegrate these areas into the western region. This was seriously opposed by the northern region.

Other areas in which political power is implicated in discourses seemingly unrelated to politics are the arts and cattle rearing. For instance, the *Citizen* in its review of the Nigerian Festival of Arts, in which the northern region did not have "large[-] scale entries," sees this trend "as dangerous for the preservation of the north's "way of life," because "surely, if the peoples of the North have any love for and faith in their own ways of life—which, after all, their culture and art should represent—they should themselves make an effort to preserve them."[13] On the surface, the idea of the "peoples of the north" tends to contest the overriding image of "one north, one people," canvassed by the leaders of the NPC. However, the image of a different "us" (northern people) against "them" (southern people) is strongly evident.

Regarding livestock, the *Citizen* refers to a report written by Mr. Thomas Shaw and Mr. Gilbert Colville, two British livestock experts, who noted, inter alia: "No matter how aesthetically attractive the race [Fulani] may be, or how deep its roots in history, they and their cattle must be settled if the large issues in Nigeria are to be solved in the interest of the Nigerian people. There can be no question of their preservation as nomadic cattle owners, owing loyalty neither to the soil nor to the territory."[14] In its reaction to this proposal, sections of which are quoted ostensibly to highlight points like the fair looks of the Fulani and their "deep historical roots," the *Citizen* stated that "there is something (almost) Machiavellian" in the suggestion of the reports. In particular, the paper takes issue with a proposal: "That the independent Fulani herds men should be lured away from his wandering life by his wife, who would be subjected to a propaganda campaign in which the good things money can buy will be dangled before her eyes."[15] The paper can be said to be defending the Fulani "nation" against subversion by foreign logic— even when the foreign power is a friendly one or a partner with the power elite, which the paper represents. This emphasis on maintaining a distinction between the Fulani, the dominant ethnic group in the north, and the rest is critical in understanding the contradictory strands of the narratives of unification and fragmentation, including the standardization and symbolization of unity of the people of the northern region and the differentiation and expurgation of the other in regard to the people of the southern regions.

In the same period that the *Citizen* focuses on all of this, the *Nigerian Tribune* focuses on the talks regarding self-government. It compares the "performances of our Northern brethren"—that is, the other—at the general conference held in Ibadan with the pre-independence Indian scene, where "the imperialist, like a drowning man clutching at a straw which might save him, made capital politics of communal difference which very nearly plunged that ancient country into chaos." The *Tribune* presents "the North" as the "problem" in the attempt to drive British "imperialists" out of Nigeria because the northern region is the "straw," a regrettable saving grace that the British held on to. The paper, therefore, puts the case "plainly and bluntly" to northerners: "Are they prepared or are they not to join hands with us in building one country and one Government?"[16] In spite of the fact that the *Citizen* does not initially devote much attention to the Ibadan conference, it still sees the press as crucial in reporting the conference because of the election that will follow the new constitution.[17] Its position is, therefore, functional.

If "they" are ready, the *Tribune* declares, they should delink themselves from their "masters" (the colonialists) and abandon their "imperialist shibboleth"; and if they are not, "well, let them go their own way and we go ours."[18] The *Tribune* also unifies the two southern regions and fragments them from the northern region, which is then narratively expunged from a "united nation" of southern Nigeria. Although the *Tribune* does not clearly identify the "we" who are against the northern "they," it is safe to assume that it is the southern "we," given that the paper goes on to mention "communal antagonism—especially between North and South," which may "spell the doom of" the grand nation, which the north is invited to join in building. This particular narrative ignores the "communal antagonism" between and within the two southern regions.

The newspaper narratives constitute constant attempts at unification and fragmentation through differentiation or expurgation of the other. The *Citizen* celebrates the opening of a new trunkline telephone system linking Kaduna with Enugu and Lagos that, "for the first time . . . enables the people of North, East and West Regions to talk with each other without having to travel long distances," and wishes that this would lead to "speedier inter-regional administrative decisions, a considerable increase of business . . . and quicker transmission of news," thereby "gaining momentum towards bringing the people of Nigeria closer together." Yet it points to differences even as it preaches unity: "As communications bring them closer together, the people of Nigeria must prepare their minds for closer contacts with other parts of the country, which have hitherto seemed remote from them. They must sink regional prejudices as much as possible for a wider patriotism. Nigeria must come first."[19] In the operation of ideology here, difference and unity are tied together in a manner that makes it difficult to disentangle one from the other. Although this narrative emphasizes unity or its potential, and validates the creation of a grand solidarity ("Nigeria must come first"), it also speaks indirectly to differences when it asks for "closer contact" with the misunderstood, misrepresented "remote" part of Nigeria—the north.

After ignoring attacks against northern leaders in the southern newspapers, the *Citizen* eventually begins to respond to accusations, such as the Tribune's, against the leaders of the northern region of colluding with "imperialists." The *Citizen* declared: "Nigerians must seriously consider whether those who are clamouring for immediate 'release from imperialist bondage' are capable of leading the country to better things. 'Imperialists' have at least given the country stability, expanding educational and medical services and some standing in the modern world[,] to name but a few advantages."[20] But the *Tribune* disagreed with the positive attitude of the *Citizen* to imperialism and colonialism. The paper argued that "British imperialism . . . has failed to fulfil the mission for which it set out. UNITY of the North, East and West they promised us. They have achieved, to our horror, DISUNITY."[21]

The *Citizen* contradicts the images of a "nation up in arms" against "imperialists," presenting the "imperialists" as "benefactors" of the country who had done so much even if "only a few" could be named. In what follows, however, the fact that the northern region could not be compared with the southern regions is betrayed by the *Citizen*—although this is shielded by the focus on all "our [northern] leaders." The paper argues under the assumption that in every section of the country, the leaders are not yet ready for responsibility: "Until, under the new Constitution, our leaders can obtain experience in national affairs and become acquainted with the heavy responsibilities of government, proving themselves efficient administrators, it would be obviously unwise for the present Government in Nigeria to hand over completely to an unproved administration."[22] The position of the northern region that it was unprepared for independence is universalized by the *Citizen* as if it were true of the two southern (eastern and western) regions. However, that the interest of the northern region was well served by the British colonial government is evident in the newspaper's celebration of British "dominion" (not imperialism) on Empire Day. The *Citizen* rejoices that British rule had served colonial Nigeria well, that is, better than any other great power could have.[23]

This editorial is significant because the press in the south, particularly in Lagos, had been historically vociferous against imperialism and British colonialism. Therefore the celebration of British "dominion" by the mouthpiece of the northern region is diametrically opposed to the condemnation and rejection of British imperialism in the south. The use of the word "dominion" by the *Citizen* and, in contrast, "imperialism" by the *Tribune* and the *Pilot*, indicate the opposing attitudes of the northern and southern newspapers to British colonialism.

Those fighting for independence from the British are "enemies and critics" of the British Empire and are "extremist nationalists and communists" in the eyes of the *Citizen*.[24] This rhetoric legitimizes British colonial enterprise through rationalization "which seeks to defend or justify a set of social relations or institutions, and thereby to persuade an audience that it is worthy of support."[25] The *Daily Times* calls on Nigerians to deal with such "extremists." The *Times* adds that "what Nigerians must do therefore, is to remove . . . the present gang of irresponsible communist-minded youths."[26] Thompson describes this type of symbolic rhetoric as one in which an enemy is constructed or identified within the ranks and "portrayed as [so] evil and harmful or threatening" as to demand collective resistance or expurgation.[27] Those dismissed by the *Citizen* and the *Times* as a "gang" of "extremists" and "communist-minded" are described by the *West African Pilot* as "filled with fine moral and ethical concepts, each reflecting the sincere, profound beliefs of workers."[28]

The representation of individuals and groups embedded in relations of domination as endowed with certain characteristics accentuates these features, for good or ill, at the expense of others, thereby assigning individuals and groups positive or negative images. As a strategy of symbolic construction, metaphors can be used both ways. This is, for instance, evident in the position expressed in southern newspapers that the "moderation" of the north is a negative factor in the push toward independence. The *Citizen* counters this, however. First, the *Citizen* reviews the state of affairs: "Whereas in other

Regions at the moment, there is considerable political activity—exaggerated, no doubt, by the organs supporting the contesting parties—the North seems hardly yet to have awakened to the new constitution." The paper then locates the problem by demeaning the nature of politics in the south: "In the East and West Regions, the political campaigns seem to be degenerating into little more than a slanging match between rival organisations."[29] The rival organizations were obviously the NCNC and the AG. This narrative differentiation in a way removes the north from the "rivalry" or "bickering" of the "slanging match." Yet the *Citizen* characterizes the positive attributes of the north as "the traditional quiet and orderly manner [of the northerner]." The north's "aloofness" is then defended and constructed as rather dignifying: "But there is one aspect of the Southern polemics which we must comment upon—the word 'moderation' has been used as a taunt. Why this should be so we cannot understand. . . . The person who practices moderation in private life is generally to be respected. The same thing we believe is true of public life and party politics. The opposite is excess—or extremism. People who go to extremes in private life, usually end in trouble. So it is in the affairs of parties and nations. . . . The *Citizen* believes in moderation, and is prepared to support those who proclaim it is politics, because we sincerely believe that the antonym—extremism—if carried into effect, ultimately means misery for the mass of the people."[30]

But the "moderation" of the northerner, for the *Pilot*, makes him a "very patient imperialist pet": "The Northerner is involuntarily bottled, corked and sealed from all manner of outside interference by his foreign caretaker, the grand idea being to keep him unsoiled and undefiled by contact with his brethren down South. That has been the imperialist game for the last fifty years where the Southerner had been mercilessly maligned, stigmatised and luridly coloured." However, the *Pilot* maintains there is hope for this "imperialist pet," as he will later be encouraged to join the "grand nation," which his "foreign caretakers" are preventing him from joining. The *Pilot* adds that "with freedom of association, the Northerner will soon come to realise that we must grow homogeneously as one nation."[31]

Taking a position similar to that of the *Pilot*'s, the *Tribune* argues that the north "should not be blamed, but rather pitied" because "West and East, the places where the healthy and enlightening sun rises and sets, have received in great abundance, their showers of applause for a noble show. . . . The rest of Nigeria beckoned to the North to join in the march but there was no response."[32]

The *Pilot* emphasizes the "stigmatisation" of the southerner in the north, overlooking or euphemizing the constant "stigmatisation" going on between the eastern and western regions (where the *Tribune*'s "healthy and enlightening sun rises and sets"), aided by the *Service* and the *Tribune*. Yet the two regions are not united in anything other than their opposition to the "imperialist pet." Even in deriding the north, in which the "imperialist has not yet been cornered in the race to perpetuate his rule in this country," the *Pilot* attacks any politician—apparently Chief Obafemi Awolowo (popularly called Awo), the leader of the Action Group—"who thinks Nigeria can be emancipated through political parties with tribal bias." The paper invites such politicians to visit Sokoto, Adamawa, and Bauchi provinces in the north to witness the "vice hold" of the imperialists: "In Sokoto Province today to be specific, the ordinary Northerner, let alone the Sultan and the Alkalis, will find it hard to understand what the NCNC, or even less, the Action Group, mean by the present struggle to break the shackles of imperialism to seek for freedom when to all appearances, he is the monarch of all he surveys." These "ignorant" Sultan and Alkalis—metonymically the whole northern region—and their limited conception of freedom constitute such a formidable "stumbling block" in the path of freedom and progress that it can hardly be righted, argues the *Pilot*: "The Northerner has been completely imbued with a false sense of security, misconceived idea of importance, or greatness, of unlimited authority and majesty—that any attempt to win his support, to enlighten or educate him, to appreciate the fact that he is not that free, is bound to fail."[33] It can be argued that the *Pilot*'s condescending attempt to deconstruct the "northerner" in this way is part of the elaborate attempts to contest and dismiss Frederick Lugard's weighty description of the Fulbe (Fulani) emirs, in the early years of the subjugation of the areas that became northern Nigeria, as "born rulers, and incomparably above the negroid tribes in ability."[34] Edmund Dene Morel, self-described as a "member of the West African Section of the Liverpool Chamber of Commerce," in his book *Affairs of West Africa*, echoes Lugard when he praises the Fulani whose "achievements . . . in Nigeria" left him "lost in wonder."[35] It is therefore interesting that the dominant ethnic group (Fulani) and their core leadership (emirs and other leaders), which

Lugard considered "incomparably above the negroid tribes," including those in the south, were considered "backward" and in need of "enlightenment" and education by the southerners.

Before dwelling on the rivalry in the southern region, a region that is sometimes presented as if it were the solid antithesis of a monolithic and backward north,[36] let us observe that barely one year earlier the *Pilot* had noted the potential of the north to join the grand nation in progress. The doubts about the north's ability to do this are transposed to the "others" (political observers) as if they were not shared by the *Pilot* and the NCNC. The paper commented: "Political observers who for long had doubted the capability of our Northern brethren to don the toga of maturity are fast jumping to the conclusion that with the restraining arm of the expatriate removed, the North can march abreast the South."[37]

This capacity to wear the "toga of maturity," in the *Pilot*'s view, is a result of contact with the north's civilized other, that is, the southern regions: "The well-nigh seven months contact with the South through the meetings of the House of Representatives has helped to remove much of the clouds of despair which for long made the Northerner a forgotten brethren in the social milieu."[38] The south is, therefore, presented as the light that will overcome the darkness of the north. The constant condescension to the northern region in the southern newspapers seems so natural or conventional that it is hardly treated with caution or caveat in the newspapers. The region is constantly presented as one that exists in a Hobbesian state.

In these narratives of power, the north is presented not only as an "inferior" in Western civilizational terms, but its readiness to join the rest of the grand nation is also rendered in a condescending manner: "The vocal section of the North is its youth. They have tomorrow and with the temper of the nation clamouring for the rewards of the morrow, no one will essay the hope that the Northern youth will watch unmoved the advance of his Southern compeer without joining the stream of progress."[39]

Expurgation of the Southern Compeer

The rivalry, however, between the eastern and western regions and the political parties dominant in both is no less vociferous than the rivalry between these two regions and the northern region. Prior to the formation of the AG in 1951, the NCNC had achieved unrivaled prominence and credibility as the only nationalist party. The formation of the AG, emerging from Egbe Omo Oduduwa (Society for Oduduwa descendants—the Yoruba) after the crisis and eventual collapse of the NYM, the organization of activists and nationalists, meant that the NCNC could no longer enjoy its position, particularly in the western region and in Lagos, without a strong challenge. Moreover, the two parties were led by the protagonists in the bitter battle for the soul of the NYM, that is, Zik and Awo.[40] This translates to the continuation of old rivalries and old accusations of "tribalism," as evident in the NYM crisis.

As regional electoral politics began in the context of the Macpherson Constitution (1951), the "unity" between the eastern and western region leaders in their attacks against the northern region—which later started a political party, the NPC, to represent its dominant interests—ended. The *Pilot* consequently regarded the AG as an "NYM-Oduduwa clique and reactionary group"[41] with a "tribal tinge" and "Pakistan-like" goals.[42]

The *Tribune* argued in this vein that "background" (the past) would come into play in the "forthcoming elections," and concluded that "we have a sure rest of mind and pride that the leader of Action Group will score heavily over Dr. Azikiwe and his train of mischief-makers." The paper placed on record past statements of a "notorious liar" (Azikiwe), with his "nefarious acts and vile propaganda" over taxation, "for the present generation and posterity to read and judge what sort of politician-capitalist he is." The word "capitalist" must be understood in context. This was a period in which socialism was very popular among anticolonial activists in Africa; it was as much praise among activists to be called a socialistas it was a smear to be called a capitalist. The subject of Zik's "sins," according to the *Tribune*, was his "empty effusions called [a] presidential address to the 'Ibo Nation' in 1949," when he reportedly said that "we [the Igbo] have been taxed without representation and our contributions in taxes have been used to develop other areas, out of proportion to the incidence of taxation in those areas." The *Tribune* charged that "in short, Zik indicated that the West and the North were living on the resources of the 'fabulous wealth' of the East . . . [and that] the East has never had amenities in proportion with her output."

The paper then narrated "the truth about the whole situation," according to the Hick's Report on the old revenue allocation system:

"In 1948–49, the East was entitled to spend 25.9 percent of the revenue, but record shows that it went beyond the provision and spent 34.6 percent. West was entitled to 30.6 percent, but spent 24.7 percent. North was entitled to 43.9 percent, but spent 40.7 percent. In 1950–51, the allocation for the East was 30.9 percent, but spent 36.4 percent. West had 27.4 percent, spent 27.9 percent; and North 41.7 percent but spent 35.7 percent. . . . Besides, the following records about the social amenities for the three regions show that East has been living quite luxuriously on the resources of other regions."[43] (See table 3.1 for the distribution of social amenities in the regions of Nigeria berween 1948 and 1949.) The *Tribune*, however, did not tell its readers what formula was used in distributing the resources. What does it mean to say a region is "entitled" to an amount? Is the allocation based on a derivative principle or on need or population?

This struggle between the two southern regions translates to a struggle between the political parties representing the interests of the two regions, the NCNC and AG, and, ultimately, the key leaders of the two parties, particularly Zik and Awo. For the *Pilot*, the AG was a party that represents evil and should therefore not be allowed to survive. The AG was dangerous to Nigerian unity, peace, and progress and all that the NCNC represented, the *Pilot* declared: "In their determination to remain difficult to Nigerian unity, in their rashness and utter disregard for the fate of millions of Westerners, in their undisguised problems to a balanced economy of the Western Region, the Action Group Government of the West blindly gropes its way in a tragedy of horrifying complications. Beset on all sides by the evils of regionalisation, it is at the moment confronted with the Lagos merger issue, the re-classification of Ilorin . . . all uniting to intensify the horror of the spectre haunting the party."[44]

This "tragedy of horrifying complications" in which the AG government "blindly gropes" is contrasted with the NCNC, which, asserted the Pilot, "nevertheless . . . will not divert from its course of action, but will relentlessly continue to pilot the nation along our economic stability road to the beautiful sunny meadows where an independent Nigeria will thrive."[45] Placing the verb *pilot* beside *the nation* has symbolic implications: the paper sought to link the fate of the nation with the efforts or activities of its pilot. The *Pilot*, in turning its name into an active verb, can therefore be regarded as providing the pathway to saving the nation. The paper added that "things have come to such a pass that soon the nation will meet

Table 3.1. The distribution of social amenities in the regions of
Nigeria between 1948 and 1949 (per million of population)

	East	West	North
Hospital beds	590	235	215
Dispensaries	49	41	25
Primary schools	654	821	106
Secondary schools	20	6	4
Teacher training institutions	9	9	2

Source: "A Notorious Liar," *NT,* July 30, 1951.

again to determine whether a halt must be called to these expensive
incursions into the heart and stability of this country,"[46] ostensibly
represented by the *Tribune* and the AG.

The elaborate policy papers with which the announcement of
the formation of a new political party, the AG, was heralded earlier in the year, according to the *Pilot,* was a ruse, as the party was
only a "weakling [that] has no blue-print to execute": "In the spate
of only nine months, the Action Group, on the national plane,
has offered students of history nothing new in spite of its claim to
'bold plans.' It started off a parochial party to enable some 'political minions' to rise into public gaze, and then begin simulating
the NCNC's national policy."[47] The term "political minions" was a
veiled reference to Awo, whose name and image, at that point, did
not compare to the towering name and image of Zik, and whose
challenges to the paper's proprietor, Zik, could not, therefore, be
tolerated by the *Pilot.* Awo's emergence as an important figure in
youth, western, and federal politics (in that order) through the
NYM, Egbe Omo Oduduwa, and the AG, by which he became a
formidable rival of Zik, was achieved by "questionable methods,"
as far as *Pilot* was concerned. If Awolowo and the AG succeed with
such methods, the "nation" would become a reflection of its "fickle
lily-livered representatives": "If to attain an objective, questionable
methods must be employed and national solidarity and coher-
ence sacrificed on the altar of personal aggrandisement—only to
change tactics and play the other way round to save our face—then
the nation itself is the nature of fickle lily-livered representatives it
has unfortunately chosen."[48]

Therefore the "political minions" and their party (Awolowo, his supporters, and the AG), the *Pilot* asserted, constitute a danger to the western region in which the "great Yoruba race" is "penned in within . . . narrow confines." The "Yoruba race," the *Pilot* concluded, has "yet to appreciate the full predicament in which it is placed through the Action Group['s] tribalistic demarcation of the country. . . . Already the evils of Action Group['s] parochial nationalism is telling on the solidarity of its precious Western Region."[49] Even though it was Igbo-led, the NCNC, in alliance with (Yoruba) township groups and parties, had become dominant in the western region before the formation of the AG, which Richard Sklar describes as "the best organized, best financed, and most efficiently run political party in Nigeria."[50] Therefore the rise of the AG was a direct threat to the position and dominance of the NCNC in the region—and the rest of Nigeria.

When the *Daily Service* was founded in 1938 as the official organ of the NYM, it was seen immediately as a business rival, if not an ideological rival as well, of the *Pilot*. Ernest Ikoli, an ethnic Ijaw and the vice president of the NYM, was its founding publisher and editor, and H. O. Davies, a Yoruba, was its founding business manager. Ikoli was later supported by Awolowo in the battle for the leadership of the NYM. It was understandable, therefore, that the *Daily Service* later became a defender of the AG, the Yoruba, and Awolowo. Championing the position of the AG against the NCNC therefore became a critical responsibility of the *Service*. Against this backdrop, the *Service* responded to the attacks on the AG and Awolowo by the *Pilot* by also attacking Zik: "After he had been assisted to find his feet, Azikiwe turned round to attack every Western leader beginning with his benefactors. . . . He created confusion among the Yorubas. . . . Before Azikiwe came to Nigeria after he had been out of the Gold Coast, the Yorubas and the Ibos lived together happily. There was no hatred, no contempt, no bitterness between them. But as soon as he arrived he began to preach his doctrine of tribal hate."[51]

The narrative of "no hatred, no contempt, no bitterness" between the Yoruba and the Igbo before Zik returned to Nigeria may be attractive, but it is largely untrue. Even though Zik, as a symbol of Igbo accomplishment and leadership, substantially affected the enthusiasm of the Igbo in national politics, he cannot be accused of being solely responsible for the mutual recriminations between the two southern majority ethnic groups. As Richard Sklar correctly argues in relation to the controversy that led to the collapse of the NYM, Zik's emergence and role "merely crystallized antagonisms that were bound to mature" between the Igbo and the Yoruba. Before Zik's return to Nigeria, as Sklar states, "In Lagos, as in other urban centers, an ever-increasing number of industrious Ibo from the densely populated East has settled in quest of economic opportunities. Invariably their presence created new social tensions." Therefore, "Azikiwe [as] the first great Ibo leader of the twentieth century," despite "his constant affirmation of non-tribal African values . . . typified [the] growing assertiveness [of the Igbo] in Nigerian affairs," which heightened "latent Ibo-Yoruba tension."[52]

The narratives in the *Service*, however, would not admit to this complex understanding of the issues. Like most narratives, it simplified things by accusing Zik of being the originator of the conflict. And given the way in which the *Pilot* also used Zik as a metonymy for the Igbo, the eastern region, and the NCNC, the argument of the *Service* seems plausible.

The *Service* ridiculed the NCNC "hush-hush" special convention in which "top secret" decisions were said to have been made to break the Macpherson Constitution—which provides for "regionalisation"—a decision strongly supported by the NCNC and the *Pilot*. The NCNC, and therefore the *Pilot*, supported the adoption of a unitary system of government for Nigeria. Because regionalization was a federal arrangement that would likely limit the party's hegemony and reach, the party attacked the Macpherson Constitution. The *Service* argued: "Those who did not know the NCNC thought there was going to be a revolution or a constitutional crisis. . . . But we knew that Dr. Azikiwe will be the very last person to give up his 420 [pounds] per annum seat in the Western House of Assembly for any idealism. . . . What will ensure the achievement of self-government is not the empty braggadocio for which the NCNC is notorious but thorough and calculated planning and systematic execution."[53] The *Service* did not need to add that the AG is noted, in contrast to the NCNC's "empty braggadocio," for "thorough and calculated planning and systematic execution." But for the *Pilot*, those who choose regionalization—that is, the "Groupers" (AG)—were "antipodes . . . sworn enemies of progress, of light and of freedom."[54] The *Pilot's* NCNC, unlike the *Service's* NCNC (and its "empty braggadocio"), was "that force that strikes terror into the hearts of the enemies of one Nigeria."[55] The *Pilot* and the NCNC were often emphatic that they are for "one Nigeria," whereas those who disagree with them represent antiunity agents.

The crisis of the NYM rears its head here again when J. O., writing in the *Pilot*, disagreed with Arthur Prest, writing in the *Service*, that Zik destroyed the NYM. According to J. O., the "Movement" (NYM) destroyed itself through the agency of the *Service*: "The edifice was nobly conceived and the designers and the architects were activated by patriotic and national motives. While the erection of this edifice was in progress, some of the builders added very bad stones from a quarry which was owned and operated through tribalism. The edifice shook and later collapsed with a crash on the tribe-barters' heads. The quarry was the *Daily Service* and the builders and stones I leave to the readers to decipher."[56] "Bad builders" is an obvious metaphor for Awo and his colleagues, whereas the stones are Egbe Omo Oduduwa and the AG.

The *Service* consistently took on Zik as much as the *Pilot* consistently took on Awo. It seems that Zik's political initiatives and actions or any around him invited negative interpretation by the *Service*, just as Awo's invited negative interpretation by *Pilot*. Even the proposed cabinet reshuffle in the eastern region was derided by the *Service*, which stated that "the proposal of the Azikiwe clique in the NCNC to reshuffle the Eastern Regional Government is an eloquent evidence of opportunism and careerism."[57]

The consequences of Zik's "politics of hate," the *Service* asserted, is helped by the way Zik is able to "hoodwink" his ethnic constituents, because "many unsuspecting Ibos and Easterners fell victims to his devilish doctrine especially when he propagated the theory that the Ibo nation was destined by God to lead the whole of Africa out of the bonds of the ages."[58] These kinds of "absurdities," as ostensibly represented by the narratives of the *Service*, among others, was narrated by the *Pilot* as introducing issues of an "entirely personal character," which "become exposed and all the more pronounced when they decry Zik, call him names and daub him a dangerous character for no other reason than that he stands for one Nigeria, convinced that tribal struggles makes scientific objectivity a crime and in principle and practice, renders impossible any agreement and progress towards our goals."[59]

The rivalry between the AG and NCNC could be said to have been conducted mainly on the pages of newspapers, at least in the intervening period between elections. Even during the elections, newspaper stories became almost as crucial as the polling centers. For example, the *Service* averred that "foolery" was intrinsic to the membership of NCNC, and asked, "When does an NCNCer cease to be an NCNCer? Answer: When he ceases to be fooled by newspaper stunts."[60] The leader of the NCNC, Zik, was described by the *Service* as "the aspiring dictator of Yaba [Lagos] . . . surrounded by raga-muffins, gutter snipes and political rouges."[61] The *Pilot* disagreed with the characterization of the NCNC by affirming that there "is a fundamental difference between the NCNC and the gang of political careerists who call themselves Action Group."[62]

The narratives in the *Pilot* upon Zik's defeat on January 10, 1952, at the Western House of Assembly in the election (by the electoral college) to the Federal House of Representatives sounded the death knell on the idea of "Nigeria" as conceived at some point by the NCNC and the AG. The action, in which Dr. A. B. I. Olorun-Nimbe, a Yoruba member of the NCNC, stood against Zik and was supported by the AG members, provoked passion in the *Pilot*. The paper asked for a boycott of the House of Representatives in the event of the "indication of the doctrine of tribalism preached by the Action Group."[63] Onitsha, Zik's hometown in the Igbo east, was "shocked" by the news, whereas a "pall of gloom hovered over" it because of what happened to "Onitsha's gift to the West," that is, Zik.[64] Zik's father reportedly stated: "I've warned my boy long ago not to cast pearl[s] before swine. It is up to him to realise that some human beings are like pigs, the more you want them to keep clean, the more they desire to remain in the sty."[65]

For Zik's father, Zik was the "pearl" that was cast before the Yoruba "swine," the "pigs" who refused to "keep clean" by voting for his son. This attitude collocated with the "consensus of opinion in the municipality" (Lagos), according to the *Pilot*, that the loss was not Zik's but that of the "electorates of Lagos and [the loss of] African prestige as a whole."[66] A strategy of dissimulation, and of displacement in particular, followed as Jesus Christ, Abraham Lincoln, and Mahatma Ghandi are referenced as having suffered a similar fate as Azikiwe, consequently investing him with their positive qualities. The *Pilot* editorialized: "How can the fate of one man be of much concern to the majority? . . . To the majority, this fact is a matter of indignation—indignation, in the sense that it was a plan by a bunch of spiteful politicians to have their revenge on a man whose towering stature in national affairs has kept them in obscurity for long."[67]

The *Tribune* seemed to answer the *Pilot*'s question concerning "the fate of one man in a majority" when it wrote: "Commenting on the spectacular overthrow of Nnamdi Azikiwe, perpetual president of the NCNC at the Western Elections, an Eastern paper warned the Yaba demagogue that in modern democratic forms of government no single individual is so powerful as to escape challenge, and no one can be regarded as indispensable."[68]

The *Pilot* captured Zik's defeat as "thunder" that rocked the NCNC. Therefore the paper asks that "the internal disintegrating forces in the NCNC [symbolized by Olorun-Nimbe, a Yoruba] should be checked and wiped out in enough time to prevent permanent harm." For the avoidance of doubt, the *Pilot* referenced the "Moscow Purge" in the Soviet Union, in which highly placed people "considered undesirable elements and enemies of the people suffered; they were either executed, imprisoned or banished to the wastes of Siberia."[69] The paper's recommendation of what should happen is a fitting example of Thompson's analysis of fragmentation as a mode of establishing relations of domination. This may take place through the expurgation of the other and involves "orienting forces . . . towards a target which is projected as evil, harmful or threatening,"[70] thereby legitimizing attacks on such targets.

Even the western region, the *Pilot* added, is "ashamed of the AG action" in the House. Though, "most nincompoops in the West talk of Ibo domination; . . . the West is ashamed of their action and the imperialists, though happy, looks on the Groupers with scorn."[71] However, the "nincompoops" in the *Tribune* responded by challenging the *Pilot*'s view: "In the Western Region where party politics has been organised on the international standard, Azikiwe found himself like a straw in mid-ocean, dejected and disserted, and ultimately failed to catch significant votes to take to the House of Reps because of his unpopularity."[72] For the *Tribune*, what happened to Azikiwe was merely the consequence of democratic electoral politics, in which an "unpopular" candidate lost, and not an example of the "tribal" politics that the *Pilot* loudly lamented.

However, the allegation of "Ibo domination" by the Yoruba press made only by "nincompoops in the West" contrasts with the *Pilot*'s condemnation of "stark Yoruba domination" by the Urhobos, a minority group in the western region, over the "humiliation" of the Oba of Benin, leading to calls for "truncation" from the west. The *Pilot*'s narrative also referred to the *Tribune*'s description of the

Yoruba people as "the great Yoruba people." This can be understood as an attempt by the *Pilot* to point to a "supremacist discourse" among the Yoruba, who are to be deconstructed later as former "vassals" of the Oba of Benin, the traditional ruler of the minority Bini of the western region. This was the *Pilot*'s indirect response to the constant accusation by the *Tribune* that Zik and the NCNC were attempting to impose "Ibo domination" on the western region and the rest of Nigeria. The *Pilot* linked the "supremacist" discourse of the *Tribune* to the "Hitlerite project." The *Pilot* asked: "But what of the name—'The Great Yoruba'? Did not Hitler begin that way with his 'great Germany' and 'superior race' and when it failed to attract attention did he not resort to mass annihilation in order to effectively establish German superiority?"[73]

Lucaites and Condit argue that a rhetorical narrative such as the above "serves as [an] interpretive lens through which the audience is asked to view and understand the verisimilitude of propositions and proof before it."[74] The content and form of this sort of narrative is conditioned by the specific audience for which it is meant, the context in which it appears, and the expected gain. Because such a rhetorical narrative operates in conflicting and competing contexts, it has a unity of direction and unity of purpose. It takes sides and offers "evidence" and "proves" a particular interpretation of the AG's behavior. Its voice is also univocal in orienting readers to a particular understanding of the situation. The narrative then requires that the "audience," in this case the people of Benin and Warri provinces (which are minority areas of the western region that contain a Yoruba majority), fight for separation from the west.

The *Pilot*, perhaps unwittingly, revealed why it has come up with the charge of a "Yoruba supremacist discourse": "In spite of sincere profession of leading Ibos, a gang of Yorubas who now club together, shielding themselves with Action Group umbrella, persisted in harping on the Ibo domination stunt thus making tribal relations to deteriorate.... Now that the Groupers' stunt of one tribe dominating another has spread to the Benins [Binis] and Itshekiris[,] who have concrete, not imaginary, proof of domination by the Action Group Yorubas, they are demanding a Central State, independent of the Yoruba Western Region."[75] The next day, the *Pilot* asserted the Binis reaction to the "national insult": "[A] Mid-Western State is the one and only effective answer to this brass-faced political jugglery."[76]

Interestingly, the *Pilot* did not see a parallel between the "great Yoruba people" and its report on the insult heaped on those it described as a "great people"—the Binis.[77] Rather, it paralleled the "righteous indignation" of the Binis to the "national pride" that sustained the British against Hitler's attempt to subjugate the British Isle.[78] It is interesting as well that the *Pilot* saw no contradiction in accusing the AG of gesturing at "mass annihilation" on the Nazi model by its reference to "the great Yoruba people,"[79] when it also called for "wiping out . . . undesirable elements and enemies of the people" in a Moscow-like purge.[80]

The *Service* responded to the *Pilot*'s attacks against the Yoruba and the AG by describing the paper's editor, Zik, as the "evil man" who disturbed the whole country because of his own "ambition": "But does it matter to him [Zik,] whose every act is dictated by his own personal ambition only?" The paper then called on "The East [to] reject this evil man as unequivocally as the West has done."[81] The *Service* justified the election that provoked heated narratives from the *Pilot*, while recommending it to the east. Even the NCNC ministers who were asked to resign by Zik were encouraged by the *Service* to stand firm against "an aspiring Hitler [Zik]," thereby deflecting back at Zik the dense, dark metaphor of unspeakable hate in the reference to the Nazis that the *Pilot* had directed at the Yoruba. The ministers were encouraged to snub Zik because "they are fighting not just for themselves but for the principle that one man shall not impose his will on the rest of the country and stifle every other opinion."[82] In pitching Zik discursively against the "rest of the country," the *Service* presented Zik as someone who is attempting to subordinate "the nation" to his "selfish ambition."

The refusal of the NCNC ministers to resign in accordance with Zik's and the party's wish was narrated by the *Service* as a refusal "to mortgage their consciences to one and only one individual . . . refusing to cooperate with evil, and . . . standing firm against confusion and dishonesty: [thus they] have dealt a heavy blow on the totalitarian ambition of Nnamdi Azikiwe. . . . And that is something for which posterity will long pay them deserving tribute." The action of Jaja Wachukwu and others who refused to resign is tied to "posterity" and rendered timeless through the assurance of the "eternal support of all decent men in all the Regions of Nigeria." Wachukwu was also said to be fighting against an "evil influence, the evil . . . which has been menacing the nation for so long under a masquerade."[83]

In spite of its own narratives of conflicts and "otherness," the *Service* accused Zik of being responsible for the entire disharmony in the west, which he was now "transferring" to the eastern region: "The tribal disharmony which Azikiwe caused in the West for over a decade is now being repeated in the Eastern Region. That is Aziki- we's trade and the trade of all aspiring dictators. If they do not cre- ate confusion and set tribe[s] against one another their chances of success are very narrow. . . . We speak from experience and we know what harm Azikiwe can do if allowed too free a hand."[84] The "expe- rience" was narrated by the *Service* in this way: "Here in the Western Region, the leaders and the people have learnt to put [Zik] in his right place. After he had been assisted to find his feet, [he] turned round to attack every Western leader beginning with his benefac- tors. . . . He created confusion among the Yorubas and gathered round him the folsam [*sic*] and jetsam of Yoruba society. . . . And because Yoruba leaders would not brook any dictatorship, they were made subjects of abuse, malicious lies and destructive criticisms."[85]

Bennett and Edelman argue that narratives such as these from both the *Pilot* and the *Service* "that embody the truths of [the politi- cal] elite and their publics seem objective" to each side because they are confirmed repeatedly by selective details that are self-fulfilling. The authors elaborate on how the *Pilot, Service, and Tribune* pres- ent "comforting fantasies" for the group and party they represent: "When a ruling group promotes its cherished ideals at the expense of critical evaluations of the actions, taken in the name of those ide- als, the telling . . . becomes comforting fantasy—escape from the otherwise unpleasant contradictions of life experience."[86]

Self-Government and the Transformation of Unity and Discord

Narratives not only provoke transformation in relations of unity and discord, they also reflect, replicate, or reproduce relations of unity and discord. In the context of late-colonial Nigeria, the politics of self-government, which led to critical transformations in the strate- gies and tactics by which ethno-regional groups and political parties pursued their interests, also led to changes in the narratives of news- papers representing ethno-regional groups and political parties.

When the NCNC and AG aligned in the fight for self-government by 1956, the "gang of political careerists" in the AG and "aspiring dictators" in the NCNC were transformed in the narratives of the *Pilot* and the *Service,* respectively. The "careerists" and "dictators," according to the *Pilot,* became "militant nationalists" who forgot "their differences and demonstrate a united front against colonial status . . . in the House of Representatives."[87] Thus the western region (and AG) and the eastern region (and NCNC) were back in their united opposition to the northern region and the NPC. Anthony Enahoro, one of the *Pilot*'s erstwhile members of a "gang of political careerists," now introduced what the *Pilot* described as a "classic motion."[88] Awo, the leader of the "gang," was transformed by the *Pilot* into a leader who gave a "pungent and critical speech . . . spotlighting the iniquitous role of the British government and the Northern members of the house."[89] Also, the resignation of the four ministers in the "gang" from the colonial federal cabinet, according to the "new" perspective of the *Pilot,* "will go down in the political history of this country as epoch-making for three reasons: First, it is a revolt against official hypocrisy; secondly, it is non-co-operation with bondage; lastly, it is an indication that Nigeria has arrived."[90] The four ministers, who were AG members, had resigned in protest against the opposition of the NPC to the 1956 proposed date for independence and the colonial government's decision to postpone the debate on independence. Consequently, the *Pilot* celebrated the action of those it had earlier dismissed, stating that "the nation must thank Messrs. [Bode] Thomas, [Arthur] Prest, [Ladoke] Akintola and the Ooni of Ife for their moral courage and patriotism."[91] The *Service* shared this sentiment with the *Pilot* and described the resignation as "the greatest event in the political and constitutional history of Nigeria."[92]

A few days before the motion for self-government was introduced on March 31, 1953, a rapprochement of sorts had started between the NCNC and AG, and therefore between the *Pilot* and the *Service* as they aligned against the northern region and the colonial government, even while asking the north to take the "reasonable" course by joining them. Argued the *Pilot:* "We believe that an issue of this nature on which outcome depends so much the future and solidarity of the great peoples of this country transcends all political party rivalries. Nationalists must vote for it." Then the *Pilot* added a "word" for the northern region: "The present session has revealed one thing, and we care not whom we offend to say it. This session has seen the alliance of the [colonial] Government and the Northern bloc. We hope this will not be repeated today. . . . There can be no reason for any Nigerian to vote against this motion today—or even to abstain from voting."[93] The *Service* agreed more or less with the *Pilot*: "The North is the only one place in this country today where the forces of imperialism are still well entrenched. . . . The time has come when they [northern leaders] must make a hard choice between Nigerian nationalism and British imperialism," adding the next day, "[so as not] give the impression that the [northern] bloc wants to constitute a stumbling block in our march to national independence. We ask our Northern brethren to think and think again."[94]

When the north "failed to think and think again," as the *Service* demanded, and so opposed the motion for self-government in 1956, all narrative hell broke loose, even as the northern representatives' faux pas, asserted the *Pilot*, "heralds New East and West[ern regional] understanding." The *Pilot* continued its narrative of what happened at the Federal House of Representatives: "British civil servants and their minions presented [an] opportunity to militant nationalists of this country to forgo their differences and demonstrate a united front against colonial status yesterday in the House of Representatives." Given this conspiratorial combine of British civil servants and their minions—a reductive combination that would otherwise look big if presented as "Her Majesty's Government and Northern leaders"—the forces of light ("militant nationalists"), including the leaders of the NCNC (Zik and Balogun) and the leaders of the AG (Awo and Bode Thomas), "shook hands heartily" after the House session, showing that, according to the *Pilot*, "a united front is possible in the struggle for Nigerian freedom." Consequently, the *Pilot* stated that "when this unity becomes a reality those responsible for [the] debacle of yesterday [the British and the members from the northern region] will have themselves to blame, because of their questionable diplomacy in pitting one brother against another."[95] The *Service* pursued essentially the same line, describing the "alliance" of the northern region and "British imperialism" as an "evil enterprise" against the possibilities of "national liberation," represented by what the *Pilot*'s called a "united front." The *Service* added: "The historical events of yesterday . . . have given the signal for the beginning of the struggle for national liberation. . . . The North has taken its place as the dutiful ally of British imperialism in Nigeria. . . . The events of yesterday were a demonstration of the evil which British intended to perpetrate in our country."[96]

Both papers (*Pilot* and *Service*), in a new understanding and rapprochement that promoted and serviced the alliance of their parties (NCNC and AG), agreed that the northern region's majority in the Federal House was the only basis for the "demonstration of evil"—that is, the defeat of the motion in the House of Representatives for Nigeria's independence in 1956. This majority was not narrated as a "fact" agreed to in 1950 at the Ibadan conference by the "militant nationalists," rather, it was narrated as an "iniquitous imposition": "The Northern members not only opposed the motion but also sought by a dilatory motion, to prevent other people from saying anything on it at all—all because they have a fifty percent majority. We have been opposed to this undemocratic way of representation in a federal parliament. [It was a demonstration] of all the evil . . . [of] this fifty percent representation which places the North in a position to impose its will on the whole country."[97] The *Pilot* added: "History was made . . . yesterday, when the Northern members used their majority to vote en bloc to defer debate on a well-conceived motion . . . on the issue of self-government in 1956. . . . It is the tyranny of the majority that made it possible for the power-drunken and dumb-driven North not only to retard freedom for Nigeria and the Cameroons but to deny our representatives the right to debate such a motion."[98]

The *Pilot*'s and the *Service*'s interpretation of what happened against the background of the Ibadan conference in 1950, in which the two regions agreed with the northern region's request for a 50 percent share of the seats in the Federal House of Representatives (based on its proportion of the population), is an excellent example of how meaning is mobilized in the service or disservice of power in the context of the relations of domination.

The images presented by the *Pilot*'s choice of phrasing had powerful consequences for the narration of national togetherness in Nigeria. From this period on, the portrayal of the north as a "retarded," "backward," and "obstructive" section of Nigeria became common in the press. This other (northern region), on the basis of the foregoing narratives, became suitably elegible for expurgation, given the "fact" that it existed outside of a standard, the "promoted ideal," which in this case was "freedom for Nigeria." Conversely, this controversy also produced the symbolization of unity. The first symbol of unity was that of the eastern and western regions "showing their oneness in the sacred cause of Nigerian freedom."[99] The *Pilot* editorialized: "The NCNC and Action Group may be as separate as the fingers in matters of details and procedure, but experience has shown that both are irrevocably committed to the solemn pledge of winning self-government for Nigeria in 1956. . . . As for the Northern bloc [read: stumbling bloc], we know that they are being led by the nose by imperialists who have no intension of releasing 'what they have.' Now, therefore, is the time for East and West to work and plan together."[100]

Now that the whole nation of "brothers" shared a "common destiny" and was separated from its foreign other, the "British imperialists," the *Pilot* argued: "Let us therefore make it plain to our brothers in the North that times have changed. The old form of propaganda which put a barrier between the Northerners and Southerners must now be exposed. Europeans may go and come, but Northerners and Southerners will continue to live together, work together and face the same destiny now or in the future."[101] But this common destiny would not hold in the "present," as the Honorable Malam Ahmadu Bello, the Sardauna of Sokoto and the "voice of the north," made a speech "which brought to a climax the crisis in the House." The *Pilot* commented: "'The mistake of 1914 [has] now come to light,' was the only sentence he [Bello] made before sitting down with apparent grief. The mistake of amalgamating Northern and Southern Regions in 1914 by Lord Lugard had, in his opinion, precipitated the crisis over the issue of political independence from Nigeria in 1956."[102] The *Service* then narrated Bello's speech in a similar vein, but added that the logic should be followed through: "The very last sentence uttered by the Northern spokesman as the climax of his previous utterances in the House of Representatives was that . . . amalgamation was a mistake—a mistake which had now come to light. We admire his frankness in that statement. . . . If it is true that the amalgamation of Nigeria is a mistake then it is time we stopped deceiving ourselves."[103] Continued the *Service*: "When the Nationalists of this country called on the central legislature to associate itself with our popular demand for self-government in 1956, the spokesman of the North repeated the threat to secede if the other regions refuse to toe the Northern line. . . . As the Sardauna himself stated, there was no Nigeria 60 years ago. If the North want to break away and remain independent of the South they may jolly well do so. . . . If the present attitude of those who now happen to find themselves on the top in the North leads to a break, the South has nothing to lose."[104]

The first joint official meeting of the NCNC and the AG Parliamentarian Council at the "much-shaking" House of Representatives, "in which matters of common interests were discussed," that is, after the self-government motion controversy led to the adjournment of the House, was described by the *Pilot* as marked by the absence of the negative other, since "this time, there were no Northerners there, no NCNC expelled men, no rebels and no reactionaries."[105] These "Northerners, NCNC expelled men, rebels and reactionaries" will no longer be tolerated in the spatial boundaries of "the free and the liberated," the *Pilot* added. They are to be expelled, as they have contacted a "contagion" that is spreading and that will end in "doom": "Now that the struggle for self-government in 1956 has assumed an active form, our infected Northerner members and Eastern Ministers may have to seek asylum in Britain or in the land of perpetual serfdom where they may continue to 'sit-tight' till doomsday."[106]

When Ahmadu Bello, the leader of the northern members of the Federal House, issued a press statement after the meeting of northern federal legislators in Kaduna "deploring the attitude of the Lagos people who hooted, booed and jeered" at them, the *Pilot* reported that "he [Bello] failed to call secession by name, but implied in his concluding sentences, that the Northerners would concentrate now on Northern development and pay less attention to the centre." But this attempt by the northern region to sever the links with the rest of Nigeria over self-government was narrated as the opinion of a leadership disconnected from the mass of its following, thus failing to reflect their aspiration for freedom and common destiny with the southern regions. The *Pilot* reported: "Kaduna, April 6—The clamour for fixing target date for self-government in this country is as loud and consistent here in the North as it is in the East and West despite the attitude of the Northern representatives in the House of Representatives. The fact [is] that the majority of those who represent the North in the central legislature today represents not the growing articulate masses of the North, but the fading class of chiefs and native administration officials who consider it "abominable sin" to depart from the advice and instruction of British District officers and Residents."

In what this narrative claimed to be news, but which was obviously opinion, the "old path" from which the youth of the north (none of whom was mentioned or quoted) were departing was presented as a path of divisiveness: "From the days of Lord Lugard, every effort has been made to keep the North and South poles apart in all matters, social, political, educational and otherwise. . . . [But] thanks to NCNC and Action Group heroes, militant nationalism has come into the North and will stay until freedom is won." Images of salvation and divine intervention in the crusade against "evil" becomes necessary in "warfare," concluded the Pilot: "The alliance of imperialism and feudalism will henceforth be fought from every nook and corner [*sic*] and Allah will surely protect the holy crusaders of the nationalist army as they enter the first phase of psychological warfare. The youth of the North stand for a united Nigeria and are prepared to die for it, whatever may be the reaction of pampered chiefs, reactionaries, imperialists and their stooge."[107]

The *Service* picked up this trope, insisting that the "real north," which it does not define, is joined to the south in a "national resolution" to be free, independent, and united. This grand solidarity, above and beyond the position of the "other north" (of "fading chiefs and native administration officials"), correlates with universal ideals. Asserting that the "Sardauna Group"—a phrase meant to diminish the popularity and legitimacy of the northern legislators led by the Sardauna—plan to "carry their threat to [its] logical conclusion," the imagined grand solidarity was summoned by the *Service*: "We believe that this country must stand together in freedom as it has remained one in bondage. We cannot afford to break ourselves into bits and pieces. The *Daily Service*—and in this we claim to speak for the Action Group—firmly believes that the salvation of the whole of the black race lies in a powerful and united Nigeria. For this reason, we would oppose any attempt by any section to break away."

But the *Service* would not mind allowing secession if it was the consensus of the people of the northern region, which the paper believed to be otherwise. The *Service* accused "Fulani imperialists" and their "British counterparts" for being responsible for the threat: "If the desire to secede came from the people of the Northern Region it would have been understandable. There is nothing anyone can do if the North, the real North, wishes to secede. But, we know it does not. . . . The threat of secession is nothing but the product of the imagination of a few Fulani imperialists actively guided by their British counterpart. The north does not want to secede." The *Service* therefore concluded on a note of hope for the imagined nation by declaring that "the North and the South will remain one country and together we shall achieve complete self-government in 1956."[108]

In many ways, these excerpts from the *Service* are a good example of the typical strategies of legitimation of the relations of power through rationalization, that is, as Thompson writes, "the construction of a chain of reasoning defending or justifying a set of social relations and institutions, persuading the audience of the desirability of supporting them," universalization, in which "relations and institutional arrangements which serve the interests of some are represented as serving all and open to being acceded by anyone," and naturalization, through which "claims are enfolded in stories that link past, present and future in a timeless tradition, inventing a community that transcends the experience of conflict, difference and division, thereby justifying the power of those who hold particular position"[109] within the sociopolitical totality. The *Pilot* and the *Service* used legitimation to defend and elaborate the interests, parties, and regions they served. In this context, the "real north" of the *Service* and the *Pilot* comes out. The *Pilot* wrote: "The actual determining factor is whether the Sardauna does carry the North with him or not. . . . The real North as represented by NEPU, [the] Askanist Movement[,][110] and the people of [the] Middle-Belt have declared that they are prepared to live or die with the South on the issue of self-government in 1956. . . . The Sardauna and his fellow aristocrats can certainly be left out without any harm to the cause."[111] These attacks on "pampered chiefs," the "Sardauna and fellow aristocrats," and emirs strike at the center of the north's values and culture, given that these people are respected in the north and, indeed, are the popular leaders of the region. The "voice" of the north, the *Citizen*, had stated earlier that "the people of the North, in particular, value these leaders who have devoted their lives to the well-being of the areas they serve and rule.[112] [The emirs] hold in their hands the destiny of the North."[113]

The northern power elite, which lacked the support of a virile and dynamic press,[114] unlike their southern "other," resorted at times to the colonial Northern Broadcasting Service to counter the "hegemonic" designs of the southern power elite. Malam Isa Kaita, the northern member of the House of Representatives, spoke regularly on the radio to defend the NPC and the region. He alleged that the southerners wanted to drive the British away so as to dominate the north. But he was dismissed by the *Pilot* as someone who, at forty-one, had spent his life "towards the buttressing of feudal autocracy" by telling "striking lies." The *Pilot* added: "Mallam Kaita . . . has not shown gumption in bringing the freedom that he had seen abroad into his own country. . . . He may succeed in deluding a few Northerners, but in the end he will have to pay the price which stooges of his type have been compelled to pay throughout history."[115]

The "price" that the *Pilot* believed Kaita will pay must be understood in the context of the fact that he was not just another northern politician speaking out, he was, as the *Citizen* described him, "one of the North's leading spokesmen."[116]

The 1953 Constitutional Talks

Narratives can unite and divide. The 1953 Constitutional Talks in London tore apart the alliance between the NCNC (the *Pilot*) and the AG (the *Service*), retuning the equation to a northeast alliance against the west. But this was not before the *Pilot-Service* "alliance" reached its peak over the self-government issue in London. It was the status of Lagos (see chapter 3) that killed the alliance. Before the delegates departed for the talks, the *Service* had warned that "the very future of [Nigeria] is dangerously poised on the outcome of the conference," thereby calling on the delegates to "express in univocal language, the true feelings of the people of this country."[117] Following this, the *Service* focused on the big problem (the Northern Region/NPC), that is, "the arch-opponent of self-government."[118] The *Service* stated: "The Sardauna and his party ought to know by now that it is not in their own interest to fall prey to the machinations of imperialist limpets. If they allow themselves to be led by the nose as usual . . . they may live to regret their toying at a crucial moment with the fate of 33 million Nigerians."[119] For the *Tribune*, the opponents of self-rule in 1956 were "unfit to exist": "The Northern aristocrats who seem to act as megaphones for imperialists see no possibility of self-government in 1956. Some say 1956 is too early . . . while our turbaned brothers from the fringe of the Sahara believe in self-government when practicable."[120] Continued the *Tribune* two days later: "We . . . view with commiseration this villainous conception and interpretation of self-government by our robed legislators of the Northern Region. . . . If there is any man who is still not ready for this objective, he is unfit to exist."[121]

The basic lines of narratives on the question of the status of Lagos as the federal capital and its relationship with the region (west) where it is located had been laid before the London Conference of 1953. The *Citizen* earlier reported this question as "a storm in a tea cup . . . accompanied with thunderbolts and lightening," which was capable of killing the Macpherson Constitution. Malam Ibrahim Imam was scheduled to raise the storm by seconding a motion by an eastern representative that Lagos be made independent of the western region. The *Citizen* reported: "There is no doubt that the Eastern Representatives will support the motion and so will the two NCNC representatives from the West. . . . The balance of power lies with the North. . . . But there is no doubt that there are many Northerners opposed to the idea." If the motion was tabled for discussion, the *Citizen* expected to see: "The Action Group representatives putting up a strong and bitter fight against the motion. The extremist members believe that if the motion is accepted, the West would ask that the capital be removed to another Region and should be 'a no man's land.' The moderates will ask the question to which there can be no effective reply: 'What has Lagos suffered so far since it has been merged with the West?'"[122]

It was therefore obvious at this point, as the *Citizen* showed, that the northern region was not opposed to retaining Lagos as part of the western region—as the western region and the AG wanted. But the NCNC and the eastern region were opposed to this. For the NCNC (the *Pilot*) and the AG (the *Service* and *Tribune*), the party was over in the heat of the Lagos controversy. As the two parties expressed opposing views on the question of the status of Lagos as a capital city, the *Service* stated: "There have been rumours of underhand tricks, one ally stabbing the other at [*sic*] the back at the London Conference. . . . The recent activities of one of the parties to the alliance seem to confirm these rumours. . . . If indeed the alliance has not broken . . . it is, at least, certain that the NCNC is not being true to the spirit in which it [the alliance] was born."[123]

Two days later, the *Pilot* addressed the emergent problems, even though it hoped that it would not affect the alliance between the NCNC and the AG over self-government in 1956: "Both the Action Group and the *Daily Service* have declared openly and have set out to demonstrate by means of statements and press articles that they will not compromise on the issue of Lagos. It is only fair, therefore, that the NCNC and its supporters should justifiably make it known that they too will not compromise. . . . This does not and should not affect the alliance or the primary objective for which it was formed."[124]

However, it was too late to save the alliance, as the *Pilot* began to call the NCNC "the only nation-wide political organisation which holds the balance of the unity of the country in its hands" and "the hope of the nation," which "reactionary elements are doing everything possible to smash." The *Pilot* consequently declared: "With the Action Group unfortunately back to the tribal shrine from which it emerged, the NCNC has been left as the only nationalist party capable of carrying on the fight for a united Nigeria. The Action Group . . . has once again started to beat the tribal drum inviting [a] . . . return to the ugly old days of hate, rancour and disunity."[125] The *Service* replied that, on the contrary, it was the alliance with the AG that brought the "much-vaunted" NCNC alive and that still this "does not mean that the truth should be suppressed and that fraud should replace honesty,"[126] because "the NCNC has failed to put forth any reasonable argument to support their own contention that Lagos should be separated from the West. Let them admit failure instead of inventing imaginary stories in order to whip up the people against what is right."[127]

The shift in the NCNC and the *Pilot*'s political calculations is evident in the narratives that signpost the end of the NCNC-AG alliance. That the NCNC is moving north is evident in the *Pilot*'s report of the "secret . . . that the NPC leaders have learnt to respect and trust Dr. Azikiwe because of the great statesmanship the National President and his party displayed in London." Those that the *Pilot* had condemned as "imperialist pets" and "allies of British imperialism" with "misconceived ideas of importance" were now transformed by the same paper into "NPC leaders."[128]

However, the *Service* saw Dr. Azikiwe's action in London as showing that he was convinced that the time to "sell out" to the British and the north had come in order to become the first prime minister of Nigeria. This is particularly so regarding Zik's support at the London Conference for granting 50 percent representation to the north. The *Service* wrote: "Let Dr. Azikiwe stand before the Nation to explain his actions. The game of deceit cannot go on indefinitely, it is bound to be exposed and from now on we will expose the hollowness of the vanity of the office-seeking man and his band of corrupt and treacherous men."[129]

With their alliance gone, the NCNC and AG turned to the north, even while still dismissing each other as undeserving of an alliance with the northern region and NPC. The "new" northern region, for the *Pilot*, was "remarkably quiet," bending "down to the urgent task of educating their people on the implications of the decisions of the London conference with particular reference to self-government in 1956," thus setting examples for the AG in "broadmindedness, tolerance and magnanimity of spirit in national affairs."[130] The *Pilot* criticized the AG for attempting to do what the NCNC was doing by planning to work with the NPC and the northern region: "Having yelled and raved in vain for a review of the decision to separate Lagos from the West . . . [the AG] has temporarily submerged its usual impulse to fulminate against the NPC in an attempt to hobnob with Northerners."[131] The experience of the AG, according to the *Pilot*, contrasted with the NCNC's experience, because the latter, "as is often the case, has been received warmly in the North." The location of the "enemy" has, therefore, shifted for both parties. Thus the *Pilot* completely obliterated its own earlier narratives of the north while accusing AG, the *Service*, and the *Tribune* of an "impulse to fulminate" against the NPC: "The forces against Nigerian unity are no longer the North but some reactionary Southern politicians. . . . That is why the North and the NCNC should keep the spirit of oneness and direct their political onslaught against such enemies of Nigerian freedom."[132]

Evidently, adjectives used for political allies and enemies were usually empty of meaning except to the extent to which they became useful in politics. The *Pilot* and the *Service*, for instance, have called virtually every opposing politician "reactionary." The two newspapers, which were earlier fighting against such reactionaries, later turned to reactionaries themselves once they no longer agreed.

It is interesting how, in this context, the relations of power determine the meaning of words. The AG, whose members (the Groupers) the *Pilot* had commended for their "patriotism" and "militant nationalism" during the debates on self-government in 1956, turned into "inimical allies" and "devils," and the NCNC's break with them was "hailed in every part of Nigeria."[133] Within the space of three years, for the *Pilot*, depending on where it stood with the NCNC, the AG moved from "a gang of political careerists" to "militant nationalists" to the "politically irresponsible." Within the same period, for the *Service* and the *Tribune*, depending on where they stood with the

AG, the NCNCers moved from "Azikiwe and his train of mischief makers" and "nefarious liars" to "militant nationalists" to "sell-outs to the British and North."[134]

Conclusion: The Nationalist Press and the Grand Nation

Although the narratives in the newspapers emphasized fractionalization and otherness, there were simultaneous as well as contradictory assumptions in the rival newspapers that (1) each side represented the *true* spirit of the nation in its narratives, and (2) despite the fractionalizing narratives of the other side, the true spirit of the nation had triumphed, or would triumph, in the end, given the collective and true aspiration of the people of Nigeria to create a grand nation. Against this backdrop, in spite of all the attacks and counterattacks, and notwithstanding the accusations against one another, the "nationalist section" of the press (including the *Pilot*, the *Service*, and the *Tribune*), in contradistinction to the "reactionary section" (including the *Times* and the *Citizen*), the *Pilot* argued, was responsible for creating a Nigerian grand nation and counteracting the subversion of this grand solidarity by imperialists. However, for the most part, the *Pilot* believed that this press fully represented the nation: "Imagine what predicament this country would be in today if there were no nationalist press to give the people the true facts. What chaos would be caused here and what impressions would be given the outside world if the nationalist press were not here to counteract the diabolical propaganda of the imperialist." The nationalist press makes the grand nation possible, argued the *Pilot*, even though it sees itself as the embodiment of that press: "It would be impossible to have any sort of a nation. It would be impossible to have any sort of unity. . . . No nation, no group, no people can survive unless they can be heard. The nationalist press is the voice of the people of Nigeria."[135]

Also, despite the narratives of division and fragmentation and narratives of standardization and symbolization of unity, both the "nationalist press" and the "reactionary press" sometimes narrated to the possibilities and, at times, to the actual existence of a grand nation, of a people with a common destiny, above and beyond the fractious ethno nations. A nation such as the one these narratives construct is one that Emerson described as "a community of people who feel that they belong together in a double sense that they share deeply significant elements of a common heritage and that they have a common destiny for the future."[136] The *Pilot* set the tone for such a narrative by using the Ghanaian "nation" as exemplar: "What is the chief factor responsible for the enormous political strides and achievement by that small nation in so short a time and with such startling rapidity? It is its dynamism in action. Its power to get together. Its determination to subordinate internal strifes, internal dissensions, internal idiosyncrasies, to the common-wealth." Such a grand nation as this, superseding lesser nations, as the *Pilot* argued, could not be achieved in Nigeria unless the logic of the grand nation was followed through: "Until Nigerians conscientiously realise that our destiny is inseparably interlocked, until they realise that they must swim or sink together, until they brush aside or learn to circumvent those little snares made to thwart our aspirations, until they cease to know each other by tribal affiliation, so long also will Nigeria continue to be a nation of heartless, docile, thoroughly domesticated pets of imperialism."[137]

Emerson argues that given the centrality of the state as the "greatest concentration of power" in modern times, the struggle to secure a coincidence between state and nation such as articulated by the *Pilot* is "inevitable."[138] Therefore, in the narratives of the press, even when the interests of the various sections—ethno nations—were served in particular contexts, these were often imagined to be in the ultimate service of the Nigerian nation. As the *Citizen* argued when the western region lost its battle to reunite with the Yoruba parts of the northern region: "We are trying to build 'regions which are integral part(s) of a single country.' . . . Yoruba in the North and Ibo in the West will make each Region feel it is a part of a family. . . . This is not a victory for the North. The North had never engaged in the 'battle.' It is also not a Regional or tribal humiliation for the West. It is a victory in the fight for a united country."[139]

H. O. Davies asserts in the *Times* that, indeed, a Nigerian nation will do better, given its potential, than even the *Pilot*'s Ghanaian exemplar: "As an African country endowed by nature and by history with all the requisite of a great nation—economic potentialities, virile and teeming population and the love of freedom—Nigeria stands shoulder high among others. It is open to us to translate these potentialities into realities." This grand solidarity is useful and crucial even beyond the Nigerian soil, argues Davies, because a "strong and united Nigeria can offer a spiritual haven to the black people of the world," given that "the unity of Nigeria [is] a sacred trust for the Negro world and civilisation."[140]

Ernest Renan's dictum is not lost on the *Pilot*. A nation remembers; a nation forgets. A "nation" such as Nigeria must, therefore, forget, as was pointed out by a famous contributor to the *Daily Times* and similarly in an editorial of the *Pilot*: "The fact of geography and economics has given us the heritage of disunity among the major tribes of Nigeria. Our duty as the leaders of our people is not to heighten but to assist in obliterating the differences."[141] "Not what we were yesterday, but where we are going to be tomorrow, should join us together as a state."[142]

The *Pilot* elided its own role and the role of other newspapers in emphasizing difference. The newspapers, however, also emphasized in other contexts that a nation is an aspiration. This was articulated by the *Times* and the *Service*: "Nigeria must be a nation. If the present-day leaders fail to make that possible, a new generation will rise to break the foundation of tribal hate to build a great nation."[143] "We are building a new nation. We cannot be too careful. We cannot take anything for granted. . . . This last opportunity must be treated as a grand one and [we must make the] best [choice]."[144] "The North and the South will remain one country and together we shall achieve complete self-government in 1956."[145] "Let us strive, therefore, to work for a unified nation, realising that never before was the adage 'united we stand, divided we fall' more true than now."[146]

The aspiration to common nationhood was thus rendered over and above the present and limiting objective conditions within the nation of aspiration. As the *Times* put it, "the importance of Nigerian unity and the creation of a great and prosperous nation"[147] was more important than any other issue, including even the issue of self-government. This hope was to be tested when Nigeria eventually achieved independence.

4

Hegemony and Ethno-Spatial Politics

"Nationalizing" the Capital City in the Late-Colonial Era

To study affiliation is to study and to recreate the bonds between texts and the world. . . . To recreate the affiliative network is therefore to make visible, to give materiality back to, the strands holding the text to society, author, and culture.

—Edward Said

This chapter examines the narratives surrounding the structure, nature, and dynamics of the spatial struggle for hegemony over a city that was seen by some "gladiators" as the social and political—perhaps also economic—equivalent of the whole of Nigeria. One of the leading nationalists of that era, H. O. Davies, captured this sentiment when he said that Lagos contained "the genius of the country."[1] Obafemi Awolowo, also a leading activists of that era, but an Ibadan resident in the same Western region, accused the nationalists in Lagos of seeing the city as "the alpha and omega of political sagacity and wisdom" and believing that "only those who lived within its confines should essay to lead the country."[2]

The above descriptions of the centrality and assumed primacy of Lagos help explain why it was important in the ethno-nationalist hegemonic and counterhegemonic politics of the period, particularly in the context of how, within that particular sociopolitical formation, these politics were geared toward the appropriation of space by the three major ethno-regional groups and their political parties, as evident in the newspapers of the period. In this chapter, two rival newspapers—the *West African Pilot* and the *Daily Service*—represent rival narratives of "ownership" and "primacy" in ethno-spatial politics to explicate a theoretical position that captures these struggles within the framework of "the political forging . . . and the institutionalization of a pattern of group activity"[3] in which idealized forms that cohere with the interests of the ethno-nationalist group are leveraged into "commonsensical" ideas in the pursuit of group's political, economic, and social interests.

The status of Lagos and its implications for national politics in Nigeria has always been a contentious issue. Therefore, as the capital of colonial Nigeria, the city was imbricated in the narratives of hegemony, counterhegemony, and domination by the main ethnic nationalities, which were folded into the struggle against colonial rule, the struggle for independence, and the struggle for national cohesion. Barely five years after the amalgamation of the northern and southern protectorates, after Lagos became the capital city, powerful ethno-regional groups and elements in the new colony and protectorates of Nigeria started a process of ending the centrality of Lagos in the nationalist struggle and nationalism discourse. One of the most important strategies for achieving this was the attempt to move the capital away from the coastal city of Lagos in Western Nigeria to somewhere more central.

The "anti-Lagos" groups and elements presented what they considered important points against the retention of Lagos as the capital city—or "administrative headquarters," as it was then known—and the removal of the capital to "an uninhabited spot in Kaduna, 570 miles away from Lagos," or somewhere behind Lokoja, which happened to be Abuja, the present Federal Capital Territory.[4] These "anti-Lagos" elements described Lagos as "the nerve-centre of political agitation and the grave of official reputations." In response, the *Lagos Weekly Record* described as "unauthorized and fallacious" the claim in some quarters that the governor-general of colonial Nigeria had ordered that "the Headquarters of the Governor-General and the central seat of Government would be the high plateau immediately behind Lokoja known as Mount Patte, situated in the very centre of the Protectorate, commanding the Niger and the Benue, within easy [reach] of Baro the starting-point of the central railway, and linked up with the western railway by a branch line to Osogbo."[5]

Consequently, upon the agitation and rumors of the impending shift in the capital, Governor-General Sir Hugh Clifford toured the southern and northern provinces and addressed the Nigerian Council on December 29, 1919. Clifford declared to the Council that Lagos, as the "radiating centre of energy, innovation and progress" in colonial Nigeria, must remain the capital city. He added: "After giving this question the most careful consideration, I have arrived at the conclusion that, at any rate, for a great many years to come, the only possible place at which the principal seat of Government can be located is Lagos. I have said that Nigeria is today standing on the threshold of great commercial expansion and development; and experience gained in other new and undeveloped countries in the Tropics shows that during the initial stages, so much depends upon the inspiration and initiative of Government and upon its close cooperation with those sections of the public which are actively engaged in the promotion of trade and of business enterprises, that is essential that the administrative Headquarters should itself be the great radiating centre of energy, innovation and progress."[6]

The City, Hegemony, and Ethno-Spatial Politics

Clifford's reasons for remaining in Lagos transcended commercial reasons—even though, as he acknowledged, these are supposed to lead to the radiation of "energy, innovation and progress." Curiously for a foreign imposition in its infancy, which the colonial government was, Clifford was also concerned about the government moving too far away from the articulation of dissent. The governor-general argued that the functions of the colonial government would suffer in its execution if it moved away from the critical appraisal that was evident in Lagos—particularly the Lagos press, which he failed to mention. "This is a function which [we] can hardly hope to fulfill unless the principal operations of the Government are carried on in the midst of the most active life and thought of the country, whence it is able to maintain the closest touch with every section of the community, and where its activities are exposed to the closest scrutiny and criticism. Such things, I contend, are aids to good government with which no administration can safely afford to dispense."[7]

Clifford did not stop there. He argued against moving the capital to what appears to be present-day Abuja or even Kaduna, both in the Northern provinces, affirming that such a move had been "definitely abandoned." He also expressed hope that the agitation would not be revived for many years: "If the seat of Government be situated in some position of comparable isolation, it must inevitably tend to become increasingly bureaucratic, and automatically deprive itself of the assistance in the framing of its measures which articulate public opinion of those whose affairs are its charge can alone efficiently supply."[8]

Yet the matter was raised again two to three decades later, in the 1940s and 1950s, as the nationalist struggle increased in tempo and as the dynamics of the concomitant political calculations for the appropriation of space and power among the three majority ethnonationalities and political parties took on new life in the leadup to independence. The debate, however, started as a contest over the rightful and constitutional "ownership" of the space by one ethnonationality, but consequently deteriorated into debate over the propriety of any ethnonationality's "vice" hold of a "common spatial heritage," which a capital city, such as Lagos, ought to be. This was the context in which one of the three major ethnonationalities, the Yoruba, insisted that Lagos belonged to them.

This chapter continues with a brief, conceptual historical background, followed by newspaper analyses of the push for ethnic counterhegemony. It examines how, as "experts in legitimation," the ethnonationalist activists and the newspapers representing their interests attempted through newspaper narratives to either render existing power structures acceptable or, on the contrary, subvert and change such power structures in the city to suit their larger political and ethnonationalist interests.

It is important to note that in spite of the centrality of "territory" as a concrete manifestation of space, in interethnic relations in Nigeria, and in the many ethnic wars sparked by the battle over territory, many of them still persisting to date, political scientists in their analysis of ethnicity in Nigeria often ignore the salience of space. Some scholars in geography have tried to remedy this.[9] But the geographers' perspectives are often not informed by the dynamics of politics. That space and politics are mixed, or that politics is also often about the appropriation and negotiation of space—in this context, ethnonationalist space—is a fact to which political scientists writing on interethnic relations in Nigeria must pay more attention.

The City and the Spatial Structure of Elaboration and Affiliation

Antonio Gramsci's political theory is centrally a discourse of the genesis and formation of the historical subject. His view of "political agents" who "posit themselves in and through historical action" led him to reject "mechanistic and deterministic" interpretations of Marxism.[10] The concept of "hegemony," which is the organizing focus of Gramscian thought on politics and ideology, is best understood as "the organization of consent—the process through which subordinated forms of consciousness are constructed without recourse to violence or coercion."[11] This concept has proved useful in understanding and explicating the organization and mobilization of interests in society—and for my purpose in this book, the narratives through which this is done.

However, there is an interesting ongoing debate in the literature as to whether Gramsci uses hegemony strictly as the noncoercive (ideological) aspect of the structure of consent or whether he uses it to understand the meshing of coercive and noncoercive aspects.[12] Gramsci is believed to be responsible for this uncertainty, given his tendency to conflate domination and hegemony and shift conceptual grounds in his writings.[13] Yet Agbaje argues that even though composed of the two dimensions, the forcible, less subtle dimension of hegemony belongs more to the drive toward dominance and domination, whereas hegemony, "at its most pristine," implies "the construction of consensus, consent, and dissent through subtle, indirect, and non-forcible means."[14]

Nonetheless, it must be conceded that Gramsci gives more weight to the nonforcible aspect of hegemony as "intellectual and moral leadership (*direzione*) whose principal constituting elements are consent and persuasion."[15] Gramsci asserts that given that reality is perceived and knowledge is acquired through cultural and ideological "prisms" and "filters," which give form and meaning in society, hegemony implies the creation of a particular structure of knowledge and particular system of values by the leadership. The group that is able to form and transform its own knowledge and values into generally applicable conceptions of the world,—the group that creates an order in which its own way of life and thought is dominant and diffused throughout society—is the one that exercises leadership.[16]

Central to this dominant ideology is the concept of "elaboration," which "aspires to the condition of hegemony," with intellectuals

playing the pivotal role. Gramsci describes their role as that of
"experts in legitimation."[17] He uses the concept of "elaboration" in
two "seemingly contradictory but actually complementary" senses.
On the one hand, elaboration connotes the refinement, or working out (*elaborare*), of a prior or more powerful idea—the perpetu-
ation of a worldview.[18] On the other hand, it means something that
Edward Said describes as more qualitatively positive. This is the position that culture or thought or art is a "highly complex and quasi-
autonomous extension of political reality," and, taken against the
backdrop of the primal importance that Gramsci gives to intellectuals, elaboration has the "density, complexity and historical-semantic
value that is so strong as to make politics possible."[19]

I argue that this is an important dimension of what political narratives can achieve. Narrative is a special kind of elaboration. And
elaboration is the "central cultural activity," which, even if passed off
as mere intellectual propaganda for the protection and furtherance
of the interests of the ruling class, constitutes the material making
a society a society. When the negative connotation of elaboration in
Marxian terms is transcended, we can see elaboration as the principal attribute of narrative in a neutral sense. Elaboration as narrative
is, therefore, "a going enterprise," the "ensemble of patterns making it feasible for society to maintain itself."[20]

Although not connected directly in the literature—particularly in
relating knowledge (narrative text) to power—elaboration is linked
to affiliation and therefore to narratives in the construction of hegemony. I formulate this linkage by drawing from Edward Said's work.
The material that is furnished by narratives as a form of elaboration,
as a core of the social web that keeps society going, is tied to social
forms by affiliation, which creates and re-creates the bonds between
texts and the structures of power.[21] In creating an affiliative network, the strand holding narrative text to society and power is given
materiality and made visible. For Gramsci, the media constitute part
of the important "material structure" for narrative elaboration and
spreading of hegemonic ideology.[22] Affiliation also releases a text
from isolation as mere text, writes Said, imposing on the scholar
or critic the "presentational problem of historically recreating or
reconstructing the possibilities from which the text arose." It is at
this juncture, argues Said, that we find a place for "intentional analysis and for the effort to place text in homological, dialogical, or anti-
thetical relationships with other texts, classes, and institutions."[23]

Intellectuals exercise hegemony over a particular location, not only because they create a particular way of life and particular conception of the world, but also because they are able to translate the interests and values of a specific social formation into general and common values and interests. One way in which this can be done is through the narrative text, which propagates a way of life and conception of the world. Here, hegemony, which resides in civil society, is translated into a bulwark in support of political society.[24] It is conceived as involving the "the political forging . . . and the institutionalization of a pattern of group activity and the concurrent idealization of that schema into a dominant symbolic framework that reigns as "common sense."[25] It is a "vehicle" with which the dominant social groups establish a system of "permanent consent" that legitimates a prevailing social order by encompassing a complex network of mutually reinforcing and interwoven ideas affirmed and articulated by intellectuals.[26]

The intellectuals, in this context, are the activists and partisans—what David Laitin calls "political entrepreneurs"—who used newspapers to legitimate or delegitimate the prevailing social order in colonial Lagos. The conflict that is inherent in the logic of hegemony, which produces counterhegemony, is captured well by Laitin, who argues that a successful hegemony does not necessarily yield "order," but it "yields a set of conflicts that automatically and commonsensically stands at the top of the political agenda."[27]

How are the foregoing arguments linked to narratives, ethno-spatial politics, and the agency of space? I intend to briefly draw a link here between ethnic hegemonic politics, the latent powers of space, and the constellations of power that spatial agency produces and reproduces.

Although the term "space" has proven remarkably difficult to define, given the significance of territory, Penrose's definition, which follows Shaefer, is illuminating. Penrose conceives of space as "structures of the real world (as identified and interpreted through experience), which are themselves slow processes of long duration."[28] From this standpoint, two latent powers of space are important. One is the latent material power of space—which is fundamental to human life—whereas the other is the latent emotional power of space.[29] When the features of the material power of space are filtered through human experience of time and process—what Penrose calls "the relational dimension of space"—they contain within them the power to invoke or provoke an emotional response. As people transform the latent material and emotional qualities of space into sources of power, they are simultaneously transformed into contexts of struggle and contention, and, therefore, into narratives.[30]

This transformation is accepted in the literature as being denoted by the term "territoriality," which a widely accepted view defines as "the attempt by an individual or group to affect, influence or control people, phenomena and relationships by delimiting and asserting control over a geographic area called a territory."[31] Consequently, territoriality enfolds into its logic the creation of boundaries, which unite and divide space—"giving symbolic meanings to notions of "us" and "them" and "ours" and "theirs"—in its entirety.[32] Space, therefore, is central to hegemony. Ethnic entrepreneurs who elaborate particular hegemonies through narratives deploy the latent emotional powers of space in affiliating particular groups to the material (physical) properties of space in order to construct the space of human existence into "our" as opposed to "their" space.

Lagos as Space of Struggle

Perhaps the modern history of Lagos—which is also called Eko[33]—began in 1851 when the British forced the King of Lagos, Kosoko, from the throne because of his slave-raiding activities. His more pliant uncle, Akintoye, replaced him. As Michael Crowder argues, the installation of a king who was not only sympathetic to British interests but also depended on the British for survival, in place of a hostile one, was "a classic example of nineteenth century colonial expansion."[34] From the 1880s on, there were four communities in Lagos: white, mainly British, civil servants, missionaries, and merchants; Saros (Creoles), black liberated slaves from Sierra Leone; Brazilians, black repatriated freed slaves from Brazil; and the indigenous Yoruba-Bini population.[35]

On July 30, 1861, Britain annexed "internally stable" Lagos because of its need for a secure base from which it could regulate trade with the interior. With the "cession" of Lagos to the British by the king, Dosunmu, who succeeded Akintoye, and Britain's subsequent annexation, a new era began "in the history of British relations with that part of the coast, an era which inaugurated the new territory of Nigeria."[36]

With the annexation of Lagos came debilitating conditions in the Yoruba hinterland as the Ijaye war flared up again. Eventually, the troubles in the interior boiled down to competition between the Egba and Ibadan to control access to Lagos. Thus while Lagos enjoyed relative peace and centrality in trade—even becoming the most prosperous colony on the West Coast, "the Queen of West African settlements"[37]—parts of the interior were engaged in war or bitter rivalry. Sir Richard Burton, the veteran traveler, had predicted that the position of Lagos "points it out as the natural key to this part of Africa and the future emporium of all Yoruba, between the Niger and the sea."[38]

Thus Lagos became the hub of economic and social activity, and with the attendant political significance of such, an emerging center of modernity. The dynamics and intensity of the politics of Lagos was so strong as to even challenge or impede the nationalist fervor generated by Herbert Macaulay over the 1923 elections in which the "natives" were allowed to elect four people into the legislative assembly—three representing Lagos and one representing Calabar in the east. It was not until the 1930s that a new generation of Nigerians looking beyond the "narrow political horizons of the capital" hijacked the control of the nationalist movement from the Macaulays.[39] From the 1930s on, the emergent educated elites in the provincial areas of Southern Nigeria demanded that political activities, as articulated by the *Eastern States Express*, extend "beyond the borders of rabid and irresponsible Lagos . . . [and] outside of the turbulent island of discord." Despite this, Lagos remained "a political prize to be won."[40]

The unique status of Lagos and the controversy over its alternative representations as a part and the whole of the imagined nation-state in late colonial Nigeria have been perceived by the political scientist and poet Odia Ofeimun as specific reflections of the fundamental nature of modern cities. Ofeimun argues: "(The city) is a poetics linked to origins, size, and geography, defined by its parts rather than by a fraction of it. . . . For the citiness of a city lies in the absorption of its many parts into a common whirlpool. Its core experience intimates a civis: a place of civilization where people who may not have the same occupation, or accept the same ancestors, and people who may not bow to the same deity, can live within a common frame of politics, thus entrenching the possibility of shared decision-making as a permanent way of life. The city is, in this sense, an ever-ready challenge because it is continually suggesting the necessity to find a common morality that can hold people together."

The political history of Lagos in the period between 1923 and 1938 revolved around the quinquennial elections for the Legislative Council and the triennial election for the Lagos Town Council, the latter of which had the elective principle partially extended to it in 1920, and the long-running issue of the status and headship of the House of Dosunmu (called "House of Docemo" by the British), the ruling house in Lagos.[41] Macaulay, who is regarded as the father of Nigerian (anticolonial) nationalism, threw himself into the fray, using his newspaper (the *Lagos Daily News*), market women, the House of Dosunmu and its supporters, and "his unique ability to fire the imagination of the semiliterate and illiterate masses of Lagos" to his advantage.[42]

The competition for the elective posts in Lagos increased the city's political awakening; the number of newspapers (five) surpassed the number of parties (two) that emerged with the awakening.[43] However, the Nigerian National Democratic Party (NNDP), led by Macaulay, emerged as the most powerful party, returning candidates to the Legislative Council in 1923, 1928, and 1933. Even though it claimed to be "national," the NNDP was a Lagos affair, notwithstanding the fact that it took a "national" stand on crucial issues, reminding Lagosians of their link to a larger territory called Nigeria.[44]

Until the 1930s, most educated Nigerians who invariably led the nationalist movement and controlled the press were from Yoruba or were Creole families who had been in long contact with Europeans. This "closed aristocracy" of the Yoruba and the Yorubalised Creoles was only intellectually challenged, in a serious and sustained manner, from the 1930s.[45] With this challenge came concrete developments in nationalist organization. The Ibo—now called Igbo—constituted the largest ethnic category that challenged the closed aristocracy. But this challenge was only possible when it was organized around the towering image and figure of Nnamdi Azikiwe, who had just returned with a string of degrees from the United States. By the early 1950s, the Ibo constituted 44.6 percent of the population of Lagos.[46]

From 1934 to 1949, Azikiwe, popularly called Zik, was "the most important and celebrated nationalist leader" on the West Coast of Africa, if not in all of tropical Africa.[47] He initiated a new era in journalism upon his return from America, first in Ghana and later in Nigeria. With the bold, daring, and sometimes shocking directness of its editorials and news, Azikiwe's *West African Pilot* displaced other newspapers and emerged as a commercial success.[48] James Coleman, the author of one of the most cited works on Nigerian history, states that Azikiwe's "combative and provocative journalism was the principal source of his fame and power, and the most crucial single precipitant of the Nigerian awakening.... Although Azikiwe's power and influence resulted partly from his fresh and militant approach (to the issue of freedom and independence), they also reflected the fact that he was the first non-Yoruba Nigerian (apart from Ernest Ikoli, an Ijaw) to emerge into prominence."[49]

Before the emergence and ascendancy of Azikiwe in Nigerian journalism and politics—which were interconnected in those days[50]—the Ibo had been on the periphery of politics, lacking a symbol and a spokesperson, even while exhibiting an unprecedented passion to catch up with their main southern rival, the Yoruba, particularly in the area of education and modernity.[51]

With the pressure exerted primarily by Azikiwe via his newspapers, the issue of Lagos became very salient. After the dissolution of the activist Nigerian Youth Movement (NYM), an offshoot of the Lagos Youth Movement, owing to internal wrangling over the choice of the Movement for the Legislative Council, the emergent parties, the NCNC and the Action Group, engaged in a battle over the status of Lagos. Azikiwe had earlier protested the domination of Lagos politics by the Yoruba, who also discriminated against non-Yoruba, particularly in the area of housing,[52] but his presidency of the Ibo State Union did not help matters. In an address to his Ibo constituents, he said: "It would appear that the God of Africa had created the Igbo nation to lead the children of Africa from the bondage of ages."[53]

Zik's main rival, Obafemi Awolowo, concedes in his autobiography that "the Ibo had never had a share in newspaper publicity before the advent of the (Zik's) *Pilot,*" but argues that "no Yoruba man of the class of Ibos publicized in the *Pilot* ever had a share of publicity in any paper either."[54] Even though it is difficult to determine what Awolowo means by "the class of Ibos," he also concedes that "the Ibos needed all the boosting they could get," ostensibly through Zik's medium. But even here, Awolowo queries the actual practice of this "ethnic boosting."[55] He writes:

But Dr. Azikiwe went about it in a manner which disgusted those of us who were used to describing citizens of Nigeria as Nigerians or Africans, and regarding their achievement as reflecting on Nigeria, indeed Africa, as a whole. . . . But as against these, the achievement of Yorubas and in particular, the academic laurels of their scholars received, if at all, inconspicuous notice in the *Pilot.* When an Ibo did or was about to do something praise-worthy, he was invariably given a two-column headline and report in the *Pilot,* and was always described by his ethnic origin in the headlines. But when the Ph.D. degree of London University, indeed of any university for that matter, was conferred on the first Nigerian ever, the historic news was given a small single-space in the *Pilot,* and the headline read: "Nigerian Economist Passes Ph.D. in London." The scholar concerned was Dr. Fadipe, a Yoruba. . . . Apart from failing to give publicity to the achievements of the Yoruba, and holding their public men to obloquy, the *Pilot* always made sure that all their misdoings received the publicity.[56]

Awolowo fails to note that given the prior advantage enjoyed by the Yoruba in the press, the *Pilot*'s attitude toward "Yoruba achievement" might only have been an attempt to "equalize" long years of publicity enjoyed by the Yoruba. Although this does not excuse the attitude as detailed by Awolowo, it partly explains the urge for the Ibo in this era to equal or balance out the Yoruba, who had had a head start. This was eventually achieved, as the Yoruba later started complaining of "Ibo domination" in metropolitan (Lagos)—and even national—politics.

With the creation—and subsequent activities—of Egbe Omo Oduduwa, a Yoruba sociocultural organization, Yoruba-Ibo tension rose in Lagos; the emergence of the Egbe heightened "tribal" antagonism between the Yoruba and the Ibo.[57] Prior to the creation of the Egbe, the immediate past years had witnessed the establishment of the Ibo ideological leadership of the pan-Nigeria movement, which operated alongside the pursuit of Ibo "cultural supremacy" organized around the Ibo State Union.[58] The Egbe seem to have unveiled this bifacial hegemony—which the *West African Pilot* derided as an "Ibo domination stunt."[59] By 1948, Oluwole Alakija, a leading member of the Egbe, made a statement typical of the rivalry and passion against Azikiwe—and by extension, the Ibo: "We were bunched together by the British who named us Nigeria. We never knew the Ibos, but since we came to know them, we have tried to be friendly and neighborly. Then came the Arch Devil [meaning Azikiwe] to sow the seeds of distrust and hatred. . . . We have tolerated enough from a class of Ibos and addle-brained Yorubas who have mortgaged their thinking caps to Azikiwe and his hirelings."[60]

The Ibo responded in kind to this intemperate statement, leading to a press (civil) war that preceded a near descent into physical violence between the two groups, as both sides descended on the local markets to purchase machetes.[61] Mahmood Mamdani's concept of "civil war" captures this well. Mamdani argues that, in the context of "tribalism" in Africa, a civil war constitutes "a continuum along which muted tension co-exist long before they break out into open confrontation."[62]

A mass meeting of the Ibo in Lagos resolved that any further personal attacks on Azikiwe would be seen as attacks on the "Ibo nation" because "if a hen were killed, the chickens would be exposed to danger."[63] The *Pilot* affirmed: "Henceforth, the cry must be one of battle against the Egbe Omo Oduduwa, its leaders at home and abroad, uphill and down dale in the streets of Nigeria and in the residences of its advocates. . . . It is the enemy of Nigeria; it must be crushed to the earth. . . . There is no going back, until the Fascist Organization of Sir Adeyemo [leader of the Egbe] has been dismembered."[64]

However, this intense rivalry was not, in terms of its intensity and implications, unusual in the history Lagos. The politics of the city had always been one of total commitment, without any fence-sitting.[65] In Lagos politics, from about four centuries preceding this era, "to lose when matters came to a head meant at least confiscation of one's property, heavy fines, a ban on trade; at worst, banishment, death or slavery. Such severe penalties were meted out, not only to the head of the losing party, but to all its members."[66]

It was against this backdrop of "civil war" that the narratives over the status and ownership of Lagos were enacted. The NCNC, and mainly Ibo, led by Azikiwe argued for the administrative separation of Lagos, as the federal capital, from the rest of the Western Region, whereas the Action Group (mainly Yoruba) led by Obafemi Awolowo rooted for the retention and merger of Lagos with the Yoruba West.[67] Whereas the *West African Pilot* represented the position of the former, the *Daily Service* represented the position of the latter in a passionate tussle for hegemony in the increasingly multicultural city. In Mamdani's phrasing, whereas the narratives in the *Service* sought to "flatten the ethnic diversity" of Lagos, the narratives in the

Pilot attempted to turn a "simple fact of heterogeneity into a source of ethnic tension."[68]

The Press and the Construction of Ethno-Spatial Hegemony

In the push and pull toward hegemony and counter-hegemony by the rival ethnic and political groups over the status and ownership of Lagos, the newspapers representing the opposing camps vented the ideas, ideals, interests, and values of the respective groups. The Yoruba elite in the AG and the Igbo elite in the NCNC saw themselves as a "determinate hegemonic force" that could transform the position, power, and privilege of their groups, including through the narratives in the newspaper press. The consequence of such consciousness, argues Fontana, "is the transformation of a subordinate, particularistic mass of disaggregated individuals into a leading and hegemonic subject whose thought and values have become the prevailing conception of the world."[69]

In Nigeria of the 1940s and early 1950s, the north was largely indifferent to the status of Lagos. Therefore, it was a straight fight between the eastern region (Igbo/NCNC) and the western region (Yoruba/AG). The reforms in the Lagos Town Council removed the independent status of Lagos and merged it with the western region. At this point, the Town Council was largely controlled by the NCNC, which produced an Igbo mayor for the city. The *Pilot* argued in this context that changes in the status of Lagos had to be be conceived along with the essence of the city: "If Lagos is still assumed to be the capital of Nigeria, surely in all its phases, institutions must exist to act as unifying media so that the centric force created will be Nigerian, neither entirely Yoruba, nor Ibo, nor Hausa. It is in this light that the proposed LTC [Lagos Town Council] reforms must again be examined."[70]

The paper made the case that it was in the "common" interest of all Nigerians to make Lagos free of any regional control. At the start of this debate, the *Pilot* came across as if it were a dispassionate observer of the trend, speaking to the seemingly "transcendental" significance of a "multicultural" city for all: "If we succeed in making Lagos Nigeria's capital, where all tribes of the nation can live without feeling themselves ostracised, where the government system of the city will not be biased in nature but based on progressive formula, if we can indeed make Lagos a sort of London, or New York, where all citizens from all parts can commingle and inhabit without animosity, then surely we would have succeeded in cementing the Nigerian ideal."[71]

What the *Pilot* called "nature" could be seen as the claim of the Yoruba to "natural ownership" of Lagos, which explains why the paper then made a case for the determination of the status of Lagos based on "progressive formula." Such a formula—"for the sake of unity"—the paper argued further, will "determine for centuries to come the graph line of peace among the people of Nigeria." The newspaper, therefore, urged Nigerians "to make this 'Atlantic City' [Lagos] a truly worthy capital of Nigeria; one that will serve as a unifying force to make three warring Nigerias impossible. And the NCNC is dedicated to this magnificent obsession."[72]

The theme of "unity" is one that resonates in any hegemonic process as the hegemonic group attempts to unify all, or at least the majority, around an organizing idea that, at its base, only serves the interest of the group. In the context of how meaning intersects with relations of domination, this is what Thompson describes as "unification."[73] A relevant strategy here is a "symbolization of unity" that involves "the construction of symbols of unity, of collective identity and identification" such as Lagos; such a symbol of unity is "created and continuously reaffirmed," as the *Pilot* did with Lagos. Therefore Lagos, for the *Pilot*, was no longer just another city but is a center of unity, a "cosmopolitan city inhabited by a more politically advanced people drawn from all sections of a federated Nigeria."[74]

The decision by the colonial government to incorporate Lagos into the western region, which would then rule the city indirectly, is consequently condemned by the *Pilot* as gratifying the "personal ambition of certain disgruntled and interested individuals" through the introduction of "a decadent and contemptible indirect rule system [that] will retard the progress of this metropolis." Therefore the *Pilot* challenged Lagosians to oppose the move, the actualization of which would mean that Lagos "has lost its status": "Shall Lagos citizens allow this retrogressive Action Group policy to jeopardise their communal interest on account of party politics? Lagos has lost its homogeneous character and should any attempt be made to revive that lost heritage, then the Central Government will be admitting our plea that Lagos is no longer the capital of a federated Nigeria."[75]

The case of Lagos was very contentious in this battle for hege-mony for a number of reasons, both economic and political. The western region needed Lagos in order to add to its size, population, and influence, as well as for economic reasons, as Awolowo repeat-edly stated. Also, the AG did not have political control of the Lagos Town Council, but would control the council indirectly if the city merged with the western region. Lagos was one the NCNC's major areas of support, and it did not desire to lose it to the AG. Related to this was the rising population of the Ibo in Lagos. The NCNC obvi-ously preferred not to place them under rival Yoruba control. This was apart from the economic benefits that would accrue to the west only if the city was placed under the western regional government, what Penrose calls the "latent material power of space."[76]

Against this background, a *Pilot* popular columnist and member of the NCNC, Mbonu Ojike, in his "Weekend Catechism," argued that the "history" of federal capitals all over the world supports the position of his party. He cited Canada, where Ottawa is independent of provincial control; Australia, where Canberra is independent of the control of any state; and the United States, where Washing-ton, DC, enjoys "political freedom" from the fifty states, to empha-size that the Action Group's terms were unacceptable: "And what is worse is that Nigerians are expected to sign away to Action Group ambition the city of Lagos which for three quarters of a century or more was developed with Eastern, Western and Northern funds."[77] When the Macpherson Constitution eventually merged Lagos with the western region, the *Pilot* stated that colonial Nigeria no longer had a capital: "The Macpherson Constitution has given us a country without a capital. Lagos though theoretically recognized as the capi-tal of Nigeria, really belongs to the West and henceforth she will be subject to legislations from the Western House of Assembly. What impudence. What a degradation of status!"[78] The *Pilot* pursued the idea that the Macpherson Constitution, by making the position of Lagos "anomalous," unsheathed one of its "greatest weaknesses": "The dual position of Lagos, described by the NCNC as anomalous, unsheathes one of the greatest weaknesses of the Macpherson Con-stitution. It is a weakness, which, perhaps, the unity if the country hinges. Theoretically, the municipality is ward and responsibility of the Western Region, but in practice the Central Government's estimates make several provisions for special expenditure for Lagos. This is because of the dual position of Lagos. Sooner or later matters are bound to come to a head in the first real test of the Macpherson Constitution over this matter of where Lagos stands."[79] This issue of Lagos evidently is one of the important reasons why the *Pilot* and the NCNC also fought the Macpherson Constitution—described as a "perfect monster"[80]—until it was superseded by the Lyttleton Constitution (1954).

The fears of the NCNC elements began to come to light shortly after the merger. The western regional government set up the Storey Commission of Inquiry to look into the affairs of the Lagos Town Council, which was controlled by the NCNC. The commission's report formed the basis of the dissolution of the Town Council The *Service* was as ecstatic about this dissolution as it was full of condemnation for the dissolved NCNC-controlled Town Council: "The dissolution of the Lagos Town Council, following the findings of the Storey Commission, is just, timely and expedient. The NCNC rascals who dominated the council since 1950 had proved themselves to be wholly incompetent, irresponsible, corrupt, shameless and utterly devoid of all sense of decency and of proportion. . . . They had . . . exposed Lagos to ridicule not only of the rest of Nigeria but of the whole civilized world. Lagos Town Council under the NCNC had long become a bedlam and a disgrace to the good name of Lagos."[81]

The *Service* then congratulated the regional government, "especially the Minister of Local Government [the Hon. Obafemi Awolowo] . . . for taking action so promptly" on the findings of the commission.[82] For the *Pilot,* the situation foretold "the encircling gloom of a not distant future ahead of Lagos," unless "all true patriots lead the isle of Nigeria's destiny out of Pharaoh's land."[83] The paper presented the position of the NCNC as that of "true patriots" who are concerned with the "collective destiny" of a Nigeria ostensibly trapped in the "land of Pharaoh" [the Western Region].

The *Pilot* asked, in the absence of the will for a reversal of the status of Lagos, for a new capital to be created: "We are no alarmists, neither do we intend to precipitate an unholy rivalry for supremacy among the three states that now constitute Nigeria. The only solution lies in the creation of a new capital unfettered by regional legislations. Meanwhile, Nigeria remains without a capital."[84] This was strictly in line with the paper's earlier warning, in which it declared the "irrevocable" position of the NCNC: "The NCNC . . . irrevocably maintains that if Lagos is to remain the capital of Nigeria, it must also be placed on a status exactly similar to what obtains in many capitals all over the world; so that any mischievous attempt to merge Lagos with the West must be vehemently opposed[,] as that would automatically strip Lagos of the glory and privilege it had hitherto enjoyed as [the] capital of Nigeria."[85]

This "glory and privilege" that Lagos had—metaphors for the political, economic, and even social significance of the city—appears to be the main reason that both sides want to keep Lagos within their sphere of influence. The *Pilot* described those canvasing "Lagos for Yorubas"[86] as "shameless gospellers," including the *Service,* whereas the *Service* described those engaging in the "stupid talk" of delinking Lagos from the west as "ne'er-do-wells."[87]

When the secretary of states for the colonies in the immediate past Labor Government expressed surprise that the matter of the Lagos merger was still alive when he met the representatives of the Egbe Omo Oduduwa, the *Service* averred that the paper would have been surprised too but for the fact that it knows "who has been holding the question in the air"—ostensibly Azikiwe, through the *Pilot.* Expletives were then directed at the person: "And it is he who has been encouraging the ne'er-do-wells to irritate the responsible section of the Nigerian community with stupid talks about Lagos. . . . The ignorant and irresponsible advocates of 'separate-Lagos' should have been silenced long before now."[88]

In what appears to point out how the capital could be moved out of Lagos, which eventually happened when the capital was moved to Abuja in 1991 (a move that, incidentally, Awolowo and the Yoruba west opposed), the *Service* stated: "The people of the Western Region are not compelling the whole country to make Lagos their capital. But, at least, it is the duty of the Governor to make it clear that the only alternative to the present situation of Lagos is for the people of Nigeria to buy a piece of land and establish on it a federal capital independent of the three regions."[89]

The two papers entered a period of "detente" when the two parties started to work together on the subject of the date of independence. They then turned on the NPC—which became "the imperialist stooge." Both the NCNC and the AG were committed to 1956 as the year of independence for Nigeria, whereas the leaders of the NPC entered a caveat that was phrased "as soon as possible." The *Pilot* captured this "detente": "What matters now is self-government first and above every other consideration. The present united front formed by militant nationalists should therefore be maintained at all costs. It is not only the responsibility of the two leaders [Zik and Awo], but that of all their followers and admirers."[90]

This "united front," however, could not be sustained beyond mid-1953 when the party leaders met in London for constitutional talks with the British government. When the issue of Lagos arose at the conference, Awolowo and his AG colleagues staged a walkout. The *Service* argued: "What should be the position of Lagos in a federal Nigeria? . . . The people of Nigeria have a right to say that their capital (not necessarily Lagos) should be independent. But neither the NCNC nor the NPC has any right to say that the town of Lagos should be truncated from the region to which it naturally belongs. All they can do is to demand that the capital of Nigeria be removed from Lagos to say, Kaduna or Port-Harcourt, which was bought with the money of Nigeria and which, in fact, should not belong to any one Region."[91]

The *Service* then presented the reasons why the western region would not agree to the severance of Lagos from it: "To submit to the severance of Lagos from the West would amount to economic and fiscal suicide on the part of the people and Government of the Western Region";[92] "The population and revenue [would be] cut down by 270,000 people and millions of pounds."[93] Again, here is a clear articulation of the material power of space containing the "basic prerequisites of human survival."[94] The *Service* added that the decision of the colonial secretary in London, Mr. Lyttleton, to "dismember" the western region—in "disregard" of "all historical facts and constitutional precedents"—for the sake of the "future of Nigeria" was not only unfair but also indefensible. Describing the western region as "the Cinderella of Nigerian unity," which has again been "called upon to bear the responsibility for uniting the conglomeration of people's that made up this vast country," the paper added that "Lagos, an indisputable Yoruba City owned by the West, is to remain a lone star. . . . And in arriving at his decision, Mr. Lyttleton disregards all historical facts and constitutional precedent."[95]

But the *Pilot* contested this. What was "indisputable" for the paper was the "joint-ownership" of the city: "There is hardly any Nigerian who does not regard Lagos with special sentimental feelings. To the Binis, it is part of their ancient empire; to the Northerner, it is not only a capital developed with the revenue from their tin, ground-nuts and cotton but the life-blood of their economic existence with particular reference to their export and import trade. Similarly,

Easterners feel that Lagos has been developed not only from their revenue but through their blood, sweat and tears as well; while a section of Westerners feel that they have an exclusive attachment to the city because of historical and geographical connections. The truth, in short, is that Lagos is very dear to all section[s] of the country."[96] This narrative is interesting in the way it negotiates the interests on the Lagos issue that the *Pilot* served, particularly the NCNC and the Igbo, through rationalization and universalization. Whereas the *Pilot's* Bini, a minority group in the western region, could claim Lagos as "part of their ancient empire" and therefore a "lost possession," for the *Pilot* the northern region, whose inadequate resources necessitated amalgamation with the southern regions, suddenly had enough resources, part of which was used in developing Lagos. The *Pilot's* eastern region is bound to Lagos with "blood, tears and toil," whereas only "a section" of the western region feels "exclusive attachment" to—not, instructively, "ownership" of—the city.

The *Service*, affronted by this, disclaimed the connections of the other parts of Nigeria. The paper stated that "the development of Lagos dates as far as the days before the amalgamation of 1924 and even from that date the contribution of which the North and East have made . . . is infinitesimal."[97] A front-page story in the *Service* even used what Azikiwe wrote in the *Pilot* on May 14, 1940, to back the claim of the Yoruba to Lagos. In attempting to eternalize the Yoruba claim to Lagos, the *Service* maintained that Zik had written that "when we speak of the Oba of Lagos, we refer to the paramount Native Ruler of Lagos Township, although Lagos is peopled mainly by the Yoruba-speaking peoples and Lagos is part of Yoruba land. And since Yoruba is part of the Western Region, Lagos should remain in Yoruba land which is part of the West."[98] Based on what it stated to be the dissatisfaction in the western region over the Lagos issue, the *Service* went further, announcing on its front page: "Motion for Secession To Be Tabled at Western House." The paper interviewed only five people in the regional capital city, Ibadan, concluding that there was "consensus of public opinion" and "wholehearted support" for "the Western Region" to "secede from the rest of Nigeria."[99]

However, the *Pilot* praised the decision of Her Majesty's Government to remove Lagos from the western region, a decision it believed tallied with the "wishes of the majority" that "Lagos should serve as the central bound of unity."[100] The paper reported that the city had, by its severance from the western region, been elevated to "an exalted position." This "majority wish," for the *Service*, was "against reason, history, logic and equity"[101] and was a reflection of the "pet[ty] jealousy and covetousness of certain malcontents."[102] Argued the *Service*: "It is not difficult for any fair-minded person to see how the present position of Lagos is inimical to the future of Nigeria ... [and] a harmonious future. ... For [Lyttleton] to disregard these facts is dangerous not only to the future but also to the very existence of Nigeria."[103] The choice, added the *Service*, "is between Lagos and Nigeria."[104]

The *Service* declared that rather than lose Lagos to the status of federal capital, the western region was prepared to contribute to building an "independent federal capital." Although Lagos could remain the commercial center, the political capital would be moved elsewhere, which would allow the western region's ownership claim over Lagos: "But to compel the West to surrender Lagos as a federal capital is to sow the seed of permanent disunity and bitterness between the West and the other regions. ... If the other Regions are not prepared to allow their federal capital to remain in the Western Region, they can remove the capital to any other place."[105] "By combining some people and certain resources and separating them from other people and resources," argues Penrose, "the creation of territories gives physical substance and symbolic meaning to notions of "us" and "them" and "ours" and "theirs."[106] But for the *Pilot*, Lagos had to remain the political and commercial capital of colonial Nigeria and the future independent Nigeria because "the political capital of any country should also be its commercial capital as well as the principal mirror of its cultural and social progress."[107]

By this time it was obvious that the alliance constructed over the date of independence between NCNC and *Pilot* and AG and *Service* had broken down. Whereas the *Service* deplored the "underhand[ed] tricks" and the "stab in the back" by the ally of the AG in the London talks, which proved that the "NCNC is not being true to the spirit in which the [alliance] was born,"[108] the *Pilot* claimed that the AG was "unfortunately back to the tribal shrine from which it emerged [with] the ugly old days of hate, rancour and disunity."[109]

Conclusion

Political parties, ethno-nationalist groups, and the newspapers representing them use narratives about space to mobilize power around emotional and material resources. The case of the rival

AG/Yoruba and NCNC/Igbo claim over Lagos reaffirms that "social processes and conditions are capable, in their own right, of generating strong links between people and place."[110] This points to the failure of the AG/Yoruba press to eliminate NCNC/Igbo attachment to the city through the imposition of the "legitimizing cloak of nature,"[111] through narratives, and through the success of NCNC/Igbo to use narratives to affirm the common ownership of a "national" space, Lagos.

The newspapers, in their support for hegemonic and counterhegemonic groups, not only tried to create a way of life and a conception of the world but they also attempted, through narratives, to translate the interests and values of the groups they represented into the "common" values and interests of the wider society.[112] As "experts in legitimation," they attempted to render existing power structures acceptable (when such structures favored the group they represented), and where they were otherwise unacceptable. They attempted to universalize the values of the social group they represented. The hegemonic and counterhegemonic moves of the two ethnic groups, Igbo and Yoruba, and the ethnic and political entrepreneurs on both sides show that, to paraphrase Mamdani, ethnicity can be a dimension of both power and resistance just as it can be a problem and a solution.[113]

Given its centrality, and the political, economic, social, and symbolic value of the city at stake, the press became a practical means of securing and resisting power over space or spatial power as well as a tool of hegemony and counterhegemony in the city. The centrality of narratives are evident in the construction of consent, dissent, and consensus as crucial ways of understanding hegemony and counterhegemony within and beyond the grand narrative of a Nigerian nation.

Part 3

Inclusion, Exclusion, and Democratic Contestations

5

Paper Soldiers

Narratives of Nationhood and Federalism in Pre–Civil War Nigeria

Narratives of conflict between antagonistic or competing communities compel the construction of simplistic binaries: good versus evil, truth versus falsehood, progress versus regression, and freedom versus oppression.[1] In reporting ethnic conflicts, the media, particularly those representing interested parties, rarely present "a coherent political analysis."[2] Yet media narratives can precipitate and exacerbate conflict. Daya Kishan Thussu and Des Freedman identify the media in the context of the communication of conflict as a "battleground."[3] Regarding the contemporary world, saturated with the media's reporting of conflict, Simon Cottle argues that the media-conflict interface needs to be understood through the perspective of "mediatized conflict." He uses this perspective to draw attention to "the more complex, active and performative ways [through which] the media are involved in conflicts today," because the media are "capable of enacting and performing conflicts as well as reporting and representing them."[4]

Against this backdrop, narratives of conflict should not be viewed as "mere reflections of reality"; indeed, they constitute "intrinsic parts of the *production* of political reality and the establishment of political truths."[5] Consequently, as studies of media coverage of conflict in Africa have shown,[6] we need to pay attention to the role of media narratives before, during, and after conflicts as a process of "history-making."[7] In Africa, students of the media and others have reflected on the function of the media in instigating and exacerbating political, ethnic, and religious conflicts. Recent examples include the activities of "hate media" such as the private radio station Radio Television Libre des Milles Collines (RTLM) and the newspaper *Kangura* during the Rwandan genocide, both of which "explicitly and repeatedly, in fact, relentlessly, targeted the Tutsi population for destruction."[8] There is also the complicity of community radio, the use of mobile phones, the Internet, and social media in the post-2007 election ethnic violence in Kenya, and the involvement of the local news media in the conflicts in nine Central African countries.[9]

Although some scholars have focused on the media's role in Nigeria in reporting political crises in general, the role of the Nigerian press in reporting and exacerbating the crises that eventually led to the country's civil war is yet to be fully acknowledged and accounted for in the literature on Nigerian history, particularly the history of the civil war.[10] As one of the most important instruments of mobilization within the context of relations of domination among the key ethno-regional and ethnic groups in late-colonial and immediate postindependent Nigeria, the press not only articulated the bases for the crises that eventually led to war but it also aggravated tension in the country and helped mobilize public opinion in crucial ways before the first shots were fired by the professional soldiers. It is in this context that I describe the newspapers in the pre-civil-war years as "paper soldiers."

In this chapter, I focus on the newspaper narratives of interregional, interethnic, and national political relations against the backdrop of the collapse of the First Republic and the tension and contradictions that led to the civil war. I concentrate on this period to point out the critical role of the press in not only narrating the challenges of national unity but also in constructing, deconstructing, and exacerbating the crisis that engulfed the young nation after soldiers attempted to seize power in January 1966.[11] The role of the press in Nigeria before the civil war is not surprising given that, globally, "organized violence requires planning" and psychological mobilization for "civilians" is as necessary "a precursor to war-waging as logistical preparedness." This is why, Susan Carruthers continues, "Media organizations play a crucial role in this process as conduits through which the case for taking up arms is advanced and sometimes contested. If we're to understand how media behave in wartime, first we must examine their contributions to processes of militarization."[12]

Given the nature of the evolution of the press in the country, and that the key political leaders and public intellectuals who defined and largely determined the character of the emergent modern public sphere in colonial Nigeria were almost always journalists and newspaper proprietors, the press has been at the vortex of every important battle around Nigeria's political history and the country's future. Starting from the struggles over modern urban formation and its governance (in Abeokuta, Benin, Calabar, Lagos, and other areas near the coast), the interventions in colonial policies, and the crusades over the proper structural and ideological approaches to the interface of the European Enlightenment and African tradition, the early press in Nigeria could be described as a battleground where ideological, cultural, and political combatants took on one another.

As discussed, during Nigeria's approach to independence from the early 1940s to the late 1950s, all the major ethno-regional blocs and the political parties representing these blocs seem to have been united in recognizing the important role of the press in the struggles for ideological and cultural validation and political victories. In most cases, newspapers thoroughly debated every major political issue before it was either adopted or rejected. It is not a surprise, therefore, that every major political leader, ethno-regional grouping, and political party in this era had its own ideological mouthpiece—a newspaper. They realized that the battle for the minds of men and women must be fought alongside other battles.

For many of the political leaders in the late colonial and early postcolonial era in Nigeria, the battle for the minds of the people was, in fact, the first battle that needed to be won. In the decade before independence, the northern region and the Northern People's Congress (NPC) and its leaders, including Sir Ahmadu Bello and Sir Abubakar Tafawa Balewa, had the *Nigerian Citizen* as their leading ideological warrior. The eastern region and the National Council of Nigerian Citizens (NCNC) and its preeminent leader, Dr. Nnamdi Azikiwe (later president of Nigeria), had the *West African Pilot* (owned by Azikiwe) as their mouthpiece. The western region and the Action Group (AG) and its preeminent leader, Chief Obafemi Awolowo, had the *Daily Service* and the *Nigerian Tribune* (the latter owned by Awolowo). In the regional, political, ideological, and personal battles of these regions, parties, and political leaders, the press, unsurprisingly, was an important instrument.

Consequently, in the first decade of Nigeria's independence, the political turmoil the country experienced was largely defined by the newspapers that represented the different groups, parties, and leaders. By this period, the *New Nigerian* emerged as the mouthpiece of the north, the NPC, and Sir Bello, whereas the *Nigerian Tribune* became the most important mouthpiece for the west, the AG, and Chief Awolowo. The *West African Pilot* remained the voice of the east, the NCNC, and Dr. Azikiwe. The *Morning Post*, owned by the federal government, reflected the position of the ruling regimes (first the Ironsi-led regime, and later the Gowon-led regime). The *New Nigerian* newspaper was founded under the premiership of Sir Ahmadu Bello in the northern region in 1966 to "truly present to the Nigeria people and the whole world a true picture of the Northern region . . . in a true and balanced manner," given the "very bad press [suffered by the region] in the hands of the Nigerian newspapers, mainly based in Lagos."[13] The paper announced in its inaugural editorial that "as a Northern newspaper, we shall seek to identify ourselves with the North and its peoples, their interest and their aspirations."[14] The paper was later acquired by the federal military government in 1975, but it continued to be the mouthpiece of the north.

The Nigerian Crisis and the Collapse of the First Republic

The Nigerian state after independence was confronted with discomforting realities in the struggle to provide a correlation between state and nation and the attempt to make the state an expression of—and a means of becoming—a nation.

At independence, the alliance between the NPC and the NCNC produced the federal government, with Alhaji Abubakar Tafawa Balewa (NPC) as prime minister and Dr. Nnamdi Azikiwe (NCNC) as president in a parliamentary system of government. Chief Obafemi Awolowo (AG), who had been the premier of the western region, left the region to become the opposition leader at the Federal House of Representatives. In the crisis that broke out within the AG in 1962, Awolowo's successor, Chief Samuel Ladoke Akintola, and his supporters left the party and formed the Nigerian National Democratic Party (NNDP), which entered into an alliance with the NPC to form the Nigerian National Alliance (NNA) in 1964. The

NCNC-NPC alliance also broke down, with the NCNC and AG entering into an alliance between 1964 and 1965 called the United Progressive Grand Alliance (UPGA). The AG crisis led to widespread violence in the western region, which resulted in a state-of-emergency declaration in the region.

During this time, Awolowo and his lieutenants were accused of planning to overthrow the federal government and charged with treasonable felony and later jailed. The national anomie that resulted from these events provoked a coup d'état by young soldiers led by Chukwuma Kaduna Nzeogwu. Nzeogwu declared, "The aim of the revolutionary council is to establish a strong, united and prosperous nation, free from corruption and internal strife." The coup leader added that the enemies are those who "have put the Nigerian calendar back by their words and deeds."[15] The young majors were later rounded up and detained while the Senate president, Nwafor-Orizu, who was acting for President Azikiwe, handed over power to the head of the army, Major-General J. T. U. Aguiyi Ironsi. In his initial broadcast General Ironsi announced, along with other measures, the suspension of the constitution while affirming the regime's readiness to honor the country's international commitments. He also asked for the cooperation of Nigerians in the task ahead.

In the foiled coup, Prime Minister Tafawa Balewa, Premier of the North Ahmadu Bello, Premier of the West Ladoke Akintola, and others were killed. There was widespread jubilation in the western and the eastern regions, but the northern region was shocked and saddened by the loss of its popular leaders, Bello and Balewa. The introduction of the unification decree by the Ironsi government later led to rumors about the return of the much-feared "Igbo domination" of Nigeria in the northern region. Efforts by the government to contest this and reassure the people of the region that there were plans to impose "Igbo hegemony" over the country proved futile in July 1966 as northern soldiers executed a counter-coup, killing the head of state, Ironsi, and his host in Ibadan, Col. Adekunle Fajuyi, the military governor of the western region. Subsequently, a northern officer, Lt. Col. Yakubu Gowon, was installed as head of state.

The Igbo-dominated eastern region, in turn, felt a deep sense of loss and fear of the return of "northern domination"; the military governor of the east, Lt. Col. Emeka Odumegwu Ojukwu, who was senior to Gowon, refused to accept that there was a central government in Nigeria or that Gowon was head of state and supreme commander of the Armed Forces. Ojukwu stated, according to a newspaper report: "That question is such a simple one and anyone who has been listening to what I have been saying all the time would know that I do not see a Central Government in Nigeria today."[16]

The pogrom against the Igbo in the north that followed this change of government precipitated a crisis that was unprecedented in Nigeria's history. This led to mass migration of the Igbo, not only from the northern region but from other parts of Nigeria as well, back to their homestead in the eastern region. However, as tension rose in the country and many expressed fear that the eastern region might secede, Ojukwu allayed the fears by declaring in August 1966 that his region "is anxious to ensure peace in the country and does not wish for secession," even though, he added, "the factors that make for true federation no longer existed."[17]

Several attempts were made to resolve the crisis and bring the estranged eastern region back fully into the union. The most important were the Aburi (Ghana) meetings in which the military governors of the regions and Lagos, together with the new head of state, Col. Yakubu Gowon, tried to reach a settlement.[18] It is significant that the military leaders at Aburi noted the role of the media in exacerbating the crisis. The following dialogue provides an example:

Lt. Col. Gowon: (head of state): I think all the Government Information Media in the country have done terribly bad[ly]. Emeka [Ojukwu] would say the *New Nigerian* has been very unkind to the East. . . .

Lt. Col. Ojukwu: (military governor of the eastern region): And the [*Morning*] *Post* [owned by the federal government] which I pay for.

Lt. Col. Gowon: Sometimes I feel my problem is not with anyone but the [*Eastern*] *Outlook* [owned by the eastern region government].

Lt. Col. Ojukwu: All the other information media have done a lot. When the Information Media in a country completely closed their eyes to what was happening. I think it is a dangerous thing.

Major Johnson: (military governor of Lagos): Let us agree it is the situation.

Lt. Col. Ejoor: (military governor of mid-west region): All of them have committed one crime or the other.

Lt. Col. Hassan: (military governor of northern region): The *Outlook* is the worst of them.

Lt. Col. Ojukwu: The *Outlook* is not the worst, the *Post* which we all in fact pay for is the worst, followed closely by *New Nigerian* [owned by the northern region government].[19]

In the end, the efforts to reconcile the opposing regions based on the Aburi Accord failed. On May 2, 1967, Ojukwu declared the secessionist Republic of Biafra, and the Nigerian civil war started thereafter.

"Paper Soldiers" and the Nigerian Crisis

The above conversation among the military leaders before the outbreak of the civil war further confirms the role of the press in the events leading up to it. It is important to examine newspaper narratives on the eve of the Nigeria-Biafra War in order to fully account for the conditions that predisposed the country to war and the role of the narratives in this context.

In this section, I compare and analyze the narratives of four newspapers on the eve of the civil war in 1966: the *New Nigerian*, which was owned by the northern regional government and thus represented the region; the *West African Pilot*, which spoke largely for the eastern region; the *Nigerian Tribune*, which spoke for the western region; and the federal government-owned *Morning Post*, which was the mouthpiece of the federal government. The main issues in the newspapers included the change in government that occurred on January 15, 1966, the unification decree promulgated by the Aguiyi-Ironsi military regime, the countercoup led by northern officers in July 1966, the pogrom in the northern region against easterners, and the "intransigence" of the eastern regional government. The Nigerian crisis of the early postindependence years, which the press had helped create and which it exacerbated by its reporting, put the various newspapers in different camps. Understandably, those whose principals had lost out in the battle that followed the granting of independence were eagerly awaiting a fundamental change that would sweep their opponents from power.

Within this political context, when soldiers took over power in January 1966, the *Tribune* and the *Pilot* were jubilant, whereas the *Morning Post* had no option but to support the new military regime, which paid its bills. However, the *Post* was transformed by the coup as much as it remained the same. Although it no longer defended some the issues and policies it had supported under the defunct Balewa administration, the *Post* still supported the power holders at the center.

Despite its earlier glorification and defense of the state of affairs under the old order, when Major-General J. T. U. Aguiyi-Ironsi became the new head of state, the *Post* announced that it "joins all lovers of peace in this country in welcoming the Military Government." The *Post*'s position was based on a simple fact: "A people deserve the type of government they get." Its image of the politicians was now that of a most contemptible bunch. The *Post* asked the new regime to be tough and to suspend all political activities: "Nigeria at this time deserves a tough and strong hand to steer her barque of state; such the Military Government now holds out every promise of supplying."[20] The next day, in an editorial titled "Best Hope for Democracy," the *Post* continued to entreat the new military regime to use force: "The new Government must suspend all political activities. Without doing this, it cannot be sure that it will get the atmosphere conducive to the re-planning that lies ahead. The trouble with this country has been over-present surfeit of politics."[21]

It took the *Post* six years to come to this conclusion about the "over-present surfeit of politics," which incidentally was also responsible for the advent of the paper itself. But in the tradition of going overboard in its support for whoever was paying its bill, the *Post* sanctioned anything and everything that the military government did or said. For instance, the statements of the military head of the regime, Aguiyi-Ironsi, were described as "words of gold," in the context of the "task of nation-building that lies ahead."[22]

For its own reasons, the *Tribune* agreed with the *Post* on the prospect of the emergence of a "Nigerian nation" from the rubbles of the First Republic, given the way the central and regional governments had dealt with the paper's owner, Awolowo, and his political party, the AG. "The spirit of oneness," editorialized the *Tribune*, "the idea of a united, detribalized country, appears to be having honest expressions in the everyday actions of our military rulers."[23] The *Post* added to this by describing politicians as the "ultimate fraudsters" whose past actions have to be obliterated so that Nigeria can start on a "clean slate."[24]

For the *Tribune*, the assassination of Premier Akintola, its founder's arch political enemy—and, by implication, the collapse of the republic in which Akintola and his principals (the NPC and the Hausa-Fulani political leaders) held sway—was a "God-send," given that "the new military regime came at a time when the ordinary people of Nigeria were wondering whether God really existed. . . . And so when God struck through our valiant army . . . the people rejoice[d]."[25] Although the *Pilot* agreed with the *Tribune* that the western region suffered most under the Balewa-led federal government, the latter asked the region to "behave," since it was the happiest for the military intervention. "After all, only God knows what would have been the fate of Westerners by now if the Army did not halt the events following the last Western Nigeria elections!"[26] In contrast, the *New Nigerian* seemed not to have reconciled itself—like the northern elite whose views it represented—to the sudden change in government and the killing of the northern region's key political and military leaders. The *New Nigerian* pointedly ignored the ensuing violent riots in the northern region in which the Igbo and others were killed.[27] However, in such narratives as the one on Ironsi's planned visit to the northern region, the position of the north on new political and ethno-regional formations in the country began to surface in the paper: "We welcome the decision of the Head of the National Military Government [Aguiyi-Ironsi] to tour parts of the republic. . . . We are particularly glad that the Supreme Commander has found time in his schedule to visit the North. With calls at Kano, Zaria, Jos and Kaduna he will obtain a cross section of opinion in the whole North. . . . He will able to re-assure any doubts they may have about the effectiveness of recent Government legislation."[28]

The *New Nigerian*, by narrating the position of the power elite as that of the "whole north," dissimulated the relations of domination through conflating a collective and its part. However, two days later, the paper argued for the building of a Nigerian grand nation that could supersede the "whole north." The paper added that every school should be made to perform the "daily ritual" of saluting the national flag, as this will help consolidate the idea of "a Nigerian nation."[29]

Unification and the Crisis of Nationhood

Unification Decree No. 34 of May 24, 1966, promulgated by the Ironsi-led regime, provided a major prism through which the newspapers narrated the tensions and contradictions of nationhood. In his speech announcing the decree, Ironsi said: "The former regions are abolished, and Nigeria grouped into a number of territorial areas called provinces. . . . Nigeria ceases to be what has been described as a federation. It now becomes simply the Republic of Nigeria."[30] Unification, in itself, is a *narrative*, and a major mode of ideology, as J. B. Thompson argues. As a mode of ideology, narratives of unification help create conditions through which relations of domination "may be established and sustained by constructing, at the symbolic level, a form of unity which embraces individuals in a collective identity, irrespective of the differences and divisions that may separate them." One of the strategies by which this is done is through what Thompson calls the "symbolization of unity." This involves "the construction of symbols of unity, of collective identity and identification," which "may be interwoven with the process of narrativization, as symbols of unity may be an integral part of the narrative . . . which recounts a shared history and projects a collective fate."[31]

The narratives of the crisis in the Nigerian newspaper press in 1966, in their various dimensions, reflect the mode and strategy of ideology in that they affirm different kinds of collective identity—national, regional, or ethnic—while simultaneously emphasizing the differences and divisions among the national, regional, or ethnic collective and the imagined other(s).

"Building one Nigeria is not an easy task by any means," stated the *Post*. "But it is not impossible either." Therefore, the announcement of the unification decree constituted for the *Post* "the first step in a journey that takes Nigeria to greatness," since "it is clear that tribalism or disunity was Nigeria's greatest bane."[32] Whereas the *Post*'s position was understandable given that it supported the official line, for the *Pilot*, support for the unitary system was a fundamental credo, given that that was the original position of Azikiwe, the NCNC, and the Igbo political elite—before they were temporarily persuaded to abandon this position by the federalists by the late 1950s. Despite this temporary position, the Igbo political elite remained committed to a unitarist political system in the early 1960s. Against this backdrop, the *Pilot* perceived unification through the unitary system, even before the unification decree was formally promulgated, as "the coming into being by natural process of a central Government [which] henceforth makes the concept of a Federal Government a misnomer."[33]

The *Pilot* hoped "that in time, the Military Government of Nigeria would consider the abolition of the word 'federal' usually attached to Nigeria." If this occurs, the *Pilot* concluded, "the name of the Military Government will be written in Gold as the only Go-Getter Government that brought unity to this country." The paper also praised Aguiyi-Ironsi for bringing a "message of hope to millions of our people" when he stated in his budget speech that "the new nation that we are creating will have a place for all people commensurate with their talent."[34] The *Pilot*'s position was a return to the fierce battle on the pages of the leading newspapers over federal versus unitary system in the 1940s and early 1950s. The *Pilot*, in that period, described the federalists as "Pakistanists." The *Pilot*'s editorials on the unification decree, therefore, totally ignored the popular resolve in the other two regions—northern and western—that Nigeria should operate the federal system.

The northern region could hardly be part of the *Pilot*'s "our people," and perhaps this was so for the western region too. Central to the northern region's "doubts"[35] about the new regime was the idea of "talent," which, for the north, generally represented a euphemism for "southern domination," and particularly "Igbo domination." A signpost of these doubts and "fears" was the piece published in the *New Nigerian*[36] that stated: "Many Northerners still need convincing that the regime is a truly national one—and not one out to replace Northern domination of the South by Southern domination of the North. Some are beginning to ask . . . why the coup leaders have not been brought to trial."[37] The narrative then set the basis for the fear of southern domination: "The North has both a lower population density and lower educational standard than the South. This leads some of the Northerners to fear that the South will somehow 'colonize' them by taking over both the jobs in the civil services and their lands. There is fear that all the current talk about administrative unity, in practice, open[s] the way to the demotion of Northerners."[38]

However, that the idea of unification constituted an ideal for the interests that the *Pilot* served was further demonstrated in the editorial devoted to defending it against the attacks or ambivalence of the other parts of Nigeria. Contrary to the *New Nigerian*'s fears about the unification decree, the *Pilot* stated that is "what Nigerians want" and that under the system "the question of one section dominating the other does not arise." Those who argue the contrary, affirmed the *Pilot,* are "tribalists" who "could not learn by the mistakes of the past, and even though many like a unitary form of Government, they still want the country to be tied up with the appendages of federalism."[39] The *Pilot* then corroborated the opinion of Lt. Col. Odumegwu Ojukwu, the military governor of the eastern region, who stated that "the present era was one of unity and solidarity for the whole country in which there were no minority areas."[40] For the *Pilot,* this was the "ideal" that had to be turned into practical reality. Though not explicitly stated, the idea of minorities in the eastern region was uncomfortable for Ojukwu and the interests that the *Pilot* represented. Stated the *Pilot:* "Indeed minority problems arise with the question of federalism no matter by what description. Before the division of the country into states, there was nothing like [a] minority problem. Nigerians want a constitution in which any section should feel at home anywhere in the country and not feel as minorities."[41]

The *Pilot* added that nothing short of a constitution that allows "free interchange of abode throughout the country" will "serve the interest of the people."[42] "The people" were primarily the Igbo, who had commercial interests in virtually every part of Nigeria, particularly Lagos and the major cities of the north. For the *Pilot* this plan for unification was therefore "far reaching" and would help Nigerians "evolve a common nationality and end sectionalism." Consequently, the paper urged the "Ironsi Regime to carry on since its doings have the unanimous support of the people. We are convinced of our national salvation under the aegis of the new Military Government."[43]

Surprisingly, despite the fact that its proprietor was the first and most eloquent of the proponents of a federal system among the country's founding fathers, the *Tribune* also shared this position on a unification decree, believing that it "would pave the way for a great and prosperous nation, which is the hope of everyone." A united nation that might emerge from this was of interest to the *Tribune:* "If the present army regime within the time-table set for itself is able to build a new Nigerian nation out of the ruins of the past, if it is able to bring together a people torn asunder by tribal trappings and narrow sectionalism which in the day of politicians became worshipped, cherished institutions, then the future of a united and progressive Nigeria is assured."[44] Perhaps the *Tribune's* position was influenced more by the fact that the new military regime upstaged the political parties and leaders who had "conspired" to defeat Awolowo's party and jailed the *Tribune*'s founder. At this point, Awolowo was still in jail.

There is no question for the *Pilot* that the unification decree would "bring together a people torn asunder by tribal trappings and narrow sectionalism," as the *Tribune* argued. In fact, for the *Pilot* the mere adoption of this form of government represented the birth of "true Nigeria." That the *Pilot* had always desired a unitary system was evident in its jubilation at the achievement of "one Nigeria, one destiny" and the "wiping out" of federalism. When the unitary system was formally announced, the *Pilot* editorialized: "Today a true Nigeria is born. Federalism has been wiped out. All the equivocation in the past about common nationality is over. Today every Nigerian is a Nigerian no matter in what part of the country he is. . . . The policy of divide and rule introduced by the British Colonial administration and perpetuated by self-seeking politicians is over. The world was made to believe that nothing could be better than a Pakistanized Nigeria because it served the interest of the few on top for the country to be so divided."[45] Also, for the new regime's mouthpiece, the *Morning Post*, the unification decree took Nigeria into "a new epoch" because "this is a thing that all true patriots of this country have eagerly looked forward to. . . . *The Morning Post* commend[s] the National Government for taking the bold step to erase all the divisive tendencies that had contributed to make Nigerians from one part of Nigeria stranger in another part."[46]

Whereas the *Tribune* hoped that the Ironsi regime would be able to perform the recommended task of unification "within the timetable set for itself,"[47] the *Pilot* did not foresee an end for the military regime: "Long live Aguiyi Ironsi's Military Government. Long live the Nigerian Republic."[48] The *Pilot* could not but wish the government long life, given the way the newspaper articulated the regime's raison d'être on its behalf: "It is the declared policy of the government to build a hate-free, greed-free nation with a contented citizenship provided with all the basic human requirements. It behooves any true lover of this country to bring these facts home to misguided Nigerians. This is the supreme task of one and all, particularly the information media at this time of national reconstruction. Anything short of this is gross disservice to the nation."[49]

That these newspapers served as "paper soldiers" for the ideological and ethno-political struggle among the contending groups is further demonstrated by how the agenda of members of particular groups was picked up and amplified by their newspapers, and how at times the agenda articulated by the newspapers was picked up and amplified by the political leaders. For example, when the military governor of the eastern region, Ojukwu, ordered that all references to "tribe or ethnic group" be "completely expunged in future from all Government records," the *Post* praised it as a "signpost of the future of Nigeria."[50] The *Pilot*, about five weeks later, asked the central government to follow the eastern region government's example by expunging "from all books and documents the vestige of colonial era regarding 'tribe' within Nigeria," while affirming, "Long live Nigeria as a nation."[51] When Ironsi obliged by announcing that "his Government will deal ruthlessly with any citizen who peddled tribalism in the new Nigeria," the *Post* declared on its front page, "No Room for Tribe."[52]

However, even as tension rose in the country, particularly in the disaffected parts of the northern region,[53] the *Pilot* praised the controversial decision to rotate military governors among the regions as a "blessing [that will] minimize tribalism,"[54] while presenting the Ironsi regime as one that was "marching on."[55] The "sixth milestone" of the Ironsi regime in its "mission of salvation," stated the *Pilot*, was producing a united country, against the odds, in that "in place of division, we are now forging a homogenous whole, instead of sectionalism, the dominant theme is now unity."[56] It is significant that the *Morning Post* and the *Pilot* were either unaware of the simmering disaffection in the northern region or chose to ignore it.

To explain the unpopular unification decree in the western and northern regions of the country, the military head of state, General Aguiyi-Ironsi, decided to embark on a tour of the country. Ironsi never returned alive from that tour, which the *Pilot* had described as the "march to progress" in the "forging of a homogeneous whole." Disaffection in the army and the political tension in the north led to a countercoup by northern officers in which Ironsi was killed in Ibadan, western Nigeria, on July 29, 1966. The *Pilot*'s somewhat arrogant earlier statement that those who lacked an "enlarged vista" will be swept away became a conundrum of sorts a few days later with the countercoup. The *Pilot*, totally impervious to the growing unpopularity of the unification decree, had declared a day before the countercoup that "the days when the pivot of nationalism began and ended with one's small sectional environment are far gone. Now the format of nationalism is broad and all embracing. Only those who are capable of showing an equally enlarged vista on public affairs will survive the clean-up campaign now taking place all around."[57]

Even on the day of the countercoup, the *Pilot*, unaware of what had happened that morning, described Ironsi's meeting with the natural rulers from all over the country the day before as a "huge success . . . in Nigeria's onward march as a nation."[58] After the countercoup, and at a period when it was not yet clear what direction Nigeria would take, the *Pilot* still narrated the "success" of the Ironsi regime, asking for peace to save the "Nigerian nation." The paper stated: "The *West African Pilot* and all Nigerians for that matter feel very much concerned that there should be trouble in the Army at a time when the national reconstruction program has advanced to very great height. . . . No matter what the source of grouse, no matter how deep and sentimental the cause of difference among the rank and file, we implore them [the soldiers] in the name of Nigeria to cease fire. . . . There is no doubt that the up-to-date [Ironsi-led] National Military Government was riding high in the estimation of the people of Nigeria. . . . In this regard, we call on all men and women of good conscience to throw in their full weight in order to halt the hand of doom before it engulfs our young nation."[59]

The next few days witnessed a vacuum in power, until Lt. Col. Yakubu Gowon was announced as the new head of state. Though the fate of the immediate past head of state, Ironsi, remained unknown, Gowon's first broadcast included the abrogation of the unification decree and the return of Nigeria to the federal system. Given its own opposition and the opposition of the northern region to the unification process under the fallen regime, the *New Nigerian* was jubilant when it reviewed what led to the collapse of the Ironsi regime. The paper editorialized: "Nigeria has a new Government. New men have accepted the arduous and difficult task of guiding the nation. . . . For the sake of the country; for the sake of our people and for the sake of our children; the new leadership must be given every support. . . . The unitary system of Government has not stood the test of time. One reason perhaps was that it was imposed hastily and without sufficient thought for the future. Unity is not something which can be imposed by force. . . . It must come about slowly and gradually and be built on goodwill."[60]

Despite the fact that such unity, as conceived by the *New Nigerian*, was not yet in place in Nigeria, the paper envisaged a "whole nation" that eagerly awaited the new measures by Lt. Col. Yakubu Gowon. Yet the *New Nigerian* rejected any suggestion that the north was jubilant over the countercoup, because "Nigeria is facing a grave situation." In an attempt to conceal its own jubilation, the paper added that "anybody who reports or gives the impression that any section of the community is jubilant is hindering the efforts to restore calm and order."[61]

Refederalization and "Warring with Words"

Despite the tension, crises, and uncertainties of the post-Ironsi era, the *Pilot* remained irrevocably committed to the sustenance of Nigeria as one indivisible entity, as it romanticized the idea of an overriding nationalism. The paper stated: "Although the armour of our National Military Government has sustained some visible dents at many points, we of the *West African Pilot* still believe that we can all rally round and begin all over again to mend it in the greatest interest of our national survival. . . . It will be a thing of joy to Nigerians if all segments of our populace will continue to feel a deep sense of national belonging borne out of justified national cohesion."[62]

However, Lt. Col. Ojukwu, the military governor of the eastern region, refused to recognize the new head of state. The *Pilot* regarded the divergent positions expressed by Gowon and Ojukwu in the aftermath of the coup as representing the depth of the "tribal sentiments in the army." Subsequently, the paper reported that "Lt. Col. Gowon said ' . . . putting all the considerations to test . . . the basis for unity is not there. . . .' The same night, Lt. Col. Odumegwu Ojukwu . . . said just as much, concluding, 'there are serious doubts as to whether the people of Nigeria . . . can sincerely live together as members of the same nation.'" In spite of all this, the *Pilot* still maintained its belief that Nigerians could swim together without bitterness and bloodshed.[63]

As part of the efforts to appease some sections of the country and isolate the eastern region, Gowon released all political prisoners, including Chief Obafemi Awolowo and Chief Anthony Enahoro. This provided another interesting context for hostilities between the newspapers. In its report of the release, the *New Nigerian* added an exclamation mark to the claim by Ojukwu that the defunct Supreme Military Council headed by Ironsi had earlier decided to release Awolowo before Ironsi was toppled. The newspaper reported that "in the telegram, Lt. Col. Ojukwu said the decision to release Chief Awolowo and other political prisoners were taken by the Supreme Council earlier on!"[64] The *New Nigerian*, whose founders were behind the imprisonment of Awolowo and the others, recalled that the imprisonment had been "a source of contention and dissension throughout Nigeria for the past few years."[65] Yet it could be argued that with the killing of northern leaders (Awo's sworn political adversaries) in the January 1966 coup, the refusal by Ironsi to put Nzeogwu and his fellow plotters to trial, and the unification decree, Ironsi would have been even more unpopular in the northern region if he had released Awolowo. But given how Awolowo's release now served the interests of the *New Nigerian* and its backers, the "merits and demerits" of Awolowo's treasonable felony trial, the paper argued, were no longer important. The paper concluded that the release of Awolowo and others should be "welcome and accepted by every Nigerian," because "their confinement provided a cause and reason for discord and differences between Nigerians of varying political beliefs."[66] The paper argued that "the future is more important than the past. The stability and prosperity of our country is more important than old political feuds and fights."[67] The stability and prosperity that the *New Nigerian* emphasized were ostensibly those of the northern region-led regime, as Gowon's statement later confirmed.

Whereas the *Post* approached the warm welcome that Awolowo received after his release as his "hour of glory," the *Pilot* narrated the release as "the triumph of truth over falsehood and victory of light over darkness."[68] On its back page, the *Post* headlined Awolowo's charge, "Don't Break the Nation," adding, "Awolowo says: I back federalism."[69] The *Tribune* reported on the arrival of the "58-year-old Nigerian nationalist, politician, philosopher and idealist [Awolowo], at this time when the nation and its people are passing through a period marked by certain vital significant events sharpening all facets of history of our great nation. . . . Therefore, the release of [Awo] we hope, marks the beginning of new crusade, of a new social and political force towards [the] building of a Nigerian nation welded together by genuine unity and strength."[70]

Even though the *New Nigerian*, in the context of Awo's imprisonment, argued that the past should be forgotten, it returned to that past to rub in the political "loss" of "a top leader" who had long preached a unitary form of government. The top leader, whom the paper failed to mention, was obviously the former ceremonial president, Nnamdi Azikiwe. The *New Nigerian* wrote: "About nine years ago, one of the top leaders in Nigeria suddenly discovered that his time-honoured fight for unitary form of government for Nigerian was a lost battle. For almost 20 years, he had advocated a unitary form of government for Nigeria. He even called for 12 states in Nigeria—all of them weak and powerless states—with a very strong centre. But to everybody's surprise . . . while in London for the 1957 Constitutional Conference, he cried out that 'federalism is imperative for Nigeria.' This was a very serious departure from an age long belief in a cause that was very unpopular."[71]

This editorial is illuminating in the indirect way in which it connects Azikiwe's and Igbo's advocacy for a unitary form of government with Ironsi's adoption of the same. The newspaper seems to suggest that this connection was in the pursuit of "Igbo domination." Without mentioning any names, the *New Nigerian* again placed a "consistent" Awolowo against the "inconsistent" Zik: "Quite in contrast with this leader, another leader advocated a federal system of government for Nigeria. He did not mince words over it. He emphasized that a country so diverse in culture and traditions—a country with many languages, and with development, educationally and otherwise, so uneven—[and] a constitution that allowed for every region to go its own pace, could only be acceptable to the majority of the people."[72]

As this point, the northern region's position in relation to the debate between the Awolowo federalists and the Azikiwe unitarists was articulated by the *New Nigerian*: "The Northern leaders of all shades of opinion . . . remained unmoved in their strong belief in a federal form of government. . . . The North thus became a late starter in the race for self-rule as it was in the race for education. The federal form of government became a blessing. Everybody came to realize that under this system no inequality and injustice could be done to anyone. That every region could progress at its own pace."[73]

However, there were some crises that confronted the "nation" in the narrative of the *New Nigerian*: "Then the Army stepped in to save us from total disintegration. We all hailed our liberators. . . . Then very soon, many things, apparently nauseating, started to happen. The military power-that-be made the most disastrous and catastrophic slip. Much against the advice of the elders of the country, the authorities decided to abolish the federation and sought to impose unitarism on the people. The result of some arbitrary decisions were chaos and confusion." The "nation" had apparently now returned to where the newspaper believed it should be. Therefore, the *New Nigerian* editorialized, "Nothing can be more reassuring than . . . that this country is to return to the federal system. . . . The decision is wise and sane." When the interests of the northern region were well served, *New Nigeria* announced that all was well with Nigeria. This was particularly true if decentralization had been encouraged in principle, argued the newspaper: "The people of this country have much in common and at stake. We can survive the strains and stresses of a lasting existence if only we return to a constitution that allows for each and every component section of the Republic to go at its own pace and to run its affairs in its own manner and light. Lt.-Col. Yakubu Gowon is certainly moving in the right direction."[74]

On its part, the *Pilot*, which had earlier celebrated the "wiping out" of federalism, shifted gears and asserted the need to put a stop to the mention of "minorities" and described the introduction of a unitary system as the "birth of a true Nigeria."[75] In the new dispensation, the Pilot maintained: "A federal system which should respect the wishes of the majority ethnic and linguistic groupings in the country and at the same time allay the fears of the minorities should appeal to the proposed consultative meetings to be drawn from all over Nigeria." The *Pilot* insisted that the "new" federalism would be "true federalism" because "there is a greater benefit to gain if we still remain one country, instead of tearing asunder by secession."[76] With this argument, the *Pilot* reintroduced the option of secession into the narrative, even though it did so by disclaiming it. A few days later, Ojukwu echoed the possibility of secession while rejecting the proposed reintroduction of federalism because, as he argued, "the factors making for a true federation of Nigeria no longer exists." Yet Ojukwu was reported by the *Pilot* to have reviewed the situation in the country in declaring that "the East is anxious to ensure peace in the country and she does not wish for secession."[77]

The *Post*, which had earlier also celebrated the promulgation of a unitary system by the Ironsi regime, and had described it as a "bold step" that all "true patriots" had looked forward to,[78] reversed itself as well by stating that "perhaps our unity lies through a federal system of government."[79] Two days later, the paper, which had described the imposition of a unitary system by the Ironsi regime as "the first step in a journey that takes Nigeria to greatness," given that, hitherto, "tribalism or disunity was Nigeria's greatest bane,"[80] added that the decision by the Gowon regime to return Nigeria to a federal system was the right one: "BUT STILL, WE ARE CONVINCED THAT FEDERALISM WOULD SUIT A SOCIETY SUCH AS OURS BETTER THAN A UNITARY GOVERNMENT. . . . WE ARE IN THE TWILIGHT ZONE AND BEFORE THE DARKNESS FALLS, WE MUST FIND THE TRUE PATH, OR FOREVER GROPE IN THE DARK. . . . We are not ashamed to admit that tribalism abounds. For we are yet to see a Nigerian who does not see himself only as Ibo, Yoruba, Hausa or Bini. We do not feel this sense of shame, not because we revel in tribalism or clanishness, but because we recognize too well that it is only a natural propensity. We believe every Nigerian is a tribalist. That doesn't matter. What matters is if tribalism succeeds to lie between Nigerians like a curtain of iron."[81]

The *Tribune*, which had welcomed the "administrative, constitutional and geographical reforms" (unitary system) in the hope that it would make Nigeria a "great and prosperous nation,"[82] also reversed its position, stating that there was "no doubt" that a federal constitution was acceptable to Nigerians, given the fact that it is "adequate to the exigencies and function of government and of course the preservation of national unity."[83] The paper then rearticulated the fundamental position of its founders: "A federal system of administration will help keep the balance of power between the component parts of the federation. Above all we are hopeful that out of all these efforts will emerge a new, powerful, progressive and united nation of our dream."[84]

The national conference that the Gowon regime planned to hold to decide the future of the country provided yet another means for the discursive negotiation of power in the troubled federation. As evident in the press, the proposed constitutional talks presented an opportunity for the narration of power from the past, presaging the negotiation of power in the present that would determine future prospects.

The *New Nigerian*, which had stated earlier in relation to Awo's release that "old political feuds and fights" should be forgotten because they were not very important, returned to the past in locating the proposed talks in the trajectory of Nigeria's history. The talks reminded the paper of the fears of "Igbo domination" in the few months under the Ironsi regime rather than the accusations of "Northern domination" (between 1960 and 1966), which preceded Ironsi's era. The paper added that "post-independent Nigeria, unfortunately, was saddled precariously with propensities of some sections of our population to lord it over the rest of the country."[85]

Given the balance of power that favored the northern region, the *New Nigerian* argued that such "wise counsel," as existed under the Lt. Col. Gowon regime, should not be lost for a return to "Igbo domination," as under General Ironsi. The paper added: "Now that our ship of state has reached another cross-roads at which point wise counsel must prevail, nothing should be done to give room for a recurrence of the events that set our hearts rumbling in January this year." The paper also established a "fact" that revealed a predilection to affirm the supremacy of the north in the area of leadership. The *New Nigerian* stated, "Northern Nigeria has been blessed with good leadership at all times and now is the time this leadership must be on show. Our place in the Republic must be unique." Despite the "sporadic and tendentious outbursts from certain quarters of the Republic"—a reference to the eastern region—the *New Nigerian* argued, in the context of the constitutional conference being held, that "we may end up in a federation or a confederation. But whatever happens the die is now cast and there should be no illusion of what is good for our people. Our [northern] leaders at this week's meeting must bear in mind that they have the support of some 29 million people [of the northern region]. They must not fail us. They must not seek concession purely for the sake of unity that cannot stand the test of time."[86]

In another editorial, the paper asked that whatever comes out of the talks must be based "absolutely on what is good for the people of the North and, of course, Nigeria."[87] This position of the *New Nigerian* was very significant in the way it compared to portions of Gowon's inaugural speech. The conclusion reads as if it is lifted from Gowon's speech, in which he states, inter alia, "I have come to strongly believe that we cannot honestly and sincerely continue in this wise, as the basis for trust and confidence in our unitary system of government has not been able to stand the test of time."[88]

Published beside the editorial "The Forthcoming Big Talks" was an opinion piece titled "A Voice from the East Pleads with Yakubu Gowon—Let's Part Our Ways." This editorial was published as if to buttress Gowon's and the *New Nigerian*'s fears. It stated in part: "It

is not possible for us to live together. The seed of bitterness has not
only been sown but has long germinated and the resulting plant is
producing its own ripe seeds which are already dispersing and ger-
minating in their own turn. If you [Gowon] really mean to give us
peace, the best and easiest way of doing that is obvious. Let each
Region go its own way." For this contributor, whose position was
given prominence in the *New Nigerian*, the idea of a Nigerian union
was vanishing and nothing needed to be done to save it: "The edifice which was erected by the British colonial administration and
which was once asked to take the name of Songhai is now a vanishing fantasy. What now remains only comprises . . . the clashing cym-
bals of our time. . . . Therefore there is a great risk in continuing
this peculiar political union. The basis for unity as a single nation
is wanting . . . tribal passion die hard. Nigeria was a chance result
of British imperial administration connoting nothing higher than
common allegiance to the British Masters."[89]

On its part, the *Tribune* was concerned more about the future and
the consolidation of the ideal and idea of the Nigerian nation in
its take on the proposed constitutional conference. But the paper
was also concerned about leadership among the Yoruba. The *Tribune* stated that the selection of its proprietor, Awolowo, to lead the
western region to the talks was vital because "Chief Awolowo, as we
know him, is a man who has dedicated his energies to the welfare
and happiness of the [Yoruba] people and by placing the burden of
the leadership of the people on him, he is only being asked to weld
together a people once wrecked by feud; and to put into service his
personal qualities and decisiveness."[90] The paper argued that the
constitutional conference was about "the nation's destiny": "This
conference is historic, it is significant. . . . It is significant because
out of these talks will emerge a charter or a philosophy upon which
rests the hopes and aspirations of a people who should live together
in a spirit of common belief and understanding; a genuine spirit
completely divorced of the past hatred, bias and ill-feelings indeed a
spirit cardinally aimed towards one destiny."[91]

The *Tribune* saw the charter and philosophy that would provide
the basis for the genuine spirit cardinally aimed toward a common
destiny for Nigerians as far more elevating than the *New Nigerian's*
focus on the "no compromise" stand the northern delegates were
urged to take in matters that—for the *New Nigerian*—were only of
a "tenuous unity." For the *Tribune*, the conference was all about the

present and future of Nigeria. Therefore, the paper stated that "all those taking part in this "people's conference . . . represent the present and the future of the Nigerian nation."[92]

Like the *Tribune*, the *Pilot* argued that it was also concerned with national unity and not sectional advantage, as advocated by the *New Nigerian*. If every section of the country had a "master plan" [like the north], the *Pilot* wondered, whose "plan" would be rejected? First, the paper reviewed what was at stake in Nigeria and then stated what it assumed to be "the truth" of the Nigerian crisis and "what is to be done": "The truth about the country is that we are lacking in those fundamental elements that make for unity—that is to say, DEFENSIVE NATIONALISM and IRON HAND LEADERSHIP. A nation requires to face foreign aggression in order to develop defensive nationalism which is a unifying factor for a common nationality. Secondly, to attain unity a nation requires a man on a horse back with a whip to keep the people together."[93] Therefore, the *Pilot*, unlike the *New Nigerian*, asked that the Lagos constitutional talks fashion a constitution "which will satisfy the aspirations of the various ethnic and linguistic groups in Nigeria."[94]

With the contending regions, particularly the northern and the eastern regions, taking diametrically opposed positions on the political structure of the country, mass killings erupted in the northern region. The *Post* argued that these two regions and the individuals representing them were not greater than "the nation."[95] The paper stated that, therefore, "we must, all of us Nigerians, accept the challenge of the times and rise as one man to the task of binding the nation's wounds in order to save her from bleeding to death,"[96] adding: "They must all agree that this country, Nigeria, can continue as one indivisible sovereign state."[97] If this was done, then a Nigerian nation would emerge as a "paradise."[98]

Whereas the *Pilot* refrained from commenting on the flight of the Igbo from the north in the wake of the riots and the killings, given its concern with the themes of unity, the *New Nigerian* used every opportunity to protect the northern region's "heritage" and attack the eastern region and its people. The *Pilot* approached the entire crisis in 1966 as a "great lesson" that taught the people "never again [to] postpone till tomorrow what they have to do today," adding that, in spite of the debacle, Nigerians "have every reason to be proud that from the still smoking rubble have emerged a new generation of Nigerians able to face the stark realities of our times."[99]

The *New Nigerian* used the stoppage of the illegal taxes being collected from fleeing easterners by the Lafia Native Authority in the northern region as an excuse to condemn the "enemies of a united Nigeria [exploiting the controversy of the illegal taxes] in their campaign of denigration against the North." As far as the *New Nigerian* was concerned, complaints over the illegal taxes were being used to "buttress [the] stupid demand for disintegration of the country." The paper further approached the complaints as a situation "in which the sins of one 'overzealous official' were visited on a whole government or region." Blaming the north for this was described by the paper as "indiscretion and insanity."[100] Furthermore, the *New Nigerian* argued that "if the communities in this country decide to part their ways, as they have the right to do, they should do so in peace and not in pieces."[101] The *Post* responded, asking if there was any need for the constituent parts of Nigeria to separate and remain enemies, if indeed separation was achieved. "There is already deep-seated bitterness among the peoples of this country. But with a little bit of good sense, time, the healer of all wounds, will ultimately ameliorate whatever bitterness may exist among the people. . . . And who knows, Nigeria may yet remain. And if she crumbles, should she do so with former Nigerians becoming inveterate enemies?"[102]

In the wake of the pogrom against easterners in the north, the *Post* asked the government to be "ruthless in maintaining peace" by "crushing the saboteurs," whereas the *Tribune* asked for restraint because Nigeria "is [sitting] on a tinder box."[103] The *Tribune* echoed the military governor of the mid-west, Lt. Col. David Ejoor: "Nigeria is now passing through a crucial and momentous stage in her history when different communities have to consider whether they can march forward as one indivisible whole in true mutual affection and concord or whether they have indeed reached the end of a once hopeful experiment in nation-building."[104]

As the number of victims of the pogrom in the north increased, the *Pilot* abandoned its earlier pleas for unity to raise what it considered critical questions: "The days of wishful thinking is over. . . . We have long deceived ourselves and no nation based on self-deception can long endure. . . . One of the major issues facing the country today is whether Nigerians can live together as one people, in peace and security. . . . Can Nigerians live together without fear of one section dominating the other? If they cannot then what is the basis of togetherness which the weeping Jeremiahs fancy can be achieved in the country?" The paper argued further that the Lagos talks could not do much in the face of the odds: "The facts as they are today, are that Nigerians are haunted by fear of domination of one section by another, by fear of insecurity of life and property, by fear of molestation. These are basic human freedoms which, lacking in a country makes nonsense of united nationhood. Under the atmosphere of apprehension and misgivings, it will be wishful thinking to feel that by a magic wand, the ad-hoc committee on Nigerian constitution meeting in Lagos can manufacture a way in which by tomorrow morning Nigerians will march along in mutual confidence as one people without suspicion of one another. Togetherness cannot be imposed."[105]

The "Mourning Day" declared by the eastern regional government on August 29—"in respect of souls lost [in the Northern region] following the events of May 15 and July 29, 1966," a mourning that the federal military government could not succeed in blocking—irked the *New Nigerian* deeply, as reflected in its reaction. Even though the paper found no problem with mourning "the death of anybody"—Ojukwu had described it as the "least honor we can do those our sons and daughters now dead"—the *New Nigerian* asserted: "Every reasonable and right-thinking Nigerian would loathe the unconstitutional action of the Military Governor of Eastern Nigeria, Lt.-Col. Odumegwu Ojukwu in selecting a day of mourning for the people of his region. . . . There is nothing wrong in mourning the death of anybody. But to do so in circumstances of defiance of lawful authority is to worsen an already bad situation. We dare ask whether those who died during the mad outrages of January this year did not deserve to be mourned." What the *New Nigerian* described as the "mad outrages of January" was the Igbo-led coup of January 15, 1966, in which two prominent Northern politicians, Bello and Balewa, and northern military officers were killed. The paper was eager to point out that the Igbo provoked the killings in the northern region by assassinating northern leaders. The paper stated, "We are surprised and rightly too, to note that the authorities in the East were so indiscreet as to have singled out the tragic events of May and July 29 as if nothing provoked or preceded those events, tragic as they were." Consequently, the paper concluded: "The declaration of a day of mourning was a flagrant incitement and whipping up of irrational emotions at a time when all reasonable people are working hard to find a solution to our present problem. . . . We can now see clearly the designs of the perpetrators of an order whereby only a section of the Nigerian community must have the right to lord things over the other sections."[106]

Even the sixteen-man delegation of northerners residing in the eastern region, which planned to visit the northern region to plead for the safety and security of easterners in the north, were told by the *New Nigerian* that, even though this is a "gesture of goodwill," it is "unnecessary" because "it is a well-known fact that Easterners, certainly all non-Northerners, have always been given protection in the North." Yet, contrary to the *New Nigerian*'s position, it was in the midst of all these "hospitable, friendly, sincere and orderly"[107] people that several hundreds of easterners, particularly the Igbo, were massacred. Two days after this narrative of normalcy and order, the *New Nigerian* itself reported that the military governor of the north "gives another STERN WARNING against lawlessness, molestation and acts of subversion."[108] Despite this, the paper insisted that these acts were perpetrated by a "small, misguided minority" of northerners. However, the *New Nigerian* later attempted to face the reality of the divisiveness of the national crisis: "We are back where we were. The uncertainties and fears which were brought about by the mad propensity of a few[109] are now being exploited to make the work of national reconstruction difficult. Acts of lawlessness, molestation, intimidation and subversion cannot do this region any good. Nations are never built or sustained by indulging in recriminations, bitterness and rancor. . . . As the Governor of the North [said, we are] most distressed over the action of the small misguided minority."[110]

This mild "internal criticism" by the *New Nigerian*, itself part of the "recriminations, bitterness and rancor" that it condemned, would certainly not do for the *Tribune*, which asked Lt. Col. Gowon to take urgent action to stop the "large scale killings" in the north because "this is savagery and sadism in their worst form." The *Tribune* added, "We condemn, in strong terms, these killings and other acts of lawlessness and disorder."[111] In an editorial titled "Whither Nigeria?" the *Post* lamented the expressions of the possible collapse of Nigeria by the head of state, Gowon, and the military governor of the east, Ojukwu, while hoping for the best: "Nigerians have watched with increasing dismay, the blood-bath of the past few months. . . . This is not the time for self-deceit. And this is not the time to pretend that the Army is free from the bug of sectionalism that bites all others outside the barracks. . . . Lt. Col. Gowon said. . . . Putting all the considerations to test . . . the basis for unity is not there." The same night, Lt. Col. Odumegwu Ojukwu, military governor of the Eastern Group of Provinces, said just as much, concluding that "there are serious doubts as to whether the people of Nigeria . . . can sincerely live together as members of the same nation. . . . We of the *Post* believe that Nigerians can swim together without unnecessary bitterness and bloodshed."[112]

It is worth noting that, unlike the *Tribune*, the *New Nigerian* did not describe the events as "killings" or a "massacre."[113] The strongest words that the *New Nigerian* used include "acts of lawlessness, molestation, intimidation and subversion"—ostensibly among otherwise "hospitable, friendly, sincere and orderly" northerners. However, for the *Pilot*, those whom the *Tribune* described as practicing "savagery and sadism" by participating in the killings were "men on the lunatic fringe"[114] who could make the country degenerate "[in]to civil war," but for the extraordinary restraint of the easterners.[115] Whereas the *New Nigerian* presented the majority of northerners as restrained, the *Pilot*, on the contrary, argued that it was the easterners who were restrained in their responses. From the *Pilot*: "Could we now face the grim realities arising from the disreputable and tragic events of recent weeks. For unless we do this, the hopes expressed both by Lieutenant-Colonel Odumegwu Ojukwu and Lt. Col. Gowon over the weekend will dash to pieces and Nigeria with it. . . . Goodwill messages cannot solve our problems which can be solved by ourselves IF WE APPROACH THESE PROBLEMS WITH TRANSPARENT HONESTY AND OPEN MIND AND STOP PLAYING THE OSTRICH WHILE OUR NATION IS ON THE BRINK OF DISSOLUTION. It is useless to sugar-coat the fact that the calamities we face are unthinkably menacing."[116]

In the context of the airlifting of easterners back to their region and Ojukwu's repeated warning that the eastern region might find itself in a situation in which the rest of Nigeria would have pushed it out of Nigeria, the *New Nigerian* reminded a fractious country of how the crisis arose. The paper often narrated this so as to emphasize that the attempt at "Igbo domination" represented by the January 15, 1966, coup was the source of all the problems of Nigeria, thereby depriving the Major Nzeogwu-led coup of its historical character. It is as if Nigeria's history began for the *New Nigerian* on that day.

Perhaps, lest people misunderstand the basis for the massacre of the Igbo, the *New Nigerian* reconstructed the past through its narration of the "genesis of the exodus [of the Igbo]": "The history of the First Republic is written in blood. . . . It stands to reason, therefore, that we should draw some conclusions from and make sober reappraisals of the events that matured into the crisis which now envelops the nation. . . . It is therefore, surprising that there are still some well-placed personalities who abuse their office by whipping up hysteria and indulging in a war of psychosis; by so doing they have unconsciously fanned the embers of hatred to the chagrin of the champions of peace and nation-building."[117]

Despite the fact that the paper had earlier reported the "molestation and harassment" of the Igbo, it now argued that the exodus of the Igbo from the northern region was "pre-planned" and "obviously" had nothing to do with what the easterners experienced in the northern region. In any case, argued the *New Nigerian*, the exodus was not only from the north. Accusations that easterners were fleeing only the north were described as "untrue and wicked." The *New Nigerian* added: "Why should we not summon courage to admit the fact that those so-called refugees have decided to migrate home out of their own volition and that the North as well as the West, the Mid-West and Lagos, have witnessed the abnormal social phenomenon."[118]

This narrative is a good example of how relations of domination are established through dissimulation, involving "the concealment, denial, obscuring, or deflection of attention away from, or glossing over, existing relations of domination and their process,"[119] as it is expressed particularly in euphemization. The massacre of the easterners was presented by the *New Nigerian* as a "misinterpretation," whereas the flights to safety were described as "pre-planned migration." Those displaced individuals who fled for dear life were described as "so-called refugees" who decided to "migrate of their own volition." Yet the *New Nigerian* considered this mass "pre-planned migration" a meaningless and thus "abnormal social phenomenon."

Before the *New Nigerian* articulated this position, the *Morning Post* acknowledged the "exodus," as earlier acknowledged by the military governor of the Northern Group of Provinces, Lt. Col. Hassan Usman Katsina. The *Post* editorialized: "There is no doubt that the past five years have confronted this country with all sorts of trying conditions. Each year had produced a phase that threatened the

solidarity of the nation." Apart from the tension in the country created by the political events of the past few years, the *Post* argued that
even the attitude of Nigerians to others of different ethnic groups
helped in creating a sense of disunity: "For instance, the pidgin English question, 'which nation you be?' which in fact, is only an attempt
by one Nigerian to find out from another what part of the country
the other came [from], auto-suggested this stranger-you-are attitude
of one Nigerian to another." The paper, therefore, suggested that
"Nigeria . . . must wage and organized war against this monster. It
has to be destroyed, or else, it will destroy the nation. And if Nigeria
survives the next five years, then she will emerge a strong, united
nation."[120] The *Post* also appealed to everyone that "Nigeria belongs
to all, and every Nigerian must begin to appreciate that he can live
and earn a living in any part of the country."[121]

But the *New Nigerian* ignored this appeal. "History," the paper
insisted, has provided many examples of how "would-be mob leaders"—ostensibly, Ojukwu and other Igbo leaders—were "eaten up"
by the "hydra-headed monster" they created. For the *New Nigerian*,
the Igbo victims of northern killings—and not the perpetrators—
constitute the "mob." The paper added: "We pray and hope that
after sober reflection the excited and ignited people will rediscover
themselves and retrace their faltering steps to the path of rectitude
and penitence."[122] Paradoxically, the *New Nigerian*, like the *Post*, was
"consoled" that a "Nigerian nation" would emerge from all these
crises in the near future: "It is consoling, however, that out of this
tragedy has emerged one great lesson and a guiding principle to
generations to come. This is that to live as a nation, the maturity
of mind, steadfastness and the appreciation of spiritual values are
desirable attitude, and that these qualities must form the philosophy
on which the new nation must subsist." While totally ignoring the
devastation suffered by thousands of easterners in the north, including the hundreds of lives lost and the move toward secession, the
mouthpiece of the northern region narrated the story of a "united
nation": "We are happy to note that those who threatened a total
disintegration of our national edifice have suddenly seen the wisdom of staying together as one united nation. . . . For the everlast-
ing glory of our nation, let us march forward as one united nation
in a federation of common destiny."[123]

However, the *Pilot* reported that Ojukwu, the governor of the
eastern region, claimed that the credit for the past unity of Nigeria

should go to the people of his region. Ojukwu reportedly stated: "This is a fact which we ourselves know and which, I am sure, our enemies minimize, but the last thing that this Region would like to do is to help destroy the edifice which they have made more sacrifice, put in greater efforts and made far-greater contributions than any other section to build."[124] However, one of the "enemies" of the eastern region, the *Tribune*, indeed "minimized" this "sacrifice" and described such a claim by Ojukwu as "in bad taste and tantamount to propaganda."[125] Even though the *Tribune* condemned the killings in the northern region and considered the reactions from the eastern region, particularly Ojukwu's, as "understandably emotional," the paper's overriding task was to protect western Nigeria in the crisis that the paper, unfortunately, reduced to a fight between the Igbo-dominated eastern region and the Hausa-Fulani-dominated northern region. Therefore, the *Tribune* announced to the two "warring" groups and regions (Igbo, eastern region, and Hausa-Fulani, northern region) that Yorubaland and the western region could be the turf for their "small skirmishes": "First, everything must be done . . . to see that no agent-provocateurs, whether Hausa or Ibo, or their agents . . . are allowed to spread foul rumors among the people of Western Nigeria. Ibos and Hausas must be warned that neither the government nor the generality of the people will allow Yoruba land to be anybody's battle-ground or arena for small skirmishes."[126]

Despite the magnitude of the tragedy that the country was witnessing, the *Tribune* was singularly devoted to ensuring that the "small skirmishes" were restricted to the eastern and northern regions—as if the western region was not in any way involved in the crisis. The paper assured the Igbo and the Hausa that the Yoruba were ready to defend their land against the outbreak of hostilities between the other two: "We would again warn potential trouble-makers, whether Hausa or Ibo and whatever their uniform or smuggled arms, that all Yorubas will rise like one man to defend their land and heritage, and that they will not allow any foolish outsider to poison the calm atmosphere of Western Nigeria."[127] The reference to "uniform" and "smuggled arms" were tropes for the northern soldiers stationed in the western region and the Igbo's rumored preparation for secession, respectively. The "smuggled arms" were in reference to the ill-fated aircraft that was allegedly flying smuggled arms to the eastern region in preparation for war.[128] Yet the *Tribune* picked up the phrase used by the *Pilot*, regarding the people who asked for mediation to be "on the lunatic fringe," while presenting the Yoruba as the "sober" and "neutral" group that could save the nation from war: "Yorubas, with other ethnic groups, are destined to restore peace and harmony between Ibos and Hausas. They must not allow people on the lunatic fringe to involve them in the present mass killings and molestation."[129]

But the *New Nigerian* disagreed that the Yoruba had a "destiny" that imposed on them the task of mediation, because the issue is not a clear-cut one between the Hausa-Fulani and the Igbo. Therefore the paper objected to those who suggested that "the Yorubas should mediate between the Eastern Region and the Northern Region, the implication being that the whole unhappy business is simply a clear-cut issue of North versus East, Hausas versus Ibos." Rather, the paper, without stating so explicitly, would have liked the matter to be seen as the Igbo against the rest of the country. The *New Nigerian* argued that the view that the crisis was between the Igbo and the Hausa "is not so [because] Yorubas lost their lives in January [in the 1966 Igbo-led coup] as well as Northerners. In addition, we should also remember that the Ibos are leaving Lagos and many towns in Western Region in large numbers."[130] This was clearly an attempt to isolate the Igbo and present the western and northern regions as a bloc united against the eastern region.

Interestingly, whereas it never used the word "killings" to describe the pogrom against the easterners in the north, when a broadcast on Radio Cotonou (Republic of Benin) "revealed" that northerners were being killed in the eastern region, the *New Nigerian* used the word "killing," even though "some [of the reports were] confirmed, [and] others yet unsubstantiated." Still, based on these confirmed and unsubstantiated reports on the killing of a few northerners, the paper declared: "The nation trembles on the brink of anarchy and despair. . . . A full-scale civil war of the most awful kind is a prospect that must be feared and avoided at all costs."[131] The pogrom against the easterners did not provoke similar "trembles on the brink of anarchy" for the *New Nigerian*.

However, about one month after this, the *New Nigerian* asked northerners to heed the appeal by the head of state, Lt. Col. Gowon, for an end to the riots and killings in the north, given the fact that northerners "have always prided themselves on their respect for constituted authority and for the maintenance of law and order."[132] This is after the mass murder of hundreds of people. In the same edition in which the paper echoed Gowon, the latter's speech addressed directly to northerners was also published. Gowon stated: "We [northerners, including himself] are known as peace-loving people and we must do everything in our power not to allow this good reputation to be soiled."[133] The very instructive appeal further stated: "Fellow Northerners. . . . You all know that since the end of July, God, in his power, has entrusted the responsibility of this great country of ours, Nigerian, to the hands of another Northerner. . . .[134] Right from the beginning of politics in this country, up to this date, whenever complications arise, the people of the North are known to champion the cause of peace and settlement.[135] Once the North remains peaceful it is easy to settle disputes arising from any other part of the country. . . . I receive complaints daily that up to now, Easterners living in the North are being killed and molested, their property looted."[136]

The *Pilot* was very charitable in its reaction to Gowon's call, in spite of Gowon's "glorification" of the northerner. The paper stated that Gowon deserved "the praise of every Nigerian" for calling a halt to the "hell let loose by men on the lunatic fringe." It even described Gowon as a "Daniel," adding that "all along, the sincere patriots of this country have been looking for a Daniel to come to the rescue of our bleeding nation."[137] This was an expression of unusual restraint after an orgy of violence, particularly in Kano, where even the indulgent *New Nigerian* stated that "the bullet holes in the airport buildings and the dark, ominously significant stains, are a reminder that blind ignorance and prejudice can have no place in a nation aspiring to greatness."[138]

The exceptional nature of the pogrom in Kano in October 1966 obviously affected the outlook of the *New Nigerian*. In a somewhat contrite manner, after the Kano killings, the paper narrated a rare "moment of truth" in Nigeria's history: "A moment of truth has been reached in Nigerian history. A moment when we have no alternative but swallow our pride and acknowledge our failings and our guilt. The legacies of hate, mistrust, bitterness and prejudices inherited from the past have exploded in our face and we now see the prospect of utter and complete chaos confronting us."[139]

Even though the paper ignored the killings that preceded these massive Kano killings, it stated that the "proud history" of a "great city" (Kano) had been stained. Yet, and instructively, the *New Nigerian* did not use the word "massacre" or "pogrom" to describe what happened in Kano, nor did it expressly accuse the Northerners of being the perpetrators. Instead, the killings were described as "black and terrible" and "full [of] horror," phrases that do not immediately suggest that the killings were against a particular group. This strategy of symbolic construction of domination had been described by Thompson as passivization in that it "delete[s] actors and agency and . . . tend[s] to represent processes as things and events [as something that] take place in the absence of a subject who produces them."[140] The paper stated: "Only those who were in Kano over this last black and terrible weekend know the full horror of what took place. It is a memory that will remain for years to come. A memory [that] besmirch[es] what, in the main, has been a proud history of a great city." Despite the magnitude of the killings and its own acceptance of complicity in the crisis, the *New Nigerian* still offered a defense of the north, even though it avoided mentioning the ethnic and regional group to which the victims belonged (easterners, Igbo), describing them rather as "those who suffered": "But with the same sincerity and intensity with which we now express our sorrow and sympathy with those who suffered, we ask that there should be no outright condemnation of the North. It is true that there have been mistakes. All of us—including this newspaper—must share some degree of blame for seeking to exploit prejudices of one kind or another. But now, albeit tragically belated, a true appreciation of the road to national suicide on which we have embarked, has been revealed in a way that we cannot, we dare not, ignore." However, beyond the sorrow and sympathy, the paper still saw the possibilities of national redemption. It appealed "to everyone with a true understanding of the situation . . . that if we must survive as a nation we must learn to live together . . . and work selfishlessly [*sic*] and honestly towards rebuilding a better and happier nation."[141]

Perhaps to ensure that this "rebuilding" was accomplished, and that the eastern region would not surprise the rest of the country with secession, the *New Nigerian* constantly focused on what the eastern region was up to in the aftermath of the pogrom. For instance, the paper asked, "Why . . . should Lt.-Col. Ojukwu . . . be at pains to reiterate that the East is not hell-bent on secession when her every move seems in that direction?"[142] Later, the *New Nigerian* returned to the issue again and again, stating in one instance that nothing had happened in Nigeria to "push" the eastern region out of the country, as Ojukwu alleged: "Which prompts us to repeat the question we asked the other day: What is the East up to? Does she mean what she says or is she playing for time? Lt. Colonel Ojukwu tells foreign diplomats that his region has no intention of seceding from the rest of the federation—not unless it is 'pushed.' And the East is behaving as if she is being pushed. We ourselves have not seen any evidence of this effect." As far as the *New Nigerian* was concerned, the east could only suffer more if it decided on secession: "We can't understand why the East is so apparently intent to inflict more hurt upon [itself]. It is in the interest of the East for her to declare right now, without further prevarications, exactly what her intentions are."[143]

Another major indication of the role of the newspapers in the crisis as ideological soldiers for the different groups and regions was indicated by the fact that, a few days after this editorial, the publishers of the *New Nigerian* were "warned" that the paper should no longer be circulated in the eastern region,[144] although the newspaper had, two weeks earlier, announced that "in spite of the crisis [the *New Nigerian*] continues to be widely circulated in the East[,] its delivery vans [going] unmolested."[145]

The *Tribune* more or less agreed with the *New Nigerian* on the implications of the statements credited to Ojukwu concerning the eastern region's position on the crisis. Stated the *Tribune:* "After strenuous denials in the past about the intentions of Eastern Nigeria to secede from the federation, the Eastern Governor has now said that the East 'might suddenly find' that it has nothing more in common with the other regions. And the question that arises from the statement is: What next?" For the paper, this only deepened the crisis and isolated the eastern region because "in our view, we cannot solve our problems by ignoring them. The problem of the East today is at the very top on the list of our national problems. It must first be solved before we can go forward." The *Tribune* then suggested "the solution," going even further than the *New Nigerian* to request a military solution: "The *Nigerian Tribune* argues the Supreme Commander [Gowon] to recognize that the time has come for a firm solution of [*sic*] the Eastern problem. If we have the force and the will to bring the East into line by armed intervention, let it be done with dispatch."[146] The *Tribune*'s position confirmed Susan Carruthers's argument that newspapers "often become de facto, if not more ardent, champions of military solutions to perceived threats, lending support to the justification for force offered by policy-makers and other war-minded parties."[147]

The *Tribune* disagreed with the *Pilot* that the proposed meeting of the army chiefs be held in Accra, Ghana, rather than in Lagos. The *Tribune's* position was that of self-interest. Ojukwu's only condition for attending the meeting in Lagos accorded with the wishes of the Yoruba people: that northern troops in the western region be withdrawn to their region and replaced by Yoruba troops. Therefore when the military governor of the northern region, Lt. Col. Hassan Usman Katsina, stated that he would not support such a withdrawal, the *Tribune* strongly condemned Katsina: "We . . . consider the statement credited to the Military Governor of the North as extremely provocative. For who does this young aristocrat in military uniform think he is to seek to draw the whole Yoruba race in battle against him and Hausas?" The "Hausa troops," who were described by the *Tribune* as "foreign troops . . . not averse to rape, murder and high-handedness," were threatening to turn Yoruba land into an "occupied territory." The *Tribune* then announced the resolve of the Yoruba, who "are determined to see that their fatherland is not turned into an "occupied territory."[148]

Clearly, by this time the narratives in the newspapers had reached a level of such divisiveness, and even hate, that Nigerian soldiers of different ethnic origins were seen as "foreign troops" and threats to certain parts of the country. That was not all. Governor Katsina would be mistaken, the *Tribune* averred, if he thought that Nigeria would continue to exist if "the East secedes or is forced to secede": "If the Northern Military Governor does not know it, he can carry this fact away: The people of Western Nigeria and Lagos have taken an irrevocable decision—if any part of Nigeria opts out of the federation, Yorubas reserve to themselves the right to determine their own future in any association."[149] It is significant that the *Tribune* did not see a contradiction between this and its earlier position in the December 14, 1966, editorial in which it asked that "armed intervention" be used "with dispatch" to ensure that the eastern region did not secede.

In the middle of all of this, the *Pilot* was not ready to let go of Lagos and refused to accept that it was a Yoruba city. While reviewing the state of the union after the collapse of the All-Nigeria Constitutional Conference, the *Pilot*, which again abandoned its support for federalism, wrote: "We whole-heartedly endorse a confederal system of government for Nigeria at least so that the inveterate enmity and bitterness existing between the North and East can be healed by time. . . . In the absence of a federation we support the suggestion of Eastern Nigeria for a Council of State, comprising equal representatives from each state or region to serve as a weak glue to hold the country together." However, the *Pilot* added, since "Lagos is jointly developed by all regions of the federation, we suggest that All-Nigeria Constitutional Conference should meet soon to decide the question of Lagos during the short spell of confederation."[150] The *Pilot*, as evident throughout the preindependence period, stood resolutely for an "independent" Lagos. The rejection by Oba Adeyinka Oyekan, the Oba of Lagos, of the planned merger plan with the western region is given prominence in the *Pilot*. Oyekan stated that "we shall fight to the last" because "our tradition is different from that of the West."[151] Even though Lateef Jakande, the leader of the Lagos delegation to the Lagos constitutional conference, described Oyekan's statement as "reckless,"[152] the *Pilot* editorialized: "The people of Lagos have the right to self-determination. It is their prerogative to decide whether the federal capital should be merged with the West or whether it should remain free from the region. This is perfectly the people's choice through a referendum." However, the *Pilot* did not leave the matter entirely to a referendum when it added: "We urge that Lagos should be a Federal territory in case the country retains its federal status. And in case of a confederation Lagos should be the country's political capital. In other words, Lagos should be a separate entity."[153]

Such territorial narratives were usually directed against rival regions. Whereas the *Pilot* fought for Lagos, the *New Nigerian* promoted minority agitations in the eastern region, where "the people of Calabar and Ogoja Provinces" suggested a strong center with "states created on the principle of ethnic grouping."[154] But although it promoted such agitation in the eastern region, the *New Nigerian* considered the "appeal" led by Josiah Sunday Olawoyin for a merger of Ilorin-Kabba province in the northern region with the western region as "irrational emotions" and a "nefarious and treacherous design to sabotage the efforts of the [constitutional conference]"—thus something that "right-thinking people" ought not to engage in.[155]

Conclusion

When a "nation" goes to war, so does the press, "wrapped in the flag no less proudly than the troops themselves."[156] The same is true as a "nation" prepares for war. Newspapers representing ethnonationalist groups become "patriotic" or "jingoistic" in gearing up for the possibility or outbreak of war, given that "dissimulation tends to begin well before the first exchange of fire," notes Carruthers. A British observer noted after World War I that "war not only creates a supply of news but also a demand for it." This is also true of the period that precedes war, in that the prewar dynamics also provoke internecine conflicts between media organizations themselves.[157]

As "paper soldiers" in the period before the civil war, the newspapers were aware that they, as well as the actual soldiers, were preparing for war. They realized that in the ensuing battle, the "soldiers" wielding the pen were as critical as the soldiers who would eventually bear arms at the outbreak of hostilities. Therefore the journalists and their media institutions regarded themselves as critical to the resolution and the exacerbation of the Nigerian crisis of nationhood. Interestingly, the *New Nigerian* noted the central role of the press in the crisis engulfing the country by "observing" the tendency of Ojukwu "to use the press . . . as a vehicle of negotiation."[158] Yet even the paper confessed in an earlier editorial that it too was an instrument of the negotiation of power and relations of domination by the northern region: "The *New Nigerian* seeks to be read throughout Nigeria but it has never lost sight of the fact that it was brought into being primarily to serve the North. It is because it considers it in the immediate as well as longer term interest of the North that it feels obliged to comment on those misguided people—we will put it no worse than that—whose actions are destined to bring nothing but dishonor and disaster to the North."[159]

In their role in the crisis as mouthpieces or ideological soldiers of the contending interests, the newspapers also waged battles against one another. In this, the *New Nigerian*, with candor, admitted that it—like the other newspapers—had failed the imagined nation: "The *New Nigerian* is conscious of its fall from grace but it has always sought to find the truth. It has not always succeeded . . . but having said that let us acknowledge that Nigeria's press . . . can do much more to restore peace in the country than they are doing."[160]

Without mentioning names, but obviously in reference to the *Eastern Nigerian Outlook* and the *Pilot*, the *New Nigerian* also pointed to the "press in certain quarters" that seemed "hell-rent [*sic*] on sensationalizing any incident which it thinks can be regarded as favorable to their own case and against the North."[161] For the *New Nigerian*, the *Pilot* would perhaps typify this predilection to "sensationalize" a case "against the North" as it suggested a meeting of all the military governors in Accra, Ghana, whose sole agenda should be "the refugee problem arising from the genocide in the North." The *Pilot* insisted that "the aggrieved East in particular, must be appeased if all parts of the country are to sit down and reason together as members of the nation." How should the east be appeased? The *Pilot* suggested a punitive tax on northerners in addition to a grant by the federal government: "Incidentally, the victims of the Eastern Nigerian origin in the last disturbances in the North have claimed 27 million [pounds] being the total loss they sustained during the riot. We believe a collective fine imposed on the taxable people of the North in addition to what the Federal Government can give to the East will calm the distressed Easterners."[162]

This raises the question of whether guilt and responsibility could be collective or personal. The *Pilot* seemed to locate the answer in what I will call the *narrative of precedence*. "A precedent for this collective fine has already been laid in Nigerian history. In 1950, the Kalabari people of Eastern Nigeria paid a collective fine of 20,000 [pounds] to Okrika people for killing Okrika fishermen on a river near Kalabar. In 1951 or thereabouts, a riot broke out between Okrika and Oguloma citizens. The former damaged the property of the later and another collective fine of 20,000 [pounds] was imposed on Okrika people which was paid to the Oguloma people as compensation. In 1958, a riot broke out in Ibadan in Western Nigeria expressing bad-blood over the death of Adekoge Adelabu. A collective fine was imposed on the affected area to compensate those whose property was lost on the affray." These examples provide a basis for a strong case to be made by the *Pilot*, which insisted that "until the East is pacified, the question of considering the future association of Nigeria is out of the question."[163]

In the period preceding the civil war, unlike the *Pilot*, the *New Nigerian* was not interested in reparation or restitution in favor of the eastern region and its people. Rather, it accused the information media of the eastern region of wagging ideological war against the rest of the country by practicing "journalism that can never do anybody any good": "They have carried news which are absolute false. They have published news which are criminally distorted. They have been saying things which are an open defiance to the National Military Government. . . . They can be used to render any country asunder, any united people disintegrating [*sic*] and any cause useless. . . . We strongly maintain that such an information medium should hang its head in shame for helping to tear this country into pieces."[164]

The federal government-owned newspaper, the *Post*, took a similar position about "certain sections of the press [that] indulge in inciting bitterness."[165] But the *Pilot* returned the salvo in response to the *New Nigerian*, which accused the newspaper press in the east and, by implication, the *Pilot:* "A Daily Paper printed in Northern Nigeria is trying very hard to introduce polemics into politics in Nigeria again. . . . At this stage in our national metamorphosis, we regard it as calculated sabotage or incitement for anybody to do any act overt or covert to engender tribal bitterness or sectional ill-feeling."[166]

By the time the civil war started on July 6, 1967, these newspapers, as well as others, became even more critical as ideological soldiers for the secessionist Republic of Biafra and the Federal Republic of Nigeria. However, the role of the press in reporting and commenting on the civil war cannot be fully understood if we do not account for how the newspapers were fully implicated in the process that led to its outbreak. As evident in the above narratives, the press in Nigeria was actively involved in reproducing the conditions that led to the outbreak of hostilities in 1967.

6

Representing the Nation

Electoral Crisis and the
Collapse of the Third Republic

What is Nigeria? A mere geographical expression or potentially a nation? And on what basis can the people who constitute it make claims on the polity? As members of different communities (ethnic or ethno-regional) or as individual rights-bearing citizens? Chapter 1 discussed the debate in Africa on whether the question of identity or that of democratic freedom should constitute the foundation for understanding belongingness within multicultural polities in Africa. This debate is mirrored in the questions above. Whereas scholars like Brendan Boyce argue that reconciling the issue of "identity redefinition" in the context of the historical limitations and opportunities in Africa is the way to go, Ivor Chipkin insists that this would lead to substituting the goal of a democratic society for that of an identity-based nation.[1] He argues, on the contrary, that "the substance of a nation must be located in the determinate history of [the] 'struggle for democracy' in which it was elaborated."[2] Chipkin assumes that "democratic practice will allow for a constant process of fashioning and re-fashioning the nation."[3] As James Sweet points out in his critique of Chipkin's position, the reality in multicultural Africa is different. "Unfortunately," Sweet notes correctly, "potential citizens do not arrive at the democratic table as social ciphers. They always bring with them racial, ethnic, religious, and class identity."[4] This reality often presents challenges to the media, particularly in terms of how to reconcile democracy with nation-building, as Cliff Barnett shows.[5]

As argued in chapter 1, the essentialization of democracy and freedom implicit in Chipkin's position is inflected differently in most African countries. This chapter provides empirical evidence for this position, as most of the newspapers and newsmagazines arrived at the democratic table seeking freedom as champions of ethnic, ethno-regional, and religious interests.

This chapter examines the narratives of the crisis of democratization in the Nigerian press in the 1990s in the context of antagonistic and competing identities within the Nigerian national space and the dangers that the subversion of democratic freedom constituted to the hopes of those who assumed that Nigeria's June 12, 1993, presidential election offered the country its greatest opportunity since the end of the civil war to begin the process of becoming a nation-state. In the context of what came to be described as the "June 12 crisis" or "June 12 debacle,"[6] between those who imagined Nigeria as a space of unfettered democratic (electoral) freedom and those who insisted that democratic freedom be tied to the fundamental interests of the constituent ethnic or ethno-regional groups in Nigeria, the country risked collapse or disintegration—or what *TheNEWS* headlined as "The Plot to Split Nigeria" (see fig. 6.1).[7]

The role of the media in the democratization process in late 1980s and 1990s Africa constitutes a core focus of the general literature on the media in Africa. This is noteworthy because it is a recent phenomenon. For a long time, the literature on democratization in Africa gave little attention to the role of the media, despite the fact that the media, as Goran Hyden and Michael Leslie argue, "have been relatively more influential in shaping the emerging, but still fledgling, democratic culture in Africa."[8] Indeed, periods of elections are key moments when the connection between not only political pluralism and media diversity but also democratic freedom and the limitations and opportunities of identity politics become very visible in Africa.[9] Also, it has been suggested, correctly, that privately owned media in Africa "have been in the forefront of creating political space for other actors in the public arena and enhancing the extent to which public officials have to consider themselves accountable to the citizenry."[10] Against this backdrop, "communicative discourses," as Ogundimu describes them, or narratives, as I approach them in this book, were "central to the democratization agenda" in late- and postauthoritarian eras in Africa.[11]

Figure 6.1. Cover of *TheNEWS*, July 20, 1998, with the photograph of the presumed winner of the June 12, 1993, presidential election, Moshood Abiola.

Transition without End

The crisis of the Nigerian union manifested in a democratic struggle between the late 1980s and mid-1990s. The context of the deep-seated dissatisfaction with the prevailing ethos was the transition to civil rule program of the Babangida regime (1985–93), which Richard Joseph described as "one of the most sustained exercises in political chicanery ever visited on a people."[12]

The transition program (described by opposition elements as a "hidden agenda"), even though aborted in 1993, continued in a new guise through the successor governments headed by Ernest Shonekan (the Interim National Government, August 26–November 17, 1993) and General Sani Abacha (November 1993–June 1998). Given the context in which the parties to the national crisis contested for power in this era, democratic discourse was central to the narratives of power and identity, even when these ultimately devolved on—or were camouflages for—ethnic or ethno-regional interests.

Against the backdrop of nation-building, General Babangida ascended to power with a promise to revive the "Nigerian nation." In his maiden broadcast, Babangida noted: "We [Nigerians] have witnessed our rise to greatness followed with the decline to the status of a bewildered nation. . . . My colleagues and I are determined to change this course of history. . . . This government is determined to *unite* this country."[13] Consequently, the regime set up the most elaborate transition program in Nigeria's history, which was to be a "supervised, gradual learning process."[14] In July 1985, Babangida defended the rationale for a long transition that would end in the election of a president in October 1992. He said the transition intended to lay "the basic foundation of a new socio-political order . . . [and the creation of] a new set of political attitudes [and] political culture aimed at ushering in a new social order."[15]

After several twists and turns, presidential elections were held on June 12, 1993. In the election in which the National Republican Convention (NRC) and the Social Democratic Party (SDP) fielded Alhaji Bashir Tofa (from the north) and Chief Moshood Abiola (from the south), respectively, the political history of Nigeria changed substantially as a southerner (specifically, a Yoruba) was generally believed to have won. This was against the long-held assumption that only a northern candidate could win a presidential election in Nigeria. When all the ploys by Babangida and his agents failed in the attempt to scuttle the election and the results, they resorted to a direct subversion of democracy. The election was annulled. As one of Babangida's close aides, Professor Omo Omoruyi, maintains in his account of the debacle, "those who wanted to create stalemate mounted ambush at the penultimate stage—the official release of the results. The ambush then assumed two dimensions: a stalemate which dragged on from June 10 to June 21 and, when this failed, the sudden death of annulment."[16] This set off a national crisis that was only second to the civil war (1967–70).

In reacting to the annulment, Abiola stated that he consulted widely to get assurance that he would not be "chasing shadows" like others before him and "assurances were given in some cases at the highest levels of government including the president himself." Consequently, Abiola rejected the annulment and affirmed that he was the president-elect and "the custodian of a sacred mandate, freely given, which I cannot surrender unless the people so demand."[17] General Babangida reacted to Abiola in a national broadcast, stating that "I feel, as I believe you yourself feel, a profound sense of disappointment at the outcome of our last effort at laying the foundation of a viable democratic system of government in Nigeria.[18] He leveled all sorts of spurious allegations against the politicians. The crisis that followed the annulment "shook the nation to its foundation, felling, on its somewhat roller-coaster journey, three regimes [Babangida, Shonekan, and Abacha] and bringing questions of 'secession,' 'disintegration,' 'self-determination,' and such terms of divisive politics to the front-burners of national discourse with unprecedented vigour."[19]

Let us now analyze the narratives in the press from late 1992 to 1994 in five magazines and newspapers: *TELL* and *TheNEWS* (representing the position of the prodemocracy coalition and, essentially, the Yoruba West), *The Guardian* (representing the south generally and the southern minorities of the oil-rich Niger Delta specifically), the *Daily Champion* (representing the Igbo east), and the *New Nigerian* (representing the north broadly and the Hausa-Fulani north essentially).

Democratization, Identity Politics, and Nation-Building

The June 12, 1993, presidential election—later described either as the "June 12 crisis" or the "June 12 debacle,"[20]—which many believed would provide a great opportunity for Nigeria to become a truly united and indivisible nation, ironically turned out to be one whose annulment polarized the country and almost degenerated into another civil war. In many parts of the country, particularly in the north and west, nonindigenes, especially the Igbo, returned to their home areas in fear of the outbreak of interethnic hostilities or full-scale civil war. The narratives in *TELL* magazine in the latter part of 1992 perhaps foreshadowed the pattern of the narratives provoked by the June 12 crisis from the second half of 1993: "Politics . . . oriental philosophers of late Mao Zedung's persuasion say . . . is 'war without the guns,' requiring, for the attainment of power, the surprise storming of the enemy and his capitulation. Both portraits are true of Nigeria's on-going politics of the presidential race. As the chips are down, what emerges . . . is master plan by the core-North to win the presidential election and thus retain power." As a mouthpiece of the "progressive" south, *TELL* placed into context the general belief in that region of the country that northerners, particularly the Hausa-Fulani, were dominating the rest and were unwilling to relinquish power to a southerner. Tanko Yakassai, a northern "irredentist" politician, was made to explain the "primacy" of the north in the overall setting of the Nigerian state. *TELL* reported: "The Northerner is not afraid to share power. Nigerians, other Nigerians, believe that they do not need to be afraid of the concentration of power in the hands of the Northerner. That is the situation many compatriots in the West, Yoruba especially, are not aware of." In the end, he said, all those who are scheming for the Southerner as president would be shocked if they did not take the Muslim North into their calculation. His reason? "Nobody can be president of Nigeria without votes of the Northern Muslims of Nigeria. Unfortunately, those who hold this view are seen as cowards and traitors of their fatherland."[21]

Ayo Opadokun, a Yoruba whose home state of Kwara was located in the middle-belt area of the north, and who had been in the vanguard of planning to ensure that the south produced the president, first under the auspices of the Committee for National Understanding (CUU), responded to Yakassai by stating that "The North . . . has carried on over the years as if they owned the country and the rest of the country were a conquered people." In the circumstances, northern sensitivity to the sensibilities of the south and middle-belt "has been largely one of contempt."

For the middle-belts, *TELL* reported that the vehicle for its resurgence against the core Hausa-Fulani north was religion: "As Middle-Belters claim, CAN [Christian Association of Nigeria] is the counterpoise to the Islamic Council with which the *Muslim North 'has been dominating us.'* . . . They seem to have . . . settled for a deal to have a Southerner, preferably a Christian, become president." The Christian challenge was narrated as a fundamental challenge in the context of the "domination" of the country by the Muslim Hausa-Fulani. As the secretary of the Kano state chapter of CAN, Joseph Fadipe, a Yoruba, articulated why the religious body joined the battle for the soul of the nation. Fadipe reportedly stated that "since the time [Sheikh Abubakar] Gumi stated that if a Muslim does not rule, there will be trouble, we have been watching out for any attempt to out-manoeuvre us." Fadipe then argued that when Christians (Generals Yakubu Gowon and Olusegun Obasanjo) ruled Nigeria, there was "more judicious use" of "our oil wealth," as against "the corruption, embezzlement, confusion and chaos Plc [public limited company]" of Muslim leaders.[22]

Yusuf advanced the argument that Nigeria was in the grip of a "tiny fraction" of the Muslim north: "Even among the Muslims, those ruling this country belong to one family. It cannot continue. Nigeria is not a feudal state. It is time for a change to allow another people to produce [the] president . . . in order to maintain the nation's integrity." However, Christian Onoh, the former governor of Anambra state, discursively threw in "the Igbo agenda" into the emerging equation. "This time around," Onoh said, "the Igbo are not prepared to play second fiddle. The Igbo heartland is, and will, not be a shopping ground for the number two position [the vice presidency]."[23]

The role of the press in setting the narrative agenda in the emerging consensus regarding the controversy over which section of the country would produce the president in the Third Republic was acknowledged by Yakassai. However, first he located his position in the "reality" of "Yoruba domination" of all key sectors of national life except political power. "My deductions [are] that the movement for a southern president is in effect a movement for Yoruba president. . . . As you know, there are two powers: one is likely to be more important than the other because you can use one to get the other. There is political power and there is economic power. All Nigerians believe that the nation's economic power today is in the hands of the Yorubas. . . . Yorubas dominate the bureaucracy . . . the Yorubas dominate the educational sector. . . . And the last powerful weapon is also controlled by the Yorubas, and that is the media. Other Nigerians believe that the Yorubas want political power to dominate the terrain." He then zeroed in on the "Yoruba press": "Have you seen the report of the *Tribune* of Tuesday, August 11? I have seen it. The editorial comment of the *Catholic Herald* was the subject of their story. The *Catholic Herald* was making conditions for the continuous existence of Nigeria as an entity, that there must be southern president. And that *Catholic Herald* actually came close to what I am saying. . . . All indications are that the threat is from the [Yoruba] West than from other part of the country. They seem to be the only section of the country that is bent on getting political power this time around."[24]

This line of narrative, which emphasized the role of the press in building or destroying the nation, found regular space in *New Nigerian*. Bala Dan Audu, for instance, accused the press in the southwest of ignoring the crisis of the fuel shortage in the north, and of "make[ing] it seem like the whole nation is on its knees, on the brink of total collapse" whenever there is such a crisis in the southwest, particularly Lagos. Audu argued that the attitude of this section of the press "worries concerned patriots": "The [Yoruba] West selfishly manipulates the media to present its position as though it represents the feeling of a cross section of the population of Nigeria. If they truly want to present a pan-Nigerian outlook, for God's sake, they should also have the courage to give the same level of publicity to the situation in the north, and other parts of the country, for that matter." Audu agreed with Yakassai that the Lagos-Ibadan (*Ngbati*) press, knowingly or unknowingly, represented only Yoruba interests, presented only "their own narrow, selfish perspective." He then submitted: "We cannot build a strong united nation when one area decide[s] to focus on its interests, to the exclusion of others."[25]

The *New Nigerian* protested the fuel crisis in the north that provoked this narrative. In the fourth editorial on the matter in one month, without clearly stating that it was defending what constituted northern interests against the silence of the dominant section of the press in the Yoruba West, the paper noted that "the social consequences [of the fuel scarcity in the north constitute] . . . an undetonated time-bomb."[26]

These narratives provide a backdrop for the battle that would soon be fought in the succeeding months as each of these powerful groups reached for the ultimate democratic prize—the presidency—in the attempts to validate group interests and counter advances by the other groups, either the duplicitous military regime that was seen as representative of the Hausa-Fulani core north or other power blocs.

Given the state of affairs in the years immediately preceding 1993, the Babangida regime and its supporters (particularly in the north) and the prodemocracy movement and human rights groups were posed for clashes. The latter constantly pointed out that "Babangida['s] most talked about hidden agenda" was unfolding by degrees. This "hidden agenda" was the belief in most parts of the country that the Babangida transition program was only a ruse and that the military ruler's real plan was to perpetuate himself in power. Consequently, *TELL* emphasized the "belief that Nigeria has so many unresolved issues threatening the nation's corporate existence," necessitating the "renewed . . . calls for a national conference.[27]

The frustration with the constant shifting of the transition goal post and its implications for ethnic and ethno-regional interests produced called for the convocation of a national conference where the various ethnic, ethno-regional, and religious interests in the "nation" would talk and develop a new national ethos. The discourse of a national conference, which was later sharpened into the Sovereign National Conference, was therefore increasingly dominant in the press at this point. The military, however, regarded such calls as strong currents geared toward upstaging the military from power. As *TELL* reported, "in its wisdom, the Babangida regime seems to have resolved that the less dialogue Nigerians do now, the better for the nation. And it does not matter what the topic of the dialogue is." This attitude, for *TELL*, constituted the beginning of "the crackdown" against the opposition.[28] The newly formed Movement for National Reformation (MNR) led by the man who moved the controversial motion for independence in 1953, Anthony Enahoro, therefore raised immediate possibilities of collision with the government. In its position paper as reported by *TELL*, the MNR "advocates a redrawing of the political, economic and administrative structure of the Nigerian nation. Anchored of the said experience, the movement observed that there is a 'need to resolve federalism as envisaged by the country's founding fathers' through 'a new Act of Union freely subscribed to by nationalities and federations.'" The movement proposed eight federations. Together these federations were to form the Union of the Federation of Nigeria (UFN) or the Union of the Federated States of Nigeria (UFSN). The proposal, the MNR asserted, would "restore self-government to the nationalities and peoples that constitute Nigeria as distinct from independence to Nigeria as a whole."[29] This proposal constituted a fundamental and radical challenge to the status quo, which the MNR and others believed was marked by the domination of Hausa-Fulani and other majority groups.

Babangida reacted to this challenge when commissioning the Nigerian Law School Hostel, as *TELL* reported it. He told the law school students: "Your nation or mine cannot do with citizens, young or old, who with antecedents littered with the debris of unutilised opportunities have recoursed to the desperate measures of wanton criticism. The military president excoriated "political fugitives of yesterday . . . who have once again become fugitives from their roots and [who] celebrate their estrangement at the altar of rabble-rousing. This was clearly an attack on Anthony Enahoro, who fled Nigeria in 1962 during the treasonable felony trial involving Oba-femi Awolowo and others and was declared a fugitive. Enahoro was later extradited to Nigeria from Britain and jailed. *TELL* wrote that, even though names are rarely mentioned in such attacks, Babangi-da's "tough posturing . . . is like preparing the slaughter slab before sweeping on the enemies."[30]

During this period, *New Nigerian* devoted itself to reflecting news and views that constantly reaffirmed the military government's "sincerity" in spite of all the attacks in the southern press, including from *TELL*, *TheNEWS*, and *The Guardian*. Regularly on the paper's front page, government spokesmen, particularly the federal information secretary, Uche Chukwumerije, defended the regime's transition program; the paper added that, if, in spite of the efforts of the regime, "Nigerians decide to mortgage consciences in exchange for a mess of political pottage, then they should have themselves to blame."[31]

Whereas the southern papers generally praised the meeting of retired generals and other prominent Nigerians convened in Otta by the former head of state General Olusegun Obasanjo to review the state of the nation, and described it as an effort "to save Nigeria," *New Nigerian*'s front-page editorial condemned the "unholy conclave at Otta," adding that "General Obasanjo had allowed his name and prestige to be exploited by junk publications to make a goldmine. . . . The cover-page complex took over from a respected statesman."[32] The paper then raised questions that suggest that the meeting of these former leaders and other prominent "conspirators" was "insurrectional": "Could be it that the real motive and goal of the Ota conclave go beyond what are contained in the communiqué? Did the participants at Ota farm house conclave want June 12 election to hold? If held, will they allow August 27, 1993, handover to be realistic? We say all these because the Otta Conclave has definitely heightened the tension in the body politic. . . . [They] give the impression of 31 super patriots in a country of 88 million Nigeria. It is an arrogance of privileges and positions that run opposite the ideals of democracy which the 31 conspirators at Otta espoused."[33] *New Nigerian* attempted to insinuate that the resolution of the "conspirators" at Otta was capable of "derailing" the transition programme—a regular official accusation against opposition elements. *The Guardian* argued to the contrary. *New Nigerian*'s "diversionary conspirators" were *The Guardian*'s "patriotic" citizens. Yet *The Guardian* quarreled with the fact that former top soldiers dominated the meeting whereas radical activists were not invited: "The patriotic impulse behind the conference is unexceptional. . . . [However] the preponderant presence of the military at this conference and the remarkable exclusion of certain ideological tendencies, has undercut its representativeness."[34]

Still, for *TELL*, Obasanjo was a concerned elder statesman "moving" with other "top Nigerian leaders" on a "mission to save motherland." Given that such a gathering was "historic," the newsmagazine gives prominence to Obasanjo's opening address at the meeting with a bold quote: "Those who could and should keep hope alive either lost or were made to lose their conscience and developed tight lips and withered hands. All that is necessary for the enthronement of evil is for good people to remain silent and inactive."[35] Obasanjo's interview published in *TELL* was described in *New Nigerian* as "characterised by extremely foul language, various unsubstantiated remarks and half-truths bordering on rumour mongering . . . unbefitting of an elder statesman." Obasanjo's interview, the paper continued, was capable of "undermining the on-going democratic transition programme."[36]

In the months immediately preceding the June 12, 1993, presidential election, the narratives in the press were dominated by issues relating to the sincerity of the military regime regarding the handover of power, the treatment of minority ethnic nationalities and their symbols, and the future of Nigeria. *TheNEWS*, for instance, focused on the Ogoni struggle for self-determination outside of the Nigerian imposition: "Ken Saro-Wiwa . . . said the Ogonis were prepared to take back their oil fields, noting '. . . Ogoniland does not belong to Nigeria.' Wiwa explained that in a situation where 300,000 Ogonis are denied bare essentials of life and their farmlands destroyed by the activities of oil companies, war was the only choice left to them, a three pronged war to reclaim their autonomy as a nation."[37]

The dissatisfaction in Ogoniland was then connected to the health and peace of Nigeria at large. "A time bomb is ticking in Ogoniland," stated *TheNEWS*, "which, if not defused by concrete and positive action by government[,] had the potential of consuming the nation in one huge avalanche of bloodletting."[38] Saro-Wiwa explained how Nigeria could be saved from collapse: "What we need is a completely new structure in the country where every nation will govern itself. That's why, to a great extent, I share the views of Chief Anthony Enahoro. . . . The Hausa/Fulani will of course want to continue with the bandit operation by forming alliance with the Yorubas and the Ibos. There's no doubt that the economic crises that have resulted from the activities of this government have led to a political crisis which would either lead to disintegration of the country or the restructuring of the country."[39]

Such narratives on ethnic division and disaffection were used by *TELL* to point to the feared disintegration of Nigeria; the newsmagazine warned that ethnic nationalities in Nigeria were "ringing the divorce bells," as the minorities were "tired of the status quo . . . threatening to go it alone." *TELL* argued that the future of Nigeria seemed to be predicated on the convocation of a national conference because "among these groups [minorities], plenty of hope now seem pinned on the proposed constitutional conference as an opportunity to articulate their positions."[40]

Related to the Ogoni disaffection was the Zango-Kataf controversy arising from violent clashes between the minority Kataf and their Hausa "guests," which resulted in the setting up of a tribunal to try Kataf leaders accused of murder and other crimes. General Domkat Bali, the former defense chief who left the Babangida regime, a man possessing "moral strength," said of the Kataf trials,

"I believe in justice and without justice in Nigeria we run the risk of not having citizens committed to the nation and not having a united nation." Bali raised many questions on the fate of the Kataf minorities: "There have been many religious crises, why is it that Zango-Kataf should get this kind of tribunal? Why was it not done for Bauchi and Kano?" He added that the trials do not "serve the country well."[41]

All of this fed into the need to contest the current arrangement in Nigeria to create a nation. As the former secessionist leader Emeka Ojukwu articulated in *TELL*, the convocation of a national conference was unavoidable: "I believe very strongly that the only legitimate cry in Nigeria today is back to the drawing boards. And that is why I say we must have a national conference. . . . We haven't created a nation. We have not created a nation. . . . I would like to show you that the interest of a group unfortunately still supersedes that of the agglomerate because I don't know what we are really. I find it difficult to call to a nation today. I would like us to sit down and let us set the parameters of our nation."[42] The insistence that Nigerians "have not created a nation" by Ojukwu, who led the secessionist Republic of Biafra, was obviously weighty.

The issue of domination and hegemony and the north's "undue advantage" at the expense of the rest of the country is another major theme reflected in the narratives. *TELL* asked Ojukwu to react to the fact that "the North . . . tends to be opposed to the idea of Nigerians or their leaders sitting down to hold [a national conference]." Ojukwu's response was full of subtle condescension in his attitude to the north: "If you are satisfied with the status quo, why would you want to shift it? This is not a church situation, it is life. . . . I mean, let's face it. When in your life, your ancestors have never seen wide expanse of water and today you can become admiral of a fleet, wouldn't you enjoy it? When you are sitting on desert sands and petrol is piped to you to exploit, wouldn't you want it? When fertilizer companies are established and you are put on top in the South to run [it] wouldn't you enjoy it? When all the services are commanded by you, when the powers—the executive, the judiciary, the legislature—are yours to take, at your command, would you really be in that situation, clamouring for change?"[43] This is a good example of *differentiation*, as Ojukwu emphasizes those things that differentiate and divide Nigerian power blocs, particularly the "exploitative" north from the rest of Nigeria.

Against the narratives of the domination of the country by the Hausa-Fulani north, the southern press continued to reflect doubt as to the sincerity of the Babangida regime to hand over power. As the parties, the SDP and NRC, prepared for their presidential primaries, *TheNEWS* described their preparations as constituting an "assumption of vacancy" in the presidential villa.[44] When two candidates, Moshood Abiola (SDP) and Bashir Tofa (NRC), emerged as the flag bearers of their parties, *TELL* described this as the "triumph of IBB's [General Babangida's] men,"[45] while *TheNEWS* asked if Abiola or Tofa could accomplish the "mission to save Nigeria." Argued the latter: "The two beneficiaries of General Babangida's 'command democracy' are Chief Abiola and Alhaji Tofa who emerged to clinch the presidential ticket of the SDP and NRC. But given the nature of partisan politics in the country and the growing clamour in certain sectors for a Sovereign National Conference and the subsequent re-ordering of the federation, Babangida's gift may soon turn into an albatross on the neck of whoever emerges as president in Nigeria."[46]

The newsmagazine avered that given the fact that "all is not well with the [Nigerian] federation and [the] dangers of its constituent parts coming unhinged," would a President Tofa or Abiola be up to the task?" For the weekly, this constituted the core question that the embattled "nation" confronted: "That rot and decay has eaten deep into the fabric of the nation and that it is tottering on the brink of collapse? That its various sub-groups are dissatisfied with the present structure of the Federation and are clamouring for a new political arrangement? Will either Abiola or Tofa, finding himself in the eye of the storm, turn out to be the man of the moment and exhibiting a presence of mind and steadfastness of purpose, steer the nation into calmer waters?"[47] *TheNEWS* believed that the global drift toward "ethnic nationalism and dismemberment of nation-states" was more salient in understanding the situation in Nigeria; democratization was only a manifestation, or a subtext, of this.

New Nigerian disagreed, arguing that such narratives were only indicative of a "new-fangled malady" of "bashing" Babangida and "holding the nation to ransom." The newspaper then accused the two leading southern weeklies of "running down" the Babangida regime: "The most guilty . . . are *TELL* and *TheNEWS*. In their effort to run down this administration . . . they would stop at nothing even if what they are doing has the potential of tearing apart the Nigerian nation. . . . As for TheNEWS they seem to have abandoned every sense of decency or ethics [w]ithin [its] short span life span. . . . They [both newsmagazines] threaten fire and brimstone if their own ideas of how the country should go is not followed. . . . These magazines must be told that they cannot hold this nation to ransom. They cannot decide for the rest of us how the country should go." The "rag sheets," as *New Nigerian* described *TELL* and *TheNEWS,* were then warned that if the "nation breaks apart," ostensibly on account of their narratives, "all of us will be engulfed in it."[48]

The Guardian argued, against the fears over the genuineness of Babangida's resolve to vacate power, that unless there were irregularities on a "wide scale," the results of the election should be respected given the fact that Nigeria's future was predicated on the outcome of the election. Given that the "journey has been long and tortuous," the "future of Nigeria requires" that the results of the forthcoming presidential elections be respected.[49] The stage was thus set for clashing narratives once the election crises erupted.

Narrating "A Date with History"

On June 15, a high court in Abuja with Chief Judge Dahiru Saleh presiding granted a petition by the Association for Better Nigeria (ABN), a shadowy organization headed by Chief Arthur Nzeribe, suspending further announcement of election results by the National Electoral Commission (NEC). NEC complied with the order of the court. By this time, election results in all the states of the federation were available publicly, even though the NEC had formally declared results in only fourteen of the thirty states. The "opposition" newspapers, in response, universalized the desirability of announcing the results, insisting that civilized conduct among the comity of nations required no less. *The Guardian* asked that the remaining results be officially declared because "we ought to demonstrate to the world that we are capable of making progress and that progress has begun" and "Nigeria is ready for democracy."[50]

New Nigerian maintained otherwise. The paper, which had earlier described the election as a "historic moment in our march towards enduring democratic polity," questioned the validity of the election in a front-page editorial instructively titled "Our Nation, Our Destiny." *New Nigerian* alluded to "some happenings that in their essence might have serious consequences for the democratic process. . . . Key among them and which are widely reported are the general apathy, low voter turn-out, the court verdict and the more insidious foreign interferences, apparent election malpractices as well as glaring lapses on the part of the [National Electoral Commission]."[51]

The paper's narrative of what transpired during the election was decidedly different from that of *The Guardian* and *Daily Champion*. For the *Champion*, "Nigeria's chequered transition process petered out towards a glorious end last Saturday, June 12, 1993, with the successful conduct of the last of the elections leading to the withdrawal of the military from civil administration. The election itself was epochal."[52] *New Nigerian* stated: "From general observation and reports, voter turn-out was very low. In at least one state, only 12.5 percent of the registered voters actually voted. . . . The situation was more serious in the Northern states where majority of the voters are peasant farmers who cannot help but attend to their farms."[53] For all of *New Nigerian*'s "general observation and reports," only one concrete example of a state among thirty could be cited for low turnout. Also, the occupational disposition of "northerners," which was not at issue for the many months preceding the election, was now responsible for the paper's rejection of the validity of the elections. But the *Champion* seemed to suggest a reason for *New Nigerian*'s about-turn, stating that the results of the election released unofficially "showed fundamental shifts in the nation's traditional pattern of loyalties and alignments,"[54] a reference to the unofficial victory of a southern candidate (Abiola) over a northern candidate (Tofa). Before this election, the heads of government in the earlier two Republics were northerners. For *The Guardian*, it was a matter of honor that the results be released and validated because Nigeria has had "enough of [these] dishonourable antics that have diminished us. . . . The way forward [is] to affirm the verdict that Nigerians delivered on June 12 [1993]."[55]

For *New Nigerian*, such views as the *Champion*'s and *The Guardian*'s and the interests they represent constitute the views of the "minority," which must not be allowed to prevail for the sake of the "destiny of our nation": "We are not apologists for military rule, but as always we want the best for the destiny of our nation. . . . To pretend that all is well with the elections is to elevate the views of the minority with a strange and unacceptable interpretation of the concept of democracy."[56]

Shortly after this editorial, the editor of the paper, Yakubu Abdul-lazeez, resigned. He stated in his resignation letter that the "sudden change on the editorial policy of the paper is geared towards fanning the embers of ethnic and regional disunity."[57] This letter received major attention from the pro-June 12 press. The *New Nigerian* in a front-page story dismissed the editor's claim as "politically orchestrated blackmail."[58]

Whereas Edwin Madunagwu, the Marxist scholar and member of *The Guardian*'s editorial board, argued that the unofficial victory of Abiola at the polls was a vote "above every other thing . . . for a revolutionary change,"[59] and that the forces against the election constituted a "neo-fascist movement,"[60] Sina Odugbemi, another member of the editorial board, wrote that, given the polarity occasioned by the election crisis, "the middle ground has vanished forever"[61] in Nigeria's politics. It was precisely the absence of the middle ground that the *Champion* deplored, while condemning the "unreasonable intolerance"[62] of such "June Twelvers," as represented by Madunagwu and Odugbemi and Olatunji Dare, *The Guardian*'s leading columnist and editorial board chair who had described *New Nigerian*'s "logic" in dismissing the validity of the election as one that it would be "courteous to call infantile."[63] In the week after the election, the *Champion*, whose publisher, Emmanuel Iwanyanwu, was a presidential aspirant under the banner of the NRC, made a volte-face. The *Champion* moved from supporting the election's validity to equivocating on this and eventually to challenging it. Although admitting that since the annulment "the nation has been thrown into tumult unprecedented in post-civil war Nigeria," it concluded that "at the level of ideas, the otherwise vibrant and vocal Nigerian society appeared to be in grave danger of fossilization between two irreconcilable extremes."[64]

On June 23, the federal military government announced the cancellation of the presidential election and suspended the electoral commission. Consequently, the narratives turned to pointing to the "dangers ahead for the nation." *TELL* narrated the state of affairs: "After 10 years of the most rapacious and destructive military interregnum in our national politics, the Nigerian people, on June 12, freely elected their new Leader, M. K. O. Abiola, in what has been universally acknowledged as the best election held in this country since independence." Yet, added TELL, "General Babangida, who anointed himself the nation's emperor August 27, 1985, and who has never intended to relinquish power, decided to so brazenly subvert the will of the people. We had severally alerted the nation about the grand fraud that is the transition programme. Many other patriotic Nigerians did the same, crying out without let about the dangers ahead for the nation."[65]

The newsmagazine universalized the acknowledgment of the free and fair nature of the election and expurgated the other, Babangida, who was identified as so evil, harmful, and threatening as to demand collective resistance and removal from office (he was an "emperor who set up" a "grand fraud [to] subvert the will of the people"). This also resulted inherently in a call for unity against the advances of the "evil other." The magazine then asked a question only to predict the "formal death" of the Nigerian nation: "The pertinent question now is: How and why did Nigerians allow the nation to come to this horrible pass? At this juncture, we can write the epithet to mark the formal death of the nation . . . : 'Here lies prostrate, Nigeria, a nation with huge potentials for greatness, but now bent and broken by the inordinate ambition of Babangida and his vile obsession with power.'"[66]

The *Champion* argued otherwise, even though its position was not equivocal. The paper stated that the issue of June 12, which could be resolved "through negotiation by the elite," should not be allowed to "threaten national survival": "Central as the mandate is to the march towards democracy, it will serve no useful purpose to allow it to threaten national survival. The nation must survive for democracy to take roots. We have no doubt that there are no obstacles this nation cannot overcome if the larger national interest forms the paramount basis of political discourse."[67]

Perhaps to further prove the "evil" of the regime, *TELL* predicted that its current edition may be the last before the regime descends on it—as it already did on *TheNEWS*—in the regime's "pacification process," which will follow Babangida's "total conquest of the nation." In dedicating the whole edition to the "stolen presidency," the magazine affirmed the eventual and ultimate triumph of that nation that has just been killed by Babangida. *TELL* declared: "We shall never give up the struggle because this country is far greater and more important than Babangida and his chorus singers. The people's will shall certainly triumph."[68]

Sani Kotangora countered this view vehemently in his interview in *TELL*. The publisher of the defunct Kaduna-based *Hotline* magazine and strident defender of northern interests argued that "no election" took place on June 12 as far as he was concerned, adding that the north was ready to go to war if Abiola became president on the basis of that election. In the interview, published ostensibly to portray the "recalcitrance" of the core North, Kotangora stated: "There was no election. . . . The whole Yoruba race voted for Abiola. Now I am beginning to believe that the problem of this country is ethnicity. . . . I believe democracy means living without any rancour or disunity and with the majority views carrying the day, but I cannot expect a candidate that is elected by about 30 percent of the people of this country, the Yoruba race, to say he's going to be my President. No way! No way!. . . . We are not afraid of war." Kotangora attempted here to *differentiate* the Yoruba from the rest of Nigeria: a minority that seeks to "overtake" the majority, the remaining 70 percent. This 30 percent minority thus separated from the majority would not be capable of constituting an effective challenge to existing patterns of political power that favor the interests that Kotangota represents. The election, for him, condemned the Yoruba as a totally "undemocratic" race that have to be stopped by the military government unless the government wants to bring chaos. "The Yorubas have shown the whole world that even if you have to take a pig, or a dog and make Yoruba marks on it," the Yoruba will choose it because "[the pig or dog] is a son of the soil."[69] The metonymy on display in this statement is very instructive when the choice of the word "pig" for the average (northern) Muslim is considered. The pig is a filthy, abominable animal for the Muslim, and the dog would pass for a bitch. Kotangora could as well be saying that the Yoruba did not care to present "abominable" candidates that would be forced on the rest of the nation, particularly the north. Kotangora also ignored the widespread popularity of Abiola in the elections, including the fact that he defeated his rival, Tofa, in his home state of Kano in the heart of the north.

After Abiola addressed a press conference at which he rejected the annulment and declared himself the president-elect, *TELL* stated that the press conference "appeared like an oasis in a desert": "It renewed the hope of the 14 million voters who on June 12 smashed the North-versus-South myth into smithereens. . . . Nigerians denounced all forms of tribalism, religion and ethnicism which divided us in the past and made military intervention possible."[70]

As Nigeria "journey[s] to the unknown" in the context of its being "on the verge of collapse as single entity" because of the annulment, *TELL* narrated a military high command that could not stand by while the nation drifted toward collapse: "The nation is at crossroads and the military will be decisive on which road is chosen to the future. General Sani Abacha, defence secretary, who until former president Ibrahim Babangida was stampeded out of office, combined the job with that of Chief of Defence Staff, said solemnly that the present calls for sacrifice and patriotism. . . . [General Oladipo] Diya [, the new chief of defense staff, was also] solemn and spare in his words."[71]

These "solemn and spare" generals were also commended by Abiola himself for their "love of the country, common sense, experience, tact and intellect" with which they "eased out" Babangida, who retired from the army and left office as military president on August 26, 1993. These qualities were also needed, *TELL* reported Abiola as saying, in easing out "Babangida's surrogates," that is, the Interim National Government (ING), which Babangida imposed on the country in his hurried exit from power. But despite the fact that "Nigeria [was] already neck-deep in political quagmire and economic depression," the *Champion* insisted that "the only way to express collective will is to support the Interim National Government,"[72] which had been undemocratically imposed on this country. Although it agreed that the annulment had "thrown the nation into a political tumult unprecedented in post-civil war Nigeria," the *Champion* condemned the violent protests following the annulment. The forces that *TELL* described as being "decisive" at the nation's crossroads were, for the *Champion*, "undemocratic forces."[73]

The *Champion* was particularly worried about the plight of the Igbo, who, fearing an outbreak of war in the heat of the crisis, had been moving en masse back to the east from different parts of the country: "It is these acts of violence that have created the state of wild panic and feeling of insecurity among Nigerian citizens. Never since the era of the civil war have Nigerians witnessed the mass exodus back home of people residing in places other than that of their origin. Given the high level of post-civil war integration of the Nigerian society, the disruption going on as a result of this panic is of phenomenal proportions."[74] The "high level of post-civil war integration" refers to the return of the Igbo to different parts of the country after the war, particularly to the north, where they suffered a widespread pogrom before the outbreak of hostilities in 1967.

For *The Guardian*, this ING was an effort to "evade the reality of the electoral verdict delivered by the people of Nigeria on June 12, 1993. It was only such a government based on that election, and not the ING, that could carry out the task of regeneration and rebuilding."[75] *The-NEWS* appeared opposed to this move toward a coup (which *TELL* predicted) to upstage the "two-month old stop-gap arrangement," that is, the ING. *TheNEWS* stated: "Against the background of a two-month old stop-gap arrangement that has failed to win the sympathy of a populace demanding respect and recognition of the democratic principle symbolised by 12 June voting . . . the military arm of the contraption might be set to foist a new dispensation on the nation thereby obscuring the electoral mandate." The newsmagazine predicted that a military coup would not be acceptable to the "civil society."[76]

It could be seen that *TheNEWS*, unlike the other pro-June 12 newspapers and newsmagazines, particularly *TELL*, did not support the line that the defense chief, General Sani Abacha, could save the situation. As opposition to Abiola's mandate festered and as the threat mounted, *TheNEWS* argued that Abacha may not be the "saviour" because he regarded "northern continued domination of the nation's military and politics as holy writ."[77] For TELL, this would "seem to suggest that, put bluntly, Nigeria's days as a single nation are numbered, especially if the hard issues of contention are not quickly addressed by way of a national conference."[78] A national conference was thus held out as the only means of saving the collapsing edifice, Nigeria. Given this, it is not surprising that the military and the core northern elite were regarded by the opposition press as perhaps the biggest obstacles to the construction and survival of the country and are constantly attacked.

The *Champion* viewed the predilection to narrate the possible extinction of the Nigerian nation as a form of "warmongering": "The nation has been trapped in a lock-jam; a prisoner to a foreboding elite power game. As the nation becomes increasingly asphyxiated, the warmongers have rolled out the drums, beating the tunes of war with a draw out captive public gyrating dangerously towards fratricide. This should stop."[79]

Democratic Setback, June-Twelvers, and Nation-Destroying

In the aftermath of the annulment of the June 12 election, particularly with the palace coup against the ING on November 17, 1993, which brought General Sani Abacha to power, *TheNEWS*, among other newspapers and newsmagazines, focused on the "Kaduna Mafia," the "dormant power vortex" of the "Northern laager," which was "set to sail again." As might be expected in a narrative that zeroed in on a power group produced by historical processes, the magazine reverted to the days of the late Sir Ahmadu Bello, Sardauna of Sokoto, the first and only premier of the northern region, who was the "very personification of the collective dream of the Northern political and economic elite to rule over the fledging Nigerian federation": "He [Bello] went further and put in place a near-perfect political and economic machinery that welded together a vast region comprised of diverse ethnic and religious groups into a single political entity so formidable in its single-mindedness of purpose that it easily trounced all other comers in the political terrain."

The "north" that had been so formidable, now a "dream empire utterly violated," *TheNEWS* stated, brought together its storm troopers in the bid to "bring back to life Alhaji Ahmadu Bello's 'single and indivisible' North as a counterforce to the South's attempt to wrest political power at the centre," as represented by Abiola's annulled victory in the June 12 presidential election. Argued the magazine: "It was the first step in a new offensive by the Northern power elite to return to the political centre stage following the rude shock it received on 12 June when the over-whelming majority of Nigerians voted for [a southerner] Chief M. K. O. Abiola as their next president. The core group . . . read in Abiola's victory a shift of political power to the south and they did not like it. 12 June also brought forcefully home to them, the harsh reality of a 'United North' that has fallen apart at the seams with the ethnic minorities of the Middle-Belt up in arms and insisting on self-determination and a political destiny distinct from Ahmadu Bello[s] 'one North, one people, one destiny.'"

Babangida's annulment of the presidential election, argued *TheNEWS*, was a "much needed breather" for this power elite, who then went into soul searching and repositioned "with power back in its enclave . . . in the safe keeping of the northern-dominated and controlled armed forces and General Sani Abacha, a Kano man of Kanuri extraction at its helm." The task that consequently faced the "amorphous and secretive group consisting of key members of the northern power oligarchy dating back to the days of Ahmadu Bello," that is, the "Kaduna Mafia," argued *TheNEWS*, was to "determine the exact point it took the wrong turn politically and re-fashion its strategy to not only block a return to 12 June but also return power to its political arm when the whistle sounds for another contest."[80]

In this same edition, the magazine published excerpts from a translated version of Maitama Sule's address at the launching of the book *Power of Knowledge* in Kaduna, where he made a statement that became highly controversial, particularly coming against the annulment. The magazine boldly quoted Sule's thesis of "divine division of labour" in Nigeria: "The northerners are endowed by God with leadership qualities. The Yoruba man knows how to earn a living and has diplomatic qualities. The Igbo is gifted in commerce, trade and technological innovation. God so created us individually for a purpose and with different gifts. . . . If there are no followers, a king will not exist."[81]

Sule also said that it was the Sardauna who had the "wisdom" and "foresight" of recruiting northern youths into the army: "Today, we are reaping the fruits of that foresight. Anything, anybody would want to say about military involvement in government; if you don't have your man at the helm of affairs, you would have been dealt with or you would have been killed."[82] *TheNEWS* argued that the power and the billions of petro dollars that this power elite hijacked could have been "carefully husbanded and utilised" to transform the northern region and Nigeria as a whole into "a flourishing and affluent federation." But this was not the case: "Greed, corruption and political opportunism intervened, turning members of the conservative Northern power elite and their compatriots in the South into billionaires overnight at the expense of the entire region. The consequence: the vicious cycle of poverty, illiteracy and disease in which Ahmadu Bello's 'One North' is trapped. Indeed, this lethal cancer has seeped into other parts of the country." The North was, therefore, depicted as the "contaminator-in-chief" among the constituent parts of the country in what Jolly Tanko Yusuf, a northern minority Christian activist, called "a stupid vision of corruption, [and] . . . of disgracing the country."[83] Adebayo Williams, a university teacher and essayist, witnessed that the disarray from which the Kaduna Mafia was recovering was a pointer to "how greed, compounded by capital political folly, can undo even the most powerful of cabals." He counseled the Mafia to support June 12 because this was the "least politically costly option for the oligarchy" after the "orphan from Minna" (General Babangida) had visited devastation on the power clique.[84] *TELL* agreed with *TheNEWS* about the opposition of "the caliphate"—which the latter called "the Kaduna mafia"—to the revalidation of Abiola's mandate. This group was informed in its activities, *TELL* disclosed, by "the need to preserve the monolithic North reminiscent of the 1960s when the late Sardauna of Sokoto, Sir Ahmadu Bello, held sway."[85]

Preoccupation with the recent past was also a major feature of the narratives regarding June 12; the newspapers and magazines regularly reminded Nigerians of the regime that brought the nation into its present crisis. *TheNEWS'* narratives of the Babangida regime after the general left office are full of attempts to finger the man as a nation destroyer par excellence, given that his "eight-years iron rule was like the extended black night of an eerie history." What could be the legacy of the man whom the magazine described as "a plague in the land?"[86] Lest history be rewritten in the future, *The-NEWS* described the years that Babangida spent in power as "years of the locust" because "for eight years . . . everywhere General Ibrahim Babangida went, he sowed chaos, grief and moral drought. Whatever he touched, he stained with his evil [aura]."[87] The news-magazine added that "the disgraced regime of Ibrahim Babangida, the military dictator . . . caused much havoc, of the Hiroshima proportions, to our country."[88] *TELL* agreed with this reading of Babangida's place in Nigeria's history because "the annulment of the June 12 presidential election by . . . Ibrahim Babangida, has not only visited on Nigerians an unprecedented trauma, it has depressed them psychologically and dampened the spirit of a people noted globally for robustness and a certain gongo-go spirit."[89] However, the *Champion* did not see the Babangida regime as roundly condemnable. According to the paper, Babangida's wife, Maryam, made "remarkable efforts to put women on the national agenda" as First Lady. Her name, therefore, would be written in gold in the annals of women's empowerment. "When the history of women movers in Nigeria is written, Mrs. Babangida will certainly get good mention for her vigorous attempts to liberate and bring to the fore-front Nigeria's down-trodden women."[90]

With the Abacha regime securely sequestered in power, the narratives of the pro-June 12 newspapers and magazine reflected the new realities. First, a major theme was disappointment with how the political class, particularly the June 12 movement, caved in, as some of its leading members, including Abiola's running mate, Babagana Kingibe, joined the Abacha regime. It was narrated as the "killing of hope" because "12 June was a beacon of hope, an intimation of greater things until the politicians conspired with military adventurers."[91]

Professor Claude Ake, the director of the Centre for Advanced Social Science (CASS), picked up this theme in an interview with *TheNEWS*, pointing out that what is left is "a popular struggle . . . to ensure the convocation of a Sovereign National Conference to save the nation."[92] *TheNEWS* confronted the question of this "historic betrayal," asking "what really went wrong" and why Abiola "readily surrendered [his] historic mandate" in endorsing Abacha's palace coup that "effectively consigned 12 June to history." The magazine's lengthy narrative picked up the myriad of reasons that were responsible for the annulment and the sustenance of the annulment, including Abiola's "personal limitations," the collusion of the party executives with the military, the General Shehu Yar' Adua's factor, and Abiola's own capitulation to the same forces that were against his ascendancy.[93]

Ojo Madueke, a politician and a columnist of *TheNEWS*, gave a conceptual cover to the shift by the erstwhile supporters of the mandate, including himself. Though Madueke considered June 12 as an "unforgettable milestone in our search for real nationhood,"[94] he argued against Sina Odugbemi's earlier submission in *The Guardian* that the "middle ground has vanished forever."[95] Madueke, after reviewing the state of affairs, which necessitated "tactical compromises and somersaults while preserving the Strategic Objective of 12 June," suggested that Nigerians embrace the "middle," that is, "the path of principled pragmatism and peaceful transition to democracy anchored on the inviolable spirit of 12 June. It is in that middle that we as a nation can recover our democratic will and purpose again."[96]

Ojo's narrative rationalized the "collaboration" of ex-June Twelvers with the military through the construction of a "chain of reasoning" that defended and justified the action and euphemized the betrayal by describing what others regarded as "capitulation" as "accommodation." Also, he universalized the action, which served the interests of those who were eager to savor the goodies of participation in governments, as if everyone shared it and endorsed the assumption of the benefits that this presented for the "nation to recover." Ojo continued his rationalization: "From that middle we can focus on a National/Constitutional conference without

debilitating anxieties concerning probable declarations of secession. . . . Those who wish to take the 12 June members of the Abacha administration to task for their decision to participate should
come forward with a principled but feasible alternative that were
open to the serious politician after the ING collapse. IT is plainly
nihilistic, if not irresponsible, to stand by and watch the nation
literally fall apart." For this narrator there was no "principled" or
"feasible" alternative to joining the Abacha train because the other
option available was for the "nation [to] literally fall apart."[97]

As 1993, which was described as Nigeria's *annus incredibilis*,
ended and 1994 began, the narratives on the fate of Nigeria as a
united entity grew desperate. *TELL* interviewed Justice Akinola
Aguda, who predicted "a war," adding that "the future of [Nigeria]
is very bleak."[98] Abiola told *TheNEWS* that Nigeria was "near disaster."[99] Aguda argued that the issue was not north versus south but
a "clique" in the north that, "because they are used to oppressing
their immediate surroundings[,] thinks the same oppression should
go round the whole country."[100] Adebayo Williams looked at the
personal limitations of the "custodian" of the June 12 mandate,
Abiola, and argued that the mandate had yet produced "significant" results. Abiola was bound to "misbehave" as he had, *TheNEWS*
essayist reasoned, because "on 12 June, the Nigerian populace delivered a resounding vote of no confidence in two principal factions
of the Nigerian ruling class: the military and the backward-looking
oligarchy that has held the nation to ransom since independence.
Bashorun Abiola, the people's arm-bearer had flirted with both." Yet
TheNEWS columnist insisted: "What is important is that the correct
lessons must be grasped. To the extent that 12 June has dealt a stag-
gering blow to the pretensions of the Nigerian ruling class, to the
extent that it has exposed the hollowness of its claims, to that extent
it remains a potent symbol of national rejuvenation, a living cause in
search of a hero."[101]

TheNEWS selected the "June 12 [election]" as "Man of the Year"
because it "represents a watershed in the history of the Nigerian
nation-state."[102] The magazine linked this with a trajectory that may
be called the triad of Nigeria's fate: the anticolonial struggle, the
civil war, and then June 12. As the latest manifestation of the fateful
triad, June 12 was constructed as: "One day in the calendar of a drab
year (that) promises the arrival of a new dawn and the eclipse of an
ancient regime—but . . . holds the destiny of a nation dangling.[103]

The military, for TELL, was responsible for the dangling destiny of the nation because: "The military came as saviour only to emerge as the scourge of the people. . . . Now, the concept of Nigerianism is seriously under contention, the nature of the state is in dispute and the national psyche is battered and beaten."[104] The annulment of this "arrival of dawn," for *TELL*, wreaked havoc on Nigeria and the nation idea because "never in [Nigeria's] brief history has one event wielded the nation solidly."[105]

Abiola, in a marathon interview published in *TheNEWS*, attacked the Abacha regime over its agenda and warned that the nation cannot move forward unless it goes back to June 12: "If only we know how near we are to disaster in this country today. They would soon know. The moment we open the Pandora box of our national relationship as a country . . . they will know that many Nigerians following the June 12 experience believe that there is no Nigeria worth living in because there can be no justice for some people."[106] "Some people" was Abiola's metaphor for southerners who were suffering from the monopoly of power by the north. Sobo Sowemimo, a lawyer speaking through *TheNEWS*, accused the north of holding "the people of this country to ransom." Given this, Sowemimo said, "secession is legitimate."[107]

Malam Lawan Dambazau seemed to be exasperated by all this as he remarked to *TELL* that "each section [of the country should] go its own way." Although Dambazau agreed that the political future of Nigeria was "doomed forever" if the June 12 debacle were not "properly addressed," he stated: "To avoid any bloodshed or civil disorder, I will suggest that we sit down peacefully round a table and ask each section of the country if they still want to belong to Nigeria. Those who want to go should be allowed to do so in peace instead of deceiving each other over a non-existent concept of one Nigeria. Honestly let us divide the country peacefully and each section goes its own way."[108]

Although Nigerians gave up the hope of redemption for their "deeply troubled nation"[109] in the hands of "an embodiment of woes," that is, General Abacha, Dambazau argued that more people in the north wanted Nigeria to remain united because they were "more nationalistic."[110] Williams could as well have been responding to these images of oneness when he argued: "The vociferous war-cries stem from [the] feeling of great betrayal, this feeling that behind the empty slogan of 'One Nigeria,' there is nothing but bare-faced hypocrisy and a grand design to sentence a part of the country to perpetual slavery."[111]

Williams claimed that "only a spirited effort can save the nation from suicide" even though the constitutional conference "will serve as a sympathetic undertaker for the nation's journey to the great beyond."[112] In this context, *TheNEWS* wondered what would happen if the conferees voted for the disintegration of Nigeria: "If at the end of the proposed constitutional conference, delegates voted that the nation pull apart for now, what would be the consequences of such a decision? Is a Czech-Slovak velvet divorce possible in Nigeria?" The magazine often used the word "nation" as synonym for Nigeria, even though it was obvious in context that this "nation" did not capture the emotional solidarity that ought to be the significant expression of a nation. Therefore, in the use of the word, *TheNEWS* may be pointing to a nation of aspiration, that is, a grand nation of intent that would also be a grand solidarity. Stated *TheNEWS:* "A million naira question hangs on the neck of the Nigerian federation: will it survive the impetuous temper of the moment or disintegrate into an unmanageable mosaic—the type of madness the world now witnesses in Bosnia? Eighty years after the amalgamation [of the northern and southern protectorates by the British], the Nigerian federation is today beset with the most challenging test of its survival." The newsmagazine then captured the dynamics of these disintegrating forces in all sections of the country, which obstructed a "collective journey of destiny," asking: "What are the consequences of the new convulsive spirit tearing down the nation? All over the country, nations and ethno-nations are putting heads together on how to redefine their place in the Nigerian federation."[113] *TheNEWS* ostensibly believed that nations and ethno nations, within the context of Nigeria, captured different types of groups. Unfortunately, there is no elaboration of which groups fit either of these tags.

On its part, *TELL* reported doubts that the confab would hold, since if it were aborted, the conservative northern political elite and General Abacha would be happy because the confab would be likely to "disturb" the balance of forces in the country. Consequently, *TELL* stated that "the scope of the on-coming talks is being teleguided and restricted to tally with the purpose of Babangida's annulment of the June 12 election to carry on with the thesis that only a northerner should, in the final analysis, rule the country." The magazine continued: "At [a] meeting, the decision of the 'Kaduna Mafia' was allegedly ratified and that Abacha was directed to seize power from [Ernest] Shonekan. Meaning that Abacha's November 17 coup was mandated by the northern ruling class to restore the north's political supremacy."[114]

This narrative of a "mandate" from the north given to Abacha conflicts with *TELL*'s earlier narratives of the "patriotic" zeal and "wisdom" of Abacha, which Abiola attested to, and the "solemnity" of the general as he dialogued with Abiola to "save Nigeria." Once Abacha failed to hand over power to Abiola, he was invested with new clothes and the events leading to his hijack of power attracted new narrations in *TELL* to suit emergent power configurations. The new configuration also transformed Abiola from the one who "betrayed" the people—as he was "wont to do given his personal limitations and ideological background"—to one who had been "betrayed by friends" and "abandoned by political associates," yet "doggedly [keeping] alive hope for the realisation of the mandate": "Two incidents last month succinctly drive home the fact that Abiola is investing his prodigious energy in keeping hope alive for June 12 and ultimately realising the mandate Nigerians gave him."[115]

It must be noted that the term mandate," used here as if it were an ordinary word that described Abiola's "legitimacy," is itself a discourse. It is complete with the baggage of settled conviction about Abiola's victory, though unannounced officially, in the June 12, 1993, election. It also accepts that whatever electoral victory Abiola won in 1993 is still tenable at this point, almost one year after the election.

TheNEWS, which had earlier narrated exhaustively why Abiola could not claim his "mandate" the year before (1993), also stated that the man "seems set" for the final push to "regain his pilfered mandate."[116] As the "forces that will chase out Abacha"[117] got ready without an answer to the question, "who will save Sani Abacha?"[118] *TheNEWS* announced that Abiola looked set to claim victory: "The very first serious evidence of a preparedness to claim the mandate was the 3 August 1993, fiery speech he [Abiola] made on the 'inviolability of June 12' where he promised to keep a date with history on the historic mandate."[119] *TELL* emphasized the likelihood of victory over the forces against the nation: "Nine months after [the] power-drunken recklessness, the ensuing political crisis draws the nation to the edge of the precipice by the day. But the symbol of June 12,

Abiola, thinks the cup will pass the nation. Rather, he told a friend last week that he would realise his mandate yet."[120]

Despite this assurance, Nigeria still faced a myriad of problems subsumed under the rubric of political and economic crises. However, these crises were narrated as resulting from the policies and attitude of the Abacha regime as "the nation [threatens to] grind to a halt."[121] As *TheNEWS* narrated it: "Abacha's political and economic agenda release a Frankenstein monster. The architect himself stands helpless as two frightening dangers confront Nigeria; the fear of disintegration and the fear of a natural economic wheel that may soon grind to a halt. Nigerians should brace up for the worst."[122]

TELL restated this line, a few weeks after *TheNEWS*, narrating "why Nigeria may collapse,"[123] as the economy "is speedily grinding . . . to a halt inflicting on the people a regime of unprecedented suffering."[124] For the magazine, these are not purely economic matters because "the problem is a leadership one which requires the nation having democratically elected rulers." The link was then explained: "The merits of this . . . are the opening up of the economy to fresh foreign investment, the pacification of the country whose diverse tempers have been over-heated, and the enthronement of peace much needed for growth. If the economic problem also boils down to having democracy, then perhaps issues like the sacredness of Abiola's June 12 mandate and the national Question suddenly becomes top-burner agenda."[125]

The two newsmagazines linked the logic of economic crisis to the June 12 crisis, the crisis of nationhood, and the manner of their resolution. For them, the state of the economy was proportional to health of the grand solidarity. As a respondent informed *TheNEWS*, the issue was not just "access to the distribution of resources, but access to distribution of power at the centre," which, for the newsmagazine, explained the north's "opposition" to even the planned "token" convocation of a constitutional confab: "If for General Abacha the decision to convene the Constitutional Conference was a token concession to the political south to enable him grab power, for the far northern politicians and technocrats, it was a major political earthquake in the mould of June 12 for the simple reason that it has the capacity of threatening the power equation in the country which is presently in their favour."[126] But *The Guardian* argued otherwise after completion of the election and selection of the members of the proposed confab. The paper averred that in the light of the imminent start of the National Conference it might appear that the country was set to move forward again, even though the reality was different. *The Guardian* stated: "It is abundantly clear right now that Nigeria is not set to move forward at all. . . . The nation is, once again, all aquiver. Tension is high."[127]

The *Champion* disagreed with *The Guardian*. As far as the *Champion* was concerned: "With the recent successful conclusion of the delegates' election, all is now set for the constitutional conference. . . . In spite of this obvious hazy start, the election went on smoothly and ended hitch-free."[128]

The Guardian disagreed still. Stating the background to the present state of affairs necessitating the national confab, the paper argued: "The idea of a re-gathering of the true representatives of the several peoples of the multi-national state of Nigeria in order to fashion an operative consensus had been propagated by this newspaper along with several other patriotic persons and institutions. The felt need for a Sovereign National Conference to tackle the complex bundle of issues popularly referred to today as the National Question. It was this idea that the present administration seized upon, and proceeded to adapt in a manner entirely of its own choosing."[129]

For the *Champion*, these purposes could still be achieved at the confab, which the military regime had set up: "To us this is the moment of truth. This is the moment when we must look ourselves in the eye, without blinking, and tell ourselves the bitter truth. This is the time to clinically treat those intractable issues that have become a cankerworm in our body-politic. Such issues as injustice, equity, marginalization, the plight of the minorities, ethnic imbalances in the military, monopoly of power by a section of the country and a host of others, should be tabled and resolved once and for all."[130]

But the version of this confab that the regime was holding, argued *The Guardian*, was "fundamentally flawed," and it had failed politically *ab initio* because "it is without legitimacy." This was because "there are whole sections of the country whose true leaders are not coming to the conference. The Constitutional Conference Election, it must be remembered, is not an election designed to produce a government. It is designed to fashion consensus. Thus, even if one tiny community only were to boycott, it would still have failed. And continuing with it will only further divide the nation."[131]

Not so, the *Champion* retorted. The paper narrateed a different reality regarding the composition of the confab: "Very credible Nigerians have thus emerged as delegates to the conference. With these calibre of personages going to the conference, we feel confident that the conference is indeed the right place to thrash out the myriad of problems currently tormenting this nation."[132]

The Guardian maintained that only two options existed for the country. The convocation of a "genuine" national conference whose recommendations would form the basis of a government of national unity based on the June 12 election, or allowing the political class to negotiate a government of national unity based on the June 12 election, which would then organize a "genuine" national conference: "The second option in our view, is the simpler of the two, to return Nigeria to peace, sanity and settled democratic governance. The fresh awakening of the demand for immediate democratisation in Nigeria shows, as nothing else can, that settled governance in Nigeria will remain a pipe-dream until the June 12 question is genuinely resolved."[133]

Any political arrangement contrary to the options offered by *The Guardian*, asserted *TheNEWS*, would result in "the portents of chaos and disintegration [which] are more real than ever before," and *TELL* agreed that "how Abacha handles them [the emergent problems] will considerably determine whether Nigeria remains one politically or [not]."[134] But the Champion insisted that "the annulment, as unjust and unfair, as it is, ought not hold the entire nation to ransom."[135]

With Abiola reaffirming the "inviolability" of June 12 as "the only way for the country to move forward," the two newsmagazines narrated a grand nation that was united against the Abacha regime because "since the mandate's annulment nothing has gone well with the nation."[136] Interestingly, the *Champion* agreed that things had not gone well with the nation since the annulment: "That the situation is gradually getting out of hand is no longer in doubt. We are passing through very grim moments in the life of our nation. For the first time since the end of the civil war, disintegration is nakedly staring us in the face. . . . Never before have we been subjected to such a protracted and precarious political stalemate as the June 12 debacle. Never before have our people been subjected to the magnitude of despondency as they are presently subjected. Never in the last 24 years, has this nation's future been so bleak and so uncertain as it is presently. The sum total is that our nation is in pillory."[137]

In this context, the pro-June 12 press reported marginal identities that were also contesting the space with the *monolith* that manifested either as the north or its dominated extension, the Nigerian state. Thus, as southern minorities threatened to secede because they were "tired of the status quo and with the convening of the constitutional conference becoming more doubtful,"[138] the middle-belt also "revolted" by setting up a "platform to challenge the hegemony of old masters [the Hausa-Fulani]" and "shake off the Hausa-Fulani yoke." In what represented a fine example of the expurgation of the other, *TheNEWS* stated that this "affirmation of defiance" by the minorities involved: "An unequivocal statement that the Middle-Belt elites had severed their binding ties with the Caliphate; now they were engaged in trying to crystallize the identity of their geopolitical zone as an independent player in the drama of Nigerian politics."[139] *TELL* linked the revolt of the minorities to the annulment of the June 12 election "that was won by Moshood Abiola who hails from the Western part of the country; "the event," added *TELL*, "has since intensified the fears of minorities who now see their chances to aspire to the presidency as non-existent, [while] the laager created has also caused the Yoruba and Ibos to call for separation at various [forums]."[140]

Twilights of the Grand Narrative

What follows the resolve of Abiola to reclaim his victory and the formation of the National Democratic Coalition (NADECO) as the vanguard for the revalidation of the mandate, as they were narrated in the press, particularly the pro-June 12 press, reflected the full "complicity" of the press with the institutions and individuals of the political society in setting the parameters of the struggle. NADECO had given the Abacha regime an ultimatum that would expire on May 30, 1994. The coalition asked the Abacha regime to fold up and allow Abiola to take over as the democratically elected president and then set up a government of national unity. In an editorial note, the editor in chief of *TheNEWS* told the story of how attention turned to the battle to revalidate the June 12 mandate: "From the grapevine, from our usually reliable sources came the information that Basorun M. K. O. Abiola, the acknowledged winner of Nigeria's 12 June Presidential election is primed up to have his long promised rendezvous with history, that is, fulfil his electoral mandate, now twice denied by the illegitimate government of Ernest Shonekan and Sani Abacha."[141] But this planned "rendezvous with history," for the *Champion,* was very "disturbing" because "it is difficult to clearly ascertain whose interests these agitations are meant to serve: that of the nation or the selfish interests of the agitators."[142]

In this "ultimate encounter," *TheNEWS* stated that Abiola was set to announce a government of national unity and a "programme of action" for which he "receives enthusiastic national support," and against which the Abacha regime could not "survive.[143] *TheNEWS* even published what Abiola, whom the magazine now called the "president-elect," would tell "fellow country men and women" in his "presidential" address. Abiola's speech published in *TheNEWS* included the following lines:

> After exhaustive consultations with fellow countrymen and women from all over Nigeria, at home and abroad, it has become clear to me that the only way forward, if we are to arrest the continuing danger- ous drift towards total economic collapse, the complete breakdown of law and order, and most importantly, the threat of political disin- tegration of our country, is to put in motion at once the machinery for actualising the mandate given to me on 12 June 1993, for a return to democratic government. . . . I call upon General Sani Abacha and his unelected and discredited team to respect the sovereign will and democratic rights of the people of Nigeria, to remove themselves forthwith from all government offices and premises over which they have exercised illegal occupancy.[144]

As the D-day for Abiola's "date with history," that is, his self-dec- laration as president, draws near, *New Nigerian* accused the mili- tary government of being "benevolent to a fault." The newspaper asked that the government be firm in dealing with the forces of the revalidation of the June 12 election.[145] The paper argued fur- ther that "June 12 can only be relevant if it is not seen in "isola- tion."[146] But *TELL* wrote, "Abacha's days are numbered," while *TheNEWS* declared that "all [is now] set for Abacha's overthrow":[147] "The Abacha junta seems cornered as the ghost of June 12 roars again in the shape of an ultimatum from pro-democracy forces."[148] "Like the proverbial Jaguar in the tale, the fiery 12 June has crashed out of General Abacha's cage and is now set to devour him. The opposition has roared back to life, spiked its guns and jumped into trenches. . . . Will it bury Sani Abacha's regime?"[149]

Whereas the *Champion* charged the Abacha regime with "giving more recognition to a very vocal minority," a "disagreeable group of people who have caused considerable tribulation for all"[150]—that is, the pro-June 12 agitators—*The Guardian* frowned at the arrest of leading politicians who "have raised poignant questions" on the eve of the threatened declaration by Abiola. The paper was particularly peeved at the arrests and "harassment" of elder statesmen Anthony Enahoro and Adekunle Ajasin, the former governor of Ondo State and leader of NADECO, because: "Every nation has its symbols and icons. . . . For the national fabric to cohere, these symbols must be treated with reverence and even under the most unsettling circumstances." The harassment of such symbols and icons, *The Guardian* declared, could only further "undermine the corporate existence [of Nigeria] whose basis is already fragile."[151]

As *TELL* and *TheNEWS* narrated the "spirit of June 12," which had returned like "the unconquerable phoenix,"[152] those opposed to the spirit, such as General Olusegun Obasanjo, were pictured as being outside of a "holy alliance." Obasanjo, *TheNEWS* stated, moved to "force his way to political relevance," even while facing a "deep credibility crisis at home."[153] The state of affairs that the likes of Obasanjo had supported was in recession, stated *TheNEWS*, as even "the most casual observer" could see that "Abacha [is] fighting desperately for dear life": "The opposition, hitherto in a slumber had in one bound, roared back to life, spiked its guns and jumped into the trenches, daring Abacha to pick up the gauntlet. As things stand, NADECO and the broad pro-democracy movement in the country is headed for certain victory in their campaign to take the wind out of Abacha's confab."[154] But for the *Champion*, Obasanjo was not a man "forcing his way to political relevance," but a "voice of reason" who in his "tireless efforts as [a statesman has] taken it upon [himself] to mediate in the crisis," risking "temporary estrangement by seeking to protect Nigeria's unity and larger national interests."[155]

NADECO proposed that the Abiola government's "primary mandate" will be to convene a Sovereign National Conference, which will restructure Nigeria and deal with the "national question." For *TheNEWS* this represented the emergence of a grand solidarity, which could give birth to a new nation: "The NADECO initiative has suddenly altered the political equation raising expectations for a truly pan-Nigerian political organisation capable of not only driving the military back to the barracks permanently, but also putting in a place, a credible platform on which the task of rebuilding the country can truly begin."[156] *TELL* added that "NADECO is the group of the moment and is not about to bend from its set objectives which is to be achieved in phases."[157] *The Guardian* argued that the division that the ultimatum by NADECO and Abacha's "intransigence" has produced is sharper and more dangerous: "It was to prevent this kind of situation that this newspaper has consistently argued that the government cannot afford to ignore the *passionate wishes* of vast segments of the polity in a multi-national society and it must be seen to play the only role for which governments are instituted—as arbiters and mediators."[158] *TheNEWS* then asked Abacha to either flee or lose his life in resistance: "General Sani Abacha may not realize it yet, but he is a mere spectator in the unfolding drama as the tide of events has swept him aside and assumed a life of its own. Will he, as General Babangida did in August 1993, smartly step aside and save his head or will he insist on riding the crest of the tide to self-destruction?"[159]

The "mere spectator" (General Abacha) in the unfolding drama of "nation assertion" was, however, able to call a halt to the battles against him as he arrested Abiola and others and shut down the protests. But before then, the opposition succeeded in "discrediting the elections [to the regime's planned Constitutional Confab] and rendering the . . . conference—if it holds—a nullity."[160]

TELL glorified and celebrated the ultimatum that NADECO handed down on the Abacha regime: "The term ultimatum is a high-calibre word in military circles. It represents the last line of warning and usually in military psyche, it does not shift easily. Next to summary decisions, it is etched indelibly in the army's lexicon, held in high-stead, a word to watch. . . . Which is why, when . . . NADECO sprang one on the government of General Sani Abacha . . . it put the junta and the nation on tenterhooks with certain ring of alarm."[161]

TheNEWS engaged the headline "What Is to Be Done" to validate June 12. Its editor in chief wrote that "although no shot have been fired yet, no petro-bombing, no sabotage of strategic installations, it is clear that the battle of wits and strength has begun."[162] The magazine could as well have been pointing out the means of fighting the battle, which had yet to be adopted. For *TELL* and *TheNEWS*, in Shuman's terms, the narratives appropriate to this context are the ones that confer victory on the opposition even though at the level of real politics the struggle is yet to make clear

gains. As "tension [mounted] in the land," with "Aso Rock in disarray" and Bashir Tofa, Abiola's opponent in the election, getting
ready to "concede victory," the "final showdown"[163] was set with
"no respite for Abacha."[164] In this context, Abiola declared Abacha "a goner" on *TELL's* cover page, with "the nation on edge as
(he) prepares to assume power." *TELL* declared, therefore, that
"Nigeria may be on the threshold of a protracted struggle for the
rebirth of democracy whose far-reaching consequences would be
difficult to predict."[165] *New Nigeria*, in the context of the threats by
NUPENG to go on strike in support of the June 12 mandate, called
on the "voices of Reason within the union . . . to oppose opportunism and despotism before the two evils destroy the union and
threaten the stability of the nation."[166]

After declaring himself president on June 10, 1994, Abiola went
into hiding. He was declared "wanted" by the Abacha regime. With
Abiola in hiding, which *TELL* described as an "11 day tactical withdrawal,"[167] the two newsmagazines reported that Abiola and Abacha "battle for control" even as pressure mounted on Abacha to
quit. *TELL* stated that "Abacha is in a fix as pressure mounts both
at home and abroad for the military to hand over to Abiola, winner
of the June 12 election[,] and give Nigeria a new lease of life."[168] As
"the cornered Abacha junta is bent on clinging to power," *TheNEWS*
asked: "Can the usurpers survive as the democratic forces queue
behind the dejure President Abiola?"[169]

Throughout this period, the two magazines called Abiola either
"the president elect" or the "dejure president." In light of this, *New
Nigerian's* Candido described the "Lagos-Ibadan Press" as having a
"strange pre-occupation with the shenanigans of June 12," in spite
of the fact that "Nigeria can move forward without June 12."[170]
The *Champion* largely agreed with Candido: "The on-going political crisis seems, more than any other incident in recent years, to
have brought to bold relief [the] unfortunate tendency of the Press
in the country. Manifesting the most petulant of disposition, some
sections of the Press became so rabid and too frenzied to make any
sober, coherent and constructive contributions in the quest for
ways of extricating the nation from the embarrassing incapacitating
quagmire into which it had been mindlessly pushed."[171]

That General Abacha was not offering an olive branch to Abiola
after his declaration worried *TELL*, which expressed its fears for the
man it called "usurper": "To say the country is in a mess would be

a gross understatement. Yet in his broadcast on Sunday, June 12, General Sani Abacha, the leader of the new gang of military usurpers, rather than attempt to provide a soothing balm for the frazzled nerves of Nigerians, threatened fire and brimstone. . . . That was the clearest indication yet that he is very determined to follow the disastrous footsteps of his disgraced predecessor, General Babangida."[172]

Yet, given the forces that the magazine discursively ranged against Abacha, *TELL* reported Abacha as "incommunicado in Aso Rock [suffering] from depression," so much so that his doctor advised him to rest, while "mallams from Kano gave him spiritual solace."[173] In spite of this "solace" for Abacha, *TELL* insisted that "the nation is being unconscionably driven to catastrophe by the Abacha junta and its collaborators."[174] When Abiola reappeared from hiding and was arrested, the magazine still "kept hope alive": "M. K. O. Abiola appeared in public Wednesday last week in Lagos to address a rally, he seemed to have a premonition of his subsequent arrest. So, he made the best use of that opportunity to restate his belief in democracy. Now in Maiduguri jail, the man who emerged victorious in last year's presidential election, tells Nigerians not to give in to coercion, a jackpot mentality."[175] For *TELL*, despite Abiola's arrest, his "dramatic public appearance" as the "elected president" "further strengthened the pro-democracy movement and put the Abacha junta on a final notice that time is up."[176] The fact that this was far from the reality did not dissuade *TELL*.

However, with Abiola behind bars, the narratives focused as much on the need for "hope" as on his "travails." *TELL* reported that "since his arrest, President-elect Abiola has been tossed round the country and treated like a criminal. But the junta is still jittery and getting desperate as it doesn't know what to do with the man whose mandate it has usurped."[177] For *TheNEWS*, "the most ridiculous, the most obnoxious happened in Nigeria when about 500 armed policemen stormed the Ikeja residence of Moshood Abiola, the man who was duly elected President."[178]

For Balarabe Abubukar, writing in *New Nigeria*, the two newsmagazines' president elect was a "tragic hero." With Abiola's self-declaration, Abubakar wrote that Abiola had made himself "an object of political mockery and ridicule . . . tearing through Nigerian's historical pages, bearing ridiculous credentials and without a sense of shame."[179] On the contrary, Abiola was presented by *TheNEWS* as a victim of an "oligarchy which feared Southern presidency": "Abiola won resoundingly the presidential election. . . . Then the criminally cruel happened. The military junta in power annulled the election on flimsy charges, but more because an entrenched Hausa-Fulani oligarchy dreaded the emergence of a Southerner as president of Nigeria. What kind of country is this?"[180]

From this point on, the narratives differentiate between those who stand for June 12, the military government that annulled and sustained the annulment of the election, and the northern "oligarchy." The fragmentation in the nation of aspiration began to manifest more clearly as *TheNEWS* confessed: "It is in this open arid land a veritable wilderness that Nigeria's democratic prospects symbolised in MKO Abiola is being caged and defiled." The newsmagazine then asked, "Would he wallow long in this Siberia of the Abacha junta?"[181] The images of "arid land" and "wilderness," where Abiola is being "defiled," are metaphors for the "caliphal North," which is opposed to Abiola's mandate and consequently defiles him and his mandate—and by a discursive extension, Nigeria.

Not prepared to give up home, *TELL* insisted that a "strange beauty" glows from the "rather weird incarceration" of Abiola as the Abacha junta was confronted with its "tenuous" hold on power while Abiola "still has the heart of the generality of the Nigerian people."[182] *New Nigerian* saw no "strange beauty" in the agitation for "the expired mandate" by those the newspaper dismissed as "CIA-backed"[183] "barbaric . . . new champions of democracy."[184] *TELL* narrated how "the caliphate"—*TheNEWS'* "oligarchy"—moved to "erect more obstacles" against Moshood Abiola: "The stress on the preservation of a cohesive and united North was informed by the desire of the hegemonists . . . to keep power perpetually in the North. . . . The urgency and desperation for power by the hegemonists of the North has found expression in the Abacha regime and two other formidable groups within the core North. . . . All owe allegiance to the preservation of the caliphal North and the status quo; all dread the prospect of a change in power base on account of the sundry privileges they are likely to lose."[185]

Despite this image of a monolithic north, however, *TELL* fragmented this monolith so as to show the lack of consensus in the north: "Far from being a monolith, the North is sundered—the abjectly poor against the extremely rich and the Middle Belt against the far North. Secondly, the clamour for the restoration of Abiola's mandate refuses to abate in spite of designs to foist on Nigerians a collective amnesia."[186] In spite of the "antics" of this oligarchy, "the nation" was still narrated as facing a "grave crisis" that might degenerate into a war. Argued *TELL*: "For a long time, Nigerians thought the dragon of national disintegration had been slain for good. The civil war of 1967–70 was supposed to have taught all the bitter lessons there were to learn—and more. But the on-going crisis bears disturbing evidence that those lessons were either never really learnt, or have been forgotten."[187]

For *The Guardian*, the past was important in understanding the present situation of things in the polity against the backdrop of the process that led to bloodshed in the past. This was a powerful way of "threatening" those in power: "Particularly worrying is the fact that it appears that the hard-liners in the ruling elite appear to have the upper hand right now. The hard-liners are not prepared to talk to the opposition. They want the opposition to surrender, meek as lambs. That, it will be recalled, was the attitude that led to the crisis in the Western Region in 1962. It was also the attitude that culminated in the civil war in 1967. Once again such tendency is on the prowl."[188]

What is equally significant in the narratives at this point is the emphasis on the "historic" injustice of the annulment, the incarceration of Abiola and his trial. This can be related to, and somewhat enables, the "grave crisis" that may lead to "national disintegration." Abiola's condition was narrated as the *most perverse* injustice by a group of soldiers who should themselves be tried for "subversion." *TheNEWS* stated: "Clearly, the illegal regime is stretching its luck too distantly. Every minute that it subjects Abiola to trial, it only indulges in self-ridicule for the junta and its civilian collaborators are actually the persons that should be tried for subverting Nigeria's democratic will."[189]

The "unjust treatment" of Abiola was set against the attempt at a "national re-awakening symbolised by the June 12 election." Taken together with the revolt to validate the election the following June, the month takes on a significance for the "nation," argued *The-NEWS*: "June 12 is now more than a median month in the calendar of a bleak year. As the recent history of our country has since proven, it is the short-hand between anomie and restoration—the metaphor of becoming."[190]

As anomie recovers itself and subdues restoration while the metaphor of becoming evaporates from the nation space, the opposition press narrated the "end of Nigeria's history." "Good-bye Nigeria!" hollered *TELL* on its cover page, as "the world turns its back on the giant."[191] This world that had turned its back on Nigeria, *New Nigeria* argued, only "refused to respect the ability and capacity of Nigerians to choose for themselves."[192] Yet another cover story in *TheNEWS* announced that "Nigeria is doomed" because, as the writer and Nobel Laureate Wole Soyinka said in an interview: "Abacha where he is sitting down and his cohorts may think that there is peace in this country. . . . It is an illusion—a complete illusion of calm. . . . Very soon, the population will be proscribed and only the government would be legal in this country."[193] The narrative in *The Guardian* regarding the state of affairs in Nigeria was even more grim: "For over a year now, it must be remembered, Nigeria has been succumbing to gravity as a result of this crisis. Severe social dislocations continue and the poor vanish into hopeless misery and the middle classes yield to dizzying poverty. The economy becomes more disarticulated by the day, and it continues to contract as investors shy away from the country and capital flight continues. Above all, the bonds of community which in spite of the strains and stresses have held the country together for decades now stands dangerously close to snapping altogether." The paper then called for the triumph of "wisdom" over "idiocy," which was typified by a situation in which "a conservative coalition with a regional core [takes] charge of the state apparatus and is using it to repress the opposition."[194]

Such positions as those represented by *The Guardian*, *TELL*, and *TheNEWS* signified for the *Champion* that the press had abandoned "sobriety and decency, adorning insensitivity, intolerance, divisiveness, recklessness and cold-calculating selfishness as a garb."[195] *New Nigerian* argued along similar lines. The foreign press, which canvassed for the restoration of democracy, were described as "unfair." The paper stated that the BBC, CNN, and the foreign press, in general, "have been less than fair in their reports about the protracted struggle between the so-called June 12 forces which are in a minority and the patriotic majority."[196]

Against the backdrop of the seizure of power by the military, General Oladipo Diya, Abacha's deputy, confessed to *TELL* that he was "ashamed of military rule."[197] Shortly after, the magazine "screamed" on its front cover, "Now, Nigeria Is Finished!"[198] It was a powerful, pithy statement of what the newsmagazine and those who shared its ideological attitude and assumptions felt about the fate of democratic Nigeria.

Conclusion: Democratic Question, Nation-Building, and Nation-Destroying

It can be argued that the press narratives of the crisis provoked by the annulment of the June 12, 1993, presidential election reflect different conceptions of what constitutes "nation-building" in a typical postcolonial state in the context of democratic struggles. These conceptions are related to the idea of "nation-destroying," as each side in the crisis assumed that any conflicting conception (and practices of "nation-building") implied an attempt at nation-destroying—as captured by *TELL*'s headline, "Now, Nigeria Is Finished!"

Walker Connor, in his significant 1972 essay "Nation-Building or Nation-Destroying?," written against the experiences of the 1960s and earlier periods, argues that those concerned with nation-building have tended to ignore the question of ethnic diversity or treat it as superficial and a mere impediment to effective state-integration.[199] G. Gigiano typifies this, defining nation-building as "the integration of communally diverse and/or territorially discreet units into the institutional framework of a single state and the concomitant transfer of a sense of common political identity and loyalty to the symbolic community defined by the founding ideology of such a state."[200]

However, Connor warns that "the problem of ethnic diversity is far too ubiquitous to be ignored by the serious scholar of "nation-building," adding that loyalty to the ethnic group and loyalty to the state "are not naturally harmonious," particularly with the elevation of the idea of self-determination to "the status of self-evident truth." When used correctly and even when misapplied, the idea of self-determination has become a doctrine that "makes ethnicity the ultimate measure of political legitimacy, by holding any self-differentiating people, simply because it *is* a people, [as having] the right, should it desire, to rule itself." This doctrine has been used not only in Africa and elsewhere to question political borders, as Connor argues, but also as a strong and viable democratic idea—and ideal—around which disaffection by any ethnic or ethno-regional group can be organized, as evident in the Nigerian case. In a postcolonial state such as Nigeria, which contains a number of nations—which Connor describes as "a self-differentiating ethnic group . . . [that is, one having] a popularly held awareness or belief that [the] group is unique in a most vital sense"—the transfer of primary allegiance from these nations (Hausa, Fulani, Igbo, Ijaw, Ogoni, Yoruba, etc.) to the state (Nigeria), which is considered a sine qua non of successful integration, argues Connor, should be approached as "nation-destroying" rather than "nation-building."[201]

Indeed, African polities have "a historical legacy of nation-building in [their] discourse, theory and praxis."[202] This is as true of the authoritarian era as it is of the democratic era, in what is touted as the search for "sustainable democracy and economic growth." However, Johan Degenaar has warned that "the nation part of nation-building fits neatly into state-nation discourse" because instead of "a nation which acquires statehood (organically) we are introduced to a concept of nation which is constructed (mechanically) by the state."[203] He cites Tamarkin, who criticizes the Jacobin nature of the state-nation as one that "assumes that Leviathan (the state) can, and is morally entitled to forge a national identity out of diverse ethnic groups."[204]

However, Degenaar argues for the Habermasian approach, which emphasizes the civic nation as a "nation of citizens" that does not derive its identity from some common ethnic and cultural properties, but rather from the praxis of citizens who actively exercise their civil rights"—such as through elections, as experienced during the June 12, 1993, election in Nigeria.[205] Since this fits well into the idea of a democratic society, Degenaar suggests that we should drop the prevailing "romantic exercise of nation-building," which is "antagonistic towards ethnicity, pluralism, regionalism, federalism—notions that play an important role in contemporary political theory and practice" in Africa, and focus on "the difficult task of democracy creation."[206]

As the narratives concerning the June 12 elections show, however, the task of democratic creation is indeed a daunting one where there is an absence of common notions of "democratic culture," which constitutes the basis for the creation of a civic nation. In the attempts to represent the nation (grand nation) within the context of a democratic debate on the future of Nigeria, the different narratives in this chapter show how "nation-building" can parallel "nation-destroying."

The narratives on the democratic crisis are significantly similar to the narratives analyzed in earlier chapters. They reflect the essential core of issues pertaining to the construction of a grand nation: issues that have to do with the democratic ethos, rule of law, justice, equity, and fairness. These issues resonate through the other cases examined earlier—and those examined in subsequent chapters. After the annulment, while reflecting issues of democracy, the rule of law, justice, equity, etc., the narratives also emphasized the possible end of the Nigerian union, given the (perceived) abandonment of the virtues and values of a democratic culture, including justice, equity, and the rule of law. Why is this so? Given the fact that the narration of the reinvention of Nigeria is predicated on the construction of a "grand nation" that abandons the authoritarian and nonegalitarian past in search of a democratic future, the annulment and the sustenance of the same represented the termination of the possibility of the emergence of a grand nation in Nigeria. The attempt to "keep a date with history" was consequently narrated as leading to the "end of history" for Nigeria. But evidently—and despite the "collapse thesis" evident in these narratives—Nigeria survived, but, despite this, questions of democracy, nation-building, and nation-destroying remain contentious.

7

The "Fought" Republic

The Press, Ethno-Religious Conflicts, and Democratic Ethos

Chapter 6 considered the relationship between identity politics and democracy in Africa and the challenge of reconciling democratic freedom with the limitations and opportunities of ethnic or eth-nonationalist (and also faith-based) claims. This chapter analyzes democratic and identitarian narratives reflecting antagonistic and competing claims within the Nigerian national space and the dangers that these represent for national democratic life in Nigeria.

Nigeria's Fourth Republic, which commenced on May 29, 1999, almost six years after the Third Republic was aborted, provided yet another opportunity for ethno-regional and religious identities to engage in simultaneous contests for supremacy or accommodation within a democratic context. A key criticism of the press in Nigeria is that it is overtly "sectional"—as demonstrated in the previous chapters—both in its coverage of events and its canvassing of perspectives.[1] For instance, although noting the critical role of the press in sustaining democracy in Nigeria, Sam Oyovbaire, the former information minister, argues that the press "could do well only if its mindset or worldview was much more robust and comprehensive than as presently designed by history." He adds that the press "should provide accommodation for the complex and pluralistic corporate Nigerian society."[2] Odia Ofeimun, poet, journalist, and political scientist, concedes that the press "has not been able to avoid a parochial edge to its reports and comments," despite that it has sometimes "displayed a certain readiness to outgrow sub-national considerations, especially in matters of political integrity and fiscal probity."[3]

The crisis precipitated by the annulment of the June 12, 1993, presidential election, which had consumed two governments—Babangida's and the Interim National Government headed by Ernest Shonekan (August 27–November 17, 1993)—also consumed the Abacha regime, its leader, General Sani Abacha, and the "symbol of June 12," Moshood Abiola, who both died in Abuja on June 8, 1998, and July 7, 1998, respectively. Whereas Abacha's death was a welcome relief to many, given the unprecedented scale of arrest, detention, execution, and assassination of dissenting figures during his rule, Abiola's death was seen by a significant section of the country as putting "Nigeria on the cross,"[4] with the attendant implications for the feared disintegration of the country. However, the death of the General Abacha and Chief Abiola could be viewed as the termination of a national debacle with potential opportunities for a new, though not necessarily fresh, beginning for a much troubled polity.[5]

A high-level negotiation that included UN Secretary-General Kofi Annan, Commonwealth Secretary General Emeka Anyaoku, and United States envoys had attempted to persuade Abiola to renounce his "mandate," which he declined before he gave up the ghost after drinking tea reportedly prepared by a member of the US delegation. An international body of medical experts later certified that Abiola died of "natural causes"—a heart attack. The new helmsman, General Abdulsalami Abubakar, Abacha's chief of defense staff, announced the resolve of his regime to move Nigeria beyond the logjam occasioned by the annulment. He released those jailed by the Abacha regime for plotting against the regime in what was dubbed the "Gwadabe coup plot," particularly the former head of state, General Olusegun Obasanjo. He also released several activists and journalists jailed by the late dictator and beckoned the press to a new lease on life in freedom. The regime then instituted a new transition program, a very short one, which was to culminate in the swearing into office of democratically elected officials by May 29, 1999.

Three political parties were registered by the regime: the People's Democratic Party (PDP), the All People's Party (APP), and the Alliance for Democracy (AD). The incarceration and eventual death of Abiola and the many casualties that the Yoruba suffered in terms of imprisonment, assassination, and exile under General Sani Abacha's murderous autocracy only served to present the other sections of the country with what could pass for a political fait accompli in the attempt to reconstitute democratic rule in 1999. The argument was stark, even if many were persuaded: the Yoruba needed to be appeased. In what Sani Kotangora described as "blackmail," northern politicians were persuaded not to run for the presidency so as not to "prove" the accusations of the northerner elites' "resolve" at perpetual headship of the Nigerian state. Apart from Alex Ekwueme, an Igbo, who made a serious run for the highest office, nobody from other ethnic nationalities seriously contested for the presidency. The PDP presented the former head of state, General Olusegun Obasanjo, whereas the APP-AD alliance presented Olu Falae, another Yoruba.

Obasanjo was the choice of core conservative elements in the north who previously had done business with him when he was in power and were particularly happy with the fact that he allowed his Fulani deputy, Yar'Adua, to run the government, while he also opposed the larger interests of his Yoruba compatriots, particularly Awolowo and later Abiola. As expected, Obasanjo did not get any significant support from the Yoruba West, apart from the few Yoruba politicians eager for national spoils and who were convinced that, as the "anointed" of the north and the generals in power, he would win the elections.

Despite the opposition to Obasanjo, the Yoruba West welcomed the transfer of power and expected a new lease on life for Nigeria, while still demanding a national conference. Rumors of Obasanjo's death before he was sworn in, however, raised his rating among his people, who suspected another "grand plan" by the core north to subvert the transfer of power. But Obasanjo's actions in the first few months in power endeared him to the Yoruba, who saw in him the potential for redressing the "vice hold" of the north on power.

The narratives that follow react to and contest this state of affairs as they serve the interests of the different nations within the Nigerian union. The past re-creates itself in new ways in the attempt by the newspapers and newsmagazines to address emergent configurations and the struggle for the soul of the Nigerian grand nation. Four newspapers and one newsmagazine are analyzed: *The Guardian* (the voice of southern minorities and, to some extent, the Yoruba West), the *Post Express* (the voice of the Igbo East), *TELL* newsmagazine (largely representing the Yoruba and the minorities), and *New Nigerian* and *Weekly Trust* (the voices of the Hausa-Fulani north). The chapter covers the first year of the new democratic government.

A New Beginning or an Old Wrath?

That the narratives of this era were as concerned with new situations and events as much as they constituted a continuation of earlier, ongoing narratives is key to understanding the enactment of power in them. The narratives can be fitted or inserted into a continuum that can at best be only new manifestations of an old wrath. Explaining the synthetic character of narratives, Louis O. Mink asserts, requires "colligation" that, as W. H. Walsh argues, involves the explanation of an event by "tracing its intrinsic relations to other events and locating it in its historical context."[6] The following narratives are constructions and elaborations of collective burdens, struggles, and destinies conditioned, as Bennett and Edelman argue, by the incentive of the privileged to justify their advantages and augment them and the need of the deprived to rationalize their disadvantages or struggle against them.[7]

In the few weeks preceding the handover of power by the "northern oligarchy" to the south in May 1999, attempts were made to provide a background to what some regarded as "national arrival." For Col. Tony Iyiam, one of the brains behind the April 22, 1990 (Orkar) coup, the important background to this is the coup that "threw a monkey's wrench into the wheel of the ruling cabal's evil work of perpetuating themselves in power forever. It sounded alarm bells on the contingency of impoverishment, brutalisation, murder and other atrocities that have been visited on Nigeria by the ascendancy of men like Badamasi Babangida, Sani Abacha and Ishaya Bamaiyi." According to Iyiam, on this "historic day"—that is, on the day of the abortive 1990 coup—Radio Nigeria, which "until then [was] permanently used by the cabal for propaganda purposes," was used by "forces of liberation . . . to expose the intensified marginalisation of the Igbo, the Yoruba, and the Southern and Northern minorities. This aroused Nigerians from their political stupor and underlined the urgent necessity to address the 'National Question' or more appropriately, to address the 'union of the countries nationalities question.'"[8]

During the brief hours in which the coup plotters held sway, continued Iyiam, Nigerians were told that the "sadistic, drug-baronish and homosexual inclined" regime of General Ibrahim Babangida had been terminated while the "dominating states" of Sokoto, Kano, Katsina, Bauchi, and Borno were excised from Nigeria by the coup plotters on behalf of the "oppressed and dominated" people of the south and middle-belt. Prior to this coup, Col. Nyiam had argued that "the concept of 'nation' was confused with that of 'country.'" The critical issues that faced Nigeria since independence therefore "still require[ed] solutions": "What are the choices before us on this [National Question] topic? In trying to posit options, it is imperative to bear a fundamental fact in mind. As of today, Nigeria is not a nation. It is a country of various nations. . . . The problem with our own entity is that we have so signally failed to imbibe a cardinal principle of fruitful co-existence, which is equity."[9] This position reflects my argument that at the core of these narratives is what can be discarded as "past continuous." As the debate on the Sharia question in the new constitution also showed, the future of Nigeria was framed in the context of her past, as *TELL* reported: "Christian Northern members of the [Provisional Ruling] Council, including those from the Middle Belt, were especially embittered by what they perceived as an attempt to remake the whole of the old North in the image of the Caliphate. They argued that the so-called North was no longer a geographic and political monolith, and that it was high time the cultural and particularly the religious diversity of the region was recognised and accepted as a reality. The fierceness of the opposition to the whole Sharia gambit has forced the opponents to retreat for now."[10]

On the eve of the return of democratic rule, the *Post Express*, as the voice of the Igbo East, was more concerned with the replacement of northern hegemony by Yoruba hegemony as the "allocation of ministerial and parastatals posts in the Fourth Republic [stirs] up a whirlwind of protests among certain political blocs in the country." According to the *Express*: "Going by the recommendations of the General Olusegun Obasanjo Transition Committee, the South-West will enjoy monopoly of the nation's communication sector. . . . Already, the proposal has drawn the wrath of some technocrats from both the Northern and South Eastern parts of the country who alleged a grand design to entrust a sector as sensitive as communications to a particular zone."[11]

Such issues and fears formed the immediate background to the restoration of democratic rule with the landmark installation of the first democratically elected president from the south. How this power shift related to the possibilities of national renewal dominated discourses in the press. Yet these discourses are fed by the southern newspapers into the need for restructuring as the basis of national renewal. After reviewing the political history of Nigeria, particularly the immediate past, *TELL* noted that "an arguably wiser nation, obviously deferring to the political imperatives of June 12, zoned the presidency to Abiola's South-West." For *TELL*, what constituted the greatest challenge of the new democratic arrangement remained the consolidation of this "wisdom" displayed by "we as a nation": "Given political courage and a good dose of statesmanship, the agenda should be simple. It lies in restructuring the Nigerian state and giving effect to a constitution that expressly makes a provision for this. This is one thing we as a nation, should not fear to do."[12]

The *Express* did not agree on the need for restructuring. Rather, the paper argued that what was most crucial at the moment was the celebration of Nigeria's survival "as a nation" in spite of the storm that had raged against the corporate existence of Nigeria in recent years: "The achievement of national survival ought indeed to be priced over other gains. This is a moment in world history when the future of large nation-states, especially federation, is being actively re-examined and even challenged in brutal conflicts. . . . In most of these cases, the continuation of nation-states that the world had come to take for granted can no longer be guaranteed."[13]

It mattered less to the *Express* in what concrete ways hope could be reinvented as national survival was celebrated. But *TELL* disagreed vehemently with this line of thinking because, since the new democratic era constituted Nigeria's "last chance" to survive as a nation, there was the need for a concrete reinvention of Nigeria beyond hope. The newsmagazine explained the rationale: "Why restructure the country? At the centre of the 'Nigerian problem' may well be the manner of the coming together of the Nigeria[n] nation, a problem which [the] late Ahmadu Bello, the first and only premier of Northern Nigeria, called 'the mistake of 1914.' Hugh Clifford . . . would, in 1922, sum up this negative aspect of the young Nigerian nation. It is 'a collection of independent native states, separated from one another . . . by great distance, by differences of history and traditions and by ethnological, racial, tribal, political, social and religious barriers.'"[14]

How has this reality played out? *TELL* asserted: "Since independence, two negative, even centrifugal forces have assailed the young republic with the devastating effect of a typhoon. One is the quest for regional, if not ethnic, hegemony over the rest of the country. The Hausa-Fulani's assertion of a divide and rule has proved unfortunate, throwing the nation into crisis. This was to lead to the emergence of the second force, namely the entry of the military in politics. . . . It did not help matters at all, again over time, that the military became absolutely controlled by the North." The "twin evil" of Hausa-Fulani domination and military rule—acting in concert and sourced from the same location, as *TELL* would have it—made the emergence of a Nigerian nation impossible. The magazine concluded: "Nothing could have been so damaging of national unity and a thriving federation. Under it [the twin evil] the south groaned and the minorities became the glorified slaves of the house that Lugard built."[15]

The strategy of expurgation of the other is used to full effect by the magazine as it identified and constructed an enemy within: the Hausa-Fulani soldiers who were portrayed as harmful, even evil, and as threats to national unity, therefore deserving of resistance and expurgation. Conversely, this also constitutes a strategy of unification, as the other ethnic nationalities are invariably summoned to a united front against the twin evils. *TELL* narratives explained Nigeria's inglorious past using the same prism as did the leaders of the abortive Orkar coup, as presented by Col. Nyiam.

Even where these twin evils constituted part of the "ignominious history" of Nigeria, the *Express* insisted that surviving against all the crises compelled Nigerians to celebrate the present and future and not mourn the past: "It is a tribute to . . . Nigerians in their own country that Nigeria weathered the storm of its recent ignominious history to endure in unity. . . . Very few nations have a second chance of re-inventing themselves. Nigeria is one. In this regard, this can indeed be said to be Nigeria's finest hour."[16]

Between Nigeria's "finest hour" (*Express*) and her "last chance" (*TELL*), the newspapers and newsmagazine disagree on how the present is to be apprehended in the context of the past and how the future should be faced: with hope or with fear? For *TELL*, "'The Mistake of 1914' could surely be corrected by restructuring. . . . Nations that choose the path of foolhardiness in resolving the . . . issues of their co-existence present the world frightening spectacles of self-implosion." Even though the power shift was a significant step, *TELL* argued, avoidance of other subsequent and crucial steps toward restructuring Nigeria could only be followed by the end of the history of the Nigerian union: "No section of the country need fear restructuring because it is not an order that be foisted on anyone. Rather, it should be the sensible outcome of a sovereign national conference of all Nigerian people at which, in freedom, a mutual consensus on a workable basis of a united Nigeria can be reached. . . . [Obasanjo] satisfies, though arguably, the requirement of power shifting to the South . . . [but] to obey this imperative in the breach could throw the Nigerian ship of state against the load-stone rock. That may well prove Nigeria's last chance."[17]

Obasanjo's ascendancy did not constitute an unqualified power shift given the fact that he was the choice of that same power bastion (Hausa-Fulani, military formation) accused by *TELL* of throwing Nigeria into crisis. But as events unfolded, this same Obasanjo became the unqualified symbol of a power shift and national reawakening for *TELL*. The magazine narrated the new state of affairs thus: "In a departure from what had become the norm, he [Obasanjo] boldly made key appointments into the government that not only stress competence and seniority but reflect the true principle of federal character. . . . For the first time since the Second Republic [1979–83], Nigeria's minority ethnic groups are being made to feel they are really part of the country and not just adjuncts of the major three. But in spite of this altruism of all he has done as president, Obasanjo is perceived by some leaders of a section of the country, to be deliberately stepping on their toes."[18]

These isolatable and isolated leaders of a section of a diverse country were accused by *TELL* of "incompetence," since the emphasis of the system against which they were complaining was "competence and seniority." This is a fine example of metonymy. The magazine then zeroed in on this section of the country: "In short, the North is grumbling, and this is threatening to become a dangerous rumble. And the only way those who believe they have first claim on political power in Nigeria settle their grievances is through a coup d'etat."[19]

From "grumbling," which conveys a negative image of an undue complaint, to a "dangerous rumble" of a coup d'état, *TELL* attempted to anticipate the perception of "the north." The north, through the strategy of synecdoche, was conflated with its part, the Hausa-Fulani (core) north, which *TELL* had earlier isolated from the rest of the north and the rest of the country. By predicting that this "north" would resort to a coup d'état as it had done in the past, since the north assumed primacy in political relations, the magazine subverted the interests of the north and nourished those of the south, which was represented as "groaning" under the "yoke" of the "conspiratorial combine" of Hausa-Fulani oligarchy and military rule.

Even the *Express*, which had earlier ignored the realities and frailties of the Nigerian union in ushering in a new dawn shortly afterward, noted—in the context of the Kafanchan communal clashes—that "Nigerians have not yet learnt the art of living together in peace." In what appeared to be a return to *TELL*'s earlier position, which it had rejected, the *Express* linked the "unpopular overlordship of Islamically imposed emirs" on non-Muslim communities in the north to the questioning of the "continued imposition of such rulers" in other parts of the country, and called for the convocation of a national conference in the future through which a "peaceful dismantling" of "alien rulership structure" could take place. "Ignoring these potential fires," concluded the *Express*, would be tantamount to stroking the embers of a future conflagration that threatened (Nigeria's) corporate integration.[20] *The Guardian* agreed that issues such as the ones that provoked the Kafanchan communal clash had to do with "the fundamentals of identity and equity in a plural ethnic setting." The paper argued against "the dimension of a nationality struggle for identity and self-determination" and asserted: "Every [ethnic] group deserves to have due recognition and political space in society. The traditional institutions of one group should not be imposed on others. Doing so will violate the principle of unity in diversity."[21]

For *TELL*, all of this feeds into the power matrix in the country, particularly because "for the first time in Nigeria's history as an independent nation, the (Northern) oligarchy saw that power has effectively eluded them." The magazine added, "They [northern oligarchy] have now been relegated to the background. . . . They regretted [their] decision . . . to concede power to the South." In resolving to "reclaim power at all cost," this "core North" (also called "northern oligarchy"), according to the magazine, decided to "sack" the Obasanjo government, which constituted for the north a "miscalculation." But the magazine argued that even in this "miscalculation" (Obasanjo's emergency as president), the "oligarchy" did not have a choice. Why? "Following the death of [Basorun Moshood Abiola] . . . the far North had grudgingly conceded that power would, out of sheer necessity and self-preservation of the northern establishment itself, have to shift to the South. But power shift, as conceived and understood by the North, was electing a Southern president they can do business with. Which is to say a person they could use to maintain the status quo and their stranglehold on power. That is, arrange a situation where they would still control all the critical and strategic levels of power without necessarily and outwardly being in charge."[22]

TELL interpreted the "signals" from the core north through the strategy of elaboration. Using phrases such as "which is" and "that is," the magazine elaborated the strategies for the acquisition of power by the north and subverts them through disclosure and by simultaneously enacting the discourse of power that served its own location in the spectrum of the relations of domination within the grand narrative.

As stated earlier, expurgation of the other as a strategy for the mobilization of meaning in the service of power has its opposite and its corollary in unification. The *Weekly Trust* returned the salvo to *TELL* and other newsmagazines and newspapers by inverting the logic. The *Trust*, in turn, isolated and expurgated the Yoruba other, unifying the other ethnic nationalities against the Yoruba and also defending "northern unity" against attempts by the southern press to divide northern groups. First, it unified all other ethnic groups against the Yoruba, as *TELL* had done against the Hausa-Fulani. The *Trust* presented the case of the rest of the country against a section of the country (southwest): "We know that the average Yoruba man and the leaders of the tribe mostly support or sympathise with OPC [Oodu'a People's Congress] and may even be secretly delighted at their heroics. The main OPC demand is Yoruba autonomy via a Sovereign National Conference. Killing people from other ethnic groups may be their method of precipitating a crisis that may lead this autonomy. Despite having one of their own [President Obasanjo] in Aso Rock, most Yoruba seem to share this desire for autonomy." From the "average Yoruba" to "most Yoruba," the *Trust* collected the whole "tribe" [a pejorative term in public discourse in Nigeria and elsewhere] in an "inordinate" pack, that is, a pack of people who are yet to be satisfied despite the fact that they have the presidency. Other ethnic groups were consequently invited to stop the Yoruba and rescue themselves: "Other regions and ethnic groups must sooner, rather than later confront this Yoruba demand and articulate their own negotiating position. As the government recognises, the constitution of Nigeria must be negotiated and each group must form and forcefully state its own position."[23] At any rate, as Aliyu Tilde, a *Trust* columnist argued, a "Yoruba nation" never existed historically and it was only a "utopia" and the "anti-thesis of Yoruba history" to talk about one: "Nothing like that ever existed in their history. While other ethnic groups could boast of having a legacy of nationhood and contribution to the advancement of nationhood this particular one [Yoruba] left only that of destruction."[24]

In articulating this allusion to the Oyo Empire, whose implosion led to a civil war in most of what constituted the Yoruba country in the precolonial era, Tilde elided the fact that the unprecedented violence of the Fulani jihad, which affected most what became the north, was part of what produced what he described as the "legacy of destruction" in the northern parts of the old Yoruba empire. It can be argued that Tilde's reference to "regions" essentially points to the idea of "one north," whereas the others are described as "ethnic groups" who must confront the Yoruba. It will also ordinarily be expected that Tilde's call for a "renegotiation" of "the constitution" by each group "forcefully" could be reconciled with similar demands by *TELL*, *The Guardian*, and the *Express*, but the reference to "the constitution" as opposed to "the [Nigerian] nation" or "the [Nigerian] state" marks the difference in perspectives. It is the constitution that Tilde wants Nigeria to renegotiate, not the state.

That the newspapers and magazines representing the broad north and south differed in their position on unity and fractionalization in the north is evident in the contradictory narratives in *TELL* and the *Trust*. The *Trust* rationalized the relations among northern ethnic groups and constructed a "chain of reasons which seeks to defend or justify the social and political relations making them worthy of being defended." It also rationalized the relations as if they exist in a "timeless and cherished" tradition, giving "northerners" a "sense of belonging to a comity and to a history that transcends the experience of conflict, difference, and division," while also glossing over the existing relations of domination in that north. On the other hand, TELL fragmented this north and, through the strategy of differentiation, emphasized "the distinctions, differences and divisions" between the groups in the north, which "disunited" them. Argued *TELL*: "Blinded by the inordinate ambition to continue to monopolise power, the (Hausa-Fulani) hegemonists are said to be alarmed that the Middle-Belt is being gradually snatched away from them. . . . Messages were sent to emirs that they should advocate their subjects on the dangers facing the 'Northern oligarchy' that is 'Southern domination.' . . . In particular, people of the Middle-Belt cannot see the sense in this . . . marginalization. . . . In spite of the fact that three of the four service chiefs are from the North[,] . . . the mafia claimed that they are not from the core North . . . that three of them are Christians. . . . Members of the mafia suddenly realized that Kano State is now the Middle-Belt. This is against their claim in the past that there is a monolithic North."[25]

The *Trust* saw this kind of narrative as an attempt to fragment the north and so rendered a counternarrative: "As at independence . . . there were 12 . . . provinces in the North. These provinces later became the 19 Northern states and Abuja Federal Capital Territory which are now referred to as 'Northern' part of the country by the Southern and (curiously by some Northern) media to deny them their cherished Northern identity and so divide them against each other to rule and dominate them." With their emphasis on the middle-belt and the Christian north, the *Trust* submits, the north's "detractors seemed to have succeeded in fragmenting the North into leadership groups," adding, "the stage is set for the domination of the North."[26]

The weekly, however, reminds northerners about how the core northern political elite, including Tafawa Balewa, Nigeria's late prime minister, Ahmadu Bello, the north's late premier, and Muhammadu Ribadu, the late federal defense minister, "battled their southern counterparts and invariably won." "When crucial issues such as date for Nigerian independence, structure of the country, etc. came up for discussion at the central legislative council or constitutional conference, the so-called illiterate backward Northerners outwitted the so-called university educated Southerners. For example, the North refused to be intimidated into accepting 1956 as the date for Nigerian independence but opted for a date 'as soon as practicable' and this saved the North from Southern domination which independence in 1956 would have entailed."[27]

The past, for the weekly, formed a basis on which the needs and opportunities of "northern solidarity" was negotiated. However, a northern "radical" and aide of President Obasanjo told *TELL* that this type of thinking, epitomized and glorified by the *Trust*, would sink Nigeria. Stated the president's aide, Ahmadu Abubakar: "Unless there is a fundamental shift in political thinking and a serious about turn by the North, the future of Nigeria cannot be guaranteed. Right now, it is the North that is posing a threat to the continued existence of Nigeria."[28]

Democracy and the Wrath of Ages

Against the backdrop of Ahmadu Abubakar's fears about the continued existence of Nigeria, barely six months after the return of democratic rule, discourses about the breakup or disintegration of Nigeria returned to the front pages as the Nobel Laureate Wole Soyinka warned in *TELL* that "if within a year, there is no rethinking in the whole process of governance, this country stands the risk of break-up."[29] Col. Abubakar Umar, a critical retired soldier from the north, disclosed to *TELL* that "if for any reason Obasanjo loses his life today in any military coup, I think that will be the end of Nigeria."[30] And Abubukar Umar asked those who doubted him: "If other countries have broken up, why do you think Nigeria will not break up[?]"[31] Voices such as these from the north who were represented in the southern narratives of power, *TELL* reported, were targets of attacks from fellow northerners who perceive them as "enemies of the [northern] cause."[32]

Whereas Abubakar in *TELL* accused the north, which "went berserk in terms of appropriation of government machinery for itself," of being responsible for the possible breakup of Nigeria, Adamu A. Mohammed in the *Trust* affirmed that it was the north that had sacrificed too much "for the corporate existence of Nigeria": "While other regions in the nation are busy adjusting their minds to the inevitable (i.e., of the balkanization of the country)[,] trying to position their people so that they won't be caught unaware, where [here] in the north all you hear or see the treachery of our elders. The North has sacrificed too much for the corporate existence of this country. We fought a 30-months civil war just to keep the nation . . . it is now evidently clear that the war fought in the first instance (a war fought out of patriotism) was a mistake. We should have asked the Biafran Republic to go, and even any other entity to have backed-out by that time." Like the "mistake of 1914," this "mistake of 1967," the writer argued, has again attracted insults to the North: "Now, look at how the other regions have constantly been abusing our efforts. They say it in point blank that the north is the only region preventing the much talked about conference of the millennium [Sovereign National Conference]. They are of the belief that we are afraid of the SNC because we have been enjoying almost all wealth at the expense of the other regions."[33]

The first one hundred days of the Obasanjo administration provides another context for evaluating the narratives of power by the different groups. When Obasanjo declared that he had been fair to all, the *Express* challenged his "concept of fairness." Even though his one hundred days had convinced Nigerians of his goodwill and his courage, the paper argued, "they have not been backed up" with the kind of "technical competence and such that produces quality public policies." More important, his "idealism is still stained with ethnicity,"[34] which the paper fails to explain here but had elaborated on earlier: "The background to this is the charge of marginalization, which various segments of the nation's population have levelled against the president. Ethnic groups, geopolitical zones, and even regional blocks [*sic*] have accused the president of being unfair to them in his appointment. What concept of fairness led the president to concentrate his security appointments . . . on the South-West zone? What fairness dictated that the military top brass come mainly from the North Central?"[35]

The *Express* ignored the question over the religious factor in the appointment of service chiefs. Three of the four were Christians, the same as most people from the Igbo East represented by the paper. As a paper biased in favor of Christianity, this factor was not considered expedient to raise. *The Guardian* agreed largely with the *Express* on political marginalization: "On the political front, the President will need to show much more greater sensitivity to concerns about marginalisation expressed by large sections of the country by adopting, and being seen to adopt a more equitable basis of power distribution among the constituent zones and states of the country. The criticism from some quarters that the President's public appointments have so far not properly reflected genuine national spread and equity in the allocation of prime portfolios should not be treated with levity. The president must take steps to redress this anomaly."[36]

In the articulation of what the *Express* called "the Igbos travails in Nigeria," which resulted in their being "hated, battered and marginalised [while seeking] an equitable share of the national cake,"[37] *TELL* stateed that the Igbo leaders presented a "feeble voice."[38]

Consequently, for *TELL*, Obasanjo's one hundred days had been full of "achievement," safe for the cry of marginalization by northern conservatives: "To many Nigerians, those [one hundred] days have been full of landmark achievement. However, some of the steps had ruffled feathers especially among the group of Northern conservatives usually referred to as the mafia." But why was the Mafia "crying" marginalization? *TELL* answered: "First, the Northern conservatives were the ones who wooed Obasanjo into joining the presidential train. He was their anointed candidate. Thus, when he became president, they expected him to pay back his IOUs."[39]

The "feeble voice" of the third leg of the Nigerian tripod—the Igbo—whose military officers were treated "at best as outsiders,"[40] attracted contempt from the *Trust*, which accused the Igbo of joining the "bandwagon" of "the Patriots," a group of eminent Nigerians canvassing for "true federalism"—a campaign the *Trust* dismissed as largely a Yoruba affair: "The four or so Igbo members jumped into the bandwagon of the 'Patriots' in order not to be left out of the corridor of power that now rules Nigeria. It was the same scenario in 1959, 1964, 1983 when Igbos played second fiddle roles to Northerners in order to secure crumbs from the master's table! Such shameful roles place the Igbos where they are today—[a] marginalised group." The patriots' proposal to reorganize Nigeria's federalism toward rectifying the imbalances that favor the north, the *Trust* argued, will only be a "prelude to the annulment of 1914 amalgamation."[41]

The Igbo did not take lightly such accusations of subservience as rendered in the *Trust*. As a letter to the editor from an Igbo published in *The Guardian* exemplifies, this accusation only fed into the overall "maltreatment" of the Igbo in Nigeria: "Even though the Igbo have suffered all manner of bastardisation, deprivation, mistrust and insult because they had the courage to defend their land and say 'No' to slavery, injustice and mass slaughter; the Igbo will rise again as a people. Someday, Ndi Igbo will be accepted, trusted and allowed to participate fully in the leadership of our country."[42]

Pressing Religious Conflict: Sharia and Secularism

The challenge to (Western) modernity and "modernist projects"—such as liberal democracy and secularism—which Islam represents, has acquired a central place in both public and academic discourse in the last two decades. The last quarter of the twentieth century produced what Manuel Castells describes as a "widespread surge of powerful expressions of collective identity that challenge globalization and cosmopolitanism on behalf of cultural singularity and people's control over their lives and environment." These challenges include "a whole array of reactive movements that build trenches of resistance on behalf of God, nation, ethnicity, family, locality" and other such "fundamental categories of millennial existence."[43]

In the literature on the developing world, the politicization, or the political instrumentalization, of religion has become part of received wisdom. In this context, Levine has argued that such instrumentalization is conditioned by the socially pervasive character of religion, which, in the developing world, makes it "a perennial source of political action and meaning."[44] This holds true for the specific case of Nigeria, where religion "has become more deeply entwined with the tissue of everyday life"[45] in the democratic era, in a way that is overdetermined by the patterns of domination in culture, politics, and economy.[46] The history of the conflict over the Sharia legal code in Nigeria and the debate surrounding it is already well documented in the literature.[47] The Sharia issue snowballed into high-tension controversy in October 1999 when the Zamfara state government inaugurated the adoption of the Islamic legal code, extending it from personal law to criminal law. Many, particularly Christians and secularists, believed the act to be in defiance of the constitution and the federal government.

The attempt to introduce Sharia law in the important state of Kaduna, where the largely Muslim Hausa-Fulani majority group had been having a running battle with Christian minority ethnic-groups, led to violent clashes that claimed several lives, with reprisal violence in other parts of the country. *TheNEWS* headlined the mutual "slaughter" among Muslims and Christians "The Road to Lebanon."[48]

The debate on secularism was linked with the "national question" and democracy, and therefore the debate about secularism was also a debate about the organizing principles of political and ethnic relations in Nigeria; it was a fight for the public space as a space of access to political power and the state. However, most of the scholarly works in Nigeria on the Sharia issue in particular and religion in general hardly pay full attention to the role of the media in igniting, exacerbating, and amplifying political-religious crises.[49] Given the characteristic "media warfare" inherent in the crisis, which drove opposing sides to the "defensive trenches,"[50] it is important to analyze media narratives of the crisis as it relates to the important quest for the control of the state, power, democracy, and secularism in Africa's biggest democracy.

The introduction of the Sharia legal code for the administration of criminal justice first in the northwestern state of Zamfara and later in the majority of northern states dominated by Muslims provoked narratives of fragmentation. The Sharia debate, however, preceded this era. It had been an issue since the struggle for independence. It arose again, fiercely, in the debates leading to the restoration of democratic rule in the Second and Third Republics. It had been easier to resolve in these two periods because soldiers were in power and could force a settlement on the political class. It was resolved that the Sharia legal system could be used for the administration of civil law in the northern states. Therefore, the introduction of the Sharia legal code for both criminal and civil justice in the Fourth Republic represented a major departure from the earlier trend and provoked a serious crisis, particularly in Christians who had always feared a "planned Islamisation" of Nigeria and the use of religion by the core north for the retention of power.

Before the military handed over power to civilians in 1999, there was a storm in the Provisional Ruling Council (PRC) over the Sharia issue. As *TELL* reported: "The pro-Sharia group wanted a provisional amendment that would fundamentally alter the status quo. The 1979 constitution only provides for states that so desire to set up a Sharia court of appeal. . . . The proposed amendment would make it mandatory for all states to set up Sharia courts."[51] The PRC eventually decided that the status quo should remain. But when the Zamfara state government under Sani Ahmed Yerima moved toward changing the status quo, debates on the implications for national unity were raised. The Zamfara state's action, according to *TELL*, constituted planting "a political bomb which may soon set the nation on fire unless care is taken."[52] The magazine editorialized: "Tick-tack! A time bomb, code named 'Sharia,' is ticking away in Zamfara State. The rest of the country is holding its breadth because its eventual explosion may shatter the dreams and aspirations of the neo-nationalists who fought with sweat and blood to have a refurbished Nigeria after the wear and tear of successive military dictatorships."[53] *The Guardian* agreed largely with this reading, emphasizing that the Sharia matter constituted a threat to democracy. The paper stated that "in a rather unfortunate twist of familiar reality, it appears the Sharia system is being turned into a factor with a potential to unleash centrifugal religious tension in our new born and still fragile democratic polity."[54] The *Express* described the Sharia law as "treasonable legislation" and the governor and the State Assembly members who approved the bill as "law breakers" who should be arrested and charged for "treason," adding that "of greater concern is that these obviously retrogressive steps are being taken in Nigeria on the eve of the 21st century."[55] In this narrative, to use Najmabadi's words, "Islam [is] consolidated with terms such as tradition and retrogression, marked as an impediment to modernity," and reproduced as "exclusive of secularism, democracy and feminism, [and] as a pollutant of these subjects."[56]

The southern papers and newsmagazines also examined the implications of "treason" and "retrogression" for the country. *TELL* editorialized: "In fact, the implications of [Governor Ahmed] Yerima's actions are too glaring to be ignored by very critical observers. The first implication is that, henceforth, no Christian or any other non-Muslim can ever become the executive Governor of Zamfara State for as long as the supreme law there is that of Sharia. . . . This is unconstitutional. The second . . . is that Zamfara has indirectly excised itself out of the federal laws of the country[,] standing close as [a] 'sovereign state within a republic.' The third, and perhaps, the most eye-opening is the fact that Zamfara has successfully 'restructured' itself within the Nigerian federation and that Northern state wants 'self-autonomy' or 'self-determination' [and] is free to adopt its own strategy to achieve same."[57]

For the *Express*, "By far the most fundamental problem which the current experimentation with the Sharia option poses is that it has the potential of bringing matters of restricted religious application into direct conflict with matters of a larger socio-political and therefore secular nature. As matters stand today, there is no way of winning the Sharia challenge without altering either the present constitution or the configuration of the territorial expression to which it refers."[58] *The Guardian* elaborated these changes in the "configuration of the territorial expression" in pointing out the implications of the Sharia issue: "There seems . . . to be an attempt to turn the Sharia into a total way of life, a kind of theocracy that supplants the law of the land. In other words, its promoters have politicised it. . . . What they are saying, in essence, is that this country cannot be one. It is a threat to national unity. It is a dangerous proposition that is abroad."[59]

TELL linked Yerima's "political crusade" with that of the late Sardauna of Sokoto, Ahmadu Bello, in the "desire" to "dip the Koran into the Atlantic Ocean [in southern Nigeria] and across Nigeria" and, ultimately, "dominate" the country eternally: "What continued to baffle most political observers is the timing of the Sharia declaration. . . . Sources told *TELL* that a Northern cabal, which has held the country to ransom for several decades but currently outside the power . . . of Aso Rock, is involved in this new plot to rattle and if possible, topple the Obasanjo administration." These "Northern leaders" who have fed on government "all their lives,"[60] as *TELL* described the core northern elite, were challenged by *The Guardian* to stop the moves that threatened national unity: "The country did not have to wait for the bloodshed in Kaduna before protesting the folly of those who want to use the Sharia as an instrument of political challenge. . . . And where are the leaders of the North. They should be courageous enough to declare it (Sharia) a monstrosity. They must say where they stand on this issue if they still harbour any hope of a united nation."[61]

A contributor to the *New Nigerian* more or less confirmed what *The Guardian* described as a "monstrosity,"[62] as he declared that the "Sharia issue . . . has today become so fundamental even to the extent of life or death."[63] This contributor also linked the Sharia debate to the caliphate, but to a contrary effect. He noted that "Muslims . . . especially the flag-bearers of [the] Shehu Usman Dan Fodio [-led] Islamic Jihad of the 19th century cherish nothing dearer to their hearts other than the Shari'a issue."[64] *The Guardian*'s lead editorialist and columnist reacted to this line of reasoning by noting that government, Christians, southerners, and secularists must not accept a "compromise" over the Sharia issue, given that "those who want to fly the flag of religion will stop at nothing."[65]

The Guardian columnist echoed, but for a contrary argument, the writer in the *New Nigerian* who saw the matter as concerning "life or death" for the "flag bearers" of the Fulani Jihad: "I have already argued that what we are confronted with is the Second Jihad. It is a religious and political project. . . . The Hausa-Fulani second-generation Jihadists are all out to remain faithful to the project of their ancestors which is to turn Nigeria into an Islamic state, to impose the Sharia on the rest of us and to question the very basis of the Nigerian nation. . . . What does the North contribute to this nation?"[66]

In the context of all the attacks against the Islamic north, the *New Nigerian* published a two-part essay ostensibly to educate "ignorant people and mischief-makers" on the Sharia.[67] It is written by the Emir of Ilorin, Sulu Gambari, a retired Federal Appeal Court judge and one of those who claimed direct descent from Usman dan Fodio, the leader of the nineteenth-century Fulani Jihad. Argued the emir: "In English/common law parlance, law is made for man and not man for law. But in Islam, it has been neither the nation nor the people, which has made the law, it is the law, which has made and molded the nation and the people. It (Shari'a) is supreme because it emanates from God who decreed its main basis in the Qur'an." The "ignorant mischief-makers" who describe Nigeria as a "secular" state, argued the emir, misunderstand the concept and are misapplying it "to confuse the citizens of the actual meaning of secularism to the effect that Nigeria or the state has no religion at all."[68]

As a medium that perceived itself as the defender of the north and Islam, the *Trust* ignored a "fundamental problem" identified by the *Express* while concentrating on Muslims and Christians who "forged unity in adversity to ward off their attackers" during the violence provoked by the imposition of Sharia on Kaduna state, whom they simply regarded as "misguided hoodlums." The responsibility for the riots, which in "several parts of Kaduna" "defied religious colouration," was, however, subtly laid by the *Trust* at the doorstep of "anti-Sharia demonstrators" who neither sought nor obtained police permit, who became "aggressive," "molested" motorists, and forced many Muslims to say "anti-Sharia slogans." However, "some" Christian demonstrators reportedly told the weekly that their "aggression" was provoked by their stoning by Muslim youths.[69]

Unlike the *Trust*'s "violent" OPC youths in Lagos (south) who exhibited "stone-age barbarism," having been "consumed by evil and employing methods some category of animals would find detestable,"[70] the Kaduna (north) youths "crafted their own agenda" only because of the "absence of leaders to guide them."[71] This contrast between "their" and "our" violence and the way in which the different newspapers euphemized "our" violence and exaggerated "their" violence is striking in the narratives. In contrast to the *Trust*'s attitude to the OPC militants, *The Guardian* argued that the OPC militants should not be dismissed because "they have an idea of what they want out of the Nigerian union. Some of their demands are fundamental to the pursuit of justice and good governance."[72]

Whereas the *Trust* expected the police to "deal decisively" with the OPC youth in Lagos, in the Kaduna riots, the paper accused the police of "going beyond their mandate by siding with one group," ostensibly Christians. The concerns of the southern press about the political implications of the religious riots were, however, not important for the *Trust*, as it argued that "terrible as the killings were, the issue goes beyond them and even the so-called political class that are always accused of manipulating people and making issues out of primordial sentiments."[73]

This stands in direct opposition to the *Trust*'s earlier argument concerning the riots in Lagos, in which Yoruba youths in OPC were implicated. In that instance, the weekly wanted a probe into the activities of those "manipulating primordial sentiments": "We hope the government will go further to find out (a) how the OPC is funded, (b) where and how it gets its supply of arms with which they overwhelm the police's feeble response. We believe that if government pursue[s] such and other relevant questions with determination and genuine desire to redress wrong and prevent future recurrence, the identity of those behind the OPC politically, ideologically and financially would be revealed. For, whatever its demand, the OPC must be made to atone for its crime."[74]

Such "atonement" was, however, not required by the *Trust* in the Kaduna case, which was reportedly worse in terms of casualties than that of Ketu, in Lagos, involving OPC. The *Trust*, which described Obasanjo's shoot-at-sight order in the Lagos (OPC) case as "indulgent . . . like a grand-father talking to wayward children rather than a commander-in-chief warning pre-meditated murderers"[75] (an order that, even if as mild as the *Trust* claimed, for *TELL* constituted a "dangerous gamble"),[76] failed to lob any names at the Kaduna youth who, under the guise of religion, killed hundreds of people and destroyed property worth billions of naira.[77] Yet the *Trust* described the retaliatory attacks in the East against Hausa-Fulani as a "massacre."[78] What happened in Kaduna was "carnage," but the violence in the East was a "massacre." Whereas carnage does not immediately convey agency, massacre clearly does. The *Trust* even accused Chief Emeka Ojukwu, the former leader of the secessionist Republic of Biafra and Igbo leader, as being partly responsible for the Kaduna riots.[79]

Like every major crisis, the introduction of the Sharia legal code and the subsequent riots again raised questions about national survival and the means of ensuring this. The *Express* offered this line of narrative in the course of the Sharia controversy: "A dangerous trend has crept into our polity. Gradually, our national discourse has been invaded by expressions of separatism and talks of ethnic self-determination. . . . Even the Sharia escapade in Zamfara is an extension of this trend. . . . In all the threats that we have seen and heard of late, there is almost always a proviso. People are saying that they would opt for self-determination if the inequities in our present system are allowed to endure."[80]

TELL presented the solution to the "inequities" in the system as tied to the convocation of an SNC, as it had always insisted: "There is no doubt that the Zamfara debacle has reawakened the people's consciousness to the need to have a sovereign national conference to resolve the primordial riddles that have negated every progressive move to make Nigeria regain its bearing in the march towards civilization."[81] After reviewing the demands of several groups, the newsmagazine affirmed that "virtually every group is talking secession if their grievances are not resolved to their satisfaction fast. And many of them are adamant that the first condition that must be fulfilled to continue to keep the country united is the convening of [a] sovereign national conference."[82]

The Politics of Restructuring: Between Secularism and Secession

Even though there was consensus among the southern newspapers about secularism, there was no consensus on the implications of the much-canvassed need for the restructuring of the federation and how the absence of such restructuring could lead to the collapse of the Nigerian union. For instance, the *Express* disagreed that the expressions of dissatisfaction within the Nigerian union captured by *TELL* constituted threats of secession. Rather, the paper stated that "we are witnessing a quickening of our patriotic instincts rather than serious and deliberate threats of secession," adding that "clearly . . . there is a case for a restructuring of the federation." However, the *Express* was convinced there was need for a sovereign national conference, given "the existence of a popularly-elected National Assembly with full powers to defend and protect the sovereignty of the Nigerian people."[83]

The reason for the absence of a threat of secession, according to the *Express*, was later explained: "On whether Nigeria is headed towards disintegration, quite a good number of political experts say that it is not likely. According to them it would have been easy for Nigeria to break-up but for the British and American interests, the fact that the South-East may not readily come out to agitate for it because of betrayal during Biafra by the very sections now campaigning the cause and the fact that the Middle-Belt which also feels, oppressed by the Hausa-Fulani oligarchy may not just support it."[84] The position of the *Express* captured the popular belief in the Igbo East that the Yoruba "betrayed" them by not fulfilling the "promise"—allegedly made by Awolowo on behalf of the Yoruba—to secede from Nigeria if the East (Biafra) did. This popular belief, virulently disputed by the Yoruba, has been one of the key sore points in Igbo-Yoruba relations. Therefore the *Express* restated the belief here as a way of announcing that the Igbo will not support the Yoruba because of the "betrayal" of the past.

The Guardian, however, agreed with *TELL* in asserting that the national conference was crucial to Nigeria's survival. Although praising the "landmark" meeting in Asaba by the six governors of the south-south states of Akwa-Ibom, Bayelsa, Cross-Rivers, Delta, Edo, and Rivers—a region described as "the economic power house of the country"—the paper found it "disturbing" that the gathering said nothing about the agitation for a national conference: "It is disturbing that the South-South leaders did not make a categorical statement on the current clamour for a national conference to address the distortions and deformities that impede the functioning of a federal system. . . . Just where does the region stand on the issue? A national conference is needed to provide a platform for a peaceful resolution of the mounting crisis. Instead of avoiding the issue, the governors and legislators of the South-South zone ought to face the challenge of preparing their various states and communities for any such conference."[85]

In what constitutes a rare admission of fundamental crisis by a medium that represents the conservative north, the *Trust* submitted that a structural problem that results in widespread dissatisfaction afflicts Nigeria: "The current cries for restructuring or [a] sovereign national conference by sections of the Nigerian federation is apparently a derivative of the patriotic desires of the people to realise self-determination and freedom to develop after having lived together since 1914. These years of the Nigerian alliance did not seem to augur well for either of the conglomeration."[86] "Either of the conglomeration" refers to the northern and southern protectorates that were amalgamated to form Nigeria in 1914.

In the editorial that echoed Ahmadu Bello's statement regarding "the mistakes of 1914," the *Trust* went further than Bello, who had said, when he made the statement, that he wished to go no further than that. Contrary to the narratives that portray the north as a "leech" feeding off the rest of the country, as *TELL* constantly alleged, the *Trust* argued that it was the north that had made most of the sacrifices for the rest of the country. "From the 1950s to date, the North has always played the role of the absorber of the shocks of the Nigerian federation. The Northern leadership [which *TELL* asserted "held the country to ransom for several decades"] at great expenses and risks has contained agitations especially from the [Yoruba] South-West."[87]

The weekly elaborated: "One pertinent question is who really is benefiting more from the logjam called Nigeria? Politically the South has persecuted Northerners in government since independence. They have been responsible for the collapse of all regimes from Balewa to Abacha. They define moments and situations. They have since become umpires of doom and never say or see anything good in and from the North be it a Christian or a Muslim."[88] Whereas *TELL* described the "power shift," that is, the emergence of a southerner as president, as a "grudging concession" by the north out of sheer necessity and self-preservation of the northern establishment,[89] the *Trust* argued that it was an "undemocratic act" for a southerner to become president: "They [southerners] forced the Northern political class to undemocratically relinquish power through their propaganda machines that were ironically aided at formation or even bankrolled by the same Northern elite and establishment." Obviously irked by the "loss of power" to the south, the *Trust* stated that Nigeria should either revert to the *status quo ante* or disintegrate. The weekly completely opposed "restructuring," which it assumed would permanently disable the northern establishment, which it represented. The *Trust* argued that the proposed SNC could only hold if that would lead to the disintegration of the "unholy alliance" that was Nigeria. Rather than restructure, declared the weekly, let Nigeria collapse: "The Nigerian national question is unending and the contradictions among the peoples are increasingly assuming primacy. The leadership is doing a lot of dis-service to the people by continuously shying away from addressing the very roots of the national calamities. . . . [A] national sovereign conference will only be relevant if it will have as its focus, the dis-memberment of this unholy alliance of incompatibles. The question of restructuring does not arise."[90]

However, the *Express* disagreed with the *Trust* on which section of the country had borne the greatest burden for Nigeria's continued existence as a single country. Against the backdrop of the efforts since the 1914 amalgamation to make Nigeria one, the *Express* sub-mitted: "In the South-East, especially among the Igbos,[91] the acute domination, suppression and marginalisation Nigeria is known to be visiting on some segments of her citizenry have been unspeak-ably pronounced. The Igbos bore the greater part of the brunt in keeping Nigeria one since the end of the war, the Igbos have been the butt of much of the ethnic and religious violence in Nigeria."[92] The paper argued further that it was against the backdrop of the recent attacks on the Igbo in Kaduna that the five governors of the southeast (Igbo) states of Abia, Anambra, Enugu, Imo, and Ebonyi demanded a "confederation as the only political arrangement that can ensure Nigeria's continuing survival as a united and indivisible country," while calling on their people to retaliate if attacked in the north. The demands, the *Express* asserted, had also been made in the southwest and the south-south. Without any categorical expression of a change of mind over its opposition three months earlier to the convocation of a national conference, the *Express* now endorsed the same in light of the call for confederation by the Igbo governors: "Nobody needs to be told that Nigerian feder-alism has been tragically defective . . . if we still sincerely believe in the possibilities of a united and indivisible Nigeria, there cannot be an attractive alternative to a confederal Nigeria which can come into being through a national conference, sovereign or otherwise." Although this betrayed the uncertainty of the *Express* on how to proceed—in that it had earlier supported the national conference, and then opposed it because it was "vitiated by the existence of a popularly elected National Assembly,"[93] only to reaffirm its impor-tance here—the editorial and the one that follows it[94] constitute examples of how the *Express* defended what it assumed to be in the best interests of the Igbo at any point in time. On the contrary, the *Trust* would not have accepted the restructuring of the federation or confederation. The paper insisted that it was either the *status quo ante* or disintegration: "The question of restructuring does not arise. The clamour for a confederation is simply an advancement of those Nigerians who want to eat their cake and have it. The basis of the alliance has been shaken to its roots. . . . Since it is the genuine desire of the people to go their ways, so let it be."[95] The reference to the "basis of the alliance" echoes Lt. Col. Yakubu Gowon's inaugural statement, in which he said, in light of the killing of northern leaders during the Igbo-led coup of January 1966 and the attacks against the Igbo in the north a few months later, that "the basis of unity is no longer there."

The *Express*, however, disagreed with the *Trust*'s interpretation of the confederal call, while accusing the latter and others opposed to it as "shadow chasers." The paper argued: "The call for confederalism is only a symptom of a more fundamental systematic failure. To quarrel with the former rather than the latter which caused it is to chase shadows in name of statecraft."[96] But Mohammed Sani Dutinma, writing in his important *Trust* column "Inside Politics," agreed with the confederation call. For him, it was good for the north: "There is nothing wrong with confederation. Was it not at a confederal level that the North produced the first political class and leadership that could not be equalled today? . . . Why then should we continue to cling to a union where we are only tolerated and regarded as parasites?"[97] When considered deeply, Dutinma's position was not so much a support for the confederal system as it was an affirmation of the capacity of the much-derided north to survive on its own when the country becomes decentralized.

Regarding President Obasanjo, who described the call for confederation as both "unpatriotic and mischievous," Dutinma restated the Igbo's "expired faith" in Nigeria and said this faith has only made them "sacrificial lambs": "[The President] would . . . be guilty of naivety if he remains insensitive to the historical circumstances that induce sections of this country to define their posture towards the Nigerian Federal Republic. The Igbos have had the strongest faith in Nigerian unity. They easily act out this faith by quickly making any part of this country they go to, their home. And yet periodically, in the history of this country, the Igbos have had to pay dearly for their faith in one Nigeria."[98]

The *Trust*'s "Inside Politics" averred that the call by Igbo governors and their kinsmen to retaliate attacks by other Nigerians was not surprising given the antecedents of "Igbo tribal leadership beginning with the January 15th 1966 bloody military coup," whose "game plan," the paper alleged, was the elimination of northern and Yoruba leaders to pave way for the imposition of "Igbo hegemony" over Nigeria. This was a return to the narratives that preceded the civil war: "When that scheme failed . . . the Igbos rebelled and seceded to form the so-called Republic of Biafra. This was crushed after a bloody civil war. It appears that history is repeating itself. This time five [Igbo] governors are playing the ignoble roles of the five majors in the 1966 infamy. This time around the 'no victor, no vanquished' slogan will not apply. The vanquished will be crushed to rise no more to afflict Nigeria's body-politic."[99] For the *Trust*, the five majors (four Igbo and one Yoruba) who planned the January 1966 abortive coup in which the leaders of the northern region and the unpopular premier of the western region were killed—an action that was the remote cause of the July 1966 countercoup and the civil war—have been "resurrected" in the five governors of the Igbo eastern states. The paper warned the Igbo that the charitable attitude of General Gowon at the end of the war (the declaration of "no victor, no vanquished") will not be repeated if the Igbo attempt to secede again and are defeated.

In light of this, *The Guardian* argued that only if all interest groups and centers of influence came together could the problems of Nigeria be solved. The crises in the country and the narratives in the press, the paper added, only proved that "all is not well with the realm." "A lasting, long term solution can only be found through the concerted effort of a variety of interest and centres of influence within the Nigerian polity. The difficulty in mobilising such adverse interests and power centres for a concerted response is, itself, a problem which underlines more deeprooted dysfunctions in our nation-building efforts." Like *TELL* and, lately, the *Express*, and unlike the *Trust, The Guardian* averred that "restructuring is the only way to save the Nigerian nation": "The opportunity for national restructuring must be seized in good spirit and with sincerity by all stakeholders, rather than continue in the pretence that we are already experiencing genuine democracy, and given efficient governance, we should simply allow sleeping dogs to lie."[100]

The *Express* strengthened the argument, given its new conviction about restructuring:

To postpone this badly needed restructuring was to condemn the Nigerian political experiment to continuous instability. The choice before the nation was clear: either true federalism or confederation.[101] The one and only way to "let sleeping dogs lie" and the only "clear choice" as far as the *Trust* was concerned was to go back to a pre-1914 structure of a united north and its other, the south. The *Trust* reaffirmed the unity of "one north," in spite of efforts to fractionalize it by the "Lagos Ibadan" (southern) press. Stated the *Trust*: "It is not true that relations between different groups in the North is antagonistic. Even the Sharia issue that is being used by the Lagos-Ibadan press axis as a tool for creating disaffection so that they [the south] may have their way in the diabolic scheme of perpetuating hegemony and holding onto both the political and economic power is not as unresolvable as it is portrayed."[102] The weekly seems to suggest here that the Sharia matter could be sacrificed at the altar of northern unity against the "southern diabolical scheme." But *TELL* restated this narrative that the *Trust* believed constituted an attempt at creating disaffection among northern groups: "The political clique [northern elite] which wants to say goodbye to Nigeria may not have it that easy. Increasingly, the Middle-Belt, a largely Christian area, may not be willing to be a part of one monolithic North."[103]

Although opposing narratives of unification in the north and promoting narratives of fractionalization, the *Express* emphasized unity in the south. The paper believed that it was the unity of the southern majority groups, the Yoruba and Igbo, that scared the north: "This unity has ordinarily put the North off and exposed its position. This is because in the event that the restructuring really takes places, the centre, which had since 1966 enjoyed the centrally collected revenue[,] will be weakened. Indeed, the North is more exposed in this than any other region."[104]

Still, the *Trust* argued that after reverting to the pre-1914 structure each of the two regions could hold a sovereign national conference to "determine what they want to do with themselves" and perhaps rectify the mistake of 1914. This not only "makes more sense," but it is also in the best interest of the north, argued the *Trust*: "The North can only realise its potentials and develop when it ceases to be a part of the present arrangement. A Northern Nigerian federation will be viable and within the first 10 years of existence be able to attain more than 90% literacy level. . . . Never mind the sea. It is only a lazy person that relies on sea-ports."[105] The reference to the viability of the north, its capacity to produce a 90 percent literacy rate and survive without access to the sea, all constitute a response to contrary positions stated throughout the history of Nigeria by the southern press. In response to the long narrative by the *Trust* and the events that provoked it, *TELL* asked if "break up is imminent" as "Northern leaders threaten Nigeria."[106] The magazine took a few symbols of the north and attacked their positions. For example, *TELL* stated: "Crises always separate real statesmen from the pretenders to that august status. . . . Shehu Shagari was the first elected executive president of the country. . . . But since . . . Northern army officers . . . sacked his government in a coup . . . Shagari's metamorphosis from a national leader to a section and ethnic leader has been swift and steady. He rarely expresses his views on national issues in public, and when he does, it is mainly to defend the so-called Northern interests. . . . [General Muhammed] Buhari's disposition and position . . . are no different from those of Shagari."[107]

The *Trust* seemed to return the "favor" by also attacking leaders from the south and southwest, such as Bola Ige, the minister of power and steel, who was described as a self-professed bastion of Yoruba interests and "apostle of ethnic hatred."[108] Despite such attacks on southern leaders, *TELL* attempted to "prove" the "bad faith" of the northern leaders: "Between October 1, 1979, and May 29, 1999, all the heads of state were Northerners and Muslims,[109] beginning from [President Shehu] Shagari himself. None of them thought then that the priority of their people was a pure, unadulterated Sharia. Which of course, clearly shows that the on-going Sharia crisis is all about politics and the control of power. The 'wrong person' is occupying Aso Rock. And the control of the seat of federal power is the exclusive preserve of Northern Muslims, as Maitama Sule . . . once implied in his weird treatise on the relative strength of the three major ethnic nationalities."[110]

The "Arewa Republic," which *TELL* said the northern "political clique" was planning to set up, was dismissed by the newsmagazine as one peopled by "a decrepit army of hungry street urchin," the *almajiris*.[111] The "clique" had decided on this path that the *Trust* advocated, *TELL* argued, because Obasanjo had blocked "their continued sucking of filthy lucre and the spoils of office." The magazine added: "Because the political clique is at the moment, in the wilderness, where it is unable to harvest the trapping and panoply of power, any longer, it is unable to come to terms with the Obasanjo presidency."[112] Contrary to the "paradise for the masses" with 90 percent literacy that the *Trust* said the "Arewa Republic" or "Northern Nigerian Federation" would become within ten years, *TELL* stated that nineteen out of the twenty *almajiris* in the north—who were used to fomenting trouble—"would go through a Hobbesian life that is short, nasty and brutish." Apart from that, "by the latest figures from the Federal Office of Statistics, FOS, the core Northern states have the highest under-five mortality rates, shortest life expectancy rates and highest population per medical doctor. . . . They have the lowest literacy levels, lack access to portable water supply, good toilet systems, electricity, and proper refuse disposal, and, have the weakest capability to generate any sort of revenue internally."[113] The final point—the incapacity to generate revenue—was a way of reemphasizing "the fact" constantly raised by the southern press that the north was a "leech" on the south.

This is precisely the situation that the *Trust* promised would be reversed in the "Northern Nigerian Federation," while it argued that "it is not true that relations between different groups in the North is antagonistic." But *TELL* insisted that the Hausa-Fulani north had lost the middle-belt and other non-Hausa-Fulani because of their "ethnic plot . . . to continue their domination of the region": "The history of events since the amalgamation of Nigeria . . . appears to lay credence to this claim. The 'core' North has always sought to be the dominant factor in the country's politics. . . . This historical antecedent is one of the reasons people say the Hausa-Fulani have continued to believe that they are in the majority. But all that fallacy is about to stop.[114] All the groups were calling for an end to internal colonisation by the "core north," which they accused of perpetually making their people "hewers of wood and drawers of water."[115]

The "belief" by the Hausa-Fulani that they were in the majority points to a perennial debate in Nigeria regarding the actual population of the Hausa-Fulani in particular, and the north of Nigeria in general. Many people in the south have always contested the north's numerical majority as "a ruse" produced initially by an "Anglo-Fulani pact" and sustained by the Hausa-Fulani "domination" of power in Nigeria. Even the census conducted under President Obasanjo, a southwesterner, failed to dispel this "belief" in the south.

As to the claim in the *Trust* that "we [northerners] fought a 30-months civil war just to keep the nation" together, *TELL* continued to factionalize the north in its reporting: "To show their deep-seated grievances nurtured by several years of marginalisation, [middle-belt] groups recalled that the bulk of their sons in the military fought the Nigerian civil war. At the end of that war, their sons were not given the desired ranks while Northern [Hausa-Fulani] officers became generals without firing a single bullet or commanding any troops."[116]

The *Trust* considered such an "onslaught" as this crucial enough for a cover story in which the paper stated: "Of late, the media have been awash with reports of various groups of political elite in the North who are championing the cause of a new identity for their people known as the Middle-Belt. The pith of this identity is the repudiation of the Far North and a desire to weld the distinct religious and ethnic minority groups in the Near North and encourage them to fancy themselves as one people." Even though it was the mouthpiece of the "far north," the *Trust* could not wish away the existence of this "near north" (usually called middle-belt), yet the paper questioned this area of the north and attempted to divide it narratively. The *Trust* noted that those making claims to speak for the people in Benue, Plateau, Adamawa, Taraba, Kogi, Kwara, Niger, Nasarrawa, and the southern parts of Kebbi, Borno, and Yobe states needed to be questioned: "Does everybody in these areas share the sentiments of a Middle Belt cause? What exactly is the Middle Belt? What is the motivation behind its resurgence? Are the pronouncements of the standard bearers of the Middle Belt truly representative of the opinions and feelings of the disparate ethnic and religious groups that populate the area." The *Trust* declared that it had found, in confronting these questions, that "the people of the place that is usually referred to as the Middle Belt are not united in their desire for a separate, independent identity," and that in any case the "media hype," such as *TELL*'s, that ostensibly accompanied "the resurgence" of the middle-belt agitation has led to the loss of the "real meaning and origins of the concept."[117]

Regarding what the *Express* gleefully announced as the revisit of the Aburi Accord by the west and the east over a newfound alliance on "confederation," the *Trust*'s "Inside Politics" columnist wishes them well, while uniting the "true northerners" in the middle-belt with the core north against this east-west (Igbo-Yoruba) alliance: "Good luck to the Yorubas, and their newly-found confederate allies east of the River Niger. The rest of us, so-called 'Middle Belters' inclusive will remain Nigerians to realise the dream of a great country on the continent of Africa. . . . The quislings and Yoruba lackeys who do not want to be addressed as Northerners should pack their bag and baggage and go to the lands of their new found 'friends' or masters in Oduduwa land or the truncated New Biafra."[118] "Quislings" and "Yoruba lackeys" are references to middle-belters championing a separate identity from that of the core north, and "Oduduwaland" and "New Biafra" are metaphors for Yorubaland and Igboland, respectively.

The move of the elder statesman and leader of NADECO Anthony Enahoro to reorganize the vanguard of pro-SNC elements also attracted opposing narratives. Whereas the *Express* described him as "a hero of Nigerian nationalism," the *Trust* dismissed him as a "77-year-old former exile" and "the big masquerade of ethnic federalism." Those joining Enahoro's "bandwagon" from the (Sahara) north, the *Trust* averred, "do not understand the complexities of life in the Savannah." It therefore submitted: "No one is begging anyone to be a Northerner. The choice for any sensible politician is dictated by hard realities. The North is big enough to survive such defections." For the avoidance of doubt, the weekly warned that once the cohesion of the north breaks, it would be the end of Nigeria. But if the north remains united, the *Trust* believed, Nigeria would survive the death of its "traducers," such as the man who first introduced the motion for independence, Enahoro: "But let nobody deceive himself about the survival of this country once the North as we know it breaks up into wrangling units. It was a united and resolute nation by the North that defeated Biafra and kept Nigeria one. . . . If the North holds together, the clamour for ethnic autonomy will begin and die on the pages of Lagos newspapers. And poor, old Enahoro may perhaps permit himself to quietly retire to Uromi for ultimate appointment with his maker."[119] With this, the *Trust* paralleled the interests of the core north with the larger interests of the country.

Given the unabating narratives of a Hausa-Fulani "threat" to the rest of Nigeria, which *TELL* articulated as the "Hausa-Fulani assertion of a divine right to rule," and the consequent attacks on the group, Muhammad Sammani, writing in the *Trust*, described the Hausa-Fulani as an "endangered" group because "virtually every ethnic group directly or indirectly attribute[s] misfortunes and disadvantages to one ethnic group—Hausa-Fulani. No ethnic group receives the seemingly endless bastion [*sic*], intimidation, harassment, insults and abuses like the Hausa-Fulani." However, though they "are the targets of attack at the slightest provocation," the Hausa-Fulani were constructed by Sammani as "the most liberal ethnic group in [Nigeria] who most often . . . only hold the 'cow' while the others milk it."[120] As the narratives show, every group in Nigeria was convinced that it was at the receiving end of an unfair deal and that others were the beneficiaries of its sacrifice.

Perhaps what best reflects the glorification of a collective past in an attempt to narrate the present and confront the future is the narrative of "Nigeria's wasted years" by *The Guardian*. All the clashing narratives of deep-seated divisions—demonstrated in the narratives since the preindependence era—are *erased* in the narration of a glorious past by *The Guardian*, in a great example of Renan's dictum that a nation forgets: "The founding nationalists had helped to inspire . . . optimism by speaking collectively of the possibility of a great nation where ethnic pluralism would constitute a source of strength, and a federalist arrangement to liberate the potentials of the constituent units of the multi-ethnic, multinational country. The euphoria seemed justifiable because indeed Nigeria is a blessed nation, endowed as it is with human and natural resources of the highest quality." However, this "glorious" past has been marred by contemporary happenings, *The Guardian* confessed, adding that "Today, sectarian identity is as sharp as a newly acquired machete, as each group resides out of the centre to the ethnic periphery. Various social groups are questioning the basis of the Nigerian union."[121]

Even though *The Guardian* presented the "questioning" of "the basis of the Nigerian union" as a problem of "today," indeed, as evident in the narratives in the previous chapters, this is a perennial process that has been ongoing since the amalgamation of the northern and southern protectorates to form the Nigerian union in 1914. But the paper is right in that the narratives of the divisions and dissention continue to return as "sharp as newly acquired machete" even though their bases are as old as the Nigerian union.

Conclusion

Margaret Scammell and Holli A. Semetko have argued that it makes no sense to continue to theorize and analyze the media-democracy interface as if "there were no contests about democratic ideals and possibilities."[122] As a major democratic institution, the press is expected to uphold democratic ideals and facilitate the expansion and deepening of democratic practices. I have used the coverage of two violent ethno-religious and ethno-political clashes to illustrate the limitations of the assumptions of liberal democratic theory on the role of the press in a democracy. The press, as an important institution in Nigeria's heterogeneous public spheres, often commits itself to further fragmentation of these publics. Despite the heroic efforts of the press in ensuring the restoration of democratic rule and its critical role in monitoring democratically elected officials and institutions, on a few critical occasions, the Nigerian press renders itself totally captive to ethno-regional and ethno-religious passions and calculations.

A postauthoritarian (democratic) press is expected to perform such specific roles as expanding the freedom of expression, acting as interlocutor for hitherto marginalized groups, disseminating the values of a democratic culture,[123] and in multicultural societies, facilitating the relegitimization of democratic cross-cultural dialogue and exchanges and "bringing all classes of the population together [thus] strengthening national social solidarity."[124] The effective performance of these functions is critical to strengthening and deepening democracy. However, the narratives of ethno-religious conflict in the press in Nigeria show the problems that arise when, as Philip Schlesinger notes, "divergent concepts of rationality, order and criminality coexists" "within the matrix of a single political domain."[125]

As Nigeria emerged from a very violent military era, the press, which was fully embroiled in the struggle to free Nigeria from this history of violence, should have shown greater restraint in its coverage of the religious and interethnic clashes that, in many respects, carried heavy historical baggage. Democratic rule is particularly constructed around the possibilities of peaceful settlement of competing social interests. Therefore, if a major democratic institution, such as the press, exacerbates the unavoidable crises that arise from this difficult process, then it would have failed in one of its most important duties. As reflected in the newspapers and newsmagazines analyzed here, the press ended up subverting the legitimacy of the democratic government and promoting, ironically, nondemocratic ways of settling social crises.

Perhaps one positive thing that can be said about the narratives of the press in the context of these violent crises is that the press re-presented the dominant standpoints regarding the fundamental questions that need to be addressed in Nigeria. However, the implications of this for democratic rule is grim; because there were no efforts to integrate the grievances and focus on the grand questions without talking past one another, the newspapers and newsmagazines failed to promote common problem solving. This is no cheering conclusion given the fact that those same questions would define and determine the future of Nigeria.

In the coverage of major ethnic and religious crises by the press, the state is often delegitimized, with regular insistence on the desirability or imminence of its dissolution. As a critical agency for the exchange of information between citizens and between citizens and the holders of state power, the media constitute "the critical lifeblood of democracy." Although it is impossible to expect that they will not reflect or maintain partisan position of the critical issues in the Nigerian society, the media are expected to rise above such partisanship in encouraging dialogue across ethnic, religious, regional, class, and gender lines so as to build a more democratic and multicultural society, which would also help to further humanize the state.

Part 4

Domination and Resistance in Majority-Minority Relations

8

Narratives, Territoriality, and Majority-Minority Ethnic Violence

As for politics . . . space, like identity, is contingent, differentiated, and relational, and . . . it thus makes little sense to conceive
of any space as stabilized, fixed, and therefore outside of the
possibility of counter-hegemony. In this view, all space-identity
formations are imbued with oppositional potential. And thus
a practical task of politics is to activate this potential through
denaturalization, exposure, and contestation so as to achieve
new appropriation and articulation of space and identity.

—J. P. Jones and P. Moss

In this chapter, I concentrate on how the symbolic manifestation
of territoriality is used to structure other manifestations. I describe
this symbolic manifestation as *discursive territoriality*, one in which
the media become resources "through which power is exercised to
produce—or disrupt—systemic regularity."[1] Discursive territoriality is a dimension of spatial politics, one in which the material and
emotional dimensions of space are harnessed in the narratives and
discourses of power, which then align particular people firmly, and
sometimes also exclusively, to particular territories and privilege
their claims to the material benefits of—and emotional attachment
to—such spaces.

Discursive territoriality emphasizes and amplifies the uniting
or divisive potentials of space and boundaries. In the process of
amplifying particular forms of sameness and difference, discursive
territoriality helps turn the material power of space, which exists
as resources for human survival, into "our" resources necessary
for "our" survival.[2] Contrary or competing claims to these spaces
and resources are, therefore, narrated as attempts to *negate* "us";

in extreme cases, they are seen as attempts to *exterminate* "us." Discursive territoriality involves the struggle over meaning enmeshed with the struggle over material resources, one in which—as Valentin Volosinov points out in his notion of "semiotic struggle"—it is hoped that changing the structure of meaning could lead to a change in specific human interactions, social organization, and the distribution of resources.[3] Discursive territoriality focuses on the representational apparatuses of space, investing them with meaning. As a reflection of power and space and spatial power, it helps in constituting and deploring meanings and reflecting them in the modulation of actual territorial contests. Such meaning can even be shared across time and space, beyond the particular territory in contention—as the case examined below shows.

Discursive territoriality is a means of discursively reifying power, given that, as Sacks avers, territoriality provides a means of reifying power because it makes potentials explicit and real by making them invisible.[4] Therefore, the imbrications of power in territoriality can be analyzed—following Anthony Giddens's conception of "power"—as "relations of autonomy and dependence between actors in which these actors draw upon and reproduce structural properties of domination."[5] Implied in this is a conception of power as a *transformative capacity* within situated social relations.

Jurgen Habermas has been very influential in attempting to understand and theorize the discursive realm in social relations and in analyzing how the socio-economic structure relates to consciousness signification. Habermas sees the interpenetration of material and subjective actions and consciousness as constituting a "lifeworld."[6] However, much of the critique of his work, *The Structural Transformation of the Public Sphere*, centers on a rejection of his assumption of a single public sphere that is grounded exclusively in rational discourse.[7] The discursive realm of the civil society, most contemporary theorists like Eley and Fraser argue, consists of multiple, often nonrational, contestatory, even *conspiratorial* public spheres.[8] These different but overlapping public spheres, which Jacobs, following Calhoun, calls "communities of discourse"—or, in fact, communities of discourse*s*—are often established and maintained by the media,[9] pointing in a Gramscian sense to the fact that "a complex web of hegemony [is] woven into the very fabric of civil society."[10]

How is the struggle over territoriality encountered discursively in the press? How is space discursively negotiated as an instrument—and as a prism—of power in dominant versus marginal ethnic groups' relations? Focusing on the narrative of violent clashes in Nigeria between a marginal minority ethnic group, the Kataf, and the dominant majority ethnic group, the Hausa—within the context of discursive territoriality—this chapter examines the "communities of discourses" that the violent clashes established and amplified.

Power and Territoriality

Conflictual relations at the level of political and civil society are usually replicated, represented, and re-presented in the media. Where such relations concern territoriality, the role of the media as "power containers," expressions of power relations, and purveyors of such power relations usually consists in rendering interpretations in which meanings are constructed in the service of power. The identification and interpretation of space in the media in ways that inscribe space with meanings also connect space to what Penrose calls "uneven and asymmetric constellation(s) of power."[11] The media, in this context, through narratives, refold space into—or rebind space with—power; consequently, they produce a territoriality that not only reflects the political economy of—as in the specific instance of this chapter—ethno-spatial struggles but also amplifies these struggles. Time, space, and power *structure* narratives and discourse and are *structured* by narratives and discourse in turn. In this chapter, in direct relation to chapter 4, I problematize space and territory in relation to narratives and discourse in an attempt to provide further insight into majority-minority relations within the grand narratives of the Nigerian nation.

Without doubt, space has referents that exist outside the parameters of narrative constitution or construction. Yet it is not immutable—given that its self-evident powers are highly complex and elusive.[12] The two types of latent power that, in Penrose's insightful analysis, space holds can be given new and particular kinds of meanings in the service of certain structures of nationalist struggles and the political economy. The first is the material dimension of space, comprising the substance that is fundamental to human life—land, water, atmosphere, etc. This dimension generated relational dynamics. The second is the emotional power of space. Filtered through human experiences of time and process, space has the capacity to invoke or release emotional responses,[13] which are crucial for nationalist imaginations and struggles.

The combination of the material and emotional dimensions of space, which turns them into sources of concrete power in society through human agency, also transforms space into territory—captured in the idea of "territoriality."[14] Territoriality, as the geographic expression of power, is one of the most common strategies for exercising political control, given that, as Hastings Donnan and Thomas M. Wilson put it, it implies social relationships and cultural identifications.[15] In this context, it is understandable that the "juxtaposition of different cultural formations in a locality," therefore, "generates multiple understandings of political space, action and thought."[16]

Penrose's elaboration of space relates to that of Kevin R. Cox. In addressing the content and form of the politics of space, Cox makes a crucial distinction between what he calls the *spaces of dependence* and the *spaces of engagement*. The first is defined by "those more-or-less localized social relations upon which we depend for the realization of essential interests, and for which there are no substitutes elsewhere; they define space-specific conditions for our material well-being [what Penrose calls the latent material dimensions of space] and our sense of significance [what Penrose calls the latent emotional dimensions of space]." The spaces are inserted in broader sets of relationships, which threaten to undermine or dissolve them. People need to "organize in order to secure the conditions for the continued existence of these spaces of engagement," but they do so by engaging with other centers of power, which may include the local, state, or national governments and the press. By doing this, another space, the space of engagement, is constructed, which becomes "the space in which the politics of securing the space of dependence unfolds."[17] In this chapter, the role of the press as the space of engagement in securing the space of dependence is useful in my analysis of spatial narrative or spatial discursivity.

Lefebvre focuses on the multiple ways in which space is experienced and identifies three types of socially produced space: perceived, conceived, and lived spaces. Perceived space, or spatial practice, "encompasses the material spaces of daily life where social production and reproduction occurs"; conceived space, or representation of space, "refers to the socially constructed discourses, signs, and meanings of space"; lived space, or representational space, "encompasses the coexistence or interaction of the first two types of spaces." The latter, as "the actually lived material and symbolic experience," can be a "terrain for the generation of "counter-spaces," spaces of resistance to the dominant order." Martin and Miller argue that Lefebvre's conceptual triad is useful in the analysis of contentious politics, "as it recognizes the material spatial dimensions of social life, the symbolic meanings of space, and the imposition of, and resistance to, dominant socio-spatial orders."[18] This is particularly true in the contentious politics between majority and minority ethnic groups in Nigeria as they struggle for or against national accommodation.

Even though there is some consensus in the literature on the theoretical importance of space, there is limited consensus on how to theorize it. A divide exists between those who seek to concretize spatiality in traditional materialist terms and those whose conceptualization locates space within a system of metaphors existing in narrative and discursive practices. However, as Natter and Jones note, this tendency to dichotomize the conceptualization of space is based on an a priori split in the representation of social life and social life *as lived*, "a distinction that fails to problematize the inter-relationships between material conditions and their reproduction by, and consequence on, representation and discourse."[19] Recognizing that material conditions of social life are connected to narrative and discursive practices is crucial to overcoming this dichotomy toward a theoretically informed social analysis.

Similarly, two views of territoriality are present in the literature. The first, now largely discredited, sees human territoriality as "a natural, instinctive phenomenon" and assumes that human beings "have an in-built territorial urge or an inner compulsion to acquire and defend space."[20] The deterministic—and inevitability-of-conflict—assumptions of this thesis are generally responsible for its widespread rejection. The second thesis ignores deterministic assumptions in spatial relations. It holds that human territoriality represents a geographic strategy that connects society and space. In stating this thesis, Robert D. Sacks posits that territoriality is "the attempt by an individual or group to affect, influence or control people, phenomena and relationships by delimiting and asserting control over geographical area . . . called a territory."[21] In line with this, Penrose states: "Territoriality is a significant form of power. This is because it creates territories which are seen to satisfy both the material requirements of life and the emotional requirements of belonging—of placing oneself in both time and space. . . . For human beings, some measure of control over a territory, whatever form it takes, has been constructed as fundamental to a sense of control over one's self and, by extrapolation, to a society's control over itself." Territoriality is therefore a spatial expression of power, which emphasizes the potency of space as a component of power.[22]

Sacks, who emphasizes that territoriality is a *relationship* and not an object, defines territoriality strictly as "as attempt by an individual or group (x) to influence, affect, or control objects, people, and relationships (y) by delimiting and asserting control over a geographical area. This area is the territory."[23] His elaboration of the tendencies of territoriality is very useful for the analysis of its manifestation in particular contexts. For Taylor, territoriality involves: (1) an interlocked system of attitudes, sentiments, and behaviors that are (2) specific to a particular, usually delimited, site or location, which (3) in the context of individuals in a group, or a small group as a whole, (4) reflect and reinforce, for those individuals or groups, some degree of excludability of use, responsibility for, and control over activities in these specific sites.[24]

In what I call Taylor's *citizenry-based* conceptualization of territoriality, inclusion, and exclusion in rights and duties are central. What happens in this case is rejection—based on nonterritorial membership—by exclusion. However, in his elaboration of various views of territorial functioning, Taylor seems to point to particular conceptualizations that present a paradox in the definition of territorial membership—relevant in the context of this chapter. For instance, territoriality conceived as "association with a place due to repeated usage or the passage of time" echoes J. J. Edney's position that territoriality implies "those places with which persons or individuals are linked by a more or less continuous association."[25] In this view, claim to territoriality is based on *long residence*—relevant to the Hausa in the case examined in this chapter—as against "original ownership" of territory, on which Kataf claims are based.

Power is at the heart of territoriality; the will to power conditions the struggle over territoriality. Anderson argues that territoriality gives relationships of power greater tangibility. It also "simplifies issues of control, and provides symbolic markers of property, possession, inclusion and exclusion." However, Anderson points out that these strengths of territoriality are, ironically, its weaknesses: "While simplifying control, territoriality oversimplifies and distorts social realities and it arbitrarily divides and disrupts social processes. . . . While giving greater tangibility to power relationships, it de-personalizes and reifies them, obscuring the sources and relations of power. It sharpens conflict and generates greater conflict as its assertion encourages rival territorialities in a 'space-filling process.'"[26] Indeed, what the narratives in this chapter illustrate is the oversimplification and distortion that are inherent in narratives of territory.

The contradictory nature of territoriality, or its inherent paradox, implies that domination and resistance, hegemony and counterhegemony, are simultaneous potentials inscribed in its practices, though not necessarily as cast-iron binaries situated differently in social polarities. The binaries may manifest at different conjectures within the same entity or group and within the same territory.

As argued in chapter 4, there is a debate in the literature on whether Antonio Gramsci in his influential exposition on the concept of "hegemony" captures the noncoercive, nonforcible (ideological) aspect of the structure of consent in society or if he meshes the coercive with the noncoercive aspect of hegemony.[27] Although the territorial conflict examined here has both the forcible and the nonforcible dimensions, and in fact represents a symbiotic relationship between the two, this chapter concentrates on how the *ideological* aspect, which "at its most pristine," as Agbaje argues, constitutes "the construction of consensus, consent, and dissent through subtle, indirect and non-forcible means,"[28] is used to respond to a crisis involving the violent push toward hegemony and the violent counterhegemonic struggle that this provokes. The attempt at the "idealization of [a group's] schema into a dominant framework that reigns as common sense"[29] becomes the basis for hegemonic and counterhegemonic struggles and narratives in the media.

Territoriality has historical, cultural, political, economic, or symbolic manifestations,[30] which are capable of polarizing territories. In some cases, it manifests as institutional divisions that set artificial limits; in others, "as economic factors (central market, single-crop economies, raw materials) or as social factors (a specific community organization); in yet others, as political factors (capital city, location of administrative centers) or as cultural factors (different languages, own customs, different worldviews)."[31]

Zango-Kataf: A Space of Struggle

The explosive nature of ethno-religious competition and rivalry, and the often-unjust reactions of the postcolonial Nigerian state, are well illustrated in the Zango-Kataf crisis. The constitutive, constraining, and mediating roles of space[32] in identity politics are also evident in this crisis. The background is important here. The grievances of the southern Kaduna minority ethnic groups in Nigeria (including the Kataf) center on their relationship with the majority Hausa(-Fulani), regarded as the dominant ethnic group in the north of the country and the country at large. The Hausa are the single most populous ethnic group in northern Nigeria. They were conquered during a jihad that started in 1804, led by the Fulani religious teacher Usman dan Fodio. The minority Fulani who conquered the Hausa and imposed the Islamic religion on the largely "pagan" Hausa adopted the Hausa language and culture. The two groups also intermarried and meshed so much so that, owing to the political sagacity of the Fulani elite, they formed an unusual ethnic amalgam that is called the Hausa-Fulani.

This ethnic amalgam sought to incorporate smaller ethnic groups in the north while imposing its political institution, culture, language, and even religion (Islam) on the minorities, some of whom had embraced Christianity. Despite its considerable success in this bid, the hegemony achieved has experienced (and still experiences) constant counterhegemonic challenges from the minority ethnic groups, particularly the non-Moslem ones. Many of the minority ethnic groups in the north of Nigeria—even though the Hausa language became their lingua franca, and the Hausa traditional dress almost became their "national costume"—were receptive to Christian conversion and education, in spite of the efforts of British colonial officials to discourage Christian proselytizing in the northern region in observance of an unwritten Anglo-Fulani pact. The adoption of the Hausa language—first by the conquering Fulani—and in a few cases the adoption of its culture by the minorities, however, did not lead to assimilation and integration of these minority groups into one cultural group.[33]

In the relationship between the dominant and the dominated groups in the north of Nigeria, political, cultural, and religious domination interconnect with economic inequality. In the resulting vortex, the minorities accused the Hausa-Fulani elite of deliberate economic underdevelopment of the non-Hausa-Fulani areas of the north. As Dear and Wolch point out, a territorially specific crisis can occur if a particular combination of economic, political, or social crises is concentrated in a single locale.[34] When the identity of those who occupy a land and space is called into question, a situation is presented in which such identity and identification with the land and space can be mobilized into a cause.[35] This situation is potentially more combustible when conflicting social groupings that are ethnically—or religiously—constituted are situated within a shared territory.

Ibrahim and Igbuzor note that the crisis created by the failure to fashion a national framework and establish justice and equity in the distribution of resources and rewards in Nigeria is "most graphically illustrated by the emergent patterns of interethnic conflicts it has engendered in relation to access to economic resources and political power at the local level": "The situation in Zango-Kataf is fairly unique and more complex as centuries of interaction between the Hausa on the one hand, and the other communal groups such as Bajju and Kataf (Atyab) have failed to produce the basis of a more enduring harmonious community life. In this respect the situation differs from other cases where the adoption of Islamic religion and inter-marriages have attenuated the level of social and cultural distance between 'immigrant' Hausa population and the 'host' communities. What one finds in the Zango-Kataf area of southern Kaduna is the tendency for ethnic boundaries to remain impervious to social and cultural exchanges such as marriages across ethnic and religious boundaries."[36]

The tension between the two communities over territoriality was a long-standing one. The Kataf, in their submission to the Cudjoe Commission of Inquiry into the February 1992 violent clashes between them and the Hausa, claimed that the Zango-Kataf land belonged to them and that they had accommodated the "Hausa immigrants" on generous terms. The Kataf claimed that, following the traditional system of landholding, the land should revert to the original owners. They were, therefore, seeking to "reclaim" their land from the "squatting" or "stranger" Hausa.[37] This historical claim to being indigenous to the land (which in Nigeria is called the principle of "indigeneity") was contested by the Hausa, who claimed to be "indigenous" to Zango-Kataf after living there for centuries. Ibrahim and Igbuzor write: "It would seem from the grievances of the Kataf who presented a deluge of complaints of injustice, socio-economic deprivations and cultural suppression, and the extent of the chains of the violent outbursts targeted at the Hausa in 1992 that the ultimate goal was to 'reclaim' their land by wiping out the Hausa community in Zango-Kataf. Otherwise, it would be difficult to come to terms with the scale of ethnic mobilisation, the sophistication of the weaponry deployed, and the scale of violence unleashed by both Hausa and Kataf [Atyab] on one another."[38]

This situation typifies Sacks's argument that territorial relationships are defined within particular social contexts in terms of differential access to things and people; a malevolent relationship occurs when differential access through territoriality benefits one group at the expense of another.[39] This comes into sharper relief as identity achieves its strongest expression in political situations of conflict over land and territory.[40]

The Zango-Kataf local government area first erupted in violence in February 1992, starting at Zango town. The local government council, under the chairmanship of Juri Babang Ayok, a Kataf, announced that the Zango weekly market would be relocated from the (Hausa-dominated) town center to a new site on the outskirts of the town. The ostensible reasons for the relocation were congestion in the old market center and little or no space to accommodate new traders, the poor hygienic conditions of the old market, and the unsuitable location of the market in the midst of residential houses belonging to the Hausa.[41] These technical reasons constitute an attempt to *displace* attention from the relationship between the controller and the controlled onto the territory, because "the local government has so decided."[42] However, the relocation, it seems, was influenced more by the felt need to reduce Hausa commercial domination and expand opportunities for emergent Kataf traders in Zango than by the reasons given—considering the demonstrated attachment of the Kataf to their soil (homeland)[43] and the resolve to benefit more than any other group from the economic potentials derivable from that soil. The reasons were, therefore, strongly territorial in both emotional and material dimensions, as the market—as a significant site—became an object or center of contestation.[44] The attempt to present the relocation as a technical decision by the local government highlights the territorial tendency toward classification. Territoriality classifies by *area* rather than by *type*,[45] making the location or relocation in space appear disentangled from, as in this case, ethnic group interest, though, as Taylor reminds us, even "small shifts in spatial location may result in major changes in territorial cognitions or behaviours, or both."[46] Social rules, such as the need to maintain hygienic conditions in the market and reduce congestion, and territorial rules, such as the need to redress the unsuitable location of the market, are mutually constitutive—a phenomenon captured by the term "spatiality." Such spatial relations invest places with power.[47]

The Hausa community opposed this move, claiming that the site for the new market was part of the Muslim praying ground. It also saw this as a "vindictive" cartographic strategy to upturn its economic advantage and strength. The Hausa, therefore, asked the courts for an injunction stopping the relocation, which was granted. As the ensuing violent territorial competition showed, it was not a competition for space per se, but a competition for things and relationships in space.[48] This "competition for things" was configured around economic relations, which then set off—within the "relationship in space"—particular patterns of political struggle and social strife.[49] On February 6, 1992, when the new market was scheduled to open, violent clashes erupted between the two groups, which led to 95 people (mostly Hausa) dead, 252 injured, and 133 houses and farmlands destroyed.

The market issue was only an avenue for the Kataf to express their rejection of the Muslim Hausa domination of political, cultural, and economic life in Zango-Kataf, which manifested in many ways, including the derogatory reference to the Kataf as "*arna*" or "kaffir" (pagans) because they were Christians. Territoriality, therefore, provided a means for the reification of power, as the potentialities of power are made explicit and real by making them visible.[50] The Commission of Inquiry into the crisis had hardly concluded its public sitting when a new riot broke out in May. These clashes spread to other places such as Kaduna, Zaria, and Ikara. This conflict was sparked by a written threat by Kataf village heads indicating their decision to repossess Kataf land "appropriated" by Hausa, the subsequent uprooting of crops on Hausa farmlands by Kataf youths, retaliatory attacks on Kataf, the alleged manipulation of the proceedings of the commission, and more.

With the violence spreading to other cities and towns, the dominant Hausa directed their attacks on Christians, specifically Christians from the south of Nigeria, who happened to be mainly Igbo.

In this way, ethno-religious groups not directly involved in the crisis were brought into it by direct attacks on them. The ongoing debates, disagreements, and polemics on interethnic relations in Nigeria, which polarize—at one level—the north and the south, and Christians and Moslems, formed the background to these attacks on nonbelligerent groups like the Igbo, Christian northerners, and some Yoruba in Kaduna. The crisis was, therefore, as much spatial as politico-religious. The various dimensions of the crisis, however, are all manifestations of the struggle over the reality or nonreality of the *grand nation* and the conditions of its reality.

This also explains why the "southern press" was inserted into the struggle as the mouthpiece of the Kataf, who did not have media outlets of their own. The "southern press," in its ongoing larger "war" against (Muslim) Hausa-Fulani "domination" of the country, appropriated the Kataf (territorial) struggle and used it to argue against and for hegemonic and counterhegemonic politics.

In the May bloody riots, Zango town was virtually reduced to rubble; several churches were burned and Christian clerics were killed. Over sixty thousand people were displaced. The casualties suffered by the Hausa in Zango-Kataf itself and in Kaduna—where it was believed that the Igbo who had been targets of incessant attacks by religious fanatics over the years were well armed to defend themselves against their attackers—were said to have shocked the northern (Muslim) power elite, who vowed to punish those responsible for the riots. The official response was also an expression of shock. Hundreds of Kataf people were arrested and held without charge for several months. Six prominent Kataf men, including the retired general Zamani Lekwot, the former military governor of Rivers State, and the former Nigerian ambassador, were charged with complicity in the riots before a special tribunal constituted by the Federal Military Government (FMG). The trial drew national attention. The prosecution later withdrew its case, but security agents rearrested the suspects as they left the tribunal. In September 1992, the Kataf men were charged before another tribunal, and fourteen of them, including the retired general, were later sentenced to death. In spite of the alleged virulent insistence—by highly placed Hausa-Fulani, both in the military and in the civil service, led by the secretary to the government of the federation, Aliu Mohammed, and the security chief, General Haliru Akilu—that the Kataf men be executed,[51] the FMG under General Ibrahim Babangida commuted the sentences to five years' imprisonment. The verdict of the tribunal sparked another national conflict as Christians and southerners condemned both the tribunal and the government for siding with the dominant Hausa, whereas northern Muslims and the Hausa-Fulani responded that the verdict should have been upheld by the FMG. In 1995, Lekwot and his constituents were released from prison.

Although the Hausa were regarded as a minority group in Zango-Kataf, where the Kataf controlled the local government, they were the majority in the larger context of the north of Nigeria—and (alongside the Fulani) in the country as a whole. The literature tends to define ethnic minorities in the context of the power spectrum in particular national and state formations in a way that mechanically fixes them at the lowest rung of the power ladder. This tendency is typified by Thomas H. Eriksen and Eghosa Osaghae. The former defines ethnic minority as "a group which is numerically inferior to the rest of the population in a society, which is politically non-dominant and which is being reproduced as an ethnic category." The latter emphasizes the relational nature of the category by stating that ethnic minorities are "usually defined in contradistinction to major groups with whom they coexist in political systems, as groups which experience systemic discrimination and domination because of numerical inferiority and a host of historical and sociological factors, and have taken political action in furtherance of their collective interest."[52] The existence of politically dominant ethnic minorities is not captured by these definitions. As Osaghae puts it, "Almost as a rule, minorities which are not subjected to domination or discrimination, and instead constitute dominant and hegemonic groups . . . are excluded from the category of proper minorities."[53] Do numerically inferior groups who are politically dominant cease to be minorities? My answer is no. Is the category of "minority" a function of numbers? I will say yes. Or is it a function of (political, economic, etc.) power? Certainly not in widely held views. Therefore, one way to get out of this bind, and yet be able to inscribe the location of power in minority-majority relations in specific contexts, is to reconceptualize the experience as "marginal-dominant" relations. In the particular case of this territorial contest, the Kataf were the majority whereas the Hausa were the minority; but in the overall context of the Nigerian state, the more consequential territorial space in which the battle for supremacy eventually was fought, that is, at the end of the violent clashes, the Hausa were the majority whereas the Kataf were a minority group. Therefore, although the Kataf were the majority in the specific locale, they were also the marginal group, whereas the Hausa, who were the minority in Zango-Kataf, were the dominant group, both in that locale and in the larger context.

What resulted from this mix was the clash of a social definition of "territory" by the Kataf, who saw themselves as the "natural" and "legal" heirs to the land, in spite of the location of "squatters" on that space and the territorial definition of "social relationship" by the Hausa, whose "ownership" was based on actual and long-term possession.[54] The narratives in the media reflect the conflicting social definition of territory and the territorial definition of social (ethnic and political) relationships.

I examine the universe of articles, news stories, and editorials on this crisis published in the newspaper *New Nigerian* and in two newsmagazines, *TELL* and *TheNEWS*, between 1992 and 1995. In their founding editorial direction, these sources reflect the conflicting ethno-religious and ethno-spatial relations in the country. The three publications were chosen because of their overt and strong support for either side in the dispute. *New Nigerian*, at the time of this crisis, was the only regular nationally distributed print medium that defended the interests of the largely Islamic north of Nigeria. *TELL* and *TheNEWS* were perhaps the most virulent in the (pro-Christian) southern media war against what was perceived to be the (Islamic) Hausa-Fulani domination of the other ethnic groups in Nigeria. The standpoint of both, therefore, recommends them for analysis in the Zango-Kataf crisis; no other medium in the north and the south focused on the crisis as much.

Admittedly, there is a clear imbalance in the location and influence of the print media in Nigeria. Most of the influential and successful newspapers and newsmagazines are located in and around Lagos, the former capital city in the south—a fact that has necessitated their description as the "Lagos-Ibadan press," "southern press," or even "*Ngbati* press."[55] *TELL* and *TheNEWS* are two of the leading organs in this "Lagos-Ibadan" press. Some professional journalists at *Newswatch*, who were dissatisfied with alleged collusion with state power by its editorial chiefs, founded *TELL* in 1991. *TELL* immediately became agitational, confronting the tyrannical military regime in power and becoming a key pillar of the eventual prodemocracy struggle. This struggle was as much against military rule as against alleged ethno-regional domination by the Hausa-Fulani power elite. The same is true of *TheNEWS*, which was founded by five editors who resigned from *African Concord* magazine, owned by the billion-aire businessman Moshood Abiola. After publishing a cover story critical of the military president, General Ibrahim Babangida,[56] the *African Concord* and its sister publication in the *Concord* Newspapers Group were proscribed by the military regime; the reopening of the publications was conditional on an apology from the *African Concord* editor. The chief editor and his senior editors refused to apologize and consequently resigned. They later founded *TheNEWS*.

In contrast, *New Nigerian* was founded in 1966 by the defunct Northern Regional Government to correct the media "imbalance" in Nigeria and as an instrument of northern power—in what one of its former managers described as a "war of unequal combat-ants." In its inaugural editorial, the paper affirmed that "as [the] Northern newspaper, we shall seek to identify ourselves with the North and its peoples, their interest and their aspirations. For that we offer no apology."[57] The data gathered are subjected to narra-tive and discourse analysis to tease out their implications in the process of constructing and deconstructing the power of territori-ality. Following Jacobs, I analyze the data through three different aspects of the discourses on the Zango-Kataf crisis. These are plot, characters, and genre.[58]

Plot is concerned with the selection, evaluation, and attribution of differential status to events.[59] It is fluid and complex in its relation-ship to events, with the capacity to "linger" on a particular event, flashback to past events, or flash forward to future events. Which events are chosen for discursive narration and which are ignored provide critical clues concerning the understanding of community in a time-space horizon that links the past, present, and future in an organic way with certain spaces.[60] Rapport and Dawson describe this as "fixities of social relations and cultural routines localized in time and space." *Character* analysis in a discourse is key to understanding the construction of heroes and antiheroes—and by extension, thesis and antithesis. Research by Rapport and Dawson has demonstrated the use of binary civil discourse to "purify" public actors and their allies and "pollute" the other, the "enemies."[61] As Jacobs elaborates, to discursively position themselves as heroic, actors cast themselves as rational, controlled in their motivation, open and trusting in their relationships, and regulated by the impersonal, whereas the other is cast as irrational and uncontrolled in its motivation, secretive, deceitful, and arbitrary.[62] *Genre* provides "a temporal and spatial link between characters and events." Of the four "archetypal" genres of Western literature, only tragedy is useful for my analysis. Usually in a tragedy "the hero typically possesses great power, but is isolated from society and ultimately falls to an omnipotent and external fate or to the violation of a moral law."[63] However, as Wagner-Pacifici and Schwartz warn, there are inconsistencies that must be found in the strictures of these different modes of presenting stories; therefore the analyst must determine how each relates to events and social settings.[64]

Kataf-strophe: The Press and the Discourse of Territoriality

Generally, before the first Zango-Kataf riots broke out in February 1992, the "Lagos-Ibadan" press (the pro-Kataf press) tended, both implicitly and explicitly, to present the minorities in the north, particularly those in the area called southern Kaduna or southern Zaria, as suffering under the yoke of Hausa-Fulani domination. *TELL* typified this tendency in its initial report on the trial of the accused Kataf men: "The trial has generated public interest and it was seen as significant in the volatile relationship between the minority Kataf people and the Hausa community in Kaduna state. The Kataf are only one of the minority ethnic groups in the state, especially in the area known as Southern Zaria, that have remained sensitive to perceived domination by the majority Hausa ethnic group."[65]

When the riots broke out, the discourse was fitted into this larger frame, given that it was the first time the majority Hausa ethnic group suffered huge losses of life in a clash with a minority ethnic group in the north. In response to such accounts, *New Nigerian* published an essay that described the "southern (pro-Kataf) press" and "their masters" as "die-hard Hausa-Fulani haters": "During and after the Zango-Kataf massacre any keen observer would have noticed the well-planned and orchestrated disinformation going on especially among the Lagos/Western (southern) axis print and electronic media. Their hatred for the North (they and their masters) has blinded them to even attempt an objective coverage of the crisis. It is a well-known fact that the hatred by the southern press and their masters is disguised as a hatred for the Hausa-Fulani."[66]

In the pro-Kataf press, the February clash was presented as a riot resulting from an attempt by a marginal and marginalized group— the Kataf—to throw off the yoke imposed on it by the dominant (Hausa). But for the pro-Hausa *New Nigerian,* "The [riot was] a conflict over land and petty jealousies over economic advantages of one tribe over the other."[67] Having stated the territorial basis of the crisis, the narratives then emphasized issues of justice and fairness as these relate to dominant-marginal relations in Nigeria.

While the press was still reacting to the first round of clashes, other, even bloodier, violence broke out in May of the same year. In his reaction, the military president, General Babangida, exaggerated that this was "the darkest chapter in the nation's history," and as such, all accused persons would be considered guilty until they could prove otherwise. This is the point at which the trial to follow began to be discursively delegitimized by the pro-Kataf press. *TheNEWS* stated, "This [Babangida's statement] is a wrong principle in law. It ought to be the other way round." It added that "the tragedy [is] deep, while the stream of emotions [are] even deeper." *TheNEWS* asserted that the federal secretary for justice and the attorney-general appointed knew "too well" that what his boss, General Babangida, said was wrong, but also realized that this was "one big assignment he had to do well."[68]

When the accused eventually came to trial in late July, it is evident in the narratives that the pro-Kataf press framed the trial of the Kataf leaders as only a necessary step toward their discharge and acquittal. *TELL* reported: "The wheel of justice grinds slowly. For Zamani Lekwot, retired major general and former governor [of] River state, who had been in detention since the May communal riots in Zango-Kataf . . . the first step forward in obtaining justice was taken last week." The trial was narrated as the first step toward reversing the history of injustice against a marginal group, the Kataf, perpetuated by a dominant group, the Hausa. *TELL* continued: "Last [week's] appearance before the Benedict Okadigbo tribunal was the first by Lekwot[,] who had been kept incommunicado since he was arrested by security agents last May. . . . As expected in such a celebrated case, the court was crowded with lawyers. . . . Among [them] . . . was Yohanna Madaki, a retired colonel and former governor of the defunct Gongola state. Like Lekwot, Madaki is a member of the Southern Zaria community that have been having testy times for many years with the Hausa-Fulani ethnic group. . . . [This] trial [is] another milestone in the testy relationship. . . . The Kataf people have protested alleged partiality of the state government."[69]

Linkages with the past constitute a regular mode of combining present events (injustice) with similar acts in the past, in a move toward the construction of a just and equitable future. In its reporting and commentaries on the clashes, the pro-Kataf press emphasized the drive toward "undue" territoriality by the Hausa. In one of the articles, *TELL* reported that Ayok Juri Babang, the chairman of the Zango Kataf local government, a Kataf who was among the accused, told the tribunal that when the May riots began, he was holding a security meeting over a letter sent by Zango-Kataf (Hausa) Muslims to the leader of northern (and Nigerian) Muslims, the Sultan of Sokoto, informing him that a jihad was about to begin in Zango-Kataf "as a result of the 100 Muslims murdered during the February riots in the town": "The letter which was signed by Aliyu Jibril of Zango-Kataf, complained that after the riots, several Muslims had lost their houses or farmlands, which they had inherited from their forefathers for more than 70 years. . . . Jibril told [Sultan] Dasuki that Nigerian Muslims are patient people, but in accordance with the injunction of the holy book, if we are cheated, and a jihad occurs in Zango, any Muslim who kills the unbeliever to heaven he will go, and if he is killed, still to heaven he will go." With this "fact" on the attempt by the Hausa to carry out a jihad—in a version of the major jihad that had started in 1804, which subjugated the "pagan" tribes in the north and established Fulani (and Hausa) ascendancy over a wide territory that became northern Nigerian—the magazine argued that the prosecution "lost steam" and "was in despair."[70]

But for the *New Nigerian*, the emphasis was on those who gave evidence that pointed to the resolve by the Kataf to "exterminate" the Hausa on shared territory. For instance, the paper reported a witness that elaborated on this alleged display of exclusionary territoriality by the Kataf: "[A] group of Katafs numbering 500 gathered and surrounded the Zango town. He said this was after uprooting the Hausas' crops on their farms, and killing many of them. He told the tribunal that the Hausas were gathered at the old market by the Katafs and were forced to sing while the Kataf danced, until when they (Katafs) were tired of dancing. They (Katafs), he said, forced the Hausas to move to the new market site where they ordered them to lie down on the ground and then set them ablaze."[71]

The allegation of the movement of the Hausa "captives" from the old market to the new market where they were allegedly "set ablaze" carries a strong image of social power over space and territory, given the opposition of the Hausa to the new market site. Similarly, the allegations of the destruction of the crops of the Hausa evokes the fact that territoriality manifests in the safeguarding or destruction of the objects of "our" or "their" material well-being, respectively. Here, through discursive territoriality, *New Nigerian* amplified a particular form of difference by emphasizing the destruction of the material power—that is, the resources—of the Hausa.

When the accused were discharged on a four-count charge of unlawful assembly, rioting with deadly weapons, causing disturbance, and arson, the pro-Kataf press celebrated the "victory" and canvassed for the immediate release of the Kataf men. But when the accused men were rearraigned on a twenty-two-count charge, including unlawful assembly, disturbing public peace, and culpable homicide punishable by death, the pro-Kataf press through its discursive presentation of the retrial implied that something other than justice would be the result of the second trial.[72] The latent theme is that of denial of justice and persecution. Such discursive structuring of the process of the trial was designed to make it easy for the pro-Kataf press to present the accused as "heroes" who are facing a tragic turn in the history of their relations with their "squatters" and "guests"—the Hausa.

But the pro-Hausa press did not see "heroes" in the Kataf men, rather they were "perpetrators of genocide," who—in spite of the fact that "going by historical precedents and facts of life, all tribes and races of the world have undergone some forms of migratory trends"—could not live peacefully with those who had settled on the same territory with them for several years: "The Kataf mobilized and armed themselves with guns, swords, knives and all kinds of dangerous weapons, descended on the unsuspecting Hausa-Fulani community in their houses, farms, mosques, etc. in a vicious attack, shooting, cutting their children, wives, looting, raping their wives and children and set[ting] the whole buildings in the community on fire."[73]

When the leading defense counsel withdrew from the case over his dissatisfaction with the process of the trial, the pro-Kataf press constructed the tribunal's chairman as a "Kataf Hangman,"[74] and the tribunal as "a law unto itself."[75] The implication of the withdrawal was presented thus: "Ordinary a sober attorney, Ajayi's [defence counsel's] lambast and resignation helped a shocked nation to visualize the political impact of the trials."[76] Not so, the pro-Hausa press (*New Nigerian*) contended as it stated its own version of the implications of the withdrawal: "The tribunal, undaunted by the withdrawal of defense counsel, assigned . . . Okhasememoh, one of the best criminal lawyers in the country, to defend the accused persons as required by law."[77]

TheNEWS also introduced an interesting dimension concerning ongoing narratives of "divide and rule" by the Hausa-Fulani against other ethnic groups in Nigeria. The magazine reported that the people of Onitsha, Okadigbo's hometown, did not "joyfully receive" the announcement of their townsman as the chairman of the tribunal because "many saw it as another attempt to use an Igbo man again" in victimizing men, particularly military officers, who had differences with those in power. The example is cited of another Igbo man, General Ike Nwachukwu, who headed the tribunal that tried and convicted the officers, including Major General Mamman Vatsa, accused of a coup plot against the Babangida regime.[78] *TheNEWS* also published a separate but related story along with the cover story on the "Kataf hangman" (Okadigbo), "on the roll of manipulated judges," detaining the cases of "judges whose verdicts have been questioned," concluding that after Okadigbo's job ends, "the nation awaits the next judge to be used like a lackey."[79]

The government's plan to rebuild Zango town, inhabited mainly by the Hausa, was another point of contention, given that the other towns in Zango-Kataf inhabited by the Kataf were not slated for reconstruction. The state governor, *TELL* wrote, had "proposed to the federal government a rehabilitation plan to include extensive development of infrastructure and a redesigning of the town's old cluster of settlement pattern." This, for the magazine, "could be another source of trouble": "The Katafs contend [that] the entire area belong[s] to them and they are in a deviant mood, waiting for the government to attempt any settlement. For one thing, they are indignant that nearly all government's pronouncements on the Zango-Kataf crisis tend to give short-shrifts to them and their age-long complaints over what they call the overbearing attitude of the Hausa community."[80]

When the "modern town" was eventually built in Zango from the "slummy settlement occupied by the Hausa," the pro-Kataf press narrated the "grouse" of the Kataf who insisted that this was yet another example of the government's "discrimination" against them: "Zango's good fortune is one of the reasons why tension runs a high temperature in Kaduna state, especially Zango-Kataf. The Kataf people point out that several houses were destroyed in Zonzon, a Kataf village bordering Zango . . . yet, up till today nothing has been done to rehabilitate or compensate the victims."[81]

Against this condemnation of "discriminatory" resettlement, the *New Nigerian* published a comment praising the rehabilitation work: "I saw the rehabilitation works, which has been carried out with extreme efficiency by any standard. That we could heal the scars in so short a period of time is a clear demonstration by the government to ensure return of peace."[82] *TELL* did not see "the return of peace," as narrated by the *New Nigerian*. On the contrary, it quoted a minority rights activist and lawyer and a retired army colonel who state that the crisis was embedded in the simple "principle of self-determination, quest for equality, freedom of religion, the right to think and dress as one likes in a normal social environment, not the one dictated by some self-appointed religious leaders." This contest was over territoriality and freedom, and therefore a question of who defines the opportunities for life and living, particularly given the "age-long complaint [by the Kataf] over what they call the overbearing attitude of the Hausa community." The market issue is captured as "a veil over the real issue," which was that "people from Southern Kaduna, including the Kataf, simply want to be on their own" and not, ostensibly, under Hausa-Fulani suzerainty: "So the market is just a tool used by the powerful people to continue to oppress the disadvantaged for their selfish end."[83]

TELL linked the matter to colonial history and the issue of traditional headship of the communities: "The British Indirect Rule policy . . . adopted the Hausa-Fulani Emirate model of native administration and, in consequence, brought many non-Hausa-Fulani groups under the rule of these two ethnic groups. . . . The Kataf, as well as many other minority groups in the north, battle with this historical antecedent. They battle daily with cultural imperialism. Their cry for self-determination is usually scuttled before it makes any impact."[84] The crisis was seen as partly a result of this. The magazine therefore reported: "The totality of the Nigerian citizenry is confused particularly now as to where power truly lies. 'Is it at the government house with the governor, emirate or chiefdom?' But since the government insisted that it cannot do without traditional rulers, 'it is only fair for each minority group to appoint its own custodian of traditions.'"[85]

Even if peace were to return, the pro-Kataf press insisted that "it will bear the legacy, a carry-over and constant reminder of these turbulent times." A key example of this, *TELL* pointed out, was the construction of police barracks at Zango, "so sited to conveniently separate the Hausa and Kataf villages. Something like a modern Berlin Wall." The newsmagazine emphasized the religious dimension of the crisis and the implications for national security and peace—given that the Kataf were mostly Christians, whereas the Hausa were mostly Muslims. It reported that whereas Christian leaders all over Nigeria were condemning the treatment of the Kataf and their leaders, the Muslim leaders were praising it. "Now," declared *TELL*, "the tension that generates from the Zango-Kataf disturbances case has snowballed into a religious hoopla, thus taking the nation again near the precipice."[86]

When the guilty verdict and death sentences were eventually passed out, the pro-Kataf press, as expected, assailed the validity of the judgment and linked the conviction of the Kataf leaders to the structural problem created by colonialism, which placed the Hausa-Fulani in an advantageous position in the north of Nigeria, and its implications for ethno-religious politics. *TELL* stated: "Many sections of Nigeria see the conviction as a direct attack on the minority ethnic groups in the North in their age-long fight against Hausa-Fulani hegemony. The Christian Association of Nigeria, CAN, has also joined the fray since most of the minorities are also Christians as opposed to the predominantly Muslim Hausa-Fulani. . . . The trouble which had its roots in pre-colonial Nigeria, may not be washed away by the shedding of Lekwot's blood. The Kataf of Kaduna State are only one of the scores of ethnic groups in the old Northern Region that have resisted Hausa or Fulani rule for centuries."[87]

The magazine was compelled to provide an even more elaborate historical context for the "subjugation" of the Kataf, which eventuated in the conviction of their leaders, a narrative that served to "justify" the demands of the Kataf and present the Hausa as "oppressors": "They [minority ethnic groups in the north] enjoyed relative freedom during the era of Habe (or old Hausa) dynasties. The coming to power of the Islamic jihadists under Shehu Uthman Dan Fodio changed the political tempo. Fodio and his successors embarked on a sometimes violent campaign of Islamisation of the minority ethnic groups. This campaign of conversion continued throughout the colonial era and up to the regime of Ahmadu Bello, the great grand-son of Dan Fodio. Bello was premier of the defunct Northern Region from 1955 until he was assassinated in 1966." The newsmagazine added that the "implications of these hundreds of years of subjugation have been profound," in that many minorities have been "almost completely assimilated" by the Hausa-Fulani with a few, such as the Kataf, resisting the assimilation by embracing "Christianity, partly as a weapon of protest," even though other Christian groups were under the "suzerainty" of "Muslim rulers." "This combustible chemistry," the magazine concluded, was the fundamental explanation for the violence and the verdict.[88]

This "fundamental explanation" of the events covering hundreds of years is a good example of what Paul Ricoeur points to in the idea of "followability" in narratives. He argues that "the fact that a story can be followed converts the paradox into a living dialect." Episodic dimension of the narrative, such as the clashes between the Kataf and the Hausa and the conviction of the Kataf leaders, draws "narrative time in direction of the linear representation of time," in that it moves from a "then, and then" of the narrative to answer the question "and then what?" But more important is the configurational dimension of such narratives in terms of their "followability." The configurational dimension—as evident in the way *TELL* presents the historical grand narrative of the Kataf-Hausa-Fulani relationship over time—deemphasizes the episodic dimensions of such encounters, as the occasional reports of the crisis did, but emphasizes their temporal features. This is done through the transformation of a "succession of events," such as the clashes, the trial, the debates, etc., "into one meaningful whole," which makes the larger story followable. Ricoeur adds that, in this context, it is the act of "retelling" (of the *longue durée*, in this case) that gives a greater significance to the narratives beyond the mere "telling."[89]

The pro-Kataf press also framed the condemned men as "freedom fighters" and "heroes." The key subtexts in the characterization of the accused as "heroes" include those of defiance (by the condemned men), honor (of the condemned men), persecution and injustice (against the condemned men and the Kataf), subversion of justice and capitulation to those in power (by the tribunal, particularly the chairman), and reprisal (by the Hausa-Fulani against Kataf and southerners).[90] The discursive task is clearly that of faulting the trial process that led to the verdict, the demonization of the tribunal (particularly the chairman, Justice Benedict Okadigbo), and condemnation of the death verdict.[91] The characterization of the chairman of the tribunal as an "antihero," a man who "seems cut and professionally spruced for the Kataf job,"[92] is meant to rob the tribunal of legitimacy and therefore dismiss the validity of the judgment. A prominent quote in *TheNEWS*, credited to the "respected jurist" Justice Akinola Aguda, stated, "I cannot see how Okadigbo [the trial judge] can really face his God." The composition of the tribunal was described by *TheNEWS* as a "patent illegality" because, even though the enabling decree, the Civil Disturbances (Special Tribunal) Decree No. 2 of 1987, "prescribes that the tribunal shall consist of one chairman and four other members making a total of five members," there were seven members appointed.[93]

The choice of Akpamgbo, "the archetypal man of controversy," to chair the tribunal was also dismissed as a nepotistic one because Okadigbo was from the same area of the country as the attorney-general, while they also shared "fellowship of the secret cult of Free masons." To show that Okadigbo was not a good judge, despite being "considered tough, courageous and single-minded," *TheNEWS* narrated the history of Okadigbo's penchant for violating the spirit of the law. It presented a few examples, including a case over the chairmanship of the Enugu local government in 1990 when the petitioner was declared the winner of an election even though he only asked the court to quash the victory of his opponent. It stated that by this, Okadigbo broke "new grounds in civil law" by granting "more relief than the petitioner had asked for." *TheNEWS* concluded that defense lawyers appearing before Okadigbo had to "deal with two prosecutors, the prosecuting counsel and the learned judge himself."[94]

The pro-Kataf press also gave prominence to the mass protest by "Bible-wielding [Kataf] women, effervescently chanting Christian songs" against the death verdict.[95] This was reportedly preceded by interdenomination church services: "The protest march began as soon as prayers ended. By six a.m. the demonstrators began to troop into the streets with the womenfolk and children in the vanguard. They barricaded the major streets carrying placards. . . . To further illustrate their anger, the women carried two coffins covered with white cloth. Inscribed on both were the words, 'Justice and Fair-play

LEKWOT: Matters Arising

Nigerians protest judicial murder

YINKA TELLA

T HE General Officer Commanding (GOC), the First Division of the Nigerian Army was simply aghast. Recently elevated to the newly created rank of Brigadier-General, John Shagaya had also held the powerful Internal Affairs portfolio in Nigeria's military government . With his wealth of experience he ought to have seen them all. Last Monday, as he led a convoy of about 10 military jeeps loaded to the hilt with armed personnel on a mission to assess the security situation in Kaduna metropolis however, he was confronted with another reality. He had not seen it all. He couldn't have seen it all.

The report he got was that thousands of Katafs, Banjus, Igbos and Yorubas had swarmed on the city on the morning of Monday, February 8, from designated centres at the secretariat of the Christian Association of Nigeria (CAN), and St. Joseph's Catholic Cathedral on Ibrahim Taiwo Road as well as the adjacent Baptist Church on Ahmadu Bello Way. There were also reports of a somewhat "impenetrable" mass of human beings said to number about a hundred thousand colonising all the main arteries and commercial, nerve-centres of the city such as Yakubu Gowon, Ibrahimn Taiwo and Ahmadu Bello Ways. They are obviously uncomfortable that Zamani Lekwot, a retired Major-General and diplomat would together with six other Katafs "hang by the neck" until death offers relief as decreed by the Benedict Okadigbo Civil Disturbances Tribunal. For somebody who is trained in the specialised art of managing violence, Shagaya, was not unduly worried. Already, he knew that the Nigerian Army depot

Figure 8.1. *TheNEWS* cover story (February 22, 1993) on the Kataf-Hausa crisis, narrating the discontent of the "'impenetrable' mass of human beings" over the death sentence imposed on Lekwot.

are dead.' The women were joined by the men after a few kilometres as they marched through the city centre. By seven a.m., they had cordoned off the major roads, singing with copies of the Bible in their hands."[96] The Bible, in this context, was constructed as a symbolic barricade, more or less signifying a symbolic (Christian) territorial defense, ostensibly against the forces of "hell." *TheNEWS* emphasized that "the predicament of Zamani Lekwot and his fellow-convicts [is] pure religious persecution."[97]

But for the *New Nigerian,* Justice Benedict Okadigbo was "not only a learned and transparently honest judge, but a devout Christian who could not have passed the sentence on Lekwot and co. without ample evidence." Therefore, "If the law is to be strictly adhered to, the federal government may have no option [than] to confirm the death sentence."[98] Here, contrary to the characterization by the pro-Kataf press, the religion (Christianity) of the chairman of the tribunal was used by the *New Nigerian* to legitimize the death sentence he passed on fellow Christians (the Kataf).

In its reports of the death sentences, the pro-Hausa press restated examples of the culpability of the condemned men, casting them firmly, in contradistinction to the discourse of the pro-Kataf press, as "antiheroes."[99] The key subthemes in the *New Nigerian* are those of proper execution of justice, deserved guilt, inhumanity (allegedly) displayed by Lekwot and other Kataf, and unjust treatment of the Hausa by the Kataf. Whereas Lekwot and the others were "Kataf leaders" and (rarely) "condemned men" for the pro-Kataf (southern) press, they were "condemned criminals" for the anti-Kataf (northern) press. The pro-Hausa press praised the death sentences,[100] reporting that "nothing should be done to put a wedge between the condemned criminals and justice."[101]

When the highest military legislative council commuted the death sentences to prison terms, the subthemes of defiance, dignity, honor, and future victory remained salient in the pro-Kataf press. *TheNEWS* typified such narratives:

> Prior to leaving Kaduna, the Zangon-Kataf six left a clear instruction about their attitude to the ruling. . . . Major-General Zamani Lekwot told his wife during one of her visits to the condemned cells, "go and tell them that I will not plead for clemency. I will not do it and nobody should plead for me because *I am not guilty.* Based on this clear resolve, [his wife] made it known to the family's associates that

nobody should make the sort of pleas for clemency the government appears interested in hearing. In fact, the mention of clemency infuriates her. A visibly angry Mrs. Lekwot asked, . . . "What is clemency? Is it not meant for people who are guilty of an offence? What offence has he committed? Was there any trial?" . . . As they [convicted Kataf leaders] languish in prison, far from their beloved wives and children, they are acting with concern for the future. In their various persons, they carry the honour of their families, a realisation that strengthens their desire to avoid the cop-out of clemency. Rather, to clear whatever stains may have attached to their names, the men wish to stand the hazards of a new trial, but this time before a regular court. . . . Beyond the honour of their families lies their consciousness of the dignity of the Kataf people . . . which remains defiant in the face of what it perceives as biased state assault on it.[102]

The pro-Hausa press was annoyed by this kind of discourse. It therefore directly attacked the "southern press" and the Christian Association of Nigeria (CAN) for being on the side of "mass murderers of innocent worshippers in the mosques," "fuelling the already volatile situation," and "crying foul over the verdict": "Since the tribunal passed its judgment, the southern press in their usual style of confusion and outright crucifixion of objectivity have began another wolf cry on what they described as 'shock inflicted by the Okadigbo tribunal verdict.' The shameless southern press . . . questioned the legality of [the] composition [of the tribunal] . . . [if Lekwot and co. escape the death verdict] it would amount to high rape of justice and a complete negation of the law."[103]

After Lekwot's release, the pro-Kataf press continued to monitor events in the area. When new chiefdoms were created in consonance with the yearning of the marginal ethnic groups, it was captured as the "clipping [of] caliphal [Hausa-Fulani] wings," which action "has rekindled a ray of hope in the hearts of the oppressed minority of Southern Kaduna and other parts of Northern Nigeria who have lived under the yoke of feudal caliphate rule for more than 200 years."[104] This was an exaggeration; even at that point, the jihad that led to the creation of the caliphate was nine years short of its bicentenary. However, in spite of its campaign against the Kataf, the pro-Hausa press still, in its narratives, insisted on a "united north" (including the Kataf and other southern Kaduna minority groups), an all-embracing territorial power that would stand against the geographical "south": "What the southerner . . . hate[s] to hear is that the north is one, a single entity. . . . Do not be deceived by the apparent hatred for the Hausa-Fulani. The hatred and contempt is for anything north and its people whether Christian or Muslim. We, the people of the North have no alternative than to stick together. We should not allow some people to reap where they did not sow. We share a common destiny."[105]

A paradox, it can be argued here, is inherent in this territorial contest—both in its actual and discursive contexts. Although the Hausa and the Fulani claim territorial rights against, and in opposition to, the minority Kataf, they nonetheless discursively insisted on a united north that incorporates the many minority groups under Hausa-Fulani suzerainty, complete with the dissimulation of the religious (Islamic) core and religious identity that was integral to the majority in the attempt to "stick together." The territorial struggle in a small locale is thus emblazoned unto the territorial struggles in the larger national space conditioned by the inherent material and emotional dynamics of space and the search for panethnic (political, economic, social, and cultural) accommodation. In the context of this north versus south narrative, *TheNEWS* linked the current crisis to some of the unresolved narratives of the Civil War: "Tension persists in Kaduna, with Igbo traders receiving quit notices from their shops in reprisal for their participation in the massive pro-Lekwot demonstrations. In the campaign for people's hearts, a revision of history is being attempted. It is now said that it was the northern minorities rather than the Hausa who fought and killed the Igbo during the war. . . . One issue . . . is the reported threat that the Igbos will have their certificate of occupancy [of lands] revoked [in Kaduna state] if they continue to support the Kataf over the Lekwot case."[106]

As evident here, the press—as a space of engagement—is discursively inserted into the localized social relations that define space-specific conditions—spaces of dependence[107]—for the material well-being and sense of significance of the Kataf and the Hausa. Although the trial was officially framed as a law-and-order matter, the press politicized this framing, pressing socioeconomic and political dynamics into the narratives.

Conclusion

Of all events that "demand narration," crisis ranks as one of the most important.[108] In territorial crisis, sociopolitical and economic contradictions are realized spatially.[109] Consequently, the contradictions of space fuel the contradictions of social relations, turning spaces, which bell hooks calls "home places," into "sources of self-dignity and agency, sites of solidarity in which and from which, resistance can be organized and conceptualised."[110] In Foucaultian terms, these "home places" are "heterotopias" or "performed spaces" that contain physical as well as social boundaries where resources are marked by their availability to some and nonavailability to others.[111] Recent scholarship has been engaged, as Neil Smith puts it, in an effort to retrieve the "spatiality of local politics" from "habitual invisibility."[112]

Thus the role of narrative discourse in understanding and analyzing such "performed spaces" and social processes has become increasingly central for social scientists.[113] This is because discourse and narration help in constituting identity and enabling social action,[114] linking disparate individuals together in a combinatorial identity formation that locates them in particular "imagined communities"—communities that then produce and reproduce what has been described as "a radically stabilized collision of competing meanings."[115] As Edward Said points out, territorial struggles are not fought only with soldiers and cannons, they are also fought at the level of ideas, images, and imaginations.[116]

Thus analyses of identity formation—particularly those based actively on territoriality—have made major contributions to our understanding of social agency. For instance, such analyses have shown the dynamics and limitations of the rigidifying aspects of (ethnic) identity by looking at these from what Somers calls the "categorically destabilizing dimensions of time, space and relationality," which emerge when identities are combined with discursivity.[117] To enliven space, as I have attempted to do in this chapter, and as Routledge correctly understands it, is "to move its discursive 'site' from that of an assumed inert backdrop against which social practices unfold to the foreground of analyses of resistance and the cultural politics of identity."[118] This is especially important in a country enmeshed in a struggle over how a grand nation can be constructed.

Locating the discourses of the Zango-Kataf crisis within the strictures of temporal and spatial configurations of dominant-marginal ethnic relations in Nigeria highlights the latent and manifest material and emotional dimensions of a territorial crisis in which both sides attempted to create differential access to resources and power based on identity. As this case indicates, the struggle over territoriality is a struggle over identity = a struggle over resources = a struggle for power. Ultimately, it is also a struggle over the proper basis of national togetherness. The discourses represent and reproduce existing patterns of power relations, given the capacity of humans to find gaps and contradictions in any social structure.[119] Such discursive formation reproduces "something which has materiality already as the result of a now past production." The resources on which power draws "have some real existence prior to their enablement of some action that constraints some other's action."[120] When discursive territoriality is understood as enmeshed in a struggle over power, our attention is drawn to what Louw describes as "the impact that 'lived battles' over hegemony have on communication."[121]

As this case indicates, a sociospatial dialectic is inherent in territoriality, in that "territorial outcomes are contingent upon the essentially unpredictable interactions of the spatial with economic and the political and social [cultural] spheres." Social life, therefore, structures territoriality and vice versa.[122] To ignore territoriality or simply assume that it has a subsidiary role is to miss a major part of the spatial manifestation of struggles for power and resources. The task of the theory of territoriality, as Sacks argues, "is to disclose the possible effect of territoriality as levels that are both general enough to encompass its many forms, and yet specific enough to shed light on its particular instances."[123] In this chapter, against the backdrop of what I call *discursive territoriality*, I pointed to the insertion of the press in the interface of power and territoriality that structures dominant versus marginal relations in Nigeria by exploring the attempts by the Kataf and the Hausa—and, by extension, their polarized supporters—to affect, influence, or control people, resources, and ethnic relationships through the delimitation and assertion of control over a particular space.

Inherent in such practices is the potential to reproduce and also to transcend existing social relations toward significant social change.[124] My argument is located within the spectrum of an agency conception of power, which sees power "to a large extent structurally determined."[125] In the discourse of dominant-marginal ethnic relations in Nigeria, the press uses the structural context in which these relations are located as resources in the mobilization of identity and the struggle to gain primacy in a territorial struggle, particularly with an eye on the political, economic, social, and cultural implications of such victory. The rival newspaper and newsmagazines supporting either side in the crisis emphasized and amplified, in different ways, the unifying and divisive potentials of territory, turning the material power of space, which exists as resources for human survival, into "our" resources that are necessary for "our" survival.[126] Space is, therefore, central to the relations between dominant and marginal groups, particularly those forced by historical or political circumstances to share the same territory. What the press does, as in this instance, is elaborate and deploy the latent emotional powers of space in affiliating the Hausa or the Kataf to the material (physical, political, and economic) properties of space toward constructing the space as "ours" as opposed to "theirs."

Finally, it must be noted that even though discursive territoriality cannot singly alter social relations in particular contexts in a way that changes the structure of the entire society, it is capable of setting in motion "unforeseen, and often undesirable, social consequences,"[127] as the Hausa-Kataf territorial struggle shows. In the next chapter, I examine similar spatial politics that also involve a minority ethnic group, but with two significant differences. The Ogoni are in the south of Nigeria and they are an oil-producing community. Therefore the Ogoni case provides an interesting comparative experience.

9

Narratives, Oil, and the Spatial Politics of Marginal Identities

The debate on the place of minority ethnic groups in Nigeria preceded the independence of the Nigerian state. However, by the 1940s and 1950s, it was evident that ethnicity in general and the struggle for the accommodation of the many ethnic nations within Nigeria would pose a major challenge to the process of nation-building. It was precisely at this point, particularly during the June 1957 London Conference on the Nigerian (Independence) Constitution, that the three dominant ethnic groups were struggling to gain advantage over one another and that ethnic minorities made it clear they would not be "pacified by the usual rhetoric and promises." These outcries from Nigeria's ethnic minorities meant that the 1957 London Conference, with its objective of independence for Nigeria in 1960, was "in dire peril." The British government, therefore, set up the Commission of Inquiry into the Fears of Minorities and the Means of Allaying Them.[1]

In the end, nothing transformative came out of this process. Ken Saro-Wiwa, the Ogoni leader, minority rights activist, writer, publisher, television producer, and former president of the Association of Nigerian Authors (ANA), notes this in *A Month and a Day: A Detention Diary*. Saro-Wiwa, who led the Movement for the Survival of Ogoni People (MOSOP), writes that "constitutional development in the wider Nigeria nation of which they [Ogoni] were only a nominal part had left them far behind."[2] As Michael Vickers notes in his important work on the Commission of Inquiry, *A Nation Betrayed*, Nigeria's minority ethnic nations were targeted as "pre-destined losers" at Nigeria's independence. Even though the British government and the colonial authorities "clearly felt that this rough, dismissive treatment of a large proportion of Nigeria's peoples could mean violence, bloodshed and retribution," they "held their breath and hoped that the bluff might work."[3] Evidently, although Nigeria has survived, the bluff hasn't worked. The minority ethnic nations continue to struggle for just and fair treatment in the Nigerian federation. Saro-Wiwa states: "As Nigeria celebrated independence [in 1960], the Ogoni were consigned to political slavery at the hands of the new black colonialists wearing the mask of Nigerianism." The struggle against his "political slavery," however, became at once more articulate and more disruptive in the late 1980s and 1990s, which, incidentally, were the years of successive transition-to-democracy programs instituted by the military regimes. "By 1990," Saro-Wiwa argues, "the Nigerian masquerade had become a real pain to the Ogoni, the more painful because Ogoni resources had gone to dress it up. And in the masquerade were bungling soldiers who mouthed platitudes about Nigerian unity and all such while they purloined the Ogoni and others."[4]

Eghosa Osaghae has argued that the management of ethnic problems in Nigeria "has tended to be complicated by the complex ethnic situations which give rise to them," particularly because these are "usually combined with other conflict-generating cleavages, such as religion . . . class and regionalism, in mutually reinforcing ways." With increased ethnic consciousness and political mobilization among the minority ethnic groups in Nigeria, based on factors such as "different perceptions of relative privileges or deprivation, history of inter-group relations, effects of state policies or actions, dispositions and strategies adopted by other competing groups . . . democratization, economic prosperity or decline, and transformatory social processes,"[5] by the early 1990s, even if they remained marginal, it was no longer possible for the majority ethnic groups and the Nigerian state to ignore the restiveness of the minority groups. As Osaghae notes, "Not since the rebellion of Isaac Adaka Boro, Sam Owonaro and Nottingham Dick, who declared a short-lived independent Niger Delta Republic in 1967 over oil-related grievances, has any oil-producing community sought redress in ways which involved mobilized mass action and direct confrontation with the state as the Ogonis did."[6]

The 1990s witnessed unprecedented "fighting back" by marginal ethnic groups as well as by other disparate interest groups in the Nigerian national space. Several marginal ethnic groups whose

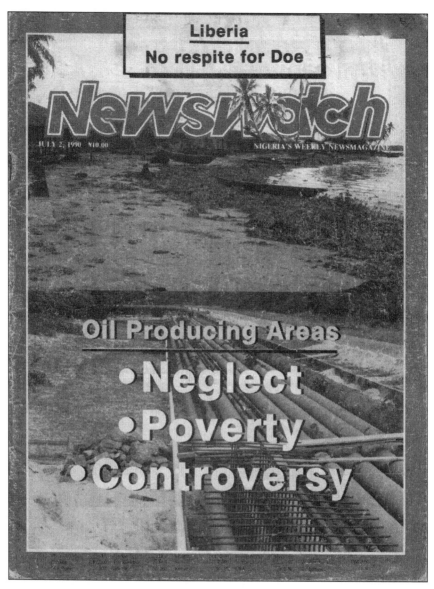

Figure 9.1. *Newswatch* cover story on the minorities in oil-producing areas of Nigeria. The bullet points on the cover constitute key narrative frames.

voices had before then been muffled raised their decibel level through sundry means. Perhaps the most prominent of these groups was the Ogoni of the oil-rich Niger delta region in the south of Nigeria. The Ogoni were campaigning principally for economic restitution, ecological rehabilitation, and, ultimately, self-determination.

The Nigerian press, being the pivot on which civil society rotates in Nigeria,[7] was centrally implicated in this struggle. It was manifestly involved in the genesis, amplification, and resolution of the crisis. This was evidently a result of the crucial role of the mass media in contemporary modern society. The mass media largely determine the cognitive and affective perceptions of the nonlocal world through their portrayal of events, issues, people, and places.[8] As Bogdanor argues, the dominant flow of political communication in the mass media eventually becomes the *definer* of what is significant in the politics of any given society at any time.[9]

The Nigerian press, with its history of agitation and its culture of dissent, which predated the formation of the Nigerian state, set the tone and tenor of the Ogoni struggle for equity, freedom, and justice, becoming one of the major sites in which the battles were fought. This chapter examines the supportive and subversive intervention of the Nigerian press in the relationship of the Nigerian state and majority groups with relatively powerless minorities, which are conceptualized here as *marginal identities*. I examine the narratives of power in the context of the construction of the sociopolitical legitimacy of a marginal ethnic group—the Ogoni—in the press and the strategic narrative support (or opposition) of the press in the battles by marginal identities against the (Nigerian) state, majority ethnic nationalities, hegemony, domination, and exploitation.

However, two points must be noted. Even though, generally speaking, the word "minority" can be seen in this context as interchangeable with "marginal," the term "marginal" is preferred because the question of who has power is not immediately clear in majority-minority relations, since there are politically—and economically—dominant minorities.[10] But the location of power is more clearly implicated in the construction of dominant-marginal discourse. Marginal identities are defined here by their subordination in political, social, and economic power structures, particularly in relation to the position and strength of dominant groups in the power matrix, and also in the politics of resource distribution. The second point is that no a priori suggestion is being made in this chapter of an all-powerful press with unmitigated effects on the political process. The role of the press is not unidimensional or unidirectional.[11]

I examine the pattern of coverage of the crisis at three stages: immediately before the outbreak of the crisis, the crisis and trials, and the aftermath. I draw inferences from the content of newspapers and newsmagazines in their narratives about the experience of the Ogoni. Two broad categories of newspapers and newsmagazines are considered. The first is the southern (Lagos-Ibadan axis) press, including *Newswatch*, *TELL*, *TheNEWS*, the *Tribune*, and *The Guardian*. The other is the northern press as represented by the *New Nigerian*. Whereas the first group was supportive of the Ogoni in their struggle for fairness, equity, and justice, the second was supportive of the status quo—the Nigerian state and the dominant ethno-regional group, the Hausa-Fulani.

Newswatch, a weekly newsmagazine founded in 1984 by four professional journalists, two from the north and two from the south, started as a liberal medium championing bold investigative reporting on January 28, 1985. *The Guardian* is owned principally by family of Alex Ibru, a minority (Urhobo) businessman, who lived most of his adult life in Lagos. He is, therefore, as much Urhobo as Lagosian. *The Guardian* is a liberal newspaper, which in its earliest years was praised as the "flagship of the Nigerian press" because of its intellectual depth and high journalistic standards.

As Rotimi Suberu argues, a "key feature of recent Nigerian politics is the strident agitation by ethnic minority communities."[12] This strident agitation became even more vociferous among the ethnic minorities in the oil-producing Niger delta region of Nigeria where the country derives about 90 percent of its national income. Given the treatment of these oil-producing minority groups, the Niger delta has been described as a place "where vultures feast."[13] It was against this backdrop that the Ogoni agitation, which started in its present form around 1990, achieved national and, subsequently, international attention. The Ogoni experience became even more widely known when four prominent Ogoni leaders were murdered, which preceded the arrest, trial, and execution of nine Ogoni activists, including the writer Ken Saro-Wiwa. The narrative period covered here spans 1992 through 1996.

Minorities in Nigeria: The Case of the Ogoni

Few terms in the social sciences and history have captured the attention of generations of politicians and scholars as has "minorities."[14] It has become one of the global indices of measuring the modernity of states and the civility of governments and other actors in the international system. This trend has led to greater attention being paid to minority problems, particularly in the context of the outbreak of nationalist struggles and struggles for self-determination around the world. Scholarly uses of this term, however, convey significant differences in meaning. Whereas the so-called ruling-elite theories of classical sociology focus on the ideological and social processes that make it possible for a minority to dominate and rule over a majority, modern sociology, particularly the American variant, focuses mainly on the way majority groups relate to relatively powerless minorities.[15] Power is central to both approaches. The second approach is useful here in its emphasis on the disadvantages experienced by minorities at the hands of majority groups who control the levers of power in the political process of any given state. In this context, ethnic minorities are usually defined "in contradistinction to major groups with whom they co-exist in political systems, as groups which experience systematic discrimination and domination because of numerical inferiority and a host of historical and sociological factors, and have taken political action in furtherance of their collective interests."[16]

The political-historical process in Nigeria has resulted in the ethnic category becoming the most stable unit of political action of all social formations arising from the colonial period.[17] The rise of consciousness of minorities, and their subsequent recognition, was a phenomenon that accompanied the hegemonic scheming and exclusionary politics of political gladiators of majority groups in the decolonization period in Nigeria. As a reaction to their marginalization at the regional level (where self-rule was granted in the 1950s prior to independence in 1960) and later at the federal center, minorities were forced to seek redress through dissenting, separatist politics that have marked their participation in the polity since then.[18] Donald L. Horwitz has famously argued that "the spread of norms of equality has made ethnic subordination illegitimate and spurred ethnic groups everywhere to compare their standing in society against that of groups in close proximity."[19]

In the early 1990s, the minority problem was concentrated largely around the Niger delta. The basic demands and grievances of the Niger delta area, the oil-producing region of Nigeria, have centered on control of resources.[20] The Ogoni protest was against "internal colonialism" by the Nigerian state (believed to be run mainly by the Hausa-Fulani elite and, to some extent, the other two ethnic nationalities, the Igbo and the Yoruba), which colluded with the multinational oil companies, particularly Shell. In the "Bill of Rights Presented to the Government and People of Nigeria" in November 1990, the Ogoni, represented by MOSOP, emphasized "the pre-colonial autonomy of the Ogoni ethnic nationality, the immense contributions of the Ogoni to the national economy, the ecological devastation of the Ogoni environment by oil exploration activities, the virtually complete marginalization of the Ogoni within the present federal structure and the need for the Ogoni people to be granted autonomous status within the Federal Republic of Nigeria."[21]

Through the activities of Ken Saro-Wiwa, MOSOP brought the deprivations of the Ogoni into the national and international limelight. Saro-Wiwa used his reputation and connections to make representations to international organizations such as the United Nations, the UN Committee for the Elimination of Racial Discrimination (CERD), the World Conference of Indigenous Peoples, the Unrepresented Nations and Peoples Organization (UNPO), the British parliamentary Human Rights Group (BHRG), Amnesty International, Green Peace, and the London Rainforest Action Group.

The Nigerian Press and Marginality

Given its advent in 1859 as a means of articulation and projection of vested interests and civil intervention in the colonial political society and state, and subsequently as the voice of the disadvantaged, the press in Nigeria has been a refuge and a site for the protection of marginalized groups in their battles against dominant interests. The fact that the press and other elements in Nigerian civil society also predate the eventual creation of a colonial (and later, postcolonial) state has made possible the development of ties, loyalties, and preferences across associational lines that later became crucial in empowering and defending nonstate and antistate action.[22] The foregoing situation encouraged links between the press and other key elements and institutions in civil society toward expanding the sphere of autonomous action vis-à-vis dominant interests in political society and the state. The Nigerian press has, therefore, played crucial roles in the overlapping conflictual and cooperative relationships among social, economic, and political forces.

Even though the first newspaper, *Iwe-Iroyin*, which was in Yoruba, was published by a missionary, the Reverend Henry Townsend, whose stated objective was "to beget the habit of seeking information by reading," the paper's demonstrable role was that of "ambitious political propaganda and [an instrument for] shrewd manoeuvring for power in Egbaland."[23] Thus, even from its supposedly pedagogic beginning, the press was located at the vortex of power, becoming "committed, agitational and, often, political."[24] However, as early as 1914 (when the southern and northern British protectorates were amalgamated to form Nigeria), the press was divided along proestablishment and antiestablishment categories. This division, which continues to the present day, was fed by developments in the north of Nigeria, where, until the colonial government established a newspaper there, most of the existing newspapers were part of chains owned by southern publisher-politicians, whose agitation for cultural dignity and the participation of the local elite in governance had increased into demands for self-rule and independence. As Agbaje notes, "the press became so enmeshed in the struggle for political power that it found it virtually an uphill task to rise above the personal, political and ethnic acrimonies of the period."[25] In the colonial period, the press in the south focused on transcending the marginality of the local elite in the socioeconomic and political life of the society and state and moving toward the domination of these spaces, whereas the press in the north was concerned with preventing the marginality that it feared would be the lot of the north if independence was granted in the context of the south's socioeconomic and educational advantage.

The issue of minority ethnic groups, as marginal identities, was yet to fully blossom until the late colonial period. When the minority groups eventually found a strong voice it was through southern politicians setting up strategically placed satellite newspapers in the northern region where minority opposition groups were located—and also in the southern region. These newspapers gave voice to the agitations of the minorities against dominant groups in each of the three regions—northern, western, and eastern—even though this also fed into the larger struggles of the three main ethnic groups against one another. Thus the newspapers were not so much genuinely committed to protecting the interests of the minority groups as they were to using minorities' agitation as ammunition against the majority political party in each region, and in the building of alliances across regions in the struggle to capture federal power.

Narratives and the Politics of Marginal Voices

As discussed in chapter 1, narratives provide a pathway for the transcultural transmission of messages about shared reality. Lucaites and Condit argue for a more complete and useful theory of narrative metacode that would render a narrative's three functions, two of which are useful here: the dialectical and rhetorical. They posit that "the primary goal of dialectic discourse is the discovery, revelation and presentation of truth." The word "truth" here is not intended to resurrect the epistemological debate between relativists and objectivists, but to distinguish between fact and fiction. Essentially, the first function of narratives, dialectical, is characterized by content that is limited by criteria of accuracy and external validity. The primary goal of the rhetorical function is "[what] persuasion achieves: the enactment of interest, or the wielding of power."[26] This wielding of power, however, relies on more than metaphors or the "mere display of truth." Rhetorical narrative is characterized not by form or content but by function; its purpose transcends its own textuality. It serves as a frame through which we are asked to view and understand the verisimilitude of propositions and proofs. Using the emphasis on content (constrained by criteria of accuracy and external validity) in the dialectical function in contrast to the emphasis on function (enactment of interest or the wielding of power) in the rhetorical function, may indicate ways in which "accuracy" and "external validity" can be used to enact interests and wield power. Marginal voices assert and legitimate their identity and intervene in the process of constituting what is important in sociopolitical discourse by appropriating what Shuman describes as "storytelling rights."[27]

These rights have three components: entitlement, tellability, and storyability. *Entitlement,* which has the clearest link to political theory, provides a means to understand how marginality can intervene in discourse, in that it is geared toward determining "who is entitled to claim a topic as legitimate discourse." As is evident, "merely because a set of events happened, even if it could be agreed what these events were, not everyone with access to this information has the 'right' to report it. This is crucial when the narrative focus is 'sensitive' material."[28] *Tellability* is about when it is appropriate for a certain person to tell a certain story. It is a matter of *discours* rather than *histoire*.[29] This is important for marginal life because the questions here are: "Is a particular event the proper basis for a narrative? Is it worthy of 'note'?"[30] Unless events that concern the marginal are seen as a basis for narratives and as worthy of note, it is unlikely that they will be publicly narrated. *Storyability*, which "might be thought of [as] a hybrid of entitlement and tellability,"[31] is about when it is appropriate for a certain person to tell a certain story, or what gets told as a story.[32] The question here is: "Given the situated encounter, what kinds of narrative are appropriate?"[33] The question can be linked to marginal life by asking: Given the encounter between marginal and dominant interests, what kinds of narratives are appropriate? Entitlement deals with *who* (the dominant or the marginal), tellability with *what*, and storyability with *how*.[34]

Narrative is central to the politics of marginal groups, particularly because the great battles in the modern world are fought in people's hearts. And since the media are the agents of reflection, contestation, and decision, it is through their narratives that people decide what to think about and, to some extent, how people think about events. Thus the fate of the marginal rests heavily on narratives. With binary divisions—between the marginal and the dominant—as the means through which the thematic significance of a narrative is signaled or conveyed, every narrative meshes a succession of events toward a goal.[35] Two categories of elementary sequence, *amelioration* and *degradation* (that which stands for and against a particular human project) are signaled at the beginning of a narrative. For the marginal, a state of deficiency (degradation) exists *ab initio*; for the dominant, a state of satisfaction (amelioration) exists. Marginal narratives are geared toward moving from the state of deficiency to satisfaction. Hendricks constructed these categories as if the transition from one to the other can only be sharp and nongradual. But I suggest that these two categories represent the endpoints of a continuum. This then creates the possibility of what I describe as quasi-amelioration and quasi-degradation. My slight reformulation basically captures tentative victories, either psychological or other kinds, that a narrative group championing a cause gains even while pursuing bigger victories (quasi-amelioration), and the "incomplete losses" that are consequently signaled by this (quasi-degradation).

Narrative analysis of this kind has in recent years grown in importance as a means for the social sciences to explain social process and social change.[36] As Jacobs, following Turner, notes, of all the events that "demand narration," crisis is one of the most crucial, since it "develops when a particular event gets narratively linked to a central cleavage in society and demands the attention of citizens as well as political elites."[37] Following Jacobs, I argue that events surrounding the assertion of marginal interests and rights—such as that of the Ogoni—are important plot elements for the different narratives (marginality framing) in the press, and they are for this reason extremely consequential for sociopolitical outcomes.

Since social reality exists in the interaction between narrative and event, code, and context, Sewell encourages social scientists to employ narratives in order to uncover this interaction, which requires the empirical study of texts, as in this chapter.[38]

Narratives of the Experiences of the Ogoni

Before the Ogoni crisis reached its crescendo between 1993 and 1995, the preoccupation of the Nigerian press in the late 1980s and 1990s was with minorities in general. By 1990, the press began an attempt at articulating the grievances of the minorities and their demands, particularly focusing on minorities in the oil-producing areas of the Niger delta. At this stage, narratives that captured general "neglect" were dominant. The Ogoni were not yet central to the narratives. Some respondents were quoted to have complained: "There is no government presence here [Niger delta]. . . . We have continued to suffer huge losses in our farmlands and fishponds because of the activities of oil-prospecting companies. Oil spillage [has] rendered almost completely useless our economic [lifeline]." These few marginal voices, *Newswatch* proposed: "Represent the collective voices of the oil-producing areas of the country crying against the neglect and poverty they have experienced in the midst of plenty. Their individual observations sum up the most telling problems that these black gold spinners have lived with since 1956 when Shell Petroleum Development Company struck oil in Oloibori, Rivers State, and set Nigeria on the road to becoming a major oil-producing country."[39]

The above typifies Condit's explication of the dialectical function of narratives: the discovery, revelation, and presentation of truth. Through such means, the press at the onset of the agitation discursively sets out the binary relations between the marginal (minorities in the oil-producing area) and the dominant (the Nigerian state, dominant ethnonationalities, Shell and other oil-prospecting companies). As the narration progresses, these divisions begin to close in on each other (discursively), leading eventually to crisis.

The language at the early stage is temperate. Even at this stage, however, two themes define the narratives: exploitation/appropriation and devastation/despoliation. As a Lagos-based engineer from one of the oil-producing states reportedly said in *Newswatch*: "What we have is a situation in which the states producing the oil wealth go cap-in-hand and the non-producing far-flung states enjoy the wealth.[40] Another commentator wrote of a "God of vengeance [who] will deal with all those whose hands are dripping with the blood of Ogonis. He will raise up soldiers who will resist native colonialism."[41]

The emphasis on appropriation and exploitation—far-flung states and native colonialism—referred to the core northern states of Nigeria. The terms are also associated with the Hausa-Fulani, the dominant ethnic nationality in Nigeria, whose assumed vice hold on political power at the center was easily linked with international finance capital as represented by oil companies such as Shell. As Said argues, *otherness* is constructed, legitimized, or delegitimized through such narrative structuring.[42] The second theme is that of devastation and despoliation: "What they [minorities] used to call upon for their livelihood and well-being have been wrecked for eternity by the coming of oil—they cannot fish because marine life has been flushed out, they cannot hunt because the game fled a long time ago, thanks to the oil hunters; and their land no longer yields good harvest. In short, neglect, poverty and deprivation."[43]

Progressively, the prominorities press increases the narrative quality of its reporting of marginal life in these affected areas, using evocative metaphors and strong images of devastation: "There was an oil spillage . . . ponds and the river in the island polluted. Animal and human beings battled with diseases which they contracted drinking polluted water. Farms were wasted. Four people died. . . . Christmas [in the village] turned into a time of mourning . . . life [in the village] mirrors the misery and plundering of the oil producing areas." In spite of this, "Shell's position is that [the company is] not legally bound to provide social infrastructure. What they offer may stem from altruism."[44] Juxtaposing Shell's cold, hard-nosed position with images of devastation, deprivation, and neglect has powerful narrative consequences. Easily, the binary image of the deprived and the criminally indifferent is created.

As Ken Saro-Wiwa stepped up his campaigns for the Ogoni, the prominorities press rose up to echo his grievances and demands on behalf of his people. The genius of Saro-Wiwa lay in his deft, functional, and successful environmentalization of a political conflict and the politicization of an environmental crisis. Simply, this involved giving resonance to the issue of environmental devastation in the area, even though this was only a manifestation of the overall political arrangement in the country; an otherwise strongly political project of gaining "self-determination" was also given an environmental expression. Both strategies, in practice, are hardly distinct.

Saro-Wiwa's credentials certainly positioned him in good stead, as the pro-Ogoni press and Saro-Wiwa himself readily admitted.[45] *TELL* underscored the fact that the Ogoni had become the spearhead of the minorities' struggle: "So far, the Ogoni . . . are the very epitome of minority fears in present day Nigeria. Not only in their anger over what they consider unjustifiable exploitation, but in the fears of how far the majority tribes are prepared to go to suppress and [repress] them . . . the experiences of Wiwa and his countrymen . . . would frighten anyone, majority or minority by tribe."[46]

Tanko Yakassai, a Hausa-Fulani politician, was often interviewed by the pro-Ogoni press to state the position of the dominant ethnic nationality and the Nigerian state on the minorities' agitation. Yakassai's view discursively raised the stakes, betraying disdain for the minorities and perhaps further legitimating their struggle. In one such interview in *TELL*, Yakassai stated: "When Biafra [the abortive secessionist Republic] attempted to take away the oil, the man from Sokoto [north] came to drive Biafra away. When next somebody comes to take it away we are going to come together again. . . . The trouble is that they [Ogonis] are not many." This attracted a reaction in the same edition from Owens Wiwa, Ken's brother, who stated: "I take my mind back to [Tanko] Yakassai's statement about Ogoni people being wiped out. . . . At that time, I thought it was the ranting of a senile fellow. But, now I realize, it is a well-planned genocide mission by the majority."[47]

In the course of the Ogoni agitation, there was a major disagreement among the leaders on the proper attitude to the forthcoming June 12, 1992, presidential election. The MOSOP leader, Saro-Wiwa, and others called for a boycott of the election to draw attention to environmental degradation and the exploitation of resources of Ogoniland by Shell and the Nigerian state. A few other Ogoni leaders, some of them members of MOSOP, were prepared to participate in the election and spoke against the planned boycott.[48] However, MOSOP voted to boycott the election. Against the backdrop of other issues, including accusations and counteraccusations of mindless rigidity (against Saro-Wiwa) and complicity, dishonesty, and venality against anti-Saro-Wiwa leaders (such as Albert Badey and Edwin Kobani), the boycott set some of the Ogoni leaders against Saro-Wiwa and MOSOP. From this point on, violence broke out intermittently in Ogoniland. While holding a meeting on May 21, 1994, the Ogoni leaders Albert Badey, Edwin Kobani, Samuel Orase, and Theophilus Orase were killed by some young people. Subsequently, Saro-Wiwa and fourteen other leaders of MOSOP were arrested and charged with the murder of the Ogoni four.

In the buildup to the murder trial, the pro-MOSOP voice was not only loud in the pro-Ogoni press, it was also consistent. Often, quotations of what MOSOP leaders and those sympathetic to their cause say were printed within the context of the narratives. In marking the first year of Saro-Wiwa detention after the multiple murders, *TheNEWS* described Saro-Wiwa as "the ebullient and liberal environmentalist" who had spent "a year in the gulag," predicting that this detention and the planned trial could mean that "the government, bent on stifling popular opinion, has finally found a way of shutting up Saro-Wiwa's persistent clamour for a better life for his people." The newsmagazine also envisaged that the conviction of Saro-Wiwa would have serious implications for the country: "As the trial gathers momentum, we cannot help but ponder the far-reaching consequences of a conviction. Pointers from the tribunal indicate that Mr. Saro-Wiwa is guilty until proven innocent instead of the other way round. To many the trial of Ken Saro-Wiwa is not just the trial of one man alleged to have committed murder, but a trial of a nation teter-ing on the verge of a catastrophic fall."[49]

The pro-MOSOP and pro-Ogoni press also persistently pro-claimed that by focusing on the activities of Ken Saro-Wiwa, it has successfully narrated the *marginality* of the Ogoni into the *center*. The Ogonis' terms, conditions, demands, and grievances were con-stantly narrated by the pro-Ogoni press, whereas the constraints and position of the dominant parties (government, Hausa-Fulani, and oil companies) rarely were. In all of the data analyzed for this chap-ter, there are few occasions in which the views of the dominant agen-cies are given much space by the pro-Ogoni press. In this, I note a stage of quasi-amelioration.

Examples of how the Ogoni interests were framed in *TELL, News-watch,* and *TheNEWS,* all pro-Ogoni newsmagazines, include: "The cry is for greater empowerment and autonomy to oversee their own affairs. And the conclusion . . . is that the federal system of govern-ment has failed across all of 33 years of nationhood to guarantee Nigeria's minorities their pride of place. The demand therefore is for a review of the present structure." Therefore: "For a multi-billion dollar oil company, Shell, to take over 30 billion US dollars from a small defenceless Ogoni people and put nothing back but degra-dation is a crime against humanity. For the Nigerian government to usurp the resources of Ogoni and legalise such theft by military decree is armed robbery."[50]

Evocative, emotive, strong words—like *heartland*—that convey images of the violation of the minority group's space by the state and dominant ethnic groups in alliance with oil companies are frequent, even while casting the minorities' intervention in the dominant's space as necessary and commendable. A few examples should suffice:

The team . . . led by . . . [the Army] camp commandant at Bori, did not back down until several villages had been levelled. They shot, killed and burnt people, animals and property.[51]

Nigeria's blessing is their collective curse. Driven from their ancestral land by oil pollution and exploitation, they hear fantastic tales of the meaning of black gold. . . . They are outlaws from the corridors of power, they are pariahs from the room where the wealth of their land is being shared.[52]

What has been happening is equivalent to [the] slave trade.[53]

Desolate towns and villages ravaged by a savage war. Weeping widows who would not be consoled. Under-aged orphans roaming the wasteland in a hopeless search for dead parents. Such ugly scars of war were the dominant feature. . . . The scope of carnage and destruction of property is even more chilling.[54]

[The government] also sent a brutal detachment of soldiers . . . into the Ogoni heartland, where they acted out the gross trappings of an army of occupation on helpless peasants. [The military administrator's] attitude . . . suggested quite clearly that the government was determined to use the affair to crush MOSOP, silencing once and for all a body that has given so loud a voice to the grievances and aspirations of . . . Ogonis.[55]

Soon after the invading force arrived, Ogoni took on the look of a conquered territory with the Nigerian Army, Air force, Navy and Police personnel as the conquerors. Entire communities were sacked and casually driven into the dense greenery. All able-bodied men that could be arrested were grabbed and locked up in putrid cells . . . women and children were routinely brutalised, and extortion rackets boomed.[56]

The environmental issue was amplified because it had international resonance, thus gaining the attention of a collection of international organization and international civil society groups. The narratives constantly proclaimed the international recognition and validity that the Ogoni struggle had gained.

Another major narrative theme was the construction of a spearhead of the Ogoni struggle: Ken Saro-Wiwa. At the start of the struggle, he was described as a "self-proclaimed" minority-rights activist. Later, he became for the pro-Ogoni press a "social crusader,"[57] "easily Nigeria's best known minority rights activist," "[a] smallish but stubborn [man who] has shown tremendous courage,"[58] and a "versatile writer and social crusader [who] almost singlehandedly, hoisted Nigeria's dire environmental problems into the agenda of global bodies."[59] This positive profiling of Saro-Wiwa provided strategic narrative support because it authenticated the leadership of the struggle. Beyond this, it constructed Saro-Wiwa and his constituents as those who had entitlements, which represents a right to claim the discourse of environmental and political wrongs as legitimate.

The trial and subsequent execution of the Ogoni nine no doubt brought out the strongest reaction in the press to the dilemma of minorities in Nigeria. From the start, the trial was deconstructed in the pro-Ogoni press as a "show trial" with "tunes of a morbidly familiar performance"[60] that was linked to the preceding trial of General Zamani Lekwot and other leaders of a northern minority group, the Kataf.

TheNEWS stated that it was yet another process of subjecting minority groups to "indignities," as experienced in the "infamous verdict" on Kataf leaders. The tribunal, its members, and the judgment were also discursively discredited by *TheNEWS* and *TELL*, which accused the tribunal of being "part of the prosecution" and of "overt acts . . . arriving at a [predetermined] conclusion." The tribunal chairman, Justice Ibrahim Auta, was described as General Sani Abacha's "hireling," who accepted the "various hearsays, embarrassing recants and strident litanies" of Saro-Wiwa's opponents for concrete evidence.[61] The whole episode involving the tribunal and its chair, the magazines averred, "flies in the face of the rule of law and justice in a civilized society."[62]

Immediately after the murder of the four prominent Ogoni leaders, the opposition press eagerly amplified the expression of innocence by Ken Saro-Wiwa and his constituents. A press conference by one of the "moderate" Ogoni leaders, Leton, who the official line described as having escaped being "hacked to death" by the accused, was captured by *TheNEWS* as "hot tirades" against the "progressively minded" Saro-Wiwa and his "heroic struggle."[63] A "pen-portrait" of Saro-Wiwa in the *Nigerian Tribune* after the death sentence stated: "No one who embarks on a 'suicide mission' like the diminutive Ken by threatening the life-line of an over-reaching, authoritarian state like the Nigerian state and the exploitation fields of a colluding international capitalism can expect to be shielded from the noose."[64]

A major theme of the narratives on the death sentences was the rejection and condemnation of the sentences by local and, particularly, international organizations, agencies, and statesmen. The pro-Ogoni press gave considerable space and prominence to these condemnations. *The Guardian* wrote: "Tirades, like a broken dam, gushed forth yesterday as international and domestic interests reacted to the death sentence imposed on . . . prominent minority leaders, among them renowned writer and social rights crusader [Saro-Wiwa]. . . . 'Travesty of justice,' 'charade,' 'hollow ritual,' and 'absence of due process' were common phrases used." The "broken dam" metaphor is followed by the phrase "unprecedented deluge of cross border correspondence . . . like torrents from an opened flood-gate."[65] The metaphor of a "broken dam" captured the discursive projection of "imminent trouble," which the pro-Ogoni press believed would follow the sentences. In the daily newspapers (*The Guardian* and *Nigerian Tribune*), these daily narratives of rejection and condemnation of the verdict continued even when the Provisional Ruling Council (PRC), the highest military ruling body, confirmed the verdict.

With reprieve foreclosed by the PRC, the pro-Ogoni press continued to narrate the possibility of saving the lives of the activists, who are hardly ever described as "condemned men." *The Guardian* stated in an editorial: "It is unfortunate that the . . . [PRC] went ahead yesterday to confirm the sentences. . . . We believe that the case of fair-hearing has not been established beyond reasonable doubt. . . . Even with the confirmation of sentence . . . there is an opportunity for government, through the office of the Head of State, to reverse the sentences in favour of committal. . . . Lest we forget, the death of more Ogoni leaders will not bring Nigeria any nearer to the solution to the serious issues of inequitable resource distribution, marginalization and environmental degradation which engendered the protests of the Ogoni and neighbouring peoples."[66]

When the nine men were eventually executed, the future of Nigeria as a united and just polity overtook the themes of respect for human rights, protection of the environment, and justice, which had predominated in the narratives before the execution. Against the backdrop of the struggle for the validation of the June 12, 1993, presidential election, the executions were narrated as yet another example of the unworkable nature of the Nigerian nation as constituted. The Abacha regime, Hausa-Fulani hegemony, and the lopsided nature of Nigeria's federalism become the targets of the pro-Ogoni press as factors that created the conditions for the "legal lynching" or "judicial murder"—as the executions were described— of Saro-Wiwa and eight others.

Arguing that the "issues thrown up by the Ogoni tragedy relate to fairness, justice and democratic governance in a plural, multinational country," *The Guardian* editorialized that the execution "has outraged the world, putting our nation's stature and reckoning at grave peril."[67] *TELL's* tone was more strident. In an unusual editorial, the newsmagazine argued that the execution would make the world see the Abacha "junta" as one "with sensibilities as pristinely unrefined as those of ruling brutes of the Stone Age." The magazine asserted that Nigeria was a "failed federation" where minorities "with all their wealth are more [like] slaves and second-class citizens." General Abacha and his men were also described as "murderers" whose "murder" of Saro-Wiwa and others has "kept Nigeria hanging from the ramparts."[68] The execution, coming at a point when the Commonwealth of Nations was meeting in Auckland, New Zealand, was narrated as a "slap in the face" of the international community, thereby bringing what Jacobs describes as the "moral dimension" to bear on the reality of the executions.[69]

Images of defiance, fortitude, and heroism, as displayed by Saro-Wiwa, his family members, and others, continued to be presented in the pro-Ogoni press side by side with the "torrents" of condemnation regarding their execution: "Lesser men would have been known to quake at that point [when the sheriff announced to Saro-Wiwa that he was about to be hanged]. But not Saro-Wiwa, who looked straight and defiantly at his accuser until the hangman behind him dropped a hood over his head."[70]

Even Saro-Wiwa's father was described as carrying himself with "grace and fortitude"[71] after the hanging of his son. The pro-Ogoni press gave full narrative expression to the plan by the international community to punish the Abacha regime for the execution. From "Abacha under fire" to Abacha as "[the] subject of global outrage," the press narrated how "Abacha and his generals are forced to embrace the cold reality that they are engaged in a fight with the rest of the world they cannot win," leading eventually to the "blinking" of Abacha. *TELL* continued, "The Abacha junta, realising the futility of fighting the rest of the world, especially President Nelson Mandela, moves to apologise to the world leader and grand patriarch of South African freedom."[72] Whereas *TheNEWS* headlined this event on its cover page as "Finally Abacha Blinks," *TELL* announced it as "Aso Rock's [Nigeria's presidential villa] hasty retreat . . . after two weeks of reckless defiance of global opinion." *Newswatch* selected Saro-Wiwa as "man of the year."[73]

On the whole, this dominant section of the press (the pro-Ogoni press) narrated the Ogoni as having gained a psychological victory even though they lost the battle. The international reaction was also constructed as a special kind of amelioration, in that it shamed the dominant regime—that is, the Abacha regime and the Hausa-Fulani and the oil companies—and forced them to concede their wrongs. In contrast, these themes were countered by the proestablishment, anti-Ogoni press, although it was not as robust as the antiestablishment (pro-Ogoni) press. The *New Nigerian* gave little or no attention to the struggle of the Ogoni until the crisis point, that is, when the trials began. In a sense, this tactic also employed the dialectical function in that, by ignoring the Ogoni events, the *New Nigerian* was more or less saying there was no truth to be discovered, revealed, or presented in the matter.

Even when the activists were sentenced to death, the *New Nigerian* presented it as a second-lead story, perhaps to capture the event as just another sentence passed on "common criminals." In the ten-paragraph story, no mention was made of the condemnation of the sentence in the local or international communities. The condemnations were totally ignored. Only pleas for clemency were constantly published by the *New Nigerian*. In the days after the verdict, the paper, as an ideological apparatus of the state and ruling elite, attempted to narrate the prevailing normality in the areas affected by the decision of the tribunal: "Ogoniland remains peaceful contrary to fears of violent reactions to the recent death sentences of the president of . . . [MOSOP] and eight others for murder. . . . Our correspondent who visited the areas yesterday reported that normal activities have been going on in spite of the verdict."[74]

Whereas the pro-Ogoni newspapers were filled with stories on the likely sanctions against Nigeria at the Commonwealth meeting, the *New Nigerian* reported: "New Zealand has refused to bow to pressure to stop Nigeria from participation in the Commonwealth Summit. . . . Prime Minister Jim Bolger[,] commenting yesterday on a call by exiled Nigerian writer, Wole Soyinka, to expel Nigeria from the summit of 52 nations[,] said such action could not advance the cause of Saro-Wiwa and eight others."[75]

This story ignored the call for sanctions by other leaders, including President Nelson Mandela of South Africa. Despite this assurance, however, perhaps suspecting that the summit might take a stand against Nigeria, the *New Nigerian* in a news analysis raised concern that Nigeria had been "set aside for demonization" at the summit. Subsequently, the Commonwealth was deconstructed by the *New Nigerian* as "an association of former British Colonies [that] today exists in times that tend to question its relevance. . . . Looking at the horrible human rights record of many Commonwealth members,

you would wonder why Nigeria had to be zeroed [in] upon. . . .
Those who insist on debating the case . . . are only politicising a serious offence which was handled by a reputable tribunal."[76]

Although the paper failed to report opposing views, it regularly
reported Nigeria's official and progovernment reactions to such
views. For instance, when Nigeria was suspended from the Commonwealth, the paper ignored it but later published two front-
page stories. The first of these concerned bishops condemning the
United States and Britain "for meddling in African affairs," and the
second centered on "popular . . . pressure on Nigeria to pull out of
[the] Commonwealth." The latter tried to persuade all "patriotic"
Nigerians to mount pressure on the military government to call the
"bluff of Britain and her 52 member neo-colonial association called
the Commonwealth."[77] By acting out the rhetorical function of narratives, the paper pursued what persuasion is geared to achieve: the
enactment of interests or the wielding and maintenance of power.

Another front-page story in the *New Nigerian* argued that "indeed
some of the agonies in our country have direct bearing on the continued servitude and regrettable nostalgic past with Britain."[78] In
contradistinction to the positive profiling of Saro-Wiwa in the antiestablishment (pro-Ogoni) press, the *New Nigerian* concluded: "What
led to their [the murdered Ogoni four] brutal murder could briefly
be summarised as follows. . . . Saro-Wiwa, instigator and promoter of
militant strategy and violent options . . . became the president [of
MOSOP]. Ever since . . . (Saro-Wiwa) had chosen the destructive
path culminating in the present unfortunate tragedy. He masterminded several other subversive wings of MOSOP." These "incontro-
vertible facts," the paper argued, were buried in the "straightjacket
of mischief, petty-politics and international meddlesomeness which
have characterized the Nigerian reality in recent time."[79] The
"meddlesome" (including Mandela, Britain, the Commonwealth,
the United States, and others in the international arena) are then
"revealed" by the paper to show their "duplicity" in a matter that
the paper saw purely as one of "law and order": "One lesson [of the
Ogoni tragedy] is the morbid and stinking hypocrisy of the Western nations[,] the worst expression of which was displayed at the
recently concluded Commonwealth conference in Auckland."[80]

Through such means, the *New Nigerian* constructed a counterhegemonic perspective against the Western other. Whereas the
antiestablishment press constantly reported the many local and

international voices calling for sanctions against Nigeria, the *New Nigerian* presented a different reality under headlines such as "Nigerians Denounce Commonwealth Decision" and "Ogonis Support FG."[81]

A major theme of opposition narratives centered on due process of law, which the trial was said to have lacked. Therefore it is understandable that the *New Nigerian* also counternarrated the legality of the process that led to the execution, reporting that the retiring Chief Justice of Nigeria stated that "the judgement was in accordance with the laws of the land which cannot be faulted anywhere in the world."[82] Whereas condemnation from Western capitals dominated the narratives of the antiestablishment press, the *New Nigerian* reported how "the Republic of Niger and Senegal . . . joined the growing league of nations that expressed support [for] the federal government over the Commonwealth."[83] Also, the paper captured the suspension of Nigeria from the Commonwealth as an example of Western powers' "premeditated, retrogressive and high-handed" conspiracy to make "Nigeria kowtow to their visions of democracy."[84]

Whereas the narratives in the pro-Ogoni press were appropriate for the simultaneous legitimation of the marginal and the delegitimation of the dominant, the narratives of the proestablishment press were appropriate for the reverse. Even though the proestablishment, anti-Ogoni press attempted to counter the narratives of the antiestablishment, pro-Ogoni press, it failed to effectively match the sheer quantity and quality of narratives emanating from the former. It was, therefore, forced to react to what, in its (proestablishment) frustration, was perceived as blackmail by the "Southern press" (pro-Ogoni press).

Conclusion

The contemporary period has, like no other time in history, witnessed the acquisition of voice by marginal (minority) groups.[85] The emergence of this trend is located not only in the transfer of marginal discourses to the mainstream but also in other factors, including the production of a cultural politics of difference, struggles around difference, and the reproduction of new identities.[86]

Marginal identities rely largely on narratives to interrupt and intervene in the process of dominant discourses. Social reality in this context is constructed around the *interaction* between these narratives and events, codes, and contexts.[87] The two diametrically opposed narrative paradigms (of support and opposition) used in the polarized sections of the press were geared toward either legitimizing or delegitimizing the struggles of the marginal ethnic group. The southern (antiestablishment, pro-Ogoni) and northern (proestablishment, anti-Ogoni) press promoted different but overlapping communities of discourse,[88] even though the *community of discourse*, built and sustained by the southern press, seemed to triumph overall.

The narratives examined above were framed largely in exclusionary modes as part of a long chain that is linked discursively to the history of dominant-marginal relations in Nigeria, which has resulted in the "arbitrary" division of the social world into "we" and "they."[89] As I have argued, focusing on how the interaction between the dialectical and rhetorical function of narratives are played out better explains the role of social and political consciousness in a given society. I have also provided examples of how narrative analysis helps in explaining social processes and social change relating to the struggle of minority groups against the state, dominant (majority) ethnic groups, and transnational capital.

Against the pattern of much theorizing and little research on such media issues as the narrative representation of ethnic minorities—an issue that has become more significant and has crucial implications—this chapter provides further evidence on the centrality of narratives in the mobilization or demobilization of marginal intervention in the socioeconomic and political life of the center in the African postcolony.

Conclusion

Beyond Grand Narratives

Narratives make "meaningful totality" out of a myriad of events.[1] Therefore they play a very important role in the struggle for control and full participation in whatever is constituted as a "totality"— particularly a political totality expressive in ethnic or ethno-national boundaries. In constructing a meaningful totality out of the mess of political life, narratives invite other narratives to validate or invalidate them. Therefore, no single narrative is adequate in representing the political world. As Campbell asserts, "only through the clash of competing narratives are we likely to assemble justifiable knowledge."[2] Indeed, although they present a more meaningful and coherent picture of the relations of domination in a particular polity, as examined in this book, the knowledge derived from clashing and competing narratives ultimately points to the illusions of grand narratives. Clashing ethno-nationalist narratives, in their attempt to provide a history of a postcolonial "nation," in the end— to use David Scott's words—"destabilize the seeming naturalness and inevitability" of national unity while accentuating the fact that such nations are "assembled contingently and heterogeneously."[3]

Yet the illusory nature of grand narratives do not vitiate their capacity to authorize action or agency or to motivate people to act one way or the other. Indeed, when grand narratives are shared, they provide "cognitive lenses" through which people can view the world.[4] This explains why people invest a lot in deconstructing grand narratives. Given that any ideological struggle is a struggle for meaning, even a grand narrative that authorizes a dominant meaning or sign cannot be invulnerable. Thus, grand narratives "can be violated and overthrown, although this is never a simple process."[5]

The preceding chapters examined how different groups in Nigeria drew on a set of "narrative schemata"[6] expressive through the print media in negotiating their interests in relation to other groups within Nigeria, while seeking to simultaneously establish and violate *the* grand narrative. In this negotiation, the struggle for or against domination constitutes the overriding motive force of these narratives.

Violence and the Struggle for National Consensus

In early 2015, as I completed the final chapters of this book, Nigeria had just successfully concluded general elections that had the potential to simultaneously disrupt as well stabilize federal power and the ethno-regional equation or balance responsible for the continued survival of Nigeria. Before the elections, the Nigerian media—including the booming local and diasporic social media—were replete with predictions of the possibility of the collapse of the Nigerian union if the elections, particularly the presidential election, went one way or the other. The international community too held its breath, while issuing veiled threats against those who might be planning to truncate the elections and precipitate violence.[7] As it turned out, and as experienced a few times in Nigeria's past, the country reached the precipice and then stopped. The elections were surprisingly peaceful, and largely free and fair.

The result of the presidential election in particular has the potential to disrupt federal power and ethno-regional balance in that, for the first time since independence, a ruling party (in this case the People's Democratic Party, PDP) and a national political party originally dominated by the northern political elite lost power at the center.[8] Also, for the first time, a political party created by a coalition of ethno-regional political interests coalescing around the core conservative Hausa-Fulani (northern) political elite and core progressive Yoruba (southwestern) political elite (the All Progressive Congress, APC), gained power at the center. Before now, these two competing ethno-regional and ideological power blocs had never succeeded in their various attempts at reaching political understanding toward jointly winning federal power.[9] Therefore the results of the 2015 elections have potentially interesting implications for the future of democracy as well as the future of Nigeria.

Similarly, the presidential election also has the potential for stabilizing federal power and the ethno-regional equation in that while the alternative coalition that has come to power in Nigeria is led by a core northerner whose politics are unarguably conservative, he ran on a progressive platform. Indeed, the strongest and most destabilizing struggle for political power in postindependent Nigeria has been between these two power elites—the northern Hausa-Fulani (conservatives) and the southern Yoruba (progressives). It is precisely because of the emergence of this unusual ethno-regional and ideological coalition that the defeat of the ruling party, the PDP—which had been allegedly "hijacked" by the southern minorities supported by the core southeastern (Igbo) elite and their political allies across the country—might *stabilize* democratic Nigeria in the short term. Even though unlikely, if the core northern (Hausa-Fulani) power elite and their strongest traducers and rivals, the southwestern (Yoruba) power elite, can find common ground in a federal government, new vistas for national accommodation might open up for Nigeria. The third leg of the Nigerian tripod, the southeastern Igbo elites, are likely to negotiate a workable accommodation in the short term within the new alliance. If this happens, then the narratives of the future—as well as the politics of memory that forms its basis—might be significantly different. Even if the memories of the past injustices by all the multiple nations of Nigeria never abate, the new ruling coalition is likely to create a new consensus and dissensus about the future, as the past is remembered in new ways.

Yet the new consensus and dissensus, paradoxically, will also constitute a guarantee that the fundamental issues of the Nigerian union will neither be confronted nor resolved, because those who are demobilized or marginalized in the short run by the ascendant order will mobilize the memories of the past in new and challenging ways. Perhaps this is an attractive thing for those who want Nigeria to survive as a single territorial unit, even if it is unable to become a nation-state in the near future. As long as these contests continue, perhaps there will be hope that the sentiments constantly expressed about the disintegration of the country, as evident in the narratives analyzed in this book, will be contained within the parameters of the constant and unremitting negotiations and renegotiations of interests through narratives.

Before he was defeated in the 2015 elections, President Goodluck Jonathan, who comes from the oil-producing minority areas of southern Nigeria, had inaugurated a national conference to discuss the future of Nigeria and write a new constitution. This was the third such conference convened within a period of two decades in

Nigeria. A constitutional conference was held in 1994 under General Sani Abacha; a national political reform conference was held in 2005 under President Olusegun Obasanjo. Nothing significant emerged from the two conferences. Jonathan's conference will most likely suffer a similar fate, as the current administration seems totally uninterested in the resolutions of the conference. The current president and the key leaders of his party, the APC, had expressed reservations about the conference before it was convened.

At the root of the agitation for a Sovereign National Conference (SNC) by most elements and groups in the south of Nigeria is the "national question."[10] This term is a shorthand description of the deep divisions and fundamental tension at the heart of the union of ethnic nationalities that constitute Nigeria. There are other facets of this "question," including the question of political power (domination, marginalization, etc.), the nature of the political union and territorial division, issues of federalism (fiscal and others), the role of religion in public life, and so on. Those canvassing for the conference stated that the way the country was constituted by the British was "lopsided" and that the country had not succeeded principally because of this. In this way, 1914 is still regarded by many as "a mistake," as Ahmadu Bello described the amalgamation of Nigeria. Although a leading Nigerian political scientist, A. D. Yahaya, stated that "the political future of the country as one indivisible nation is resolved with the end of the civil war" and "the major political issue today is, therefore, not the unity of the country,"[11] it is obvious that the critical issue remains the unity of Nigeria. Many in the south, as expressed in the narratives analyzed in earlier chapters, believe that the north has dominated political power (notwithstanding the fact that, before 2015, a northerner had been president for only about three out of a total of sixteen years of the Fourth Republic). Therefore, they continue to call for a restructuring of Nigeria through the process of a national conference. The idea of "restructuring" is not popular in the north, where there is also widespread belief that the south has dominated the economy. Most of the voices from the north, particularly the core north, have expressed the position that there was no need to restructure Nigeria. Even though those opposed to the need for a national conference in the north always attended the national conferences, they often frustrate any attempt by southerners to ensure a fundamental restructuring of Nigeria.

However, some key interest groups in the south were convinced that the 2014 conference held under a president from the minority areas of the south would be different. More than six hundred resolutions were passed at the conference, which produced a 10,335-page report. President Jonathan promised to implement the resolutions. The fears that the conference might lead to the disintegration of Nigeria was dismissed by the chairman of the conference, the retired Chief Justice Idris Kutigi. He told the press that "we have held a National Conference and we are more united today than ever."[12]

The unity was obviously only in the imagination of Kutigi. As Mohammed Haruna, a famous journalist and former managing director of the *New Nigerian* who unapologetically defends the interests of the north, said, "virtually every constitutional conference in this country has come with a hidden agenda by its convener and virtually all of them have come to grief."[13] What Haruna described as a "hidden agenda" is the attempt to restructure Nigeria. Those who disagree with Haruna would insist that Nigeria might still come to grief in the end if it was not restructured. The narratives in the preceding chapters articulate this struggle for and against restructuring in different ways, indicating the absence of a common horizon that can lead to the creation of a grand narrative.

But while the debate about the resolutions of the 2015 national conference is ongoing, a different kind of restructuring has been forced on Nigeria by the terrorist group Boko Haram (translated as "Western education is forbidden"), which calls itself Jana'atu Ahl as-Sunnar li-Da'awati wal-Jihad and the "Nigerian Taliban." The group, which has existed in various forms since the 1990s, seeks to overthrow the Nigerian government and impose an Islamic regime based on the Sharia.[14] A leading scholar on Islam in northern Nigeria, Murray Last, has suggested that the logic of attacks by Boko Haram against the state and its agencies of legitimate violence "followed a pattern that goes back at least some 200 years in northern Nigeria, and has a logic to it that is understandable given the conditions of life for the poorly educated young today in . . . Nigeria."[15] Moreover, "Boko Haram has grown at a time when there are many national issues that draw anger and feed the group."[16] The group has carried out terrorist attacks in the northeast and parts of northwestern Nigeria. Since May 2011, the group has killed over eleven thousand people.[17] The Nigerian military has failed to subdue the group. This is a cause for worry around the world, especially with the group's claims of links to the Islamic State (ISIS). The US State Department, after much hesitation, eventually designated the group as a Foreign Terrorist Organization (FTO) in November 2013.

Not surprisingly, the print media in Nigeria has given prominence to the Boko Haram insurgency, not only because of the security challenges it presents but also because of the challenges it poses to the territorial integrity of Nigeria and the country's continued corporate existence. Indeed, the crisis of the 2015 national conference is not unrelated to the Boko Haram insurgency. However, whereas the conference opened up a space of negotiation for the contending forces in Nigeria, Boko Haram seeks to "seal politics off from the play of contending differences."[18] Yet both positions are reflections of the unfinished nature of the Nigerian union and the tensions that continue to show that the amalgamation of 1914 has failed to discourage centrifugal forces in Nigeria. Although this book does not focus on the 2014 national conference and the Boko Haram phenomenon, the implications of both for the grand narrative are evident in the cases examined in the book. Nigeria's new president, Mohammadu Buhari, has committed himself to ending the "Boko Haram menace." Some have even predicted that Buhari is the "man to defeat Boko Haram."[19]

If Buhari defeats Boko Haram, can he defeat the conditions that not only produced it but continue to defeat every effort to truly unite the country and call off the incessant actual and discursive struggles to *end* Nigeria's history?

The Past in the Future

"Just what a nation can be, its very possibility and desirability, how it is to be imagined, and who is going to generate such processes," argues Charmaine McEachern, "are all very much constrained and enabled by what had gone before."[20] As this book shows, what has gone before for a nation is largely a function of narratives. Narratives link the nation's past, present, and future, while articulating its possibility and desirability or its impossibility and nondesirability. Thus narratives and counternarratives about the reality of shareable and enduring national sentiments, as examined in this book, will end only if and when Nigeria is no longer a single territorial unit. As

Joshua Dienstag states, "a narrative that ends is without a future . . . in politics, the idea of a final end point can be a dangerous one." Indeed, the end of narrative would also translate into the end of politics, given that narratives are articulations and negotiations of meaning in relation to conflict, power, interest, change, and development. Therefore, argues Dienstag, "to imagine a political narrative that ends may be to imagine a too-perfect satisfaction with the present and therefore an end to politics as the realm of conflict, change, and growth."[21] Indeed, because the (unending) possibility of conflict is integral to the political,[22] political narratives are always already inherently and permanently conflictual.

One of the central questions that provoked this book is the extent to which the idea of a Nigerian "grand nation" is evident in the narratives of the Nigerian press over the last seven decades, roughly between 1941 and 2011. Against the backdrop of the narratives examined, this book contests the assumption in much of the literature that ideology functions *only* as a kind of "social cement," a glue that binds people in collectively shared values and norms. The book shows that specific social-historical circumstances determine the meaning, parameters, and salience of the concept of "nation" (ethnic group) and "grand nation" (nation-state) in the narratives of the Nigerian press. In their interpretation and articulation of the notion of "nation," the Nigerian newspapers and newsmagazines cross registers, from the notion of "nation" as ethnic group (Igbo, Yoruba, Hausa, Efik, Fulani, Tiv, etc.), ethno-regional group (Hausa-Fulani, northerners, southerners, etc.), or political region (north, west, southwest, east, southeast, south-south, middle-belt, etc.), to the Nigerian union (nation-of-aspiration). Therefore, although people can be glued to any of these registers, such commitment, while reinforcing or fortifying certain notions of "togetherness" in the postcolonial context, also serves to separate and undermine other notions of togetherness. In this way, it is evident that ideology can function both as social cement that binds people together and as a tool for dividing people into separate communities of shared values and norms.

In their narratives of power, the Nigerian press mobilizes "the nation" for the strategic interest of whatever power the various newspapers and newsmagazines serve. Therefore the nation can be either a Nigerian grand nation whose existence some take for granted and others approach as an aspiration that motivates action, or an ethnic nation (such as Hausa-Fulani, Igbo, or Yoruba nation) whose *reality* as a basis for action, reaction, and relation is constantly affirmed through the narratives. However, even these ethnic nations are contested: some narratives attempt to limit their frontiers, whereas others contest their actual existence in history, beyond the imaginary or the aspirational. The dynamics of the relations of domination at each point determine which of these contesting notions and narrative practices of "nation" is glorified and sanctified as meaning is deployed in the service or disservice of power. In this context, as some of the narratives show, the reality or consolidation of either the ethno nation or the grand nation depends on the building of one and the destroying of the other. In this sense, as Walker Connor points out, nation-building in one instance would also mean nation-destroying in another, and vice versa. I suggest that one way of approaching the narratives examined in this book, despite their often strident and highly divisive tone, is to understand them as ultimately constituting attempts to reduce "competing loyalties to manageable proportions."[23] In a country in which there are very few institutionalized, accountable, and transparent processes of conflict resolution and representation of diversity, the media narratives constitute perhaps the most open and most unrestrained avenues for the ventilation of national grievances and the articulation of dominant as well as marginal interests.

Yet in all of the narratives, clearly the Nigerian grand narrative, even where it is discursively combated, subverted, and disparaged, is still assumed to be an ideal, but a conditional ideal. In the light of Connor's argument, it seems that the press in Nigeria desires building a grand nation without destroying ethnic nations. Not surprisingly, the conditions that would transform Nigeria into a grand narrative are expressed in different and often conflicting ways. The press exhibited—in the cases studied from the 1950s to the early twenty-first century—a tendency toward affirming the primacy of the Nigerian grand narrative if and where it serves the common interests, defined primarily by contending narratives in light of the ethnic, ethno-regional, or even religious interests that they represent.

Grand Narrative and the Prose of Power

Language in particular and communications in general, and the interactions they foster or impede, constitute the lifeblood of politics. Therefore, as James P. Gee argues, it is within interactive communication that "social goods are created, sustained, distributed and redistributed. It is there that people are harmed and helped."[24] In this sense, the language of those who write about the nation and the lives of those who live it are connected.[25] Thus narratives, which are central to interactive communication, are crucial in the total organization of national life. Against this background, in examining the narratives of nations, I have conceptualized the "Nigerian nation" as a grand narrative.

In the struggles over what constitutes the symbolic boundaries of the Nigerian nation and the other existing nations as expressed in the press, discursive narratives become what Homi Bhabha has described as "the grim prose of power that each nation . . . wield[s]." The effects of the "conceptual indeterminacy" of the "nation" and the fact that it "wavers between vocabularies," as evident in the relationship among Nigeria's many ethnic nationalities and the idea of a "Nigerian grand nation," have implications for the "narratives and discourses that signify a sense of 'nationness'"—and the struggles that define the *sense* of nationhood. To encounter the nation "as it is written"[26] is to capture the nation in its myriad, and often clashing, narratives, it is also to capture the nation itself as a grand narrative. Where the myth of the nation is an aspiration that seeks to override competing ethnic nations—based, in turn, on longer surviving myths—within a territorial boundary, I have argued, the narratives of such a nation, and the nation itself, constitute a grand narrative. In this a context, as Homi Bhabha maintains: "The boundary that marks the nation's selfhood interrupts the self-generating time of national production and disrupts the signification of the people as homogeneous. The problem is not simply the 'self-hood' of the nation as opposed to the otherness of other nations. We are confronted with the nation split within itself, articulating the heterogeneity of its population. The barred Nation It/Self, alienated from its eternal self-generation, becomes a liminal signifying space that is internally marked by the discourses of minorities, the heterogeneous histories of contending peoples, antagonistic authorities and tense locations of cultural difference."[27]

Given that every (real or imagined) nation already contains within it elements of its own heterogeneity, including the minorities, even a grand narrative necessarily invites counternarratives that mobilize meaning in the service or disservice of power. The conflict that is embedded in narrative, particularly in the context of the validity of its existence in its contradistinction from other narratives, is captured by Barthes, who argues that narrative discourse moves "in its historical impetus, by clashes."[28] As a grand narrative, Nigeria, like most other postcolonial grand narratives, has existed throughout its history in and by narrative clashes, and in its present and its move toward the future, Nigeria continues to exist through narrative clashes.

Pêcheux presents an argument similar to Barthes' in *Language, Semantics and Ideology*, in which he examines the relationship of discourses to ideological practices and language. He avers that narratives as discourses "are not peaceful; they develop out of clashes with one another, and because of this there is a political dimension to each use of words and phrases."[29] In these clashes, meaning becomes crucial. This is particularly true of multinational states that are already fundamentally alienated from their unending attempts at self-generation. Therefore, as different notions and narratives of nations within a grand nation antagonistically mobilize meaning in the service or disservice of power, the press becomes an even more critical instrument for the negotiation of relations of domination.

However, it is important to note that I am not arguing that newspapers and newsmagazines representing ethno-regional groups and parties in Nigeria speak always and only for the interests they represent. Sometimes the press speaks for interests that are not necessarily ethno-regional: it may defend the narrow interests of its proprietors in terms of their personal, class, or political privileges. But even when the press protects such narrow interests, these interests are often subsumed—even if not absolutely and always—into the overall fundamental ethno-regional, ideological, and party-political interests that have been at stake since the preindependence era. Despite the several mutations of these fundamental interests since late-colonial-era Nigeria, the fault lines created in the colonial period are still clearly traceable in the narratives of the press in Nigeria in early twenty-first century. This is especially true during periods of political crisis when most of the newspapers and newsmagazines identify threats to the ethno-regional and political party interests they represent. This book explores these fault lines so as to expose the alternative articulations of unity and division that underwrite the politics of a postcolonial formation.

One implication of the above is that further studies will be required on how the Nigerian press narrates the idea of a "Nigerian nation" when there are no crises. It can be argued that the fundamental perspectives on how the various interests see the Nigerian union are likely to be more strongly and acutely articulated in periods of political crisis than at any other time. Yet it will be interesting to analyze periods where there are no crises, so as to capture, for comparative analysis, the narratives of everydayness when there is not much immediately at stake. It might also shed light on what is repressed when there is no narrative crisis—in Nigeria or any other multinational postcolonial state.

In a terrain in which power, interest representation, and sociopolitical relations are concealed, and in which attempts are made to conceal the very process of concealment, teasing out meaning in the service of power in press narratives cannot but be susceptible to further analysis that might correspond with or differ from the interpretations and the conclusions reached in this book. There is, therefore, no limit to the interpretation of the symbolic forms that I have analyzed. Given the centrality of the media in the making or sustenance of nationhood in Africa, more comparative studies are needed regarding how meaning is mobilized in the service and disservice of power through the African media.

Notes

Chapter 1

1. Quoted in "Leaders and Self-Government for Nigeria," *Vanguard*, January 14, 2000, 20.
2. Quoted in Coleman, *Nigeria*, 399.
3. "North Not Ready for Self-Rule in 1956—Sardauna," *Vanguard*, January 9, 2000, 32.
4. Ibid.
5. "Hand in Hand," *Nigerian Tribune* (hereafter *NT*), February 2, 1950, capitals in original.
6. "Nigeria First," *Nigerian Citizen* (hereafter *NC*), April 6, 1951, 8.
7. Editorial, "Elections," *NC*, August 23, 1951, 8.
8. "The Bottled Northerner," *West African Pilot* (hereafter *WAP*), November 24, 1952, 7.
9. "Northern Youth React to Crisis in Central Legislature . . . ," *WAP*, April 7, 1953, 1.
10. Ibid.
11. Editorial, "What Blind Ambition Can Do!," *WAP*, July 19, 1952, 2.
12. Michael Hanne states that "Nations and groups in antagonistic relations generally hold to contrary and competing grand political narratives and metaphors of identity, which interpret situations and events in ways that justify their own position." "An Introduction to the 'Warring with Words' Project," 15.
13. "Tribalism," *Daily Times* (hereafter *DT*), September 8, 1953, 5.
14. Hammack and Pilecki, "Narrative as a Root Metaphor for Political Psychology," 77, 97.
15. Mayer, *Narrative Politics*, 3.
16. I thank one of the anonymous reviewers for encouraging me to point this out.
17. Schlesinger, *Media, State and Nation*, 172.
18. Law, "Near and Far," 229.
19. Renan, *Qu'est-ce qu'une nation?*
20. Anderson, *Imagined Communities*, 62.
21. Volosinov, *Marxism and the Philosophy of Language*, 95.
22. Cf. Law, "Near and Far," 300.

23. Billig, *Banal Nationalism.* Billig's idea of "banal nationalism" has also been contested with some evidence from the Scottish case by Law, "Near and Far," 299–317, 2001.

24. Law has argued thus using Terry Eagleton's idea that the nation is both "densely corporeal and elusively spectral at the same time." However, I think that in the African context it is the state that is "densely corporeal," whereas the nation is "elusively spectral." See Eagleton, *Ideology of the Aesthetic,* 208.

25. Casmir, *Communication in Development,* x.

26. Ibid.

27. Doornbos, "African State in Academic Debate," 180.

28. Casmir, *Communication and Development,* x.

29. Degenaar, *Myth of a South African Nation.*

30. Degenaar, "Beware of Nation-Building Discourse," 24.

31. Young, *African Colonial State in Comparative Perspective,* 241.

32. Neuberger, "State and Nation in African Thought," 231–32.

33. Tamarkin, *Nationalism, Nation-Building and Society in Africa,* 18–19.

34. Ibid.

35. Smith, *National Identity,* 106.

36. Young, *African Colonial State,* 241; Casmir, *Communication and Development,* x.

37. Casmir, *Communication and Development,* x; Anderson, *Imagined Communities,* 169.

38. Casmir, *Communication and Development,* x.

39. The term "psuedo-nation" is used here to point to a country that pretends that the project of "nation formation" is complete and so is regarded as "nation." The term "nation-state," in contrast, connotes a state that either has congruity with a nation or one in which the different nations have resolved to subsume their nations to a state that is then invested with the status of nation.

40. De Goor, Rupesinghe, and Sciarone, *Between Development and Destruction,* 67–68.

41. Cited in Chipkin, "South African Nation," 27.

42. McEachern, *Narratives of Nation,* xii.

43. Boyce, "Nation-Building Discourse in a Democracy," 23.

44. Sweet, "South Africans Exist," 144.

45. Chipkin, *Do South Africans Exist,* 60, 119, 27, 26. Cf. McEachern, *Narratives of Nation,* xii–xx.

46. Sweet, "South Africans Exist," 141.

47. Casmir, *Communication and Development,* x.

48. Condon, "Nation Building and Image Building in the Tanzanian Press," 354.

49. Ibid.

50. Kaplan, "American Press and Political Community," 331.

51. Ibid., 331.

52. Billig, *Banal Nationalism*, 6.

53. Ginsbur, Abu-Lughod, and Larkin, "Introduction," 11.

54. Kirk-Greene, "Ethnic Engineering and the 'Federal Character' of Nigeria," 458–78; Smith, *National Identity*, 111–12.

55. Joseph, Taylor, and Agbaje, "Nigeria," 272; Adebanwi and Obadare, "Introducing Nigeria at Fifty," 381.

56. Joseph, Taylor, and Agbaje, "Nigeria," 272.

57. See Ekeh, "Colonialism and the Two Publics in Africa" and "Political Minorities and Historically Dominant Minorities in Nigerian History and Politics."

58. See the debate between Ajayi and Ekeh on whether colonialism was an episode (Ajayi) or an epoch (Ekeh) in African history. Ajayi, "Colonialism," and Ekeh, "Colonialism and the Two Publics in Africa."

59. Smith, *National Identity*, 112.

60. There is an assumption that the narratives of ethnic nationalities within an aspiring nation-state are lesser narratives.

61. Thompson, *Ideology and Modern Culture*.

62. The Hausa and Fulani are two different ethnic groups. However, against the backdrop of the eighteenth-century Fulani jihad through which the latter came to dominate the Hausa, and through intermarriages and shared religious, cultural, and political interests, the two have come to be identified—and also self-identify—as a single ethnic nationality in Nigeria.

63. Nicolson, *Administration of Nigeria*, 180.

64. Awolowo, *Path to Nigerian Freedom*, 47.

65. Ibid., 16.

66. Omu, *Press and Politics in Nigeria*, 204–5.

67. Ibid.

68. "Lugard," *Lagos Weekly Record*, February 1, 1919.

69. For an examination of newspapers published in the local language (Yoruba), see Oduntan, "*Iwe Irohin* and the Representation of the Universal in Nineteenth-Century Egbaland"; Barber, "Translation, Publics and the Vernacular Press."

70. Crowder, *Story of Nigeria*, 228.

71. Awolowo, *Awo*, 166.

72. Coleman, *Nigeria*, 361; Legislative Council Debates, March 4, 1948, 227.

73. Bennett and Edelman, "Towards a New Political Narrative," 157. It is interesting to note that the divisions that occasioned these narratives mirrored the struggle toward independence and the attendant fears of domination by the components groups in the Nigerian union. In the early twentieth century, one of the pioneer journalists in Nigeria and publisher

of the *Lagos Weekly Record,* John Payne Johnson, reflected the opposite sentiments (that of unity, even for all West Africans) when he wrote in his newspaper: "West Africans have discovered today what the Indians . . . discovered 35 years ago, that, placed as they were under the controlling influence of a foreign power, it was essential to their well-being that they should make a common cause and develop a national unity. . . . We hope the day will soon come when . . . Hausas, Yorubas, and Ibos will make a common stand and work hand in hand for their common fatherland." Cited in Coleman, *Nigeria,* 185.

74. Papastergiadis, "Reading Dissemination," 517.

75. Dienstag, *Dancing in Chains,* 211.

76. Bennett and Edelman, "Towards a New Political Narrative," 169, 171.

77. Herman, Jahn and Ryan, *Routledge Encyclopedia of Narrative Theory,* ix; Lucaites and Condit, "Re-constructing Narrative Theory," 90.

78. Herman, Jahn, and Ryan, *Routledge Encyclopedia of Narrative Theory,* ix.

79. Gerbner, *"Homo Narrans,"* 73.

80. Fisher, "Narrative Paradigm," 86.

81. Lucaites and Condit, "Re-constructing Narrative Theory," 103–5.

82. Bormann, "Symbolic Convergence Theory," 128–38; quote on 128.

83. See ibid., 130.

84. Herman, *Basic Elements of Narrative,* 2.

85. Bennett and Edelman, "Towards a New Political Narrative," 170–71.

86. Emerson, *From Empire to Nation,* 90, 102.

87. Chatterjee, *The Nation and Its Fragments,* 5.

88. Smith, *National Identity,* 74. Cf. Yumul and Özkirimli, "Reproducing the Nation," 801.

89. Connor, "A Nation Is a Nation," 377.

90. Ekeh, "Colonialism and the Two Publics in Africa," 1975.

91. Cited in Omu, *Press and Politics in Nigeria,* vii.

92. Ibid. This is true for most parts of Africa regarding not only newspapers but also other media. Abu-Lughod makes a similar point about television and radio in Egypt under President Nasser. See Abu-Lughod, "Finding a Place for Islam," 499–500.

93. Billig, *Banal Nationalism,* 11.

94. Tennekoon, "Newspaper Nationalism."

95. For some examples, see Gershoni and Jankowski, *Redefining the Egyptian Nation;* Hagen, "'Read All About It'"; Harrison, Newspapers and Nationalism in Rural China; Inthorn, "Death of the Hun?"; Legg, *Newspapers and Nationalism;* Wardle and West, "Press as Agents of Nationalism"; Watenpaugh, "Cleansing the Cosmopolitan City."

96. Postill, *Media and Nation Building.*

97. Madanou, *Mediating the Nation*, 5; see also, Costelloe, "Discourses of Sameness," 315–40; Dhoest, "Negotiating Images of the Nation," 393–408.

98. Rhoodie and Liebenberg, "Preface," 2.

99. Nyamnjoh, *Africa's Media*, 63.

100. Lila Abu-Lughod, "Finding a Place for Islam," 493–94, 509–10.

101. Ives, "Mediating the Neoliberal Nation," 153. 159.

102. McEachern, *Narratives of Nation*, xii, xv.

103. Spitulnik, *Producing National Publics*.

104. Spitulnik, "Radio Cycles and Recycling in Zambia," 12, 14–16.

105. Ibid; see also Spitulnik, "Social Circulation of Media Discourse," 161–87.

106. Edmondson, *Performance and Politics in Tanzania*, 5.

107. Askew, *Performing the Nation*, 6.

108. Chick, "Nigerian Press and National Integration"; Okonkwor, *Press and Nigerian Nationalism*. Idemili, *The West African Pilot and the Movement for Nigerian Nationalism*.

109. Omu, *Press and Politics in Nigeria*, 240.

110. Thompson, *Ideology and Modern Culture*.

111. Scholars include McDowell, *Gender, Identity and Place*; Yuval-Davis, *Gender and Nation*; and Marston, Jones, and Woodward, "Human Geography without Scale." Quote from Ives, "Mediating the Neoliberal Nation," 155.

112. Wittman, "Various Concepts of Power," 449.

113. Dahl, "Concept of Power," cited in ibid., 449.

114. van Dijk, "Social Cognition, Social Power and Social Discourse," 16.

115. Fairclough, *Media Discourse*, 2.

116. van Dijk, "Social Cognition, Social Power and Social Discourse," 16.

117. Fairclough, *Critical Discources Analysis*, 6.

118. Thompson, *Ideology and Modern Culture*, 7. 8, 71.

119. Bhabha, *Nation and Narration*, 2, 3.

120. Said, *Culture and Imperialism*, 11.

121. Brennan, *Salmon Rushdie and the Third World*, 4.

122. Papastergaidis, "Reading DissemiNation," 513; Bhabha, "DissemiNation," 305.

Chapter 2

1. As Schütz captures it, this "is a controversy which for more than half a century has split not only logicians and methodologists but also social scientists into two schools of thought." Schütz, *Phenomenology of the Social World*, cited in Blaikie, *Approaches to Social Enquiry*, 31.

2. See Fay, "An Alternative View," 82–88; Blaikie, *Approaches to Social Enquiry*, 122–24.

3. Gibbons, "Introduction," 1–2.

4. Ibid.; see also Taylor, "Language and Human Nature," 101–32.

5. Taylor, "Interpretation and the Sciences of Man," 24.

6. Gibbons, "Introduction," 1–2.

7. Fay, "An Alternative View," 83.

8. Ibid., 84–88.

9. Thompson, *Ideology and Modern Culture*, 21.

10. Ricouer's relevant works include *Hermeneutics and the Human Sciences, The Conflict of Interpretations: Interpretation Theory*, and *Time and Narrative*.

11. Thompson, *Ideology and Modern Culture*, 278.

12. Habermas, *Theory of Communicative Action*, 107.

13. Giddens, *New Rules of Sociological Method*, 158.

14. Fay, "An Alternative View," 89.

15. Habermas, "Hermeneutic Claim to Universality," xvi.

16. Lukács, *Geschichte und Klassenbewusstsein*, cited in Dröge, "Social Knowledge," 49.

17. Dröge, "Social Knowledge," 49.

18. Hegel, *Werke*, Band 16, *Religionsphilosophie*, 156, cited in Dröge, "Social Knowledge," 49–50.

19. Dröge, "Social Knowledge," 49.

20. Ibid.

21. Helle, *Soziologie und Symbol*, cited in Dröge, "Social Knowledge," 51.

22. Dröge, "Social Knowledge," 54, 57.

23. See Kreimeier, "Fundamental Reflections," 37–47.

24. Mannheim, *Ideology and Utopia*, xv.

25. Modern philosophy and science, Mannheim argues, have been somewhat trapped in the concerted drive toward objectivity. This concern with the bases and processes of the search for valid knowledge has influenced the writings of Western thinkers from Plato, Aristotle, Descartes, and Bacon, through Locke, Hume, Bentham, Mill, Adam Smith, Marx, Comte, and Verba, to Popper, Kunn, Manheim, Max Scheler, and the more contemporary thinkers and writers like Dilthey, Husserl, Heidegger, Foucault and Derrida. Mannheim, *Ideology and Utopia*, xv–xxi. For a review of the progression of the history of thought, see also Mckenzie, "Age of Reason," 8–24.

26. Mannheim, *Ideology and Utopia*, xxviii, xxxix–xxxx. This makes the sociology of knowledge indeed relevant to our task in this book, given the different "heritage of groups," which the different newspapers seek to protect and project. The question that the sociology of knowledge seeks to answer is therefore very important to understanding the different narratives.

27. Mannheim merely describes it as a "suitable method for the description and analysis of . . . thought" (*Ideology and Utopia*, 2).

28. Ibid.

29. It is important to note the caution offered by Thompson regarding the fact that the language of *explanandum* and *explanans* is inadequate for the methodology of the sociology of knowledge. See Thompson, *Ideology and Modern Culture*.

30. Mannheim, *Ideology and Utopia*, 3.

31. Ibid.

32. Thompson, *Ideology and Modern Culture*, 29.

33. Ibid., 28–29. I avoid the intricate details of the development of the term "ideology" from 1796 when de Tracy first used it. Only significant changes in the meaning of the term over time are addressed. For a more detailed account, see Thompson, *Ideology and Modern Culture*, 29–60.

34. Ibid., 32, 30. Destutt de Tracy's definition of the science of ideas is cited in Mannheim, *Ideology and Utopia*, 71.

35. Thompson, *Ideology and Modern Culture*, 31.

36. Ibid., 32.

37. Ibid.

38. Mannheim, *Ideology and Utopia*, 72.

39. Thompson, *Ideology and Modern Culture*, 34–38.

40. Ibid., 37–38.

41. Mannheim, *Ideology and Utopia*, 55–56.

42. Thompson, *Ideology and Modern Culture*, 44. 45, 46, 49, 50.

43. Ibid., 56.

44. Ibid., 57.

45. Ibid., 58.

46. Ibid., 59.

47. Thompson states that his task is not "to provide a comprehensive account" of the ways in which meaning intersects with relations of domination but to stake out a rich field of analysis. Ibid., 60.

48. Ibid., 61.

49. Ibid., 71.

Chapter 3

1. Quoted in "Leaders and Self-government for Nigeria," *Vanguard*, January 14, 2000, 20.

2. Quoted in Coleman, *Nigeria*, 399. Emphasis added.

3. Ibid.

4. "North Not Ready for Self-Rule in 1956—Sardauna," *Vanguard*, January 9, 2000, 32.

5. Coleman, *Nigeria*, 399; see also Crowder, *The Story of Nigeria*, 234.

6. "North Not Ready for Self-Rule in 1956—Sardauna," *Vanguard*, January 9, 2000, 32.

7. Ibid.

8. Quoted in "Leaders and Self-Government for Nigeria," *Vanguard*, January 14, 2000, 20.

9. Mannheim, *Ideology and Utopia*, xxix.

10. "Zik to Leave Politics: N.E.C. Leaders View," *NC*, January 19, 1952, 3.

11. Editorial, "Literacy," *NC*, January 26, 1951.

12. "Points from Your Letters," *NC*, February 2, 1951, 8.

13. Editorial, "Northern Art," *NC*, February 16, 1951, 6.

14. "Reservation for Fulani Urged: Livestock Mission Proposal," *NC*, March 2, 1951, 1.

15. "Nigerian Livestock Mission Report: And the Women," *NC*, March 2, 1951, 4.

16. "Imperialist Trump Card," *NT*, February 16, 1951.

17. "The Press," *NC*, March 30, 1951, 6.

18. "Imperialist Trump Card," *NT*, February 16, 1951.

19. "Nigeria First," *NC*, April 6, 1951, 8.

20. "Give and Take," *NC*, April 27, 1951.

21. "Hand in Hand," *NT*, February 2, 1950. Capitals in original.

22. "Give and Take," *NC*, April 27, 1951.

23. "Empire Day," *NC*, May 18, 1951.

24. Ibid.

25. Thompson, *Ideology and Modern Culture*, 61.

26. "Workers Beware," *DT*, January 20, 1951, 5.

27. Thompson, *Ideology and Modern Culture*, 65.

28. "Labour in a Dependency," *WAP*, January 1, 1952, 1.

29. "Moderation," *NC*, June 1, 1952, 6. The organs supporting the contesting parties refers, ostensibly to *WAP* (NCNC), *Daily Service*, and *Nigerian Tribune* (AG).

30. Editorial, "Elections," *NC*, August 23, 1951, 8.

31. "The Bottled Northerner," *WAP*, November 24, 1952, 7. Cf. "Surprise from the North," editorial, *WAP*, February 19, 1952: "The Northern legislators are proving equal to the task before them. . . . Whatever may be the opinion in the North, it is nevertheless a sign of political awakening made more so by Southern influence. We wish the speed be accelerated to cover up the gap left by many years of lagging. . . . Northern conservatism is breaking. When that is consolidated, a free and more dynamic North will indeed emerge."

32. "Hand in Hand," *NT*, February 2, 1950. The adjectives "healthy" and "enlightening" qualifying the sun could be regarded as speaking to the backwardness of the north and the attendant problems.

33. "North and Our Freedom," *WAP*, November 19, 1952, 2.

34. Perham, *Lugard*, 46–47.

35. Morel, *Affairs of West Africa*, 127.

36. Despite its "misconceived idea of importance, or greatness . . . and majesty," as the *Pilot* states.

37. "Even the North Is Ready," *WAP*, October 15, 1952, 2.

38. Ibid.

39. Ibid.

40. Azikiwe had described the NYM as founded to "lay a solid foundation for the development of the nationalist spirit in Nigeria" (*My Odyssey*, 144). For details on the NYM crisis, see Coleman, *Nigeria*; Sklar, *Nigerian Political Parties*; and Awolowo, *Awo*.

41. "Lagos Belongs to All Alike," *WAP*, January 14, 1952.

42. Editorial, "We Will Have No Pakistan," January 12, 1952. Interestingly, the *Pilot* had welcomed the AG when it was formally launched in March 1951: "Its aims and objects are laudable and its programme of action is varied and wide. From all appearances it is an awakening consciousness in the West." *WAP*, March 29, 1951. "Pakistan" is a metaphor for secession or separation.

43. "A Notorious Liar," *NT*, July 30, 1951.

44. Editorial, "What Blind Ambition Can Do!" *WAP*, July 19, 1952, 2.

45. Ibid.

46. Ibid.

47. Ibid.

48. "Members of One Family," *WAP*, October 7, 1952.

49. "Evils of Narrow Nationalism," *WAP*, October 1, 1952.

50. Sklar, *Nigerian Political Parties*, 422.

51. "Confusion Goes East," *Daily Service* (hereafter *DS*), January 26, 1953.

52. Sklar, *Nigerian Political Parties*, 54, 55.

53. Editorial, "Empty Braggarts," *DS*, January 8, 1953.

54. Editorial, "Latest Fashion in Antipodes," *WAP*, October 9, 1952.

55. Editorial, "Short Cuts to Independence," *WAP*, October 10, 1952.

56. "Unification of Nigerian Tribes," *WAP*, January 3, 1952.

57. Editorial, "Opportunism," *DS*, January 10, 1953.

58. Editorial, "Will the East Surrender?," *DS*, January 27, 1953.

59. Editorial, "The Fallacy of Regionalisation," *WAP*, January 12, 1952.

60. "An NCNCer," "Wit and Humour," *DS*, January 3, 1953.

61. Editorial, "Reject Confusion," *DS*, January 29, 1953.

62. Editorial, "A Fundamental Difference," *WAP*, January 8, 1953.

63. "Boycott of Centre as Way Out," *WAP*, January 14, 1952, 1.

64. "Zik's Father Speaks on the Western House Election Issue," *WAP*, January 14, 1952, 1.

65. Ibid.

66. Ibid.

67. Ibid. The reference to those who Zik's stature held in "obscurity" can be read as a reference to Awo.

68. "Why Inter-Tribal Antagonism," *NT*, February 19, 1952.

69. "Time for a Shake Up," *WAP*, January 16, 1952.

70. Thompson, *Ideology and Modern Culture*, 65.

71. "West Is Ashamed of the Groupers," January 22, 1952.

72. "Why Inter-Tribal Antagonism," *NT*, February 19, 1952.

73. "Urhobos Condemn Action Group for Humiliating Oba of Benin: Truncation from West Demanded," *WAP*, February 4, 1952, 1.

74. Lucaites and Condit, "Re-constructing Narrative Theory," 94.

75. "The Evil Gospel Spreads," *WAP*, February 4, 1952.

76. "Groupers to Study Democracy at Work in the Eastern Provinces. Binis React to National Insult," *WAP*, February 5, 1952, 1.

77. "Oh, Thou Shade of Overami," *WAP*, February 5, 1952.

78. "Groupers to Study Democracy at Work in the Eastern Provinces. Binis React to National Insult," *WAP*, February 5, 1952, 1.

79. "Urhobos Condemn Action Group for Humiliating Oba of Benin: Truncation from West Demanded," *WAP*, February 4, 1952, 1.

80. Time for a Shake Up," *WAP*, January 16, 1952.

81. "The Evil Man," *DS*, February 2, 1953.

82. "Stand Firm!" *DS*, February 2, 1953.

83. "Commendable Courage," *DS*, February 3, 1953.

84. "The Dictators Trade," *DS*, February 9, 1953.

85. "Confusion Goes East," *DS*, January 26, 1953.

86. Bennett and Edelman, "Towards A New Political Narrative," 158.

87. "Motion on Self-Govt. Heralds New East and West Understanding," *WAP*, April 1, 1953, 1.

88. Ibid.

89. "NCNC and Action Group Stage Dramatic Joint Walk Out. Northern Majority is A Bogey," *WAP*, April 1, 1953, 1.

90. "What Is Right for Our Country?," *WAP*, April 2, 1953, 1.

91. Ibid.

92. "West Central Ministers Resign! No Compromise on Self-Govt," *DS*, April 1, 1953, 1.

93. "Self-Government in 1956," *WAP*, March 31, 1953.

94. "The Major Test," *DS*, March 30, 1953, 1; and "Let the North Think," *DS*, March 31, 1953.

95. "Motion of Self-Government: Herald New East and West Understanding," *WAP*, April 1, 1953, 1.

96. Editorial, "The Struggle Begins," *DS*, April 1, 1953, 1.

97. Ibid.
98. "The Tyranny of the Majority," *WAP*, April 1, 1953, 1.
99. Ibid.
100. "Now Is the Time," *WAP*, April 12, 1953.
101. "North and Official Influence," editorial, *WAP*, April 1, 1953.
102. "Sardauna of Sokoto Recalls 1914 Issue," *WAP*, April 2, 1953, 1.
103. Editorial, "The Mistake of 1914," *DS*, April 4, 1953.
104. Editorial, "These Threats of Secession," *DS*, April 2, 1953.
105. "NCNC And AG Parliamentary Council Hold Joint Meeting. They Issued Statement of S.G.," *WAP*, April 4, 1953, 1.
106. "The Contagion Spreads," *WAP*, April 4, 1953.
107. "Northern Youth React to Crisis in Central Legislature. They Are for Freedom in 1956," *WAP*, April 7, 1953, 1.
108. "The Voice of the Real North," *DS*, May 15, 1953.
109. Thompson, 61.
110. NEPU and the Askanist Movement were NCNC's allies. Interestingly, before the NPC emerged, the *Citizen* did not think these parties, particularly NEPU, existed for the north. It hoped that "the North may evolve an effective organization more solid and enduring than NCNC, Action Group, or any of the other parties classified as 'national.'" See "Not Indifferent," *NC*, July 12, 1951, 8. And when the NPC was formed, the *Citizen* described it as "an act of major significance in the North," because "before last week, there was only one political party in the North, the Northern Elements Progressive Union [which the paper had earlier narrated out of existence by nonrecognition] which is now undergoing one of its periods of afflation with Dr. Azikiwe's National Council of Nigeria and Cameroons. It is a matter of regret that the [NPC] could not have come out into the political arena three or four months earlier." See "A New Party," *NC*, October 11, 1951, 8. The *Citizen* at this point conveniently forgot that it had praised the absence of party politics in the north barely two months earlier, when it stated that "fortunately, the North has not become the victim of the inter-party mud-slinging, slander, and libel which is characterizing elections in some other parts of country." Yet it wished in October that the party had been born three or four months earlier. See "Elections," *NC*, August 23, 1951, 8. Consequently, when NEPU "quite unexpectedly" gained seventeen seats in the Kano city elections (in alliance with the NCNC), with the implication that it might gain control of the Northern House of Assembly, the *Citizen* averred that the "red light is showing," "if the farcical position at Kano, where a minority group looks like getting control against the declared interests of the overwhelming majority of people, is repeated elsewhere."
111. "The Truth Is Out," *WAP*, May 14, 1953. "In the North, there must be the most strident heart-searching particularly at the top, to find the cause." "Elections," *NC*, October 25, 1951, 6.

112. "Keeping in Touch," *NC*, June 14, 1951, 6.

113. "Education," *NC*, September 13, 1951.

114. Even though there was the *Nigerian Citizen*, it did not have the reach and dynamism of the southern press.

115. "Isa Kaita's Lies on the Air," *WAP*, April 17, 1953, 1.

116. "Neglect of the North Is Deliberate, Says Isa Kaita," *NC*, March 20, 1952, 1.

117. "The Country's Fate," *DS*, July 21, 1953.

118. "Sardauna and NPC Colleagues Rewarded for Services Rendered," *DS*, June 1, 1953, 1.

119. "The Country's Fate," *DS*, July 21, 1953.

120. "Self-Government in 1956," *NT*, May 8, 1953.

121. "E-Stand By," *NT*, May 10, 1953.

122. "North Member May Throw Political Bomb in Lagos," *NC*, March 13, 1952, 6.

123. "Action Group-NCNC Alliance," *DS*, September 10, 1953.

124. "NCNC-Action Group Alliance," *WAP*, September 12, 1953.

125. "Secret of *Daily Times* Drive to Break the NCNC Revealed. Action Group Enters Its Trap," *WAP*, September 21, 1953.

126. "Dredging the Drains," *DS*, September 23, 1953.

127. "NCNC and Lagos," October 6, 1953.

128. "Secret of *Daily Times* Drive to Break the NCNC Revealed. Action Group Enters Its Trap," *WAP*, September 21, 1953.

129. "Dredging the Drains," *DS*, September 23, 1953.

130. Editorial, "The North Keeps Silent," *WAP*, October 2, 1953.

131. Editorial, "Late Appeal to North," *WAP*, October 31, 1953.

132. Editorial, "NCNC Delegates Visit North," *WAP*, November 4, 1953.

133. "No Alliance with the Devil," *WAP*, November 18, 1953.

134. "Groupers and Irresponsible Gossip," *WAP*, December 1, 1953.

135. "Nationalist Press, Voice of the People," *WAP*, May 21, 1953.

136. Emerson, *From Empire to Nation*, 102.

137. "Nigeria—A Nation of Barkers," *WAP*, July 9, 1952.

138. Emerson, *From Empire to Nation*, 102.

139. "Middle-West Settlement," *NC*, September 4, 1952, 6.

140. H. O. Davies, "The Common Sense of Nigerian Politics," *DT*, February 15, 1951.

141. "Homogeneity Is Merely a Nonsensical Fancy," *DT*, February 24, 1951, 5.

142. "We Will Have No Pakistan," *WAP*, January 12, 1952, 2.

143. "Tribalism," *DT*, September 8, 1953.

144. "Our New Deal: An Opportunity," *DT*, September 1, 1953, 5.

145. "The Voice of the Real North," *DS*, May 15, 1953.

146. "A Unified Nigeria," *DT*, January 6, 1953, 5.

147. "Unity," *DT*, April 8, 1953, 1.

Chapter 4

Epigraph. Said, *The World, the Text and the Critic,* 174–75.
1. Awolowo, *Awo,* 154.
2. Ibid.
3. Laitin, *Hegemony and Culture,* 19.
4. The capital formally moved to Abuja in 1991 under the regime of General Ibrahim Babangida, even though the project was started under the regime of General Murtala Mohammed in 1975.
5. *Lagos Weekly Record,* February 14, 1920, 1.
6. Ibid.
7. Ibid.
8. Ibid.
9. See, for instance, Abumere, *Distributional Inequality.*
10. Fontana, *Hegemony and Power,* 1.
11. Gramsci, in Barrett, *Politics of Truth,* 54.
12. Ibid., 54–55.
13. Agbaje, *Nigerian Press,* 11.
14. Ibid., 10–11.
15. Fontana, *Hegemony and Power,* 140.
16. Ibid.; Laitin, *Hegemony and Culture,* 105.
17. Said, *The World, the Text and the Critic,* 170, 172.
18. Ibid., 170.
19. Ibid., 170–71.
20. Ibid., 171.
21. Ibid., 174.
22. Mouffe, "Hegemony and Ideology in Gramsci," 217.
23. Said, *The World, the Text and the Critic,* 174.
24. Laitin, *Hegemony and Culture,* 105.
25. Ibid., 19.
26. Fontana, *Hegemony and Power,* 141.
27. Laitin, *Hegemony and Culture,* 100, 107.
28. Penrose, "Nations, States and Homelands," 278. As Penrose notes, writers on the subject, including Storey (in *Territory*), Sack (in *Human Territoriality*), and Taylor and Flint (in *Political Geography*) fail to offer any definition of the term "space." Storey offers no definition at all, whereas Taylor and Flint, who note that "space itself is an area of contention . . . there is nothing neutral about any spatial arrangement," avoid defining the term itself although they attempt to define it in relation to something else, thereby ignoring the agency that is integral to space. See Penrose, "Nations, States and Homelands," 294.
29. Ibid., 278–79.
30. Ibid., 279.

31. Sacks, *Human Territoriality*, quoted in Penrose, "Nations, States and Homelands," 279.

32. It is important to recognize that, as Anssi Paasi in "Constructing Territories" argues, "boundaries may be simultaneously historical, natural, cultural, political, economic, or symbolic phenomena and each of these dimensions may be exploited in diverging ways in the construction of territoriality" (42). See Penrose, "Nations, States and Homelands," 280.

33. A Bini word meaning "camp."

34. Crowder, *Story of Nigeria*, 120.

35. Cole, *Modern and Traditional Elites*, 1.

36. Ibid., 133, 136.

37. Even the colonial governor Young said, as early as 1885, that Lagos was his first contact with civilization since he left England. Ibid., 6, 47.

38. Burton, *Wandering in Africa*, quoted in Cole, *Modern and Traditional Elites*, 8–9.

39. Cole, *Modern and Traditional Elites,*, 217.

40. Quoted in Zachernuk, *Colonial Subjects*, 131.

41. Coleman, *Nigeria*, 197.

42. Ibid. See also Adebanwi, "Colonial Modernity and Tradition."

43. Coleman, *Nigeria*, 198.

44. Ibid., 199.

45. Coleman, *Nigeria*, 217.

46. Population census figures in ibid.

47. Ibid., 220.

48. Ibid., 222–23.

49. Ibid., 223–24.

50. Adebanwi, "Nigerian Press and the National Question."

51. This seems to have been achieved by the 1930s and 1940s when the Igbo were considered to have superseded the Yoruba in the embrace of Western education. See Coleman, *Nigeria*, 224, 226.

52. Ibid., 340.

53. Ibid., 347.

54. Awolowo, *Awo*, 139.

55. Coleman, *Nigeria*, 342–43.

56. Awolowo, *Awo*, 140–41.

57. Sklar, *Nigerian Political Parties*, 68–70.

58. Ibid.

59. "The Evil Gospel Spreads," *WAP*, February 4, 1952.

60. Quoted in Coleman, *Nigeria*, 346.

61. Ibid.

62. Mamdani, *Citizen and Subject*, 292.

63. Coleman, *Nigeria*, 346.

64. Ibid.

65. Cole, *Modern and Traditional Elites*, 41.

66. Ibid.

67. Interestingly, merging Lagos with another place was not novel. In 1883, the Colonial Office in London decreed a union between Lagos and Accra, which reduced the powers of the administrator of Lagos; this was followed by the 1884–85 agitation for the separation of Lagos and Accra and the return of a separate Legislative Council for Lagos. By 1883, the three Lagos newspapers, including the *Lagos Times*, *Lagos Observer and Eagle*, and *Lagos Critic*, had opened a concerted attack on the merger. Cole, *Modern and Traditional Elites*, 53.

68. Mamdani, *Citizen and Subject*, 292.

69. Fontana, *Hegemony and Power*, 32.

70. "Symbol of Nigeria," *WAP*, July 16, 1952.

71. Ibid.

72. Ibid.

73. Thompson, *Ideology and Modern Culture*, 64.

74. "Native Authority in Lagos," *WAP*, July 16, 1952.

75. Ibid.

76. Penrose, "Nations, States and Homelands," 279.

77. "Lagos Merger Issue" ("Weekend Catechism"), *WAP*, July 19, 1952.

78. "Country without Capital," *WAP*, February 11, 1953.

79. "The Anomalous Position of Lagos," *WAP*, October 11, 1952.

80. "The Perfect Monster," *Pilot*, October 14, 1952.

81. "The Nuisance If Removed," *DS*, February 7, 1953.

82. Ibid.

83. "Lagos Loses Its Temper Again!" *WAP*, October 11, 1952.

84. "Country without Capital," *WAP*, February 11, 1953.

85. "The Bone of Contention," *WAP*, August 4, 1952.

86. "Lagos Belong to All Alike," *WAP*, January 14, 1952.

87. "Facing Facts," *DS*, January 12, 1953.

88. Ibid.

89. Ibid.

90. "What Matters Now!" *WAP*, April 21, 1953.

91. "Lagos," *DS*, August 20, 1953.

92. "West Cannot Submit to Separating Lagos," *DS*, August 21, 1953.

93. "Nigeria's Cinderella," *DS*, August 21, 1953.

94. Penrose, "Nations, States and Homelands," 278.

95. "Nigeria's Cinderella," *DS*, August 21, 1953.

96. In fact, a letter published in the "Public Opinion" column of the *Pilot*, written by D. V. Edebwin, argued that "the Binis are by historical fact, the owners of Lagos, and naturally they should be the most interested in the question of its future state" ("We Own Lagos," *WAP*, September 15, 1953). Quote from "Lagos Is Dear to All," *WAP*, September 10, 1953.

97. "Nigeria Funds in Lagos," *DS*, September 8, 1953.
98. "Zik Supports Lagos-West Merger—Odebiyi," *DS*, October 17, 1953.
99. "Ibadan People Oppose," *DS*, August 24, 1953.
100. "Lagos Is Dear to All," *WAP*, September 10, 1953.
101. "Mr. Lyttleton's Decision," *DS*, August 22, 1953.
102. "Nigeria's Cinderella," *DS*, August 21, 1953.
103. "Mr. Lyttleton's Decision," *DS*, August 22, 1953.
104. "Lagos or Nigeria," *DS*, September 3, 1953.
105. "A Neutral Capital," *DS*, August 24, 1953.
106. Penrose, "Nations, States and Homelands," 280.
107. "Action Group Fails Again," *WAP*, September 2, 1953.
108. "Action Group-NCNC Alliance," *DS*, September 10, 1953.
109. "Secret of *Daily Times* Drive to Break the NCNC Revealed. Action Group Enters Its Trap," *WAP*, September 21, 1953.
110. Harvey, *Justice, Nature and the Geography of Difference*, in Penrose, "Nations, States and Homelands," 282.
111. Penrose, "Nations, States and Homelands," 282.
112. Fontana, *Hegemony and Power*, 140–41.
113. Mamdani, *Citizen and Subject*, 8.

Chapter 5

1. See Hanne, "An Introduction to the 'Warring with Words' Project," 16; Charteris-Black, *Politicians and Rhetoric*.
2. Allen and Seaton, "Introduction," 2.
3. Thussu and Freedman, "Introduction," 4.
4. Cottle, *Mediatized Conflict*, 9.
5. Rosland, "Constructing Legitimacy," 28. Emphasis in original.
6. See Atkinson, "Deconstructing Media Mythologies of Ethnic War in Liberia"; Leopold, "The War in the North"; Alexander and McGregor, "Representing Violence in Matabeleland, Zimbabwe"; McNutty, "Media Ethnicization and the International Response to War and Genocide in Rwanda"; and Styan, "Misrepresenting Ethiopia and the Horn of Africa?"
7. Allen and Seaton, "Introduction," 4.
8. Thompson, "Introduction," 2; see also Forges, "Call to Genocide"; Kabanda, "*Kangura*"; Higiro, "Rwandan Private Print Media"; Li, "Echoes of Violence."
9. Howard, "Community Radio"; Goldstein and Rotich, "Digitally Networked Technology"; Makinen and Kuira, "Social Media"; Frère, *Media and Conflicts in Central Africa*.
10. Akinyemi has examined the role of the British press and the civil war. See *The British Press and the Nigerian Civil War*.

11. I could also have focused on the civil war years, but I was unable to gain access to the newspapers published in the short-lived Republic of Biafra. This is an area of research that other students of media and politics in Nigeria should take up in the future.

12. Carruthers, *Media at War*, 16.

13. Joda, "Foreword," ii. See also Mohammadu, "Introduction," v–viii.

14. Cited in Mohammadu, "Introduction," v.

15. Quoted in "First Coup: Nzeogwu's Speech," *Vanguard*, February 10, 2000, 30.

16. Quoted in "Attitudes at Aburi: How the Military Viewed Politicians," *Vanguard*, February 15, 2000, 32.

17. "Ojukwu Speaks: East Wants Peace, No Wish to Secede," *Morning Post* (hereafter *MP*), August, 19, 1966, 1. See the cover of this *Morning Post* issue.

18. Quoted in "Attitudes at Aburi: How the Military Viewed Politicians," *Vanguard*, February 15, 2000, 32.

19. Exchanges among Nigeria's military chiefs, quoted in "Views and Counter Views at Aburi," *Vanguard*, February 17, 2000, 30.

20. "Road to Survival," *MP*, January 19, 1966, 1.

21. "Best Hope for Democracy," *MP*, January 20, 1966, 1.

22. "Words of Gold," *MP*, January 21, 1966, 5.

23. "Path to True Unity," *NT*, March 9, 1966, 1.

24. "Without Bitterness," *MP*, February 9, 1966, 5.

25. "Forward with Our Army," *NT*, January 29, 1966, 1.

26. "Help Fajuyi," *WAP*, April 7, 1966, 2.

27. For instance, editorial headlines in the *New Nigerian* as late as July 1966 give indications of this. They include "Meeting the People," July 1, 1966; "(U.S.) Independence," July 4, 1966; "Putting Teeth into the Rent Legislation," July 4, 1966; "Get Expert Advice to Build Exports," July 13, 1966; "Incentive for Self-Help," July 15, 1966.

28. "Meeting the People," *New Nigerian* (hereafter *NN*), July 16, 1966.

29. "A Symbol of National Unity," *NN*, July 18, 1966, 6.

30. "The Regions Are Abolished." Ironsi's broadcast to the nation banning political parties and introducing decree no. 34, May 24, 1966.

31. Thompson, *Ideology and Modern Culture*, 60, 64.

32. "One Nigeria," *MP*, February 15, 1966. Yet *MP* states that the "demarcations" between Nigerians were "artificial." See "This Accra Victory," *MP*, February 15, 1966, 1.

33. "The Budget," *WAP*, April 2, 1966.

34. Ironsi, quoted in ibid.

35. As expressed in the editorial "Meeting the People," *NN*, July 16, 1966.

36. The article by Walter Schwarz was supposedly meant to be published in the London *Sunday Observer*, but was not. See "Strangers within Our Gates," *NT*, May 18, 1966, 1.

37. Major Chukwuma Kaduna Nzeogwu and the other majors who planned and executed the January 15, 1966, coup in which prominent northern leaders were killed. They had been arrested and detained by the Ironsi regime after power was handed over to Ironsi. "Nigeria Back in Politics?," *NN*, May 12, 1966, 1.

38. Ibid.

39. "What Nigerians Want," *WAP*, April 19, 1966, 1. "Govt Must Be Firm," May 31, 1966, 1.

40. "In the Bid for a United Nigeria . . . There Is No Talk of a Minority—Ojukwu," *WAP*, April 9, 1966, 1.

41. "What Nigerians Want," *WAP*, April 19, 1966, 1.

42. Ibid.

43. "Recrimination?," *WAP*, April 25, 1966.

44. "A United Nigeria," *NT*, May 26, 1966, 1.

45. "One Nigeria, One Destiny," May 26, 1966, 2.

46. "*Civis Nigerianus Sum*," *MP*, May 26, 1966, 1.

47. "A United Nigeria," *NT*, May 26, 1966, 1. The *Tribune* notes elsewhere that when the Ironsi regime announced that it had prepared a twenty-year plan for Nigeria, "this does not fall within the programme of a corrective government." "Twenty Years," *NT*, July 22, 1966.

48. "One Nigeria, One Destiny," May 26, 1966, 2.

49. "Govt Must Be Firm," May 31, 1966, 1.

50. "We Must Unite," *MP*, May 10, 1966, 1.

51. "Long Live United Nigeria," *WAP*, June 25, 1966.

52. "No Room for Tribe," *MP*, July 15, 1966, 1.

53. The *Tribune* and the *Pilot* report "92 killed . . . 506 wounded, 300 arrested." *NT*, June 2, 1966; *WAP*, June 2, 1966.

54. "Transfer of Army Governors," *WAP*, July 5, 1966.

55. "Marching to Progress," *WAP*, July 18, 1966, 1.

56. "The First 6 Months," *WAP*, July 18, 1966.

57. "Test For Rulers," *WAP*, July 28, 1966.

58. "A Huge Success," *WAP*, July 30, 1966.

59. "Plea for Calm," *WAP*, August 1, 1966, 1.

60. "Our Hope for the Future," *NN*, August 2, 1966, 1.

61. Ibid.

62. "Let's Begin Again," *WAP*, August 2, 1966.

63. Ibid.

64. "Ojukwu Congratulates Chief Awolowo," August 4, 1966, 1.

65. "Releasing Goodwill through the Prison Gates," *NN*, August 4, 1966.

66. This is an example of euphemization. The three years these three men had served out of the ten-year term (or less) was described as "confinement," which glosses over the hardship and psychological trauma of imprisonment.

67. "Releasing Goodwill through the Prison Gates," *NN*, August 4, 1966.

68. "Awo's Hour of Glory. . . ." *MP*, August 4, 1966. "Awo At Ibadan," *WAP*, August 9, 1966.

69. "Don't Break the Nation," *Post*, August 5, 1966, back page.

70. "Release for Awo," *NT*, August 3, 1966, 1. "Welcome, Awolowo," *NT*, August 4, 1966.

71. Interestingly, Gowon later created twelve states and part of the rationale was to break the "recalcitrance" of the east. "Federalism Only Answer," *NN*, August 10, 1966, 1.

72. Ibid.

73. Ibid.

74. Ibid.

75. "One Nigeria, One Destiny," May 26, 1966, 2.

76. "True Federalism," *WAP*, August 10, 1966.

77. Factors for True Federation No Longer Exists: Ojukwu," *WAP*, August 19, 1966.

78. "*Crisis Nigerianus Sum*," *MP*, May 26, 1966, 1.

79. "Peace in Our Time," *MP*, August 6, 1966.

80. "One Nigeria," *MP*, February 15, 1966, 1.

81. "This Is No Time to Kid," *MP*, August 8, 1966, 5. Capitals in original.

82. "A United Nigeria," *NT*, May 26, 1966, 1.

83. "A New Constitution," *NT*, August 10, 1966, 1.

84. Ibid.

85. "The Forthcoming Big Talks," *NN*, August 23, 1966, 6.

86. Ibid.

87. "The Issue at Stake," *NN*, August 29, 1966.

88. Gowon's inaugural speech. See Obotetukudo, *The Inuagural Addresses and Ascenson Speeches*, 60–65.

89. Raymond E. Okorie, "A Voice from the East Pleads with Yakubu Gowon—Let's Part Our Ways." *NN*, August 23, 1966, 6.

90. "A New Chapter," *NT*, August 16, 1966, 1.

91. "The Nation's Destiny," *NT*, September 12, 1966, 1.

92. Ibid.

93. "The Problem of Unity," *WAP*, September 6, 1966, 2. Capitals in original.

94. "The Task before Us," *WAP*, September 12, 1966, 1.

95. "The Nation before Self," *MP*, August 16, 1966.

96. "Best Yet to Come," *MP*, August 12, 1966.

97. "The Nation before Self," *MP*, August 16, 1966.

98. "Best Yet to Come," *MP*, August 12, 1966.

99. "The March of History," *WAP*, September 2, 1966.

100. "An Example of Reasonableness," *NN*, August 25, 1966.

101. "Restraint, Please," *NN*, August 24, 1966.

102. "Freedom of Movement," *MP*, August 26, 1966.

103. "Crush the Saboteurs," *MP*, August 31, 1966. "Restraint Please," *NT*, August 30, 1966, 1.

104. "To Be or Not to Be?," *NT*, August 27, 1966, 1.

105. "When Our £-o-v-e Is Tied to the Pound," *WAP*, September 19, 1966, 1.

106. "Indiscreet," *NN*, August 31, 1966.

107. "That Delegation from East," *NN*, September 10, 1966.

108. "Lt. Col. Hassan Gives Another STERN WARNING—Against Lawlessness, Molestation and Acts of Subversion," *NN*, September 12, 1966, 1.

109. Ostensibly, the five majors led by Nzeogwu, who masterminded the January 16, 1966, coup.

110. "Let's Watch and Pray," *NN*, September 13, 1966, 1.

111. "Action, Gowon," *NT*, October 4, 1966, 1.

112. "Whither Nigeria?," *MP*, August 5, 1966.

113. "What Next, Gowon?," *NT*, October 5, 1966, 1.

114. "A Daniel, a Daniel," *WAP*, October 5, 1966.

115. "Hitting the Bull's Eye," *WAP*, Octber 3, 1966, 1.

116. "States for Sale," *WAP*, October 3, 1966, 1. Capitals in original.

117. "Genesis of the Exodus," *NN*, September 28, 1966, 1.

118. Ibid.

119. Thompson, *Ideology and Modern Culture*, 62.

120. "Exodus," *MP*, June 18, 1966, 5.

121. "Genesis of the Exodus," *NN*, September 28, 1966, 1.

122. Ibid.

123. "Genesis of the Exodus," *NN*, September 28, 1966, 1.

124. "Well Not Destroy the Edifice We Helped to Build: 3,000 Easterners Dead in May Riots—Ojukwu," *WAP*, October 20, 1966, 1.

125. "Enough Is Enough," *NT*, October 26, 1966, 1.

126. "Warning and Vigilance," *NT*, October 6, 1966, 1.

127. Ibid.

128. "Stop the Gas," *NT*, October 27, 1966.

129. "Warning and Vigilance," *NT*, October 6, 1966, 1.

130. "Not Such a Clear Cut Issue," *NN*, September 29, 1966.

131. "Peace—We Must Find an Answer," *NN*, September 30, 1966, 1.

132. "Above All Keep Calm," October 3, 1966.

133. "Appeal by Gowon. North's Role in Peace Moves," *NN*, October 3, 1966, 1.

134. Gowon could have added: "after the last northerner in power, Balewa, was killed by the Igbo."

135. He does not cite even one example of when the north had compromised its position in the interest of "peace and settlement."

136. "Appeal by Gowon. North's Role in Peace Moves," *NN*, October 3, 1966, 1.

137. "A Daniel, a Daniel," *WAP*, October 5, 1966.

138. "On the Spot Report: Kano—A City of Hurt Yet New Hope," *NN*, October 4, 1966, 1.

139. "Moment of Truth in Our History," *NN*, October 4, 1966.

140. Thompson, *Ideology and Modern Culture*, 66.

141. "Moment of Truth in Our History," *NN*, October 4, 1966.

142. "Why Not?," *NN*, October 15, 1966.

143. What Is the East Up To? (with No Apologies for Repeating the Question)," *NN*, October 21, 1966. Incidentally, Zik had also warned the north in 1953 that secession would be "calamitous to its corporate existence." "Dr. Zik Warns the North Secession Prophets and Propagandists: It Would Be Capital Blunder," *WAP*, May 15, 1953, 1.

144. "Motor, Carrying New Nigerian Turned Back at Onitsha," *NN*, October 28, 1966.

145. "Footnote: On the Spot Report," *NN*, October 4, 1966, 6.

146. "What Next?," *NT*, December 14, 1966, 1.

147. Carruthers, *Media at War*, 17.

148. "What Next?," *NT*, December 14, 1966, 1.

149. Ibid. The *Tribune*, which had earlier asked that the east be brought into line by force, changed its tone, asking: "Will Nigeria continue as a political unit? If so, in what form? To assume that these questions do not arise since Nigeria MUST remain one is to fly in the face of the facts. . . . The truth . . . is that Eastern Nigeria is gradually breaking its links with the rest of the country. There are powerful elements in the Region who advocate its complete secession from Nigeria. Equally, there are powerful elements in Northern Nigeria who are anxious to see the Ibos out of Nigeria. How do we reconcile these opposing forces?" The paper then called for "reconciliation" rather than "forcing" the east back into the union. See "Wanted: A Happy New Year," *NT*, December 31, 1966, 1.

150. "Nigerian Confederation," *WAP*, November 22, 1966.

151. "We Shall Fight against Merger with West . . . ," *WAP*, November 28, 1966.

152. "'Oyekan's Attack Is Reckless': Jakande Defends Lagos Delegation . . . ," *WAP*, November 29, 1966, 1.

153. "Lagos State?," *WAP*, November 30, 1966, 2–3.

154. "Calabar, Ogoja Want a Strong Centre: New Memo to Ojukwu," *NN*, November 24, 1966, 1.

155. "Unwarranted Agitation," *NN*, September 16, 1966, 1.
156. Marvin Kalb, "A View from the Press," 1995, 3.
157. Carruthers, *Media at War*, 16, 5, 10.
158. "Action Not Words," *NN*, November 22, 1966.
159. "At Stake—The Future of the North," *NN*, September 26, 1966.
160. "Responsibility of the Press," *NN*, September 27, 1966.
161. Ibid.
162. "Meet in Ghana," *WAP*, December 16, 1966, 1.
163. Ibid.
164. Ibid.
165. "To the Future," *MP*, August 30, 1966, 1.
166. "Keep Polemics Away," *WAP*, April 21, 1966.

Chapter 6

1. Boyce, "Nation-Building Discourse in a Democracy," 23. Chipkin, *Do South Africans Exist: Nationalism*, 60, 119.
2. Ibid., 26.
3. Sweet, "South Africans Exist," 146.
4. Ibid.
5. Barnett, "Broadcasting the Rainbow Nation," 274–303.
6. See Dare, *Diary of a Debacle*.
7. "The Plot to Split Nigeria," *TheNEWS* (hereafter *TN*), July 20, 1998.
8. Hyden and Leslie, "Communications and Democratization in Africa," 1; see also Nyamnjoh, *Africa's Media*.
9. Frère, *Elections and the Media in Post-conflict Africa*, 1.
10. Hyden, Leslie, and Ogundimu, "Preface," vii.
11. Ogundimu, "Media and Democracy in Twenty-First Century Africa," 236.
12. Richard Joseph, testimony before the Africa Sub-Committee of the US House of Representatives, August 1993. See Adebanwi, "Construction and Deconstruction of Political Reality." The section heading refers to the edited volume *Transition without End* by Diamond, Kirk-Greene, and Oyediran, which captures the crisis of democratic transition in Nigeria.
13. General Ibrahim Babangida, maiden broadcast as head of state, August 28, 1985.
14. Olagunju, Jinadu, and Oyovbare, *Transition to Democracy in Nigeria*, 93.
15. Quoted in Akande, "Machiavellian Statecraft," 258.
16. Omoruyi, *Tale of June 12*, 98.
17. See *TG*, June 25, 1993, 1.
18. See *TG*, June 26, 1993, 1.

19. Adebanwi, *June 12 Crisis.*

20. For instance, one of Nigeria's most respected columnists, Olatunji Dare, published a weekly record of the events of this era in "Diary of Debacle." These were later collected into the volume *Diary of a Debacle.*

21. "Who Succeeds Babangida," cover story, *TELL,* September 1992, 12, 15.

22. Ibid., 18. A public limited company in Nigeria is equivalent to a limited liability company (LLC) in the United States. The term is used here in the press to denote the "incorporation" or systematic institutionalization of "corruption, embezzlement, confusion and chaos."

23. Ibid., 15.

24. "Nobody Can Be President without Muslims," interview, *TELL,* September 7, 1992, 16.

25. Bala Dan Audu, "Western Press and National Issues," *NN on Sunday,* May 2, 1993, 5.

26. "Still on the Fuel Scarcity in the North," editorial, *NN,* May 6, 1993, 1.

27. "The Crackdown Begins," cover story, *TELL,* January 4, 1993, 10.

28. Ibid.

29. "Wanted! Another Country," *TELL,* January 4, 1993, 17.

30. "The Crackdown Begins," cover story, *TELL,* January 4, 1993, 10.

31. "FMG Has Lived Up to Expectations—Chukwumerije," *NN,* February 3, 1993, 1.

32. The "unholy conclave at Otta" is a reference to southern-based newspapers and magazines that praised the Otta meeting, including *TELL, The-NEWS,* and *The Guardian. TELL* put Obasanjo on the cover in its reports of the meeting. "The Unholy Conclave at Otta," *NN,* June 12, 1993, 1.

33. Ibid.

34. "The Otta Elders Conference," *TG,* June 4, 1993.

35. "The People's Verdict: Go, IBB, Go," *TELL,* May 3, 1993.

36. Yusuf A. Mohammed, "Anti-democratic 'Democracy': Obasanjo's Recipe for National Confusion," *NN,* May 11, 1993, 5.

37. "A Call to Arms," *TN,* March 29, 1993, 16–17.

38. Ibid.

39. "Sharpville Will Be Child's Play," *TN,* March 29, 1993, 18.

40. "Ringing the Divorce Bells," *TELL,* May 2, 1994, 10, 15.

41. "I Have Serious Doubt That IBB Will Hand Over," *TN,* March 29, 1993, 21. The "many religious crises" that Bali refers to was as much a religious clash as it was an ethnic clash: the Kataf were dominantly Christians whereas the Hausa were dominantly Muslims. Bali remarked: "I think it is more of a coincidence that the Hausas are assumed to be all Moslems and the Katafs are mainly Christians[;] one would well say that it's a religious conflict—you can also say it is a tribal conflict. So, it could be both." Bali was a middle-belter and Christian.

42. "Yes, I Will Fight Again. If . . . ," *TELL*, March 1, 1993, 22.

43. Ibid., 23.

44. "The Last Lap," *TN*, March 22, 1993, 19.

45. "The Triumph of IBB's Men," *TELL*, April 12, 1993.

46. "Mission to Save Nigeria," *TN*, April 12, 1993.

47. Ibid.

48. "*TELL, TheNEWS*, and the Transition," *NN*, May 20, 1993.

49. "Facing June 12," *TG*, June 9, 1993.

50. "The Results, Now," *TG*, June 18, 1993.

51. "Our Nation, Our Destiny," *NN*, June 16, 1993.

52. "The People's Mandate," *Daily Champion* (hereafter *DC*), June 18, 1993.

53. "Our Nation, Our Destiny," *NN*, June 16, 1993, 1.

54. "Victory Pattern Emerges: Presidential Poll Latest," *DC*, June 14, 1993, 1.

55. "A Matter of Honour," *TG*, July 5, 1993, 8.

56. "Our Nation, Our Destiny," *NN*, June 16, 1993.

57. Yakubu Abdulazeez, "Letter of Resignation," June 16, 1993, see "*New Nigerian* Editor Resigns," *DC*, June 18, 1993, 2; "NNN Debunks Editor's Claim," *NN*, June 19, 1993, 1 & 3. See also, Adebanwi, "Construction and Deconstruction of Political Reality."

58. "NNN Debunks Editor's Claim," *NN*, June 19, 1993, 1.

59. "A Vote for Revolutionary Changes," *TG*, June 17, 1993, 13.

60. "Understanding the Present Situation," *TG*, June 24, 1993, 13.

61. "The New Governing Class," *TG*, June 30, 1993, 25.

62. "Nigeria: Way Forward," *DC*, August 2, 1993.

63. Olatunji Dare, "Diary of a Debacle (1)," *TG*, June 22, 1993.

64. "Nigeria: Way Forward," *DC*, August 2, 1993, 1, 4.

65. "From the Editor," *TELL*, July 5, 1993, 9.

66. Ibid.

67. "Nigeria: Way Forward," *TELL*, July 5, 1993.

68. "From the Editor," *TELL*, July 5, 1993.

69. "No Way for Abiola," *TELL*, July 5, 1993, 24–25.

70. "Dictatorship Unbound," *TELL*, July 5, 1993, 28.

71. "A Nation in Distress: Threat of Break-Up Real," *TELL*, October 4, 1993.

72. "Moving Ahead," *DC*, September 10, 1993, 1. Significantly, a few weeks after this, the editor of the paper, Emma Agu, was appointed the chief press secretary to the chairman of the Interim National Government, Ernest Shonekan.

73. "Nigeria: Way Forward," *DC*, August 2, 1993, 1.

74. Ibid.

75. "An Evasion of Reality," *TG*, August 6, 1993, 8.

76. "What Is the Army Up To?," *TN*, November 15, 1993, 13.

77. "Can Abiola Make It?," *TN*, October 11, 1993, 14–20.

78. "I'll be President—Abiola," *TELL*, October 11, 1993.

79. "Nigeria: Way Forward," *DC*, August 2, 1993, 1.

80. "The Mafia Moves," *TN*, November 22, 1993, 18–25.

81. "Why the North Leads," *TN*, November 22, 1993, 16–17.

82. Ibid.

83. "The Mafia Moves," *TN*, November 22, 1993, 18–25.

84. "The Last Oligarchs," *TN*, November 15, 1993, 33–35.

85. "June 12: North's Grand Design against Abiola," *TELL*, July 18, 1994, 8–14.

86. "A Plague in the Land," *TN*, October 18, 1993.

87. "The Years of the Locust," cover story, *TN*, October 18, 1993.

88. "If Nigeria Breaks . . . ," *TN*, February 21, 1994.

89. "The New Political Gamble," *TELL*, May 9, 1994.

90. "Honouring Mrs. Babangida," *DC*, September 20, 1993.

91. "A Game for Chameleons," *TN*, December 6, 1993, 22.

92. "A New Reality Is Emerging," *TN*, November 13, 1993, 28.

93. "June 12: What Really Went Wrong? Inside Account," *TN*, December 13, 1993.

94. "Is There Life after 12 June?," *TN*, November 13, 1993, 10.

95. "The New Governing Class," *TG*, June 30, 1993.

96. "Is There Life after 12 June?," *TN*, November 13, 1993, 10.

97. Ibid.

98. "We May Have a War—Aguda," *TELL*, January 17, 1994.

99. "We Are Near Disaster—Abiola," *TN*, January 10, 1994, 29–39.

100. "We May Have a War—Aguda," *TELL*, January 17, 1994.

101. A Cause in Search of Hero," *TN*, January 10, 1994, 21–23.

102. "Backstage," *TN*, January 10, 1994.

103. "Man of the Year: June 12," *TN*, January 10, 1994.

104. "Still in Babylon," *TELL*, January 24, 1994.

105. "The New Gamble," *TELL*, January 24, 1994.

106. "We Are Near Disaster—Abiola," *TN*, January 10, 1994.

107. "Secession Is Legitimate," *TN*, January 17, 1994, 53.

108. "Let Each Section Go Its Own Way," *TELL*, February 14, 1994, 18–19.

109. "The Great Betrayal: Abacha's 100 Days of Drift," *TELL*, March 7, 1994, 10.

110. "Let Each Section Go Its Own Way," *TELL*, February 14, 1994.

111. "An Arewa Liaison," *TN*, February 21, 1994.

112. Ibid.

113. "If Nigeria Breaks . . . ," *TN*, February 2, 1994, 19.

114. "Abacha and the Kaduna Mafia: Their Plot to Derail Constitutional Conference," *TELL*, March 14, 1994, 10–11.

115. "The Travails of Abiola," *TELL*, April 11, 1994, 8–13.

116. "Abiola Tackles Abacha. Forms Govt. Cabinet List Out Soon. Asks Abacha to Pack Out," *TN*, May 16, 1994, 17.

117. "Forces That Will Chase Out Abacha," *TN*, March 28, 1994.

118. "Who Will Save Sani Abacha?," *TN*, March 28, 1994.

119. "Abiola Tackles Abacha. Forms Govt. Cabinet List Out Soon. Asks Abacha to Pack Out," *TN*, May 16, 1994.

120. "A Letter Cannot Annul the Mandate," *TELL*, April 11, 1994.

121. "Get Set for the Worst," *TN*, February 14, 1994.

122. "Prepare for the Worst," *TN*, February 14, 1994.

123. "Why Nigeria May Collapse," *TELL*, April 18, 1994.

124. "Staring Collapse in the Face," *TELL*, April 18, 1994.

125. Ibid.

126. "Prepare for the Worst," *TN*, February 14, 1994, 27.

127. "If Peace Must Return," *TG*, June 6, 1994, 12.

128. "Onward, Democracy," *DC*, June 6, 1994, 4.

129. "If Peace Must Return," *TG*, June 6, 1994.

130. "Onward, Democracy," *DC*, June 6, 1994.

131. "If Peace Must Return," *TG*, June 6, 1994.

132. "Onward, Democracy," *DC*, June 6, 1994.

133. Ibid.

134. "Staring Collapse in the Face," *TELL*, April 18, 1994, 16.

135. "In Whose Interest?," *DC*, June 10, 1993, 1.

136. "Abacha in Trouble. His Problems Mount Despite Eagles' Victory," *TELL*, April 25, 1994.

137. "In Whose Interest?," *DC*, June 10, 1993.

138. "Ringing the Divorce Bells," *TELL*, May 2, 1994.

139. "Middle Belt Revolts," *TN*, May 23, 1994, 15.

140. "The Big Revolt: Minorities Threaten to Secede," *TELL*, May 2, 1994, 15.

141. "Backstage," *TN*, May 16, 1994, 4.

142. "In Whose Interest?," *DC*, June 10, 1993, 1.

143. "The Ultimate Encounter," *TN*, May 16, 1994, 17.

144. "Reading Abiola's Lip," *TN*, May 16, 1994.

145. "Government Must Be Firm (1)," *NN*, June 6, 1994, 1.

146. "Let Sanity Prevail," *NN*, June 11, 1994, 1.

147. "Abacha's Days Are Numbered," *TELL*, May 30, 1994. "All Set for Abacha's Overthrow," *TN*, May 30, 1994.

148. "Red Card for the General . . . ," *TELL*, May 30, 1994.

149. "Abacha's Game Is Up," *TN*, May 30, 1994.

150. "That Abacha Speech," *DC*, June 18, 1994, 4.

151. "An Unacceptable Response," *TG*, June 11, 1994.
152. "On the March Again," *TN*, June 6, 1994, 12.
153. "Obasanjo's Game," *TN*, May 30, 1994.
154. "Abacha's Game Is Up," *TN*, May 30, 1994, 18.
155. "Nigeria: Way Forward." August 2, 1993.
156. Ibid.
157. "Tightening the Noose," *TELL*, June 6, 1994, 11.
158. "The Conference," *TG*, June 27, 1994, 12.
159. "Abacha's Game Is Up," *TN*, May 30, 1994.
160. "Tightening the Noose," *TELL*, June 6, 1994.
161. Ibid.
162. "June 12: What Is to Be Done," *TN*, January 13, 1994.
163. "'Abacha Is a Goner'—Abiola," *TELL*, June 13, 1994.
164. "Part of the Grand Conspiracy," *TN*, June 27, 1994.
165. "The Final Showdown," *TELL*, June 13, 1994, 10.
166. "Kokori's Threat," *NN*, July 4, 1994.
167. "Abiola's Triumph," *TELL*, July 4, 1994, 10.
168. "Walking a Tight Rope," *TELL*, June 27, 1994.
169. "No Respite for Abacha," *TN*, June 27, 1994.
170. "The June 12 Papers," *NN*, July 6, 1994.
171. "The Nigerian Press," *DC*, August 29, 1994.
172. "From the Editor," *TELL*, June 27, 1994.
173. Ibid.
174. "The Final Showdown," *TELL*, June 13, 1994.
175. "Don't Lose Hope, Detained Abiola Tells Nigerians," *TN*, July 4, 1994.
176. "Abiola's Triumph," *TELL*, July 4, 1994.
177. "Abiola's Ordeal in Detention," *TELL*, October 17, 1994, 10–14.
178. Backstage, "Abiola's Travails," *TN*, July 4, 1994.
179. Balarabe Abubukar, "Abiola: A Tragic Hero?," *NN*, July 22, 1994, 7.
180. Backstage, "Abiola's Travails," *TN*, July 4, 1994.
181. "In Abacha's Gulag," *TN*, July 11, 1994.
182. "Abiola's Ordeal in Detention," *TELL*, October 17, 1994.
183. "CIA and Confab," *NN*, September 23, 1994, 1–2.
184. "The Triumph of Madness," *NN*, July 26, 1994, 1.
185. "Plots to Kill June 12," *TELL*, July 18, 1994, 10.
186. Ibid.
187. "On the Brink," *TELL*, July 25, 1994, 9.
188. "Time for Genuine Dialogue," *TG*, July 18, 1994, 10.
189. "Backstage," *TN*, July 18, 1994, 4.
190. "Backstage," *TN*, July 11, 1994.
191. "Goodbye Nigeria! The World Turns Its Back on the Giant," *TELL*, October 31, 1994.

192. "Unacceptable," *NN*, August 30, 1994.
193. "Nigeria Is Doomed," *TN*, November 28, 1994.
194. "Time for Genuine Dialogue," *TG*, July 18, 1994.
195. "The Nigerian Press," *DC*, August 29, 1994.
196. "Foreign Media Nonsense," *NN*, August 24, 1994, 1.
197. "I Am Ashamed of Military Rule," *TELL*, August 8, 1994.
198. "Now, Nigeria Is Finished," *TELL*, December 6, 1993.
199. Connor, "Nation-Building or Nation-Destroying?," 319.
200. Gagiano, "The Contenders," 32.
201. Connor, "Nation-Building or Nation-Destroying?," 321, 331, 337, 336.
202. Liebenberg, "Nation-Building and Community Reconciliation," 14.
203. Degenaar, "Beware of Nation-Building Discourse," 24.
204. Tamarkin, *Nationalism, Nation-Building and Society in Africa*, 18.
205. Habermas, "Citizenship and National Identity," 3.
206. Degenaar, "Beware of Nation-Building Discourse," 25, 26, 28.

Chapter 7

1. Obadare, "The Press and Democratic Transition," 38.
2. Oyovbaire, "The Media and Democratic Process." Cf. Ado-Kurawa, *Sharia'h and the Press in Nigeria.*
3. Obadare, "The Press and Democratic Transition," 38.
4. There are different cover stories and others reflecting this view. For example, "The Drift to Chaos," *TN*, October 11, 1993; "If MKO Should Die . . . Nigeria Is Finished—Kudi Abiola," *TELL*, May 27, 1996; "The Plot to Split Nigeria," *TN*, July 20, 1998; "Nigeria's Cross: Abiola's One Year Behind Bars," *Newswatch*, June 26, 1995.
5. See Dare, *Diary of a Debacle.*
6. Mink, "The Anatomy of Historical Understanding," 32. Walsh, *Philosophy of History*, 59–64.
7. Farrell, "Narrative in Natural Discourse," 110. Bennett and Edelman, "Towards a New Political Narrative," 165–66.
8. Tony Iyiam, "No Easy Walk to Freedom," *TELL*, May 3, 1999, 46.
9. Ibid., 46, 47.
10. "War over Sharia: PRC Divided," *TELL*, May 10, 1999, 20–25.
11. "North, South-East Protest Ministerial Allocations . . . ," *Post Express* (hereafter *PE*), May 11, 1999, 1.
12. "Nigeria's Last Chance," *TELL*, May 31, 1999, 16.
13. "Celebrating Survival, Re-inventing Hope," *PE*, May 29, 1999, 6.
14. "Nigeria's Last Chance," *TELL*, May 31, 1999.
15. Ibid.

16. "Celebrating Survival, Re-inventing Hope," *PE*, May 29, 1999.

17. "Nigeria's Last Chance," *TELL*, May 31, 1999.

18. "From the Editor," *TELL*, July 5, 1999, 17.

19. Ibid.

20. "The Kafanchan Communal Unrest," *PE*, June 4, 1999, 8.

21. "The Kafanchan Communal Unrest," *TG*, June 4, 1999, 16.

22. "The North Fights Back," *TELL*, July 5, 1999, 22, 21.

23. "The Killings in Ketu," *Weekend Trust* (hereafter *WT*), December 3–9, 1999, 1.

24. "The Only Solution to OPC," "Friday Discourse," *WT*, January 7, 13, 2000, 14. Tilde describes the Yoruba as an "ethnic group," yet argues that they never constituted a "nation" in their history.

25. "The North Fights Back," *TELL*, July 5, 1999, 21. "The Mafia Bares Its Fang," *TELL*, September 20, 1999, 15.

26. "Constitution Reviews—Wither Northern Nigeria," *WT*, November 3–9, 1999, 31.

27. Ibid.

28. "'The Trouble with the North . . .' Ahmadu Abubakar, Presidential Aide," *TELL*, September 6, 1999, 17.

29. "What the President Must Do," *TELL*, July 5, 1999, 30.

30. "Nigeria May Break-Up . . . ," *TELL*, July 12, 1999, 13.

31. "'The Trouble with the North . . .' Ahmadu Abubakar, Presidential Aide," *TELL*, September 6, 1999.

32. "The Mafia Bares Its Fang," *TELL*, September 20, 1999.

33. "The North: Where Do We Stand?," *WT*, January 18–24, 2000, 37.

34. "100 Days of Obasanjo," *PE*, September 6, 1999, 8.

35. "Obasanjo's Theory of Fairness," *PE*, August 18, 1999, 8.

36. "Obasanjo's First 100 Days," *TG*, August 30, 1999, 20.

37. "Nigeria: Hope for the Southeast? (11)," *PE*, December 24, 1999, 24.

38. "Wounds That Won't Heal," *TELL*, September 20, 1999, 24.

39. "The Mafia Bares Its Fang," *TELL*, September 20, 1999.

40. Wounds That Won't Heal," *TELL*, September 20, 1999.

41. "'Patriots' Proposal: A Prelude to the Annulment of 1914 Amalgamation," *WT*, January 18–24, 2000, 37.

42. "Ndi Igbo and the Nigerian Union," *TG*, June 17, 1999.

43. Castells, *Power of Identity*, 2.

44. Levine, "Religion and Politics in Contemporary Historical Perspective," 97.

45. Obadare, "In Search of a Public Sphere," 177.

46. Kamrava, *Politics and Society in the Developing World;* Levine, "Religion and Politics," 97.

47. See Ilesanmi, *Religious Pluralism*; Suberu, "Religion"; Kalu, "Safiyya and Adamah."

48. "The Road to Lebanon," *TN*, March 6, 2000, 12–13.
49. A noteworthy exception is Kukah, *Religion, Politics and Power in Northern Nigeria*. Kalu and Obadare, at different times, make a brief allusion to the "media hype [on the Sharia that] also heated up the political temperature" and "rankled," and the "southern suspicion of the northern desire" to "deep the Quran into the sea," which "resonates in the western (Yoruba)-based and dominated print media" in Nigeria. Kalu, "Safiyya and Adamah," 396–97; Cf. Obadare, "In Search of a Public Sphere," 183.
50. Kalu, "Safiyya and Adamah," 397.
51. "War over Sharia: PRC Divided," *TELL*, May 10, 1999.
52. "Sharia Akbar! Sharia Ak-bomb!!" *TELL*, November 15, 1999.
53. "From the Editor," *TELL*, November 15, 1999, 11.
54. "The Sharia Controversy," *TG*, November 4, 1999, 16.
55. "Democracy and Order," *PE*, October 21, 1999. "Sharia, Civil Rights and National Question," *PE*, November 11, 1999.
56. Najmabadi, "(Un)veiling Feminism," 34, 41. For a very strong view that condemns the notion of "secularism" as canvassed by the press in the south of Nigeria, see Ado-Kurawa, *Shari'ah and the Press in Nigeria*.
57. "From the Editor," *TELL*, November 15, 1999, 11.
58. "Sharia, Civil Rights and National Question," *PE*, November 11, 1999.
59. "Sharia and the Kaduna Riots," *TG*, February 28, 2000, 20.
60. "Sharia Akbar! Sharia Ak-bomb!!" *TELL*, November 15, 1999.
61. "Sharia and the Kaduna Riots," *TG*, February 28, 2000.
62. "Sharia and the Kaduna Riots," *TG*, February 28, 2000, 20.
63. "Governor Mu'azu, A Word on Sharia," *NN*, February 16, 2000, 15.
64. Ibid.
65. "Obasanjo and the Jihadists," *TG*, March 3, 2000, 41.
66. Ibid.
67. "Understanding Shari'a Law," pt. 1, *NN*, February 16, 2000, 14.
68. "Understanding Shari'a Law," pt. 2, *NN*, February 18, 2000, 15.
69. "Kaduna Carnage. Eye Witnesses Accounts," *WT*, February 25, 2000.
70. "The Killings in Ketu," *WT*, December 3–9, 1999, 1.
71. "Shariah: The Way Out," *WT*, March 3–9, 2000, 1.
72. "The Problem of Ethnic Militias," *TG*, September 23, 1999, 16.
73. "Shariah: The Way Out," *WT*, March 3–9, 2000, 1.
74. "The Killings in Ketu," *WT*, December 3–9, 1999.
75. Ibid.
76. "OPC: Obasanjo's Dangerous Gamble," *TELL*, January 31, 2000.
77. "Shariah: The Way Out," *WT*, March 3–9, 2000, 1.
78. "Massacre in the South-East—As Returnees Told Tales of Happenings in Kaduna," *WT*, March 3–9, 2000, 6.
79. "Kaduna Riots: The Ojukwu Connection," *WT*, March 3–9, 2000.

80. "Threats of Secession," *PE*, November 22, 1999.

81. "From the Editor," *TELL*, November 5, 1999.

82. "Tension Escalates. . . . Over Secession Threat," *TELL*, November 22, 1999.

83. "Threats of Secession," *PE*, November 22, 1999.

84. "21st-Century Nigeria: A Threatened Federation," *PE*, December 12, 1999, 10–11.

85. "Landmark Meeting at Asaba," *TG*, April 7, 2000, 16.

86. "Towards a Northern Nigeria Federation," *WT*, March 24–30, 2000, 15.

87. "Towards a Northern Nigerian Federation," *WT*, March 24–30, 2000, 15. Quote in "Sharia Akbar! Sharia Ak-bomb!!" *TELL*, November 15, 1999.

88. This is an attempt to *unify* all northerners, irrespective of religion, against the south. "Sharia Akbar! Sharia Ak-bomb!!" *TELL*, November 15, 1999.

89. "The North Fights Back," *TELL*, July 5, 1999.

90. "Towards a Northern Nigerian Federation," *WT*, March 24–30, 2000, 15.

91. The *PE* preferred a southeast that subsumed the south-south, otherwise there would have been no need to mention the Igbo once reference had been made to its synonym, the southeast.

92. "For a Confederal Nigeria," *PE*, March 15, 2000, 8.

93. "Threats of Secession," *PE*, November 22, 1999.

94. "Obasanjo and Confederation," *PE*, March 20, 2000, 9.

95. "Towards a Northern Nigerian Federation," *WT*, March 24–30, 2000, 15; "Threats of Secession," *PE*, November 22, 1999.

96. "Obasanjo and Confederation," *PE*, March 20, 2000.

97. "North: The Party If Over," *WT*, March 31–April 6, 2000, 37.

98. Ibid.

99. "From the Five Majors to the Five Governors?," *WT*, March 31–April 6, 2000, 37.

100. "Communal Clashes: Beyond Crisis Management," *TG*, August 1999, 20.

101. "The Truth about Nigeria," *PE*, March 27, 2000, 8.

102. "Towards a Northern Nigerian Federation," *WT*, March 24–30, 2000, 15.

103. "A Dangerously Agenda," *TELL*, March 20, 2000.

104. "Confederacy—East/West Reviews the Aburi Accord," *PE*, March 25, 2000, 11.

105. "Towards a Northern Nigerian Federation," *WT*, March 24–30, 2000, 15.

106. "Break-Up Imminent? Northern Leaders Threaten Nigeria," *TELL*, March 20, 2000.

107. "From the Editor," *TELL*, March 20, 2000.

108. "G. G. Darah's Diatribe and Ethno-Religious Hatred," *WT*, March 31–April 6, 2000, 1.

109. *TELL* had never accepted that Ernest Shonekan was a head of state and always discountenanced the eighty-four days he spent in office as head of the Interim National Government. Shonekan was a Yoruba and a Christian.

110. "From the Editor," *TELL*, March 20, 2000.

111. "The Other Side of Sharia," *TELL*, March 20, 2000, 17.

112. "A Dangerous Agenda," *TELL*, March 20, 2000, 14.

113. "The Other Side of Sharia," *TELL*, March 20, 2000.

114. "The Middle Belt Revolt," *TELL*, March 27, 2000, 20.

115. "Defusing the Sharia Bomb," *TELL*, April 17, 2000, 12.

116. Ibid. The *Trust* quote is in: "The North: Where Do We Stand?," *WT*, January 18–24, 2000.

117. "Middle Belt: One 'Region,' Many Voices," *WT*, June 23–29, 2000. See also, "Middle-Belt Is Meaningless,'" *WT*, April 28–May 4, 2000, 13–14.

118. "Ooni's Outburst," *WT*, May 12–18, 2000, 27.

119. "For a Confederal Nigeria," *PE*, March 15, 2000. "One North or Anarchy," *WT*, April 21–27, 2000, 1.

120. "Endangered Hausa-Fulani," *WT*, April 7–13, 2000, 34. Even the idea of the Hausa-Fulani as a single ethic group is problematic. Peter Ekeh argues that the term "Hausa-Fulani" is largely a political construct. The Hausa and Fulani are two separate but interrelated groups that have fused in the power configuration in Nigeria. Ekeh, "Political Minorities," 33–63.

121. "Nigeria: The Wasted Years," *TG*, October 1, 1999.

122. Scammell and Semetko, *Media, Journalism and Democracy*, xiii.

123. Tironi and Sunkel, "Modernization of Communications," 174.

124. Anthony and Gunther, "Media in Democratic and Nondemocratic Regimes," 10–11.

125. Schlesinger, *Media, State and Nation*, 19; and Leach, *Custom, Law and Terrorist Violence*, cited in Schlesinger, *Media, State and Nation*, 19.

Chapter 8

Epigraph. Jones and Moss, "Guest Editorial: Democracy, Identity, Space," 256.

1. Clegg, *Frameworks of Power*, 143.

2. Paasi, "Constructing Territories, Boundaries and Regional Identity," 42, in Penrose, "Nations, States and Homelands," 280.

3. Volosinov, *Marxism and the Philosophy of Language*, cited in Louw, *Media and Cultural Production*, 24.

4. Sacks, *Human Territoriality*, 33.

5. Giddens, *A Contemporary Critique of Historical Materialism*, 29.

6. Louw, *Media and Cultural Production*, 24.

7. Jacobs, "Civil Society and Crisis," 1238.

8. Eley and Fraser, cited in ibid., 1238–39.

9. Calhoon, "Indirect Relationship," cited in Jacobs, "Civil Society and Crisis," 1238.

10. Clegg, *Frameworks of Power*, 160.

11. Penrose, "Nations, States and Homelands," 278.

12. Sacks, "Power of Place and Space," 326.

13. Penrose, "Nations, States and Homelands," 278–79.

14. Ibid., 279.

15. Donnan and Wilson, "Territoriality, Anthropology, and the Interstitial," 13.

16. Sam Kaplan, "Territorializing Armenians," 400.

17. Cox, "Spaces of Dependence," 1–23.

18. Lefebvre, *The Production of Space*, cited in Miller and Martin, "Space and Contentious Politics," 146.

19. Van Lieu and Jones, "Discursive Limits to Agency," 150.

20. Penrose, "Nations, States and Homelands," 279.

21. Sacks, *Human Territoriality*, 19.

22. Penrose, "Nations, States and Homelands," 282.

23. Sacks, *Human Territoriality*, 56.

24. Taylor, *Human Territoriality Functioning*, 81.

25. Ibid.

26. Anderson, "Questions of Democracy, Territoriality and Globalization," 27, cited in Donnan and Wilson, "Territoriality, Anthropology, and the Interstitial," 13.

27. Barrett, *Politics of Truth*, 54.

28. Agbaje, *Nigerian Press*, 11.

29. Laitin, *Hegemony and Culture*, 19.

30. Paasi, "Constructing Territories, Boundaries and Regional Identity," 42, cited in Penrose, "Nations, States and Homelands," 280.

31. Dawson, "Territoriality," 883.

32. Dear and Wolch, "How Territory Shapes Social Life," 9.

33. Isumonah, "Migration, Land Tenure," 15.

34. Dear and Wolch, "How Territory Shapes Social Life," 11.

35. Saltman, "Introduction," 3.

36. Ibrahim and Igbuzor, "Memorandum submitted to the Presidential Committee on Provisions and Practice on Citizenship and Rights in Nigeria."

37. Isumonah, "Migration, Land Tenure, Citizenship," 15.

38. Ibrahim and Igbuzor, "Memorandum."

39. Sacks, *Human Territoriality*, 57–58.

40. Saltman, "Introduction," 3.

41. Suberu, *Ethnic Minority Conflicts*, 54.

42. Sacks, *Human Territoriality*, 59.

43. Tuan has pointed to the deeply significant nature of homeland; almost every human grouping regards its own homeland as "the centre of the world" (*Space and Place*, 149).

44. Pfaff-Czarnecka, "Ritual, Distances, Territorial Divisions," 26.

45. Sacks, *Human Territoriality*, 58.

46. Taylor, *Human Territoriality Functioning*, 4.

47. Sacks, "Power of Place and Space," 327.

48. Sacks, *Human Territoriality*, 59.

49. See Dear and Wolch, "How Territory Shapes Social Life," 11.

50. Sacks, *Human Territoriality*, 59.

51. Personal discussions with a government-owned media chief who doubled, at this period, as an unofficial security adviser to the Babangida regime. Toronto, Canada, July 15, 2004.

52. Eriksen, *Ethnicity and Nationalism*, 121. Osaghae, "Managing Multiple Minority Problems," 3.

53. He cites the examples of white colonial regimes in Africa and Asia, the Afrikaner whites in apartheid South Africa, the Tutsi in post-1994 Rwanda, and the Fulani in Nigeria. Osaghae, "Managing Multiple Minority Problems."

54. Sacks, *Human Territoriality*, 60, 61.

55. The latter term was first used as a positive description of the Nigerian press as "a press that is voluble if not cantankerous, a press that is buoyed by a no-holds-barred approach to matters of national interest, and with a capacity for advocacy and adversarial haggling against those it considers guilty of malfeasance objective." See Ofeimun, "The *Ngbati* Press," *TN*, February 14, 1994, 15. "Ngbati" is a pejorative word for the Yoruba of western Nigeria, where Lagos—and Ibadan—is located. However, the term "Ngbati press," as later used by a *THISDAY* columnist, Waziri Adio, captures popular sentiments in the north—and to some extent, among the Igbo—that the dominant sections of the press in Nigeria pander to the interests of the Yoruba. Adio, who is Yoruba, states: "Some of us have fooled ourselves that this is a fair, independent press. Now we know better." See "Hypocrisy of the *Ngbati* Press," *THISDAY*, September 5, 1999, back page. *Hotline*, the defunct ardently pro-north newsmagazine, also argued that the "Lagos-Ibadan Press axis" gives "prominence" to "distortions about the North," concluding that "certain . . . people in the old Western region are, through their media establishments, hell-bent on seeing that Nigeria as a geographical entity is torn to shreds." See Mohammed Momoh Otu, "Lagos-Ibadan Press and Eccentricism," *Hotline*, January 11–24, 1998, 15.

56. "Has Babangida Given Up?," *African Concord*, April 13, 1992. See Adebanwi, *Trials and Triumphs*, 3–12.

57. Muhammed, *Courage and Conviction*, v.

58. Jacobs, "Civil Society and Crisis."

59. Steinmetz, "Reflections on the Role of Social Narratives," 497–501.

60. Giddens (*Central Problems in Social Theory; A Contemporary Critique of Historical Materialism;* and *The Constitution of Society*) has noted the importance of time-space relations in the structuration of society. He argues that time unfolds at three levels that recursively connect it to spatial locales. These include the *durée, dasein,* and *longue durée.* For an exposition of Giddens's views on this, see Lieu and Jones, "Discursive Limits to Agency," 10. Time-space relations concerns "specific sets of human relationships, located within concretized localities and within identifiable periods." Louw, *Media and Cultural Reproduction*, 4.

61. Rapport and Dawson, "Topic and the Book," 4.

62. Jacobs, "Civil Society and Crisis," 1244–45.

63. Ibid.

64. Wagner-Pacifici and Schwartz, "The Vietnam Veterans Memorial," cited in ibid., 1246.

65. "Witnesses of Zango-Kataf," *TELL*, August 17, 1992, 5.

66. "On Zango-Kataf Massacre and National Security," *NN*, March 5, 1993, 5.

67. "The Okadigbo Verdict," *NN*, February 13, 1993, 1.

68. "Cut for the Job," *TN*, March 8, 1993, 30.

69. "The Trial of Lekwot," *TELL*, August 10, 1992, 31.

70. "Trial of a General," *TELL*, August 24, 1992, 16.

71. "Zango-Kataf Crisis: Prosecution Closes Case," *NN*, March 5, 1993, 1.

72. "More Woes for Lekwot," *TELL*, August 21, 1992.

73. "On Zango-Kafat Massacre and National Security," *NN*, March 5, 1993, 5.

74. "Kataf Hangman: Why Justice Okadigbo Was Picked for the Job," cover headline, *TN*, March 8, 1993.

75. "Cut for the Job," *TN*, March 8, 1993, 34.

76. Ibid.

77. "The Okadigbo Verdict," *NN*, February 13, 1993.

78. "Cut for the Job," *TN*, March 8, 1993, 34.

79. "Are They Lackeys?," *TN*, March 8, 1993, 32–33.

80. "Trial of a General," *TELL*, August 24, 1992, 17.

81. "Tension Mounts over Lekwot," *TELL*, March 8, 1993, 10, 11.

82. "Lekwot, Jusice," *NN*, March 3, 1993, 13.

83. "Trial of a General," *TELL*, August 24, 1992, 17.

84. "Tension Mounts over Lekwot," *TELL*, March 8, 1993, 14.

85. "Trial of a General," *TELL*, August 24, 1992, 17-18.

86. "Tension Mounts over Lekwot," *TELL*, March 8, 1993, 10, 11, 13.

87. "It's a Kangaroo Affair," *TELL*, February 15, 1993, 11.

88. Ibid., 12.

89. Ricoeur, *Time and Narrative*, 1: 67.

90. See, for instance, "Lekwot: Matters Arising," *TN*, February 22, 1993, 26.

91. "A March for Lekwot," *TELL*, February 22, 1993, 16.

92. "Cut for the Job," *TN*, March 8, 1993, 29.

93. Ibid., 31, 30.

94. Ibid., 31.

95. "Lekwot: Matters Arising," *TN*, February 22, 1993, 25.

96. "A March for Lekwot," *TELL*, February 22, 1993, 17.

97. "Lekwot: Matters Arising," *TN*, February 22, 1993, 25.

98. "The Okadigbo Verdict," *NN*, February 13, 1993, 1.

99. "Zango-Kataf: Accused Sentenced to Death," *NN*, February 2, 1993, 1; 4.

100. "The Okadigbo Verdict," *NN*, February 13, 1993, 1.

101. "Zango-Kataf Communal Clashes: Justice Must Take Its Course – Sheik Lemu," *NN*, February 12, 1993, 1.

102. "I won't beg," *TN*, March 8, 1993, 25–26.

103. "The Okadigbo Verdict," *NN*, February 13, 1993, 1.

104. "Clipping Caliphal Wings: Colonel Isa sets the ball rolling for the liberation of ethnic minorities in Southern Kaduna," *TN*, November 13, 1995, 11.

105. "On Zango-Kataf Massacre and National Security," *NN*, March 5, 1993, 5.

106. "I Won't Beg," *TN*, March 8, 1993, 26.

107. Cox, "Spaces of Dependence," 2.

108. Jacobs, "Civil Society and Crisis," 1241.

109. Routledge, "A Spatiality of Resistances," 70.

110. bell hooks, cited in ibid., 71.

111. Pile and Thrifts, "Conclusions: Spacing and the Subject," 374, cited in Routledge, "A Spatiality of Resistances," 71.

112. Smith, cited in Moore, "Remapping Resistance," 101.

113. Sawyer, "A Discourse on Discourse," 433.

114. Jacobs, "Civil Society and Crisis," 1240; cf. Somers, "Narrative Construction of Identity," 606.

115. Donnan and Wilson, "Territoriality, Anthropology, and the Interstitial," 18.

116. Said, *Culture and Imperialism*, 7.

117. Somers, "Narrative Construction of Identity," 605–6.

118. Routledge, "A Spatiality of Resistances," 101.

119. Louw, *Media and Cultural Production*, 12.
120. Clegg, *Frameworks of Power*, 144, 145.
121. Louw, *Media and Cultural Production*, 106.
122. Dear and Wolch, "How Territory Shapes Social Life," 4.
123. Sacks, *Human Territoriality*, 55, 216.
124. Dear and Wolch, "How Territory Shapes Social Life," 4.
125. Callinicos, cited in Stewart Clegg, *Frameworks of Power*, 145.
126. Penrose, "Nations, States and Homelands," 280.
127. Sacks, *Human Territoriality*, 215.

Chapter 9

1. See Vickers, *A Nation Betrayed*, 3, 4, for more details on the content of this paragraph.
2. Saro-Wiwa, *A Month and a Day*, 185.
3. Vickers, *A Nation Betrayed*, 292.
4. Saro-Wiwa, *A Month and a Day*, 186, 187.
5. Osaghae, "Managing Multiple Minority Problems," 1.
6. Osaghae, "Ogoni Uprising," 326.
7. Adebanwi, "Construction and Deconstruction of Political Reality."
8. Agbaje, "Mass Media," 98, following Schramm, *Mass Media and National Development*, 127.
9. Bogdanor, *Blackwell Encyclopedia of Political Science*, 443.
10. This dilemma has led to the construction of different kinds of minorities in Nigeria: southern, northern, and middle-belt minorities; ethno-linguistic minorities; religious minorities; regional minorities; and national minorities, including a subset of economically strategic minorities. See Osaghae, *Crippled Giant*. Even though this list is not exhaustive, as Osaghae readily admits, it nonetheless indicates the complexity of the minority question in Nigeria. Examples of minorities that have constituted dominant hegemonic groups in Africa include the Afrikaners in apartheid South Africa, the Tutsi in post-1994 Rwanda, and the Fulani in Nigeria.
11. Agbaje, "Mass Media," 99.
12. Suberu, *Ethnic Minority Conflicts*, 1.
13. Okonta and Douglas, *Where Vultures Feast*.
14. Ekeh, "Minorities in Nigerian History and Politics," 33.
15. Ibid.
16. Osaghae, "Managing Multiple Minority Problems," 3.
17. Ekeh, "Minorities in Nigerian History and Politics," 35.
18. Ibid., 37; Osaghae, "Managing Multiple Minority Problems," 5.
19. Horwitz, *Ethnic Groups in Conflict*, 5.

20. See Osaghae, "Ogoni Uprising"; Naanen, "Oil-Producing Minorities," 46–78; Welch, "Ogoni and Self-Determination," 635–50; Obi, "Globalisation and Local Resistance," 137–48.

21. "Ogoni Bill of Rights," in Saro-Wiwa, *A Month and a Day*; Suberu, *Ethnic Minority Conflicts*.

22. Agbaje, "Beyond the State," 458.

23. Omu, *Press and Politics in Nigeria*, 8.

24. Agbaje, "Beyond the State," 459.

25. Agbaje, *Nigerian Press Hegemony*, 144.

26. Lucaites and Condit, "Re-constructing Narrative Theory," 91.

27. Shuman, *Storytelling Rights*, 1–2.

28. Gary, "Review of *Storytelling Rights*," 1275.

29. Shuman, *Storytelling Rights*, 2, 54, 74.

30. Gary, "Review of *Storytelling Rights*," 1275.

31. Ibid.

32. Shuman, *Storytelling Right*, 2, 54.

33. Gary, "Review of *Storytelling Rights*," 1275.

34. Ibid. Although Fine uses *when* as the type of question that captures storyability, I think *how* better captures the manner in which Shuman constructs her inquiry.

35. Bremond, "La logique des possible narratifs," 62–63, cited in Hendricks, "Structural Study of Narration," 102.

36. Abbott, "From Causes to Events," 428–55; Jacobs, "Civil Society and Crisis," 1240; Sewell, "Introduction Narrative and Social Identities," 479–89.

37. Jacobs, "Civil Society and Crisis," 1242. Turner, *Drama, Fields and Metaphors*, 39.

38. Sewell, "Introduction: Narrative and Social Identities," 485. Jacobs, "Civil Society and Crisis," 1243.

39. "Sticky, Oily Problem," *Newswatch*, July 2, 1990, 15–19; quote on 19.

40. Ibid.

41. "Uncle Bola's Column," *Sunday Tribune*, November 3, 1995.

42. Said, *Culture and Imperialism*, 7.

43. "Sticky, Oily Problem," *Newswatch*, July 2, 1990, 15–19.

44. Ibid.

45. Saro-Wiwa, *A Month and a Day*, 139–40.

46. "The Big Revolt: Minorities Threaten to Secede," *TELL*, May 2, 1994, 12.

47. "Interview with Tanko Yakassai," *TELL*, January 10, 1994.

48. See Hunt, *Politics of Bones*, 100–104.

49. "A Year in the Gulag," *TN*, May 29, 1995, 16.

50. "The Big Revolt: Minorities Threaten to Secede," *TELL*, May 2, 1994, 12.

51. Ibid., 13.

52. Ibid.

53. "Revolt of the Lawmakers," *TELL*, February 8, 1993, 28.

54. "Wasteland," *Newswatch*, November 1, 1995, 25.

55. "Another Show Trial," *TN*, November 28, 1994, 15.

56. "Saro-Wiwa, Others Get Death Sentence," *The Guardian*, November 1, 1995, 1.

57. "Abacha's Revenge," *TELL*, November 13, 1995, 12.

58. "Another Show Trial," *TN*, November 28, 1994, 15.

59. "Saro-Wiwa, Others Get Death Sentence," *The Guardian*, November 1, 1995, 1.

60. "Another Show Trial," *TN*, November 28, 1994, 15.

61. "Auta Tribunal Was Biased," *TELL*, November 27, 1995, 10.

62. "Ken Saro-Wiwa Will Live," *Sunday Tribune*, November 19, 1995, 3.

63. "Tension Mounts: Can Komo Cope with the Aftermath of the Ogoni Tragedy?," *TN*, June 13, 1994, 10.

64. "Saro-Wiwa: On a Darkling Plain," *Sunday Tribune*, November 1995, 14.

65. "US, Anyaoku, Others Fault Ruling, Seek Clemency," *TG*, November 2, 1995, 1.

66. "Don't Kill Saro-Wiwa, Others," *TG*, November 9, 1995, 10.

67. "Aftermath of Ogoni Trial," *TG*, November 14, 1995, 10.

68. "The Way Forward," *TELL*, November 20, 1995, 8–9.

69. Jacobs, "Civil Society and Crisis."

70. "The World vs. Abacha," *TELL*, November 7, 1995, 17.

71. "Saro-Wiwa's Father Speaks," *TG*, November 27, 1995, 1.

72. "Panic Grips Aso Rock," *TELL*, December 4, 1995, 8–12.

73. "Finally Abacha Blinks," *TN*, December 11, 1995, 8–12. "Aso Rock's Hasty Retreat," *TELL*, December 11, 1995, 8–14; *Newswatch*, January 7, 1996.

74. "Commonwealth Summit and the Nigerian Situation," *NN*, November 10, 1995, 1.

75. Ibid.

76. "Bishops Condemn US and Britain for Meddling in African Affairs," *NN*, November 13, 1995, 1.

77. "Pressure on Nigeria to Pull Out of Commonwealth," *NN*, November 13, 1995, 1.

78. "Call Commonwealth Bluff—Don," *NN*, November 13, 1995.

79. "The Ogoni Issue (1)," *NN*, November 14, 1995, 1, 5.

80. "The Ogoni Issue (2)," *NN*, November 15, 1995, 1.

81. "Commonwealth Decision: Mammoth Support for FG," *NN*, November 22, 1995, 1. "Nigerians Denounce Commonwealth Decision," *NN*, November 15, 1995, 1. "Ogonis Support FG," *NN*, November 21, 1995, 1.

82. "Commonwealth Decision: Mammoth Support for FG," *NN*, November 22, 1995, 1.

83. "Senegal, Niger Daily Found FG," *NN*, November 25, 1995.

84. "Nigeria and the Commonwealth (1)," *NN*, November 27, 1995.

85. Hall, "What Is This 'Black' in Black Popular Culture."

86. Ssewakiryanga, "New Kids on the Blocks," 4–8.

87. Jacobs, "Civil Society and Crisis."

88. Jacobs, "Civil Society and Crisis," following Calhoon, "Indirect Relationship and Imagined Communities," 108–11.

89. Jacobs, 1242, following Alexander, "Citizen and Enemy as Symbolic Classification,"166.

Conclusion

1. Anchor, "Narrativity and the Transformation of Historical Consciousness," 133–34, cited in Hanne, "An Introduction to the 'Warring with Words' Project," 19.

2. Campbell, *Writing Security*, 281, cited in Hanne, "An Introduction," 20.

3. Scott, *Refashioning Futures*, 70.

4. Hanne, "An Introduction," 12–13.

5. Tomaselli, Tomaselli, and Muller, "A Conceptual Framework," 18.

6. Hanne, "An Introduction," 16.

7. Michael R. Gordonjan, "Kerry Meets with Nigerian Leaders to Encourage Peaceful Election," *New York Times*, January 25, 2015; Jeffrey Scott Shapiro, "Kerry Breaks Protocol, Flies to Nigeria to Discourage Election Violence," *Washington Times*, January 25, 2015; "Kerry Urges Nigerians to Refrain from Post-presidential Election Violence," *The Guardian*, January 25, 2015; Kevin Sieff, "U.S., Britain Fear Possible 'Political Interference' in Nigerian Election," *Washington Post*, March 30, 2015.

8. The northern political elites have, perhaps temporarily, lost their dominance in the PDP, principally to the Ijaw leaders represented by President Goodluck Jonathan.

9. Earlier efforts include the attempts at political understanding or alliance between the Northern People's Congress (NPC) and Action Group (AG) in the First Republic (eventually, a breakaway faction of the AG formed the Nigerian National Democratic Party, NNDP, which allied itself with the NPC); the understanding between the northern leaders, led by Major-General Shehu Musa Yar'Adua, and the Unity Party of Nigeria (UPN), led by Obafemi Awolowo in the Second Republic; the People's Solidarity Party (PSP), the putative north-south alliance in the abortive Third Republic (the party was not even registered by the Babangida military

regime); and the failed alliance between the Sunday Awoniyi-led northern group, All Nigerian Congress (ANC), and the Adekunle Ajasin-led Yoruba group, People's Consultative Forum (PCF), later known as Afenifere.

10. Mustapha, "National Question"; Ake, "Theoretical Notes on the National Question"; Watts, "Black Gold, White Heat"; Momoh and Adejumobi, *National Question in Nigeria*; Gana, "Federalism and the National Question."

11. Cited in Mustapha, "National Question," 81.

12. Abdullahi Tasiu Abubakar, "Analysis: What Did Nigeria's National Conference Achieve?," *BBC*, August 26, 2014.

13. Ibid.

14. See Walker, "What Is Boko Haram?," 14; and Solomon, "Counter-Terrorism in Nigeria."

15. Last, "Pattern of Dissent," 11.

16. Walker, "What Is Boko Haram?," 14.

17. John Campbell, "Buhari Is the Man to Defeat Boko Haram," *Foreign Policy*, April 10, 2015.

18. Scott, *Refashioning the Future*, 20.

19. Ibid.

20. McEachern, *Narratives of Nation Media*, 2.

21. Dienstag, *Dancing in Chains*, 18–19.

22. Van Der Zweerde has pointed to "the ubiquitous possibility, in everything social, of real conflict," in "Friendship and the Political," 151.

23. Connor, "Nation-Building or Nation-Destroying?," 321.

24. Gee, *An Introduction to Discourse Analysis*, 2.

25. Bhabha, "Introduction," 1.

26. Ibid., 2.

27. Bhabha, *Location of Culture*, 212.

28. Macdonell, *Theories of Discourse*, 3.

29. Pêcheux, *Language, Semantics, and Ideology*, cited in ibid., 43.

Bibliography

Abbott, Andrew. "From Causes to Events: Notes on Narrative Positivism." *Sociological Method and Research* 20, no. 4 (1992): 428–55.

Abu-Lughod, Lila. "Finding a Place for Islam: Egyptian Television Serials and the National Interest." *Public Culture* 5 (1993): 493–513.

Abumere, S. I. *Distributional Inequality and the Problem of National Integration.* Ibadan: Vantage Press, 1998.

Adebanwi, Wale. "The Carpenter's Revolt: Youth, Violence and the Reinvention of Culture in Nigeria." *Journal of Modern African Studies* 43, no. 3 (2005): 339–65.

———."Colonial Modernity and Tradition: Herbert Macaulay, the Newspaper Press and the (Re)production of Engaged Publics in Colonial Lagos." In *African Print Cultures*, edited by Stephanie Newell, Emma Hunter, and Derek R. Peterson. Ann Arbor: University of Michigan Press, forthcoming.

———. "Construction and Deconstruction of Political Reality: The Nigerian Press and the June 12 Crisis." MSc diss., University of Ibadan, 1995.

———. *June 12 Crisis (1993–1998): An Annotated Bibliography.* Kano: CRD, 2009.

———. "The Nigerian Press and the National Question." In *The National Question in Nigeria*, edited by Abubakar Momoh and Said Adejumobi, 201–15. Burlington, VT: Ashgate, 2002.

———. *Trials and Triumphs: The Story of TheNEWS.* Lagos: West African Book Publishers, 2008.

Adebanwi, Wale, and Ebenezer Obadare. "Introducing Nigeria at Fifty: The Nation in Narration." *Journal of Contemporary African Studies* 28, no. 4 (2010): 379–405.

Adekanye, Bayo J. "Interactions of Ethnicity, Economy and Society in Separatist Movement in Africa." In Anderson, Bull, and Duvold, eds., *Separatism: Culture Counts, Resources Decide*, 72–105.

Ado-Kurawa, Ibrahim. *Shari'ah and the Press in Nigeria: Islam versus Western Christian Civilization.* Kano: Hudahuda Press, 2001.

Agbaje, Adigun. "Beyond the State: Civil Society and the Nigerian Press under Military Rule." *Media, Culture & Society* 15, no. 3 (1993): 455–72.

———. "Mass Media and the Shaping of Federal Character: A Content Analysis of Four Decades of Nigerian Newspapers (1950–1984)." In *Federal Character and Federalism in Nigeria*, edited by Peter P. Ekeh and E. E. Osaghae, 98–127. Ibadan: Heinemann Educational Books, 1989.

———. *The Nigerian Press: Hegemony and the Social Construction of Legitimacy, 1960–1993.* Lewiston, NY: The Edwin Mellen Press, 1992.

Ajayi, Ade J. F. "Colonialism: An Episode in African History." In *Colonialism in Africa, 1870–1960*, vol. 1, *The History and Politics of Colonialism, 1870–1914*, edited by L. H. Gann and Peter Duignan, 137–46. Cambridge: Cambridge University Press, 1969.

Ajibade, Kunle. *Jailed for Life: A Reporter's Prison Notes.* Ibadan: Heinemann, 2003.

Akande, Adeolu. "Machiavellian Statecraft, State Corporatism and the Social Construction of Neo-Patrimonialism: Nigeria under General Babangida," PhD diss., University of Ibadan, Nigeria, 1995.

Ake, Claude. "Theoretical Notes on the National Question in Nigeria" (mimeograph). Port Harcourt, Nigeria: University of Port Harcourt, 1987.

Akinyemi, Bolaji. *The British Press and the Nigerian Civil War: The Godfather Complex.* Ibadan: University Press in association with Oxford University Press, 1979.

Alexander, J. C. "Citizen and Enemy as Symbolic Classification: On the Polarizing Discourse of Civil Society." In *Where Culture Talks: Exclusion and the making of Society*, edited by Marcel Fournier and Michele Lamont, 289–308. Chicago: University of Chicago Press, 1992.

———. "The Mass Media in a Systemic, Historical and Comparative Perspective." In *Mass Media and Social Change*, edited by E. Katz and T. Szecsko, 17–52. London: Sage Publications, 1981.

Alexander, J. C., and Phillip Smith. "The Discourse of American Society: A New Proposal for Cultural Studies." *Theory and Society* 22, no. 2 (1993): 151–207.

Alexander, Jocelyn, and JoAnn McGregor. "Representing Violence in Matabeleland, Zimbabwe: Press and Internet Debates." In Allen and Seaton, *Media of Conflict*, 244–67.

Allen, Tim, and Jean Seaton, eds. "Introduction." In Allen and Seaton, *Media of Conflict*, 1–8. London: Zed Books, 1999.

———, eds. *Media of Conflict: War Reporting and Representations of Ethnic Violence*, 1–8. London: Zed Books, 1999.

Anderson, Benedict. *Imagined Communities.* London: Verso, 1983.

Anderson, James. "Questions of Democracy, Territoriality and Globalization." In *Transitional Democracy: Political Spaces and Border Crossing*, edited by James Anderson, 6–38. London and New York: Routledge, 2002.

Andersen, Trude, Beate Bull, and Kjehl Duvold. *Separatism: Culture Counts, Resources Decide.* Bergen, Norway: Chr. Michelsen Institute, 1997.

Askew, Kelly. *Performing the Nation: Swahili Music and Cultural Politics in Tanzania.* Chicago: University of Chicago Press, 2002.

Atkins, Douglas G., and Laura Morrow. *Contemporary Literary Theory.* Amherst: University of Massachusetts Press, 1989.

Atkinson, Phillipa. "Deconstructing Media Mythologies of Ethnic War in Liberia." In Allen and Seaton, *Media of Conflict,* 192–218.

Awolowo, Obafemi. *Awo: The Autobiography of Chief Obafemi Awolowo.* London: Cambridge University Press, 1960.

———. *Path to Nigerian Freedom.* London: Faber and Faber, 1947.

Ayoob, Mohammed. "State-Making, State-Breaking and State Failure: Explaining the Roots of 'Third World' Insecurity." In Van de Goor, Rupesinghe, and Sciarone, *Between Development and Destruction,* 67–86.

Azikiwe, Nnamdi. *My Odyssey: An Autobiography.* London: C. Hurst, 1970.

Bal, Mieke. *Narratology: Introduction to the Theory of Narrative.* Toronto: University of Toronto Press, 1999.

Banerjee, Subhabrata Bobby, and Goldie Osuri. "Silences of the Media: Whiting Out Aboriginality in Making News and Making History." *Media, Culture & Society* 22, no. 3 (2000): 263–84.

Barber, Karen. "Documenting Social and Ideological Change through Yoruba *Oriki*: A Stylistic Analysis." *Journal of the Historical Society of Nigeria* 10, no. 4 (1981): 39–52.

———. "Translation, Publics and the Vernacular Press in 1920s Lagos." In *Christianity and Social Change in Africa: Essays in Honour of J. D. Y. Peel,* edited by Toyin Falola, 187–208. Durham, NC: Carolina Academic Press, 2005.

Barnett, Cliff. "Broadcasting the Rainbow Nation: Media, Democracy, and Nation-Building in South Africa." *Antipode* 31, no. 3 (1999): 274–303.

Barrett, Michèle. *The Politics of Truth: From Marx to Foucault.* Cambridge: Polity Press, 1992.

Barthes, Roland. "Introduction to the Structural Analysis of Narratives." In Bennett et al., *Culture, Ideology and Social Process,* 165–84.

Barthsch, Renate. "Semantic and Pragmatical Correctness as Basic Notions of the Theory of Meaning." *Journal of Pragmatics* 3, no. 1 (1979): 1–43.

Bauman, Z. *Hermeneutics and Social Science.* London: Hutchinson, 1978.

Becker, Karin. "Media and the Ritual Process." *Media, Culture & Society* 17, no. 4 (1995): 629–46.

Bennett N. L. "Myth, Ritual and Political Control." *Journal of Communication* 30, no. 4 (1980): 166–79.

Bennett, Tony, Graham Martin, Colin Mercer, and Janet Woollacott, eds. *Culture, Ideology and Social Process: A Reader.* Berkshire, UK: Open University Press, 1981.

Bennett, W. Lance, and Murray Edelman. "Towards a New Political Narrative." *Journal of Communication* 35, no. 4 (1985): 156–71.

Bhabha, Homi K. "DissemiNation: Time, Narrative and the Margins of the Modern Nation." In Bhabha, *The Location of Culture*, 199–244.

———. "Introduction: Narrating the Nation." In Bhabha, *Nation and Narration*, 1–7.

———. *The Location of Culture*. New York: Routledge, 1994.

———. ed. *Nation and Narration*. New York: Routledge, 1990.

Billig, Michael. *Banal Nationalism*. London: Sage Publications, 1995.

Black, Max. *The Labyrinth of Language*. Middlesex, England: Penguin Books, 1968.

Blaike, Norman. *Approaches to Social Enquiry*. Cambridge: Polity Press, 1993.

Bogdanor, Vernon. *The Blackwell Encyclopedia of Political Science*. Oxford, UK: Blackwell Publishers, 1991.

Bonjour, Laurence. *The Structure of Empirical Knowledge*. Cambridge, MA: Harvard University Press, 1985.

Bormann, Ernest G. "Symbolic Convergence Theory: A Communication Formulation." *Journal of Communication* 35, no. 4 (1985): 128–38.

Bourdieu, P., and J. S. Coleman, eds. *Social Theory for a Changing Society*. Boulder, CO: Westview Press, 1991.

Boyce, Brendan. "Nation-Building Discourse in a Democracy." In *National Identity and Democracy in Africa*, edited by Mai Palmberg, 231–43. Pretoria, South Africa: HSRC, 1999.

Breen, M., and F. Corcorcin. "Myth in the Televisions Discourse." *Communication Monographs* 49, no. 2 (1982): 127–36.

Bremond, Claude. "La logique des possible narratifs." *Communications* 8 (1966): 60–76.

Brennan, Timothy. *Salmon Rushdie and the Third World: Myths of the Nation*. London: Macmillan, 1989.

Brookes, Rod. 1999. "Newspapers and National Identity: The BSE/CJD Crisis and the British Press." *Media, Culture & Society* 21, no. 2 (1999): 247–63.

Brown, Richard Harvey. *Social Science as Civil Discourse: Essays on the Invention, Legitimation, and Uses of Social Theory*. Chicago: University of Chicago Press, 1989.

Buchanan, Allen. "Separatism, Citizenship and State System." In Anderson, Bull, and Devold, *Separatism*, 192–228.

Burgess, Jacquelin. "News from Nowhere: The Press the Riots and the Myth of the Inner City." In Burgess and Gold, *Geography, the Media and Popular Culture*, 192–228.

Burgess, Jacquelin, and John R. Gold, eds. *Geography, the Media and Popular Culture*. London: Croom Helm, 1985.

Calhoun, Craig C. "Indirect Relationship and Imagined Communities: Large-Scale Social Integration and the Transformation of Everyday Life." In Bordieu and Coleman, *Social Theory for a Changing Society*, 95–120.

Carruthers, Susan L. *The Media at War.* New York: Palgrave-Macmillan, 2000.

Casmir, Fred, ed. *Communication and Development.* Norwood, NJ: Ablex, 1991.

Castells, Manuel. *The Power of Identity.* Oxford: Blackwell Publishers, 1997.

Caton, Charles E., ed. *Philosophy and Ordinary Language.* Urbana: University of Illinois Press, 1963.

Cerlisten, R. O. "Power and Meaning: Terrorism as a Struggle over Access to the Communication Structure." In *Contemporary Research on Terrorism,* edited by P. Wilkinson and A. M. Stewart, 419–50. Andersen, Scotland: Aberdeen University Press, 1987.

Charteris-Black, Jonathan. *Politicians and Rhetoric: The Persuasive Power of Metaphor.* New York: Palgrave-Macmillan, 2005.

Chatterjee, Partha. *The Nation and Its Fragments: Colonial and Postcolonial Histories.* Princeton, NJ: Princeton University Press, 1993.

———. "Whose Imagined Community?" *Millennium: The Journal of International Studies* 20, no. 3 (1991): 521–25.

Chick, John D. "The Nigerian Press and National Integration." *Journal of Commonwealth Political Studies* 9, no. 2 (1971): 115–33.

Chipkin, Ivor. *Do South Africans Exist? Nationalism, Democracy and the Identity of the People.* Johannesburg, South Africa: Wits University Press, 2008.

———. "The South African Nation." *Transformation: Critical Perspectives on Southern Africa* 51 (2003): 25–47.

Chisholm, Roderick M. *Theory of Knowledge.* New Delhi: Prentice-Hall of India, 1987.

Clay, Jason W. "Epilogue: The Ethnic Future of Nations." *Third World Quarterly* 11, no. 4 (1989): 223–33.

Clegg, Stewart R. *Frameworks of Power.* London: Sage Publications, 1989.

Coker, Increase. *Landmarks of the Nigerian Press: An Outline of the Origins and Development of the Newspaper Press in Nigeria, 1859 to 1965.* Lagos: Nigerian National Press. 1968.

Cole, Patrick. *Modern and Traditional Elites in the Politics of Lagos.* Cambridge: Cambridge University Press, 1975.

Coleman, James S. *Nigeria: Background to Nationalism.* Berkeley: University of California Press, 1958.

Condon, John C. "Nation Building and Image Building in the Tanzanian Press." *Journal of Modern African Studies* 5, no. 3 (1967): 335–54.

Connolly, William E. "Appearance and Reality in Politics." In Gibbons, *Interpreting Politics,* 148–74.

———. *Why I Am Not a Secularist.* Minneapolis: University of Minnesota Press, 1999.

Connor, Walker. "Ethnic Identity: Primordial or Modern?" In Anderson, Bull, and Duvold, *Separatism,* 27–40.

———. *Ethnonationalism: The Quest for Understanding.* Princeton, NJ: Princeton University Press, 1994.

———. "Nation-Building or Nation-Destroying?" *World Politics* 24, no. 3 (1972): 319–55.

———. "A Nation Is a Nation, Is a State, Is an Ethnic Group, Is a. . . ." *Ethnic and Racial Studies* 1, no. 4 (1978): 377–400.

———. "The Politics of Ethnonationalism." *Journal of International Affairs* 27, no. 1 (1973): 1–21.

Corbey, Raymond. "Ethnographic Showcases, 1870–1930." In *The Decolonization of Imagination*, edited by Jan Nederveen Pieterse and Bhikhu Parekh, 57–80. London: Zed Books, 1995.

Costelloe, Laura. "Discourses of Sameness: Expressions of Nationalism in Newspaper Discourse on French Urban Violence in 2005." *Discourse and Society* 25, no. 3 (2014): 315–40.

Cottle, Simon. *Mediatized Conflict: Understanding Media and Conflicts in the Contemporary World*. Berkshire, UK: Open University Press, 2006.

———. "The Production of News Formats: Determinants of Mediated Public Contestation." *Media, Culture & Society* 17 (1995): 275–91.

———. *TV News, Urban Conflicts and the Inner City*. Leicester, England: Leicester University Press, 1993.

Couldry, Nick. "Disrupting the Media Frame of Greenham Common: A New Chapter in the History of Mediations?" *Media, Culture & Society* 21, no. 3 (1999): 337–58.

Cox, Kevin R. "Spaces of Dependence, Space of Engagement and the Politics of Scale, or: Looking for Local Politics." *Political Geography* 17, no. 1 (1998): 1–23.

Crotty, Michael. *The Foundations of Social Research: Meaning and Perspective in the Research Process*. London: Sage Publications, 1998.

Crowder, M. *The Story of Nigeria*. London: Faber and Faber, 1962.

Curran, James. "Rethinking the Media as a Public Sphere." In Dahlgren and Sparks, *Communication and Citizenship*, 27–56.

Curran, James, and Michael Gurevith, eds. *Mass Media and Society*. London: Arnold, 1996.

Dahl, Robert A. "The Concept of Power," *Behavioral Science* 2, no. 3 (1957): 201–15.

Dahlgren, Peter, and Colin Spark, eds. *Communication and Citizenship: Journalism and the Public Sphere*. London: Routledge, 1991.

Dare, Olatunji. *Diary of a Debacle: Tracking Nigeria's Failed Democratic Transition (1989–1994)*. Ibadan: Agbo Areo Publishers, 2010.

Dare, Sunday. *Guerilla Journalism: Dispatches from the Underground*. Bloomington, IN: Xlibris Corporation, 2007.

Dawson, Richard W. "Territoriality." In *Encyclopedia of World Geography*, edited by R. N. McColl, 883–85. New York: Godson Books, 2005.

Deacon, David, Natalie Fenton, and Alan Bryman. "From Inception to Reception: The Natural History of a News Item." *Media, Culture & Society* 21 (1999): 5–31.

Dear, Michael, and Jennifer Wolch. "How Territory Shapes Social Life." In *The Power of Geography: How Territory Shapes Social Life*, edited by Jennifer Wolch and Michael Dear. Abingdon, England: Routledge, 1989.

Degenaar, Johan. "Beware of Nation-Building Discourse." In Rhoodie and Liebenberg, *Democratic Nation-Building in South Africa*, 23–29.

———. "The Myth of a South African Nation." Occasional Paper, no. 40. Institute for a Democratic Alternative in South Africa. Cape Town: IDASA, 1991.

Der Derian, James. "S/N: International Theory, Balkanisation and the New World Order." *Millennium: The Journal of International Studies* 20, no. 3 (1991): 485–506.

Derrida, Jacques. *Of Gramatology*. Translated by Gayatri C. Spivak. Baltimore, MD: Johns Hopkins University Press, 1976.

Des Forges, Allison. "Call to Genocide: Radio in Rwanda, 1994." In Thompson, *Media and Rwanda Genocide*, 41–54.

de-Shalit, Avner. "National Self-Determination: Political, Not Cultural." *Political Studies* 44, no. 4 (1996): 906–20.

de Silva, Kingsley M. "Ethnicity and Nationalism." In Van de Goor, Rupesinghe, and Sciarone, *Between Development and Destruction*, 109–25.

Dhoest, Alexander. "Negotiating Images of the Nation: The Production of Flemish TV Drama, 1953–1989." *Media, Culture & Society* 26, no. 3 (2004): 393–408.

Diamond, Larry. "Nigeria's Search for a New Political Order." *Journal of Democracy* 2, no. 2 (1991): 54–69.

Diamond, Larry, Juan J. Linz, and Seymour Martin Lipset. *Democracy in Developing Countries: Latin America*. Boulder, CO: Lynne Rienner Publishers, 1988.

Diamond, Larry, Anthony Kirk-Greene, and Oyeleye Oyediran. *Transition without End: Nigerian Politics and Civil Society under Babangida*. Boulder, CO: Lynne Rienner, 1996.

Dienstag, Joshua Foa. *Dancing in Chains: Narrative and Memory in Political Theory*. Stanford, CA: Stanford University Press, 1997.

Director, Osa. *Suicide Journalism*. Ibadan: Bookcraft, 2008.

Doherty, Thomas, ed. *Postmodernism: A Reader*. New York: Columbia University Press, 1993.

Donnan, Hastings, and Thomas M. Wilson. "Territoriality, Anthropology, and the Interstitial: Subversion and Support in European Borderlands." *Focaal—European Journal of Anthropology* 41, no. 3 (2003): 9–25.

Doornbos, Martin. "The African State in Academic Debate: Retrospect and Prospect." *Journal of Modern African Studies* 28, no. 2 (1990): 179–98.

Dowding, Keith. *Power*. Minneapolis: University of Minnesota Press, 1996.

Dreyfus, Hubert L. "Beyond Hermeneutics: Interpretation in Late Heidegger and Recent Foucault." In Gibbons, *Interpreting Politics*, 203–20.

Dröge, Franz. "Social Knowledge and the Mediation of Knowledge in Bourgeois Society." *Media, Culture & Society* 5, no. 1 (1983): 49–63.

Dunn, John. "Does Separatism Threaten the State System?" In Andersen, Bull, and Duvold, *Separatism*, 130–45.

Eagleton, Terry. *The Ideology of the Aesthetic.* Oxford: Blackwell, 1990.

Edmondson, Laura. *Performance and Politics in Tanzania: The Nation on Stage.* Bloomington: Indiana University Press, 2007.

Ekecrantz, Jan. "Journalism's 'Discursive Events' and Sociopolitical Change in Sweden, 1925–87." *Media, Culture & Society* 19, no. 3 (1997): 393–412.

Ekeh, Peter P. "Colonialism and the Two Publics in Africa: A Theoretical Statement." *Comparative Studies in Society and History* 17, no. 1 (1975): 91–112.

———. "Political Minorities and Historically Dominant Minorities in Nigerian History and Politics." In *Governance and Development in Nigeria*, edited by Oyeleye Oyediran, 33–63. Ibadan: Oyeleye Consult, 1996.

Eley, Geoffrey. "Nations, Publics, and Political Cultures: Placing Habermas in the Nineteenth Century." In *Habermas and the Public Sphere*, edited by Craig Calhoun, 289–339. Boston: MIT Press, 1992.

Fraser, Nancy. "Rethinking the Public Sphere: A Contribution to the Critique of Actually Existing Democracy." In *Habermas and the Public Sphere*, edited by Craig Calhoun, 109–42. Boston: MIT Press, 1992.

Emerson, Rupert. *From Empire to Nation: The Rise to Self-Assertion of Asian and African People.* Cambridge, MA: Harvard University Press, 1960.

Eriksen, Thomas H. *Ethnicity and Nationalism: Anthropological Perspectives.* London: Pluto Press, 1993.

———. "Rethinking Ethnicity: An Alternative Approach to the Study of Identification." In Andersen, Bull, and Duvold, *Separatism*, 41–55.

Evans, Martin. "Languages of Racism within Contemporary Europe." In Jenkins and Sofos, *Nation and Identity in Contemporary Europe*, 30–49.

Fairclough, Norman. *Critical Discourse Analysis: The Critical Study of Language.* London: Longman, 1995.

———. *Media Discourse.* London: Edward Arnold, 1995.

Farrell, Thomas B. "Narrative in Natural Discourse: On Conversation and Rhetoric." *Journal of Communication* 35, no. 4 (1985): 109–27.

Fasehun, Frederick. *Frederick Fasehun: The Son of Oodua.* Lagos: Inspired Communication, 2002.

Fay, Brian. "An Alternative View: Interpretive Social Science." In Gibbons, *Interpreting Politics*, 82–100.

Feyerabend, Paul. 1975. *Against Method.* 3rd ed. London: Verso, 1993.

Fine, Gary Alan. Review of *Storytelling Rights: The Uses of Oral and Written Texts by Urban Adolescents*, by Amy Shuman. *American Journal of Sociology* 94, no. 5 (1989): 1274–76.

Fisher, Walter R. "Narration as a Human Communication Paradigm." *Communication Monographs* 51, no. 1 (1984): 1–22.

———. "The Narrative Paradigm: In the Beginning." *Journal of Communication* 35, no. 4 (1985): 74–89.

Fiske, John. "Postmodernism and Television." In Curran and Gurevith, *Mass Media and Society*, 55–67.

Fleischman, Suzanne. "Evaluation in Narrative: The Present Tense in Medieval 'Performed Stories.'" *Yale French Studies* 70 (1986): 199–251.

Fontana, Beneditto. *Hegemony and Power: On the Relation between Gramsci and Machiavelli*. Minneapolis: University of Minnesota Press, 1993.

Foucault, Michel. *Power/Knowledge*. Edited by C. Gordon. Brighton: Harvester, 1980.

Fowler, Roger, Bob Hodge, Gunther Kress, and Tony Trew. *Language and Control*. London: Routledge, 1979.

Fraser, Nancy. "Rethinking the Public Sphere: A Contribution to the Critique of Actually Existing Democracy." *Social Text*, nos. 25–26 (1990): 56–80.

Freeden, Michael. "Editorial: What Is Special about Ideologies?" *Journal of Political Ideologies* 6, no. 1 (2001): 5–12.

Freeman, Michael. "Democracy and Dynamite: The Peoples' Right to Self-Determination." *Political Studies* 44, no. 4 (1996): 746–61.

Frère, Marie-Soleil. *Elections and the Media in Post-conflict Africa: Votes and Voices for Peace?* London: Zed Books, 2011.

———. *The Media and Conflicts in Central Africa*. Boulder, CO: Lynne Rienner, 2007.

Gagiano, Jannie. "The Contenders." In *The Myth Makers: The Elusive Bargain for South Africa's Future*, edited by Pierre du Toit and Willie Esterhuyse, 10–35. Stellenbosch, South Africa: University of Stellenbosch, 1990.

Gana, Aaron T. "Federalism and the National Question in Nigeria: A Theoretical Exploration." In *Federalism in Africa: Framing the National Question*, vol. 1, edited by Aaron Tsado Gana and Samuel G. Egwu, 17–46. Trenton, NJ: African World Press, 2003.

Gee, James Paul. *An Introduction to Discourse Analysis: Theory and Method*. London: Routledge, 1999.

Genette, Gerald. 1980. *Narrative Discourse: An Essay in Method*. Translated by Jane E. Lewin. Ithaca, NY: Cornell University Press, 1995.

Gerbner, G. "*Homo Narrans*: Story-Telling in Mass Culture and Everyday Life." *Journal of Communication* 35, no. 4 (1985): 73–74.

Gershoni, Israel, and James P. Jankowski. *Redefining the Egyptian Nation, 1930–1945*. Cambridge: Cambridge University Press, 2002.

Gibbons, Michael T., ed. *Interpreting Politics*. Oxford: Basil Blackwell, 1987.

———. "Introduction: The Politics of Interpretation ." In Gibbons, *Interpreting Politics*, 1–31.

Giddens, Anthony. *Central problems in Social Theory: Action, Structure and Contradiction in Social Analysis.* London: Macmillan, 1979.

———. *The Constitution of Society: Outline of the Theory of Structuration.* Cambridge: Polity, 1984.

———. *A Contemporary Critique of Historical Materialism.* Vol. 1, *Power, Property and the State.* London: Macmillan, 1981.

———. *A Contemporary Critique of Historical Materialism*, vol. 2, *The Nation State and Violence.* Cambridge: Polity Press, 1985.

———. *New Rules of Sociological Method: A Positive Critique of Interpretive Sociologies.* 2nd ed. Stanford, CA: Stanford University Press, 1976.

———. *Politics, Sociology and Social Theory: Encounters with Classical and Contemporary Social Thought.* Stanford: Stanford University Press, 1995.

Ginsburg, Faye D., Lila Abu-Lughod, and Brian Larkin. "Introduction." In *Media Worlds: Anthropology on New Terrain*, edited by Faye D. Ginsburg, Lila Abu-Lughod, and Brian Larkin. Berkeley: University of California Press, 2002.

Glaserfeld, Ernst Von. "On the Concept of Interpretation." *Poetics* 12 (1983): 207–18.

Glynos, Jason. "The Grip of Ideology: A Lacanian Approach to the Theory of Ideology." *Journal of Political Ideologies* 6, no. 1 (2001): 191–214.

Goldberger, Nancy, Jill Tarrule, Blythe Clinchy, and Mary Belenky, eds. *Knowledge, Difference, and Power: Essays Inspired by Women's Ways of Knowing.* New York: Basic Books, 1996.

Golding Peter, and Graham Murdock. "Culture, Communications and Political Economy." In Curran and Gurevitch, *Mass Media and Society*, 60–83.

Goldstein, Joshua, and Juliana Rotich. "Digitally Networked Technology in Kenya's 2007–2008 Post-election Crisis." Berkman Center Research Publication. The Berkman Center for Internet and Society, Harvard University, Cambridge, MA, September 2008.

Gotz, Wienold. "On Deriving Models of Narrative Analysis from Models of Discourse Analysis." *Poetics* 1, no. 3 (1972): 15–28.

Gramsci, Antonio. *Selections from the Prison Notebooks.* Edited and translated by Q. Hoare and G. Nowell-Smith. New York: International Publishers, 1971.

Gross, Larry, John Stuart Katz, and Jay Ruby, eds. *Image Ethics: The Moral Rights of Subjects in Photography, Films and Television.* New York: Oxford University Press, 1988.

Gunther, Richard, and Anthony Mughan, eds. *Democracy and the Media: A Comparative Perspective.* Cambridge: Cambridge University Press, 2000.

Gunther, Richard, and Anthony Mughan. "The Political Impact of the Media: A Reassessment." In Gunther and Mughan, *Democracy and the Media*, 402–47.

Habermas, Jürgen. "Citizenship and National Identity: Some Reflections on the Future of Europe." *Praxis International* 12, no. 2 (1992): 1–19.

———. "The Hermeneutic Claim to Universality." In Gibbons, *Interpreting Politics*, 175–202.

———. *On the Logic of the Social Sciences*. Translated by Shierry Weber Nicholsen and Jerry A. Stark. Cambridge, MA: MIT Press, 1994.

———. *The Structural Transformation of the Public Sphere: An Inquiry into a Category of Bourgeois Society*. Translated by Thomas Burger. Cambridge, MA: MIT Press, 1989.

———. *The Theory of Communicative Action*, vol. 1, *Reason and the Rationalization of Society*. Translated by Thomas McCarthy. Cambridge: Polity Press, 1986.

Hackett, Rosalind I. J. "Managing or Manipulating Religious Conflict in the Nigerian Media." In *Mediating Religion: Conversations in Media, Religion and Culture*, edited by Jolyon P. Mitchell and Sophia Marriage, 47–63. London: T & T Clark, 2003.

Hagen, J. M. "'Read All About It': The Press and the Rise of National Consciousness in Early Twentieth-Century Dutch East Indies Society." *Anthropological Quarterly* 70, no. 3 (1997): 107–26.

Hall, Stuart. "Culture, the Media, and the 'Ideological Effect.'" In *Mass Communication and Society*, edited by James Curran, Michael Gurevitch, and Janet Woollacott, 315–48. London: Sage Publications, 1977.

———. "What Is This 'Black' in Black Popular Culture?" In *Black Popular Culture*, edited by Gina Dent, 21–33. Seattle: Bay Press, 1992.

Hammack, Phillip L., and Andrew Pilecki. "Narrative as a Root Metaphor for Political Psychology." *Political Psychology* 33, no. 1 (2012): 75–103.

Hanne, Michael. "An Introduction to the 'Warring with Words' Project." In *Warring with Words: Narrative and Metaphor in Politics*, edited by Michael Hanne, William D. Crano, and Jeffery Scott Mio, 1–49. New York: Psychology Press, 2014.

Harris, Peter B. *Foundations of Political Science*. London: Hutchinson, 1983.

Harrison, Henrietta. "Newspapers and Nationalism in Rural China, 1890–1929." *Past & Present* 166 (2000): 181–204.

Harvey, David. *Justice, Nature and the Geography of Difference*. Oxford: Basil Blackwell, 1996.

Hegel, G. W. F. *Lectures on the Philosophy of Religion*. Translated by E. B. Speirs and J. Burdon Sanderson. London: Oxford University Press. 1971.

Helle, H. J. *Soziologie und Symbol*. Cologne: VS Verlag für Sozialwissenschaften, 1969.

Hendricks, William O. "The Structural Study of Narration: Sample Analysis." *Poetics* 1, no. 3 (1972): 100–123.

Herman, David. *Basic Elements of Narrative*. Malden, MA: Blackwell Publishing, 2009.

Herman, David, Manfred Jahn, and Marie-Laure Ryan. "Introduction." In Herman, Jahn, and Ryan, *Routledge Encyclopedia of Narrative Theory*, ix–xi.

———. *Routledge Encyclopedia of Narrative Theory*. Oxfordshire, England: Routledge, 2005.

Hertz, L. *Nationalism in History and Politics*. London: Routledge and Kegan Paul, 1944.

Higiro, Jean-Maria Vianney. "Rwandan Private Print Media on the Eve of the Genocide." In Thompson, *Media and Rwanda Genocide*, 73–88.

Hindess, Barry. *Philosophy and Methodology in the Social Sciences*. Sussex, England: The Harvester Press, 1977.

Hobsbawm, Eric. "Introduction: Inventing Traditions." In Hobsbawm and Ranger, *Invention of Tradition*, 1–13.

Hobsbawm, Eric, and Terence Ranger, eds. *The Invention of Tradition*. Cambridge: Cambridge University Press, 1983.

Horwitz, Donald L. *Ethnic Groups in Conflict*. Berkeley: University of California Press, 1985.

Hoskin, Goeffrey, and George Schöpflin. *Myths and Nationhood*. London: Hurst, 1997.

Howard, Sam. "Community Radio and Ethnic Violence in Africa: The Case of Kenya." MA diss., University of East Anglia, UK, 2009.

Howarth, David. "Discourse Theory." In *Research Strategies in the Social Sciences: A Guide to New Approaches*, edited by Elinor Scarbrough and Eric Tanebaum, 268–92. Oxford: Oxford University Press, 1998.

Hughes, John A., and Wes Sharrock. *The Philosophy of Social Research*. 2nd ed. London: Longman, 1997.

Hunt, J. Timothy. *The Politics of Bones: Dr. Owens Wiwa and the Struggle for Nigeria's Oil*. Toronto: McClelland & Stewart, 2005.

Hyden, Goran, and Michael Leslie. "Communications and Democratization in Africa." In Hyden, Leslie, and Ogundimu, *Media and Democracy in Africa*, 1–27.

Hyden, Goran, Michael Leslie, and Folu F. Ogundimu, eds. *Media and Democracy in Africa*. New Brunswick, NJ: Transaction Publishers, 2002.

Hyden, Goran, Michael Leslie, and Folu Ogundimu. "Preface." In Hyden, Leslie, and Ogundimu, *Media and Democracy in Africa*, vii–ix.

Idemili, Samuel Okafor. *The West African Pilot and the Movement for Nigerian Nationalism, 1937–1960*. Madison: University of Wisconsin Press, 1980.

Ihwe, Jens. "On the Foundations of a General Theory of Narrative Structure." *Poetics* 3 (1972): 2–14.

Ilesanmi, S. O. *Religious Pluralism and the Nigerian State*. Athens: Ohio University Press, 1997.

Inthorn, Sanna. "The Death of the Hun?: National Identity and German Press Coverage of the 1998 Football World Cup." *European Journal of Cultural Studies* 5, no. 1 (2002): 49–68.

Isumonah, Adefemi V. "Migration, Land Tenure, Citizenship and Communal Conflicts in Africa." *Nationalism and Ethnic Politics* 9, no. 1 (2003): 1–19.

Ives, Sarah. "Mediating the Neoliberal Nation: Television in Post-Apartheid South Africa." *ACME: An International E-Journal for Critical Geography* 6, no. 1 (2007): 153–73.

Jacobs, Ronald N. "Civil Society and Crisis: Culture, Discourse, and the Rodney King Beating." *American Journal of Sociology* 101, no. 5 (1996): 1238–72.

———. "Producing the News, Producing the Crisis: Narrativity, Television and News Work." *Media, Culture & Society* 18 (1996): 373–97.

———. *Race, Media and the Crisis of Civil Society: From Watts to Rodney King.* Cambridge: Cambridge University Press, 2000.

Jakubowicz, Karol. "Media within and without the State: Press Freedom in Eastern Europe." *Journal of Communication* 45, no. 4 (1995): 125–39.

Jones, J. P. and P. Moss. "Guest Editorial: Democracy, Identity, Space." *Environment and Planning D: Society and Space* 13 (1995): 253–57.

Jameson, Fredric. *The Political Unconscious: Narrative as a Socially Symbolic Act.* Ithaca, NY: Cornell University Press, 1981.

Jamieson, Neil L. "Communication and the New Paradigm for Development." In *Communication in Development*, edited by Fred L. Casmir. Norwood, NJ: Ablex, 1991.

Jenkins, Brian, and Spyros A. Sofos, eds. *Nation and Identity in Contemporary Europe.* London: Routledge, 1996.

———. "Nation and Nationalism in Contemporary Europe: A Theoretical Perspective." In Jenkins and Sofos, *Nation and Identity in Contemporary Europe*, 7–29.

Jenkins, Richard. "Rethinking Ethnicity: Identity, Categorization and Power." *Ethnic and Racial Studies* 17, no. 2 (1994): 197–223.

Joda, Ahmed. "Foreword." In Mohammadu, *Courage and Conviction*, i–iv.

Joseph, Richard, Scott Taylor, and Adigun Agbaje. "Nigeria." In *Comparative Politics at the Crossroads*, edited by Mark Kesselman, Joel Krieger, and William A. Joseph, 613–89. Lexington, MA: DC Heath, 1996.

Joseph, William A., Mark Kesselman, and Joel Krieger, eds. *Third World Politics at the Crossroads.* Lexington, MA: DC Heath, 1996.

Kabanda, Marcel. "*Kangura*: The Triumph of Propaganda Refined." In Thompson, *Media and Rwanda Genocide*, 62–72.

Kalb, Marvin. "A View from the Press." In *Taken By Storm: The Media, Public Opinion, and the U.S. Foreign Policy in the Gulf War*, edited by W. Lance Bennett and David L. Paletz, 3–7. Chicago: University of Chicago Press, 1994.

Kalu, Ogbu U. "Safiyya and Adamah: Punishing Adultery with Sharia Stones in Twenty-First Century Nigeria." *African Affairs* 102 (2003): 389–409.

Kamrava, Mehran. 1993. *Politics and Society in the Developing World.* 2nd ed. London: Routledge, 2000.

Kaplan, Richard. "The American Press and Political Community: Reporting in Detroit, 1865–1920." *Media, Culture & Society* 19 (1997): 331–55.

Kaplan, Sam. "Territorializing Armenians: Geo-Texts and Political Imaginaries in French Occupied Cilicia, 1919–1922." *History and Anthropology* 15, no. 4 (2004): 399–423.

Kerkvliet, Benedict J. Tria. "An Approach for Analysing State-Society Relations in Vietnam." *Sojourn: Journal of Social Issues in Southeast Asia* 16, no. 2 (2001): 238–78.

Kirk-Greene, A. H. M. "Ethnic Engineering and the 'Federal Character' of Nigeria: Boon of Contentment or Bone of Contention?" *Ethnic and Racial Studies* 6, no. 4 (1983): 457–76.

Kitzinger, Jenny. "Media Templates: Patterns of Association and the (Re)construction of Meaning over Time." *Media, Culture & Society* 22, no. 1 (2000): 61–84.

Kreimeier, Klaus. "Fundamental Reflections on a Materialist Theory of the Mass Media." *Media, Culture & Society* 5, no. 1 (1983): 37–47.

Krejci, Jaroslav, and Vitezslav Vilimsky. *Ethnic and Political Nations in Europe.* London: Croom Helm, 1981.

Krog, Antjie. *Country of My Skull: Guilt, Sorrow, and the Limits of Forgiveness in the New South Africa.* New York: Times Books, 1998.

Kukah, Matthew H. *Religion, Politics and Power in Northern Nigeria.* Ibadan: Spectrum Books, 1993.

Laitin, David. *Hegemony and Culture: Politics and Religious Change among the Yoruba.* Chicago: University of Chicago Press, 1986.

Larrain, Jorge. *Marxism and Ideology.* London: Macmillan, 1983.

Last, Murray. "The Pattern of Dissent: Boko Haram in Nigeria 2009." *Annual Review of Islam in Africa,* no. 10 (2008–9): 7–11.

Law, Alex. "Near and Far: Banal National Identity and the Press in Scotland." *Media, Culture & Society* 23, no. 3 (2001): 299–317.

Leach, E. *Custom, Law and Terrorist Violence.* Edinburgh: Edinburgh University Press, 1977.

Lefebvre, Henri. *The Production of Space.* Trans. by Donald Nicholson-Smith. Cambridge, MA: Blackwell, 1991 [1974].

Legg, Marie-Louise. *Newspapers and Nationalism: The Irish Provincial Press, 1850–1892.* Dublin: Four Courts, 1999.

Leopold, Mark. "'The War in the North': Ethnicity in Ugandan Press Explanation of Conflict, 1996–97." In Allen and Seaton, *Media of Conflict,* 219–43.

Leopold, Peeters. "Why Do We Need Interpretation?" In Mouton and Joubert, *Knowledge and Method in the Human Sciences,* 156–67.

Lerner, Adam J. "Introduction to Reimagining the Nation." *Millennium: The Journal of International Studies* 20, no. 3 (1991): 351–52.

———. "Transcendence of the Nation: National Identity and the Terrain of the Divine." *Millennium: Journal of International Studies* 20, no. 3 (1991): 407–27.

Levin, David Michael. "Sanity and Myth in Affective Space." *Philosophical Forum* 14 (1982–83): 157–89.

Levine, Daniel. "Religion and Politics in Contemporary Historical Perspective." *Comparative Politics* 19, no. 1 (1986): 95–122.

Li, Darryl. "Echoes of Violence: Considerations of Radio and Genocide." In Thompson, *Media and Rwanda Genocide*, 90–109.

Liebenberg, Ian. "Nation-Building and Community Reconciliation in an Embattled South African Society." In Rhoodie and Liebenberg, *Democratic Nation-Building in South Africa*, 9–22.

Linz, Juan J., and Alfred Stepan. *Problems of Democratic Transition and Consolidation: Southern Europe, South America, and Post-Communist Europe.* Baltimore, MD: Johns Hopkins University Press, 1996.

Lipski, John M. "From Text to Narrative: Spanning the Gap." *Poetics* 5, no. 3 (1976): 191–206.

Louw, Eric. *The Media and Cultural Production.* London: SAGE Publications, 2001.

Lucaites, John L., and Celeste M. Condit. "Re-constructing Narrative Theory: A Functional Perspective." *Journal of Communication* 35, no. 4 (1985): 90–108.

Lukacs, Georg. *Geschichte und Klassenbewusstsein.* Amsterdam: Munter.gut erhalten, 1967.

———. *History and Class Consciousness: Studies in Marxist Dialetics.* Translated by Rodney Livingstone. London: Merlin Press, 1971.

Lukes, Steven. "On the Social Determination of Truth." In Gibbons, *Interpreting Politics*, 64–81.

Lyman, Stanford M. *Ethnicity, Pluralism and Their Implications for Africa and the World.* Maiduguri, Nigeria: University of Maiduguri Press, 1988.

Macdonald, Myra. *Representing Women: Myths and Feminism in the Popular Media.* London: Edward Arnold, 1995.

Macdonell, Diane. *Theories of Discourse: An Introduction.* Oxford: Blackwell, 1986.

Madanou, Mirca. *Mediating the Nation: News, Audiences and the Politics of Identity.* London: UCL Press, 2005.

Makinen, Maarit, and Mary Wangui Kuira. "Social Media and Post-election Crisis in Kenya." *Information and Communication Technology—Africa* 13. Annenberg School for Communication, University of Pennsylvania, 2008.

Mamdani, Mahmood. *Citizen and Subject: Contemporary Africa and the Legacy of Late Colonialism.* Princeton, NJ: Princeton University Press, 1996.

Manheim, Karl. *Ideology and Utopia: An Introduction to the Sociology of Knowledge.* Translated by Louis Wirth and Edward Shils. New York: A Harvest Book, 1936.

Marston, Sallie A., John Paul Jones III, and Keith Woodward. "Human Geography without Scale." *Transaction of the Institute of British Geographers* 30 (2005): 416–32.

Martin, Wallace. *Recent Theories of Narrative.* Ithaca, NY: Cornell University Press, 1996.

Marx, Karl. *The Poverty of Philosophy.* Chicago: Progress Publishers, 1910.

Mayer, Frederick W. *Narrative Politics: Stories and Collective Action.* Oxford: Oxford University Press, 2014.

Maschiio, Thomas. "The Narrative and Counter-Narrative of the Gift: Emotional Dimensions of Ceremonial Exchange in Southwestern New Britain." *Journal of the Royal Anthropological Institute* 4, no. 1 (1998): 83–100.

McCrone, David. "Explaining Nationalism: The Scottish Experience." *Ethnic and Racial Studies* 7, no. 1 (1984): 129–37.

McDowell, Linda. *Gender, Identity and Place: Understanding Feminist Geographies.* Minneapolis: University of Minnesota Press, 1999.

McEachern, Charmaine. *Narratives of Nation: Media, Memory and Representation in the Making of the New South Africa.* New York: Nova Science Publishers, 2002.

McGee, Michael Calvin, and John S. Nelson. "Narrative Reason in Public Argument." *Journal of Communication* 35, no. 4 (1985): 139–55.

Mckenzie George. "The Age of Reason or the Age of Innocence." In *Understanding Social Research: Perspective on Methodology and Practice*, edited by George Mckenzie, Jackie Powell, and Robin Usher, 8–23. London: The Falmer Press, 1997.

McNair, Brian. *An Introduction to Political Communication.* London: Routledge, 1995.

McNulty, Mel. "Media Ethnicization and the International Response to War and Genocide in Rwanda." In Allen and Seaton, *Media of Conflict,* 268–86.

Miller, David. *Market, State and Community.* Oxford: Clarendon Press, 1989.

Miller, Deborah G., and Bryan Martin. "Space and Contentious Politics." *Mobilization: An International Journal* 8, no. 2 (2004): 143–56.

Mink, Louis O. "The Autonomy of Historical Understanding." *History and Theory* 5, no. 1 (1966): 24–47.

Mitchell, Timothy. "Everyday Metaphors of Power." *Theory and Society* 19, no. 1 (1990): 545–77.

Mitchell, W. J. T., ed. *On Narrative.* Chicago: University of Chicago Press, 1980.

Mohammadu, Turi. *Courage and Conviction—New Nigeria: The First 20 Years.* Kaduna: Hudahuda Publishing, 2000.

———. "Introduction." In Mohammadu, *Courage and Conviction*, v–viii.

Mohammed, Danladi Adamu. "Why Newspapers Fail in Northern Nigeria." Paper presented at Graduate Seminar, Centre for Journalism Studies, Wales, February 2002.

Momoh, Abubakar, and Said Adejumobi, eds. *The National Question in Nigeria: Comparative Perspectives.* Surrey, UK: Ashgate, 2002.

Moore, Donald S. "Remapping Resistance: 'Ground for Struggle' and the Politics of Place." In *Geographies of Resistance*, edited by Michael Keith and Steven pile, 87–106. London: Routledge, 1997.

Morel, Edmund Dene. *Affairs of West Africa.* London: William Heinemann, 1902.

Moufee, Chantal, ed. *Gramsci and Marxist Theory.* London: Routledge and Kegan Paul, 1979.

———. "Hegemony and Ideology in Gramsci." In Bennett et al., *Culture, Ideology and Social Process*, 219–34.

Mouton, Johann, and Dian Joubert, eds. *Knowledge and Method in the Human Sciences.* Pretoria: HSRC, 1991.

Mughan, Anthony, and Richard Gunther. "The Media in Democratic and Nondemocratic Regimes: A Multilevel Perspective." In Gunther and Mughan, *Democracy and the Media*, 1–27.

Mumbi, Dennis K. *Communication and Power in Organisations: Discourse, Ideology and Domination.* Norwood, NJ: Ablex, 1988.

Murray, Martin J. "Moralising the Agrarian Question: Concealed Meanings and Competing Master Narratives in the Construction of an Imagined South African Countryside." *Journal of Contemporary African Studies* 14, no. 1 (1996): 5–28.

Mustapha, Abdul Raufu. "The National Question and Radical Politics in Nigeria." *Review of African Political Economy* 13, no. 37 (1986): 81–96.

Naanen, Ben. "Oil-Producing Minorities and the Restructuring of Nigerian Federalism: The Case of the Ogoni People." *Journal of Commonwealth & Comparative Politics* 33, no. 1 (1995): 46–78.

Najmabadi, Afsaneh. "(Un)veiling Feminism." *Social Text* 18, no. 3 (2000): 29–45.

Neuberger, Benjamin. "State and Nation in African Thought." In *Nationalism—A Reader*, edited by J. Hutchinson and A. Smith, 231–36. Oxford: Oxford University Press, 1994.

Neuman, W. Russell, Marion R. Just, and Ann N. Crigler. *Common Knowledge: News and the Construction of Political Meaning.* Chicago: University of Chicago Press, 1992.

Nicholson, I. F. *The Administration of Nigeria, 1900–1960: Men, Methods and Myths.* Oxford: Clarendon Press, 1969.

Nnoli, Okwudiba. *Ethnic Politics in Africa.* Ibadan: Vantage Publishers, 1989.

Nyamnjoh, Francis. "Africa's Media: Democracy and Belonging." In *Media and Identity in Africa,* edited by Kimani Njogu and John Middleton, 62–75. Edinburgh: Edinburgh University Press, 2009.

———. *Africa's Media: Democracy and the Politics of Belonging.* London: Zed Books, 2005.

Obadare, Ebenezer. "In Search of a Public Sphere: The Fundamentalist Challenge to Civil Society in Nigeria." *Patterns of Prejudice* 38, no. 2 (2004): 177–98.

———. "The Press and Democratic Transition in Nigeria: Comparative Notes on the Abacha and Abubakar Transition Programs." *Issue: A Journal of Opinion* 27, no. 1 (1999): 38–40.

Obi, Cyril I. "Globalisation and Local Resistance: The Case of the Ogoni Versus Shell." *New Political Economy* 2, no. 1 (1997): 137–48.

Obotetukudo, Solomon W. *The Inuagural Addresses and Ascenson Speeches of Nigerian Elected and Non-elected Presidents and Prime Minister, 1960–2010.* Lanham, MD: University Press of America, 2011.

Odamah, Aliyu Musa. "Reporting Religion and Enemy Images in the Nigerian Press." *Networking Knowledge: Journal of the MeCCSA Postgraduate Network* 3, no. 1 (2010): 1–13.

O'Donnell, Guillermo, and Philippe C. Schmitter. *Transitions from Authoritarian Rule: Tentative Conclusions about Uncertain Democracies.* Baltimore, MD: Johns Hopkins University Press, 1991.

Oduntan, Oluwatoyin B. "*Iwe Irohin* and the Representation of the Universal in Nineteenth-Century Egbaland." *History in Africa* 32 (2005): 295–305.

Ofeimun, Odia. "Imagination and the City." *Glendora: A Quarterly Review on the Arts* 3, no. 2 (2000): 11–15, 137–41.

Ogundimu, Folu F. "Media and Democracy in Twenty-First Century Africa." In Hyden, Leslie, and Ogundimu, *Media and Democracy in Africa,* 207–37.

Ojo, Emmanuel. "The Mass Media and Sustainable Democratic Values in Nigeria: Possibilitics and Limitations." *Media, Culture & Society* 25 (2003): 821–40.

Okonkwor, Raphael Chude. *The Press and Nigerian Nationalism, 1859–1960.* Minneapolis: University of Minnesota, 1976.

Okonta, Ike, and Oronto Douglas. *Where Vultures Feast: Shell, Human Rights and Oil In the Niger Delta.* New York: Sierra Book Club and Crown Publishers, 2001.

Olagunju, Tunji, Adele Jinadu, and Sam Oyovbaire. *Transition to Democracy in Nigeria, 1985–1993.* London: Safari Books, 1993.

Olagunju, Tunji, Adele Jinadu, and Sam Oyovbaire. *Transition to Democracy in Nigeria (1985–1993).* Ibadan: Spectrum Books, 1993.

Olukotun, Ayo. "Authoritarian State, Crisis of Democratization and the Underground Media in Nigeria." *African Affairs* 101, no. 404 (2002): 317–42.

———. "Media Accountability and Democracy in Nigeria." *African Studies Review* 47, no. 3 (2004): 69–90.

———. "The 1999 Nigerian Transition and the Media." *African Journal of Political Science* 5, no. 2 (2000): 33–44.

———. *Repressive State and Resurgent Media under Nigeria's Military Dictatorship, 1988–1998.* Research Report No. 126. Uppsala: Nordiska Africainestitutet, 2004.

Omoruyi, Omo. *The Tale of June 12: The Betrayal of the Democratic Rights of Nigerians (1993).* London: Press Alliance Network, 1999.

Omu, Fred I. A. *Press and Politics in Nigeria, 1880–1937.* London: Longman, 1978.

Osaghae, Eghosa E. *Crippled Giant: Nigeria since Independence.* London: C. Hurst, 1998.

———. "The Crisis of National Identity in Africa: Clearing the Conceptual Underbush." *Plural Societies* 19, nos. 2–3 (1990): 116–32.

———. "Managing Multiple Minority Problems in a Divided Society: The Nigerian Experience." *Journal of Modern African Studies* 36, no. 1 (1998): 1–24.

———. "The Ogoni Uprising: Oil Politics, Minority Agitation and the Future of the Nigerian State." *African Affairs* 94, no. 376 (1995): 325–44.

Ostergard, Uffe. "'Denationalizing' National History—The Comparative Study of Nation-State." *Culture and History* 9, no. 10 (1991): 9–41.

Overing, Joanna. "The Role of Myth: An Anthropological Perspective, or the Reality of the Really Made-Up." In Hoskin and Schopflin, *Myths and Nationhood*, 1–18.

Owolabi, E. O. "Herbert Macaulay's *Lagos Daily News* and the Development of Nigerian Nationalism." BA essay. University of Ibadan, 1984.

Oyovbaire, S. "The Media and Democratic Process in Nigeria." Paper presented at the National Institute for Policy and Strategic Studies, Kuru, Jos, Nigeria, August 7, 2001.

Paasi, A. "Constructing Territories, Boundaries and Regional Identities." In *Contested Territory: Border Disputes at the Edge of the Former Soviet Empire*, edited by Thoman Forsberg, 42–61. Aldershot: Edward Elgar, 2000.

Papastergiadis, Nikos. "Reading Dissemination." *Millennium: Journal of International Studies* 20, no. 3 (1991): 507–19.

Pasternack, Gerhard. "Interpretation as Methodical Procedure—Methodological Fundaments of Normed Hermenuetics." *Poetics* 12 (1983): 185–205.

Pavel, Thomas G. "Some Remarks on Narrative Grammars." *Poetics*, no. 4 (1973): 5–30.

Pearson, Raymon. "Separatism: Nationalist Theory and Historical Practice." In Anderson, Bull, and Duvold, *Separatism*, 17–26.

Pêcheux, Michel. *Language, Semantics and Ideology.* Translated by Harbans Nagpal. New York: St. Martin's Press, 1982.

Penrose, Jan. "Nations, States and Homelands: Territory and Territoriality in Nationalist Thought." *Nations and Nationalism* 8, no. 3 (2002): 277–97.

Perham, Margery. "Foreword." In Awolowo, *Path to Nigerian Freedom*, 9–16.

———. *Lugard: The Years of Authority, 1895–1945.* vol. 2. London: Collins, 1960.

Pfaff-Czarnecka, Joanna. "Ritual, Distances, Territorial Divisions: Land, Power and Identity in Central Nepal" In Saltman, *Land and Territoriality*, 113–34.

Pfeiffer, Ludwig K. "Interpretation: Anthropological and Ecology of Mind." *Poetics* 12 (1983): 165–83.

Phelan, James. *Narrative as Rhetoric: Technique, Audiences, Ethics, Ideology.* Columbus: Ohio State University Press, 1996.

Philip, Mark. "Foucault on Power: A Problem in Radical Translation?" *Political Theory* 11 (1983): 29–52.

Phillips, Louise. "Media Discourse and the Danish Monarchy: Reconciling Egalitarianism and Royalism." *Media, Culture & Society* 21 (1999): 221–45.

Pile, Steven, and Michael Keith, eds. *Geographies of Resistance.* London: Routledge, 1997.

Pile, Steve and Nigel Thrift. "Conclusions: Spacing and the Subject." In Steve Pile and Nigel Thrift, eds., *Mapping the Subject: Geographies of Cultural Transformation*, 371–80. New York, NY: Routledge, 1995.

Pillai, Poonam. "Tracking the Nation: Discourses of Internationalism and Transnational Agricultural Corporations." *Media, Culture & Society* 20, no. 4 (1998): 593–608.

Polkinghorne, Donald E. *Narrative Knowing and the Human Sciences.* Albany: State University of New York Press, 1988.

Postill, John. *Media and Nation Building: How the Iban Became Malaysian.* New York: Berghahn Books, 2006.

Prince, Gerald. *A Grammar of Stories.* The Hague: Mouton, 1973.

———. "Narrative Pragmatics, Message, and Point." *Poetics* 12, no. 6 (1983): 527–36.

———. "Narrative Signs and Tangents." *Diacritics* (Fall 1974): 2–8.

Quintilian. *The Institutio Oratoria of Quintilian.* 4 vols. Translated by H. E. Butler. Cambridge, MA: Harvard University Press, 1966.

Rahnema, Majid. "Power and Regenerative Processes in Micro-Spaces." *International Social Science Journal* 117 (1988): 361–75.

Ranger, Terence. "The Invention of Tradition Revisited: The Case of Colonial Africa." In *Legitimacy and the State in Twentieth-Century Africa: Essays in Honour of A. H. M. Kirk-Greene*, edited by Terence Ranger and Olufemi Vaughan, 62–111. London: Macmillan Press, 1993.

Rapport, Nigel, and Andrew Dawson. "The Topic and the Book." In *Migrants of Identity: Perceptions of Home in a World of Movement*, edited by Nigel Rapport and Andrew Dawson, 3–17. London: Berg, 1998.

Renan, Ernest. *Qu'est-ce qu'une nation?* Translated by Ethan Rundell. Paris: Presses-Pocket, 1992.

Rhoodie, Nic, and Iam Liebenberg, eds. *Democratic Nation-Building in South Africa*. Pretoria, South Africa: HSRC Publishers, 1994.

———. "Preface." In Rhoodie and Liebenberg, *Democratic Nation-Building in South Africa*, 1–5.

Richards, Robert J. "Review of *Narrative Knowing and the Human Sciences* by Donald E. Polkinghorne." *American Journal of Sociology* 95, no. 1 (1989): 258–60.

Ricouer, Paul. *The Conflict of Interpretations: Interpretation Theory*. Edited by Don Ihde. Evanston, IL: Northwestern University Press, 1974.

———. *Hermeneutics and Human Sciences: Essays on Language, Action and Interpretation*. Edited and translated by John B. Thompson. Cambridge: Cambridge University Press, 1981.

———. *Interpretation Theory: Discourse and the Surplus of Meaning*. Fort Worth: Texas Christian University Press, 1976.

———. *Lectures on Ideology and Utopia*. Edited by George H. Taylor. New York: Columbia University Press, 1986.

———. *The Rule of Metaphor: Multi-disciplinary Studies of the Creation of Meaning in Language*. Translated by Robert Czerny with Kathleen McLaughlin and John Costello. London: Routledge and Keagan Paul, 1978.

———. *Time and Narrative*. Vol. 1. Translated by Kathleen McLaughlin and David Pellauer. Chicago: University of Chicago Press, 1983.

Robinson, Francis. "Nation Formation: The Brass Thesis and Muslim Separatism." *Journal of Commonwealth and Comparative Politics* 15, no. 3 (1977): 215–30.

Rorty, Richard. "Method, Social Science and Social Hope." In Gibbons, *Interpreting Politics*, 241–59.

Rosland, Sissel. "Constructing Legitimacy in Political Discourse in the Early Phases of Trouble." In *Political Discourse and Conflict Resolution: Debating Peace in Northern Ireland*, edited by Katy Hayward and Catherine O'Donnell, 16–30. New York: Routledge, 2011.

Rotberg, R. I. "African Nationalism: Concept or Confusion?" *Journal of Modern African Studies* 4 (1966): 33–46.

Routledge, Paul. "A Spatiality of Resistances: Theory and Practice in Nepal's Revolution of 1990." In Pile and Keith, *Geographies of Resistance*, 68–86.

Russell, Betrand. *Power.* London: Unwin Books, 1975 [1938].

Rustow, D. A. *World of Nations.* Washington, DC: The Brookings Institution, 1967.

Sacks, R. *Human Territoriality: Its Theory and History.* Cambridge: Cambridge University Press, 1986.

Said, Edward W. *Culture and Imperialism.* London: Vintage Publishers, 1994.

———. *The World, the Text and the Critic.* Cambridge, MA: Harvard University Press, 1983.

Salamone, Frank. "Playing at Nationalism: Nigeria, a Nation of 'Ringers.'" *Geneve Afrique* 30, no. 1 (1992): 55–75.

Saltman, Michael. "Introduction." In *Land and Territoriality,* edited by Michael Saltman, 1–8. Oxford: Berg, 2002.

Saro-Wiwa, Ken. *A Month and a Day: A Detention Diary.* Ibadan: Spectrum Books, 1995.

Sawyer, Keith R. "A Discourse on Discourse: An Archeological History of an Intellectual Concept." *Cultural Studies* 16, no. 3 (2002): 433–56.

Scammell, Margaret, and Holli Semetko, eds. *The Media, Journalism and Democracy.* Surrey, England: Ashgate, 2000.

Schlesinger, Philip. *Media, State and Nation: Political Violence and Collective Identities.* London: Sage Publications, 1991.

Schmid, Herman. "On the Origin of Ideology." *Acta Sociological* 24 (1981): 57–73.

Schmidt, Siegfried J. "Interpretation Today—Introductory Remarks." *Poetics* 12, nos. 2–3 (1983): 71–81.

Schmitter, Philippe C. *Some Propositions about Civil Society and the Consolidation of Democracy.* Vienna: Institut für Hohere Studien, 1993.

Schöpflin, George. "The Functions of Myth and a Taxonomy of Myths." In Hoskin and Schöpflin, *Myths and Nationhood,* 19–35.

Schramm, Wilbur. *Mass Media and National Development: The Role of Information in Developing Countries.* Stanford, CA: Stanford University Press, 1964.

Schudson, Michael. "Sending Political Message: Lessons from the American 1790s." *Media, Culture & Society* 19 (1997): 311–30.

Schütz, Alfred. *The Phenomenology of the Social World.* Translated by George Walsh and Frederick Lehnert. Evanston, IL: Northwestern University Press, 1967.

Scott, James. *Refashioning Futures: Criticism after Postcoloniality.* Princeton, NJ: Princeton University Press, 1999.

Sewell, William H., Jr. "Introduction: Narrative and Social Identities." *Social Science History* 16, no. 3 (1992): 479–89.

———. "A Theory of Structure: Duality, Agency and Transformation." *American Journal of Sociology* 98, no. 1 (1992): 1–29.

Sherwood, Steven. "Narrating the Social." *Journal of Narratives and Life Histories* 4, nos. 1–2 (1994): 69–88.

Shook, John R. *Dewey's Empirical Theory of Knowledge and Reality.* Nashville, TN: Vanderbilt University Press, 2000.

Shuman, Amy. *Storytelling Rights: The Uses of Oral and Written Texts By Urban Adolescents.* New York: Cambridge University Press, 1986.

Sinnott, Richard, and E. E. Davis. "Political Mobilisation, Political Institutionalization and the Maintenance of Ethnic Conflict." *Ethnic and Racial Studies* 4, no. 4 (1981): 398–414.

Sklar, Richard. *Nigerian Political Parties: Power in an Emergent African Nation.* Princeton, NJ: Princeton University Press, 1963.

Slaatta, Tore. "Media and Democracy in the Global Order." *Media, Culture & Society* 20 (1998): 335–44.

Slater, Ian. "Orwell, Marcuse and the Language of Politics." *Political Studies* 23, no. 4 (1974): 459–73.

Smith, Anthony D. *The Ethnic Origins of Nations.* Oxford: Blackwell, 1986.

———. *National Identity.* Reno: University of Nevada Press, 1991.

———. "Nationalism: A Trend Report and Annotated Bibliography." *Current Sociology* 21, no. 3 (1973): 1–178.

———. "The Nation: Invented, Imagined, Reconstructed?" *Millennium: The Journal of International Studies* 20, no. 3 (1991): 353–68.

———. "The Origins of Nations." *Ethnic and Racial Studies* 12, no. 3 (1989): 340–67.

———. *Theories of Nationalism.* New York: Holmes & Meier, 1971.

Smith, Dorothy E. *The Conceptual Practices of Power: A Feminist Sociology of Knowledge.* Toronto: University of Toronto Press, 1990.

Smith, Neil. "Contours of a Spatialized Politics: Homeless Vehicles and the Production of Geographical Scale." *Social Text* 33 (1992): 54–81.

Solomon, Hussein. "Counter-Terrorism in Nigeria." *The RUSI Journal* 157, no. 4 (2012): 6–11.

Somers, Margaret R. "The Narrative Construction of Identity: A Relational and Network Approach." *Theory and Society* 23, no. 5 (1994): 605–49.

Soyinka, Wole. *Open Sore of a Continent: A Personal Narrative of the Nigerian Crisis.* Oxford: Oxford University Press, 1996.

Spitulnik, Debra. *Producing National Publics: Audience Constructions and the Electronic Media in Zambia.* Durham, NC: Duke University Press, 1991.

———. "Radio Cycles and Recycling in Zambia: Public Words, Popular Critiques, and National Communities." *Passages*, no. 8 (1994): 10, 12, 14–16.

———. "The Social Circulation of Media Discourse and the Mediation of Communities." *Journal of Linguistic Anthropology* 6, no. 2 (1996): 161–87.

Ssewakiryanga, Richard. "'New Kids on the Blocks': African-American Music and Ugandan Youth." *CODESTRIA Bulletin*, nos. 1–2 (1999): 24–28.

Steinmetz, George. "Reflections on the Role of Social Narratives in Working Class Formation: Narrative Theories in the Social Sciences." *Social Science History* 16, no. 3 (1992): 489–516.

Steinmetz, Horst. "On Neglecting the Social Function of Interpretation in the Study of Literature." *Poetics* 12 (1983): 151–64.

Storey, David. *Territory: The Claiming of Space*. Harlow, UK: Prentice Hall/ Pearson Education, 2001.

Styan, David. "Misrepresenting Ethiopia and the Horn of Africa? Constraints and Dilemmas of Current Reporting." In Allen and Seaton, *Media of Conflict*, 287–304.

Suberu, Rotimi T. *Ethnic Minority Conflicts and Governance in Nigeria*. Ibadan: Spectrum Books, 1996.

———. "Religion: A View of South." In Diamond, Kirk-Greene, and Oyediran, *Transition without End*, 477–508.

Sweet, James H. "South Africans Exist: Identity, Nationalism, and Democracy." *Safundi: The Journal of South African and American Studies* 11, nos. 1–2 (2010): 141–48.

Tagil, Sven. "Ethnic and National Minorities in the Nordic Nation-Building Process: Theoretical and Conceptual Premises." In *Ethnicity and Nation Building in the Nordic World*, edited by Sven Tagil, 8–32. London: Hurst, 1997.

Tamarkin, M. *Nationalism, Nation-Building and Society in Africa: Fateful Connections*. Cape Town: Centre for African Studies, University of Cape Town, 1992.

Taylor, Charles. "Interpretation and the Sciences of Man." *Review of Metaphysics* 25, no. 1 (1971): 3–51.

———. "Language and Human Nature." In Gibbons, *Interpreting Politics*, 101–32.

Taylor, Peter, and Colin Flint. *Political Geography*. 4th ed. London: Pretice Hall, 2000.

Taylor, Ralph B. *Human Territoriality Functioning: An Empirical, Evolutionary Perspective on Individual and Small Group Territorial Cognitions, Behaviours and Consequence*. Cambridge: Cambridge University Press, 1988.

Tennekoon, Serena. "Newspaper Nationalism: Sinhala Identity as Historical Discourse." In *Sri Lanka: History and the Roots of Conflict*, edited by Jonathan Spencer, 205–26. New York: Routledge, 1990.

Thompson, Allan, ed. "Introduction." In Thompson, *Media and Rwanda Genocide*, 1–11.

———. *The Media and Rwanda Genocide*. London: Pluto Press, 2007.

Thompson, John B. *Ideology and Modern Culture: Critical Theory in the Era of Mass Communication.* Cambridge: Polity Press, 1990.

———. *The Media and Modernity: A Social Theory of the Media.* Stanford, CA: Stanford University Press, 1995.

Thussu, Daya Kishan, and Des Freedman. "Introduction." In *War and the Media: Reporting Conflict 24/7*, edited by Daya Kishan Thussu and Des Freedman, 1–12. London: Sage Publications, 2003.

Tironi, Eugenio, and Guillermo Sunkel. "The Modernization of Communications: The Media in the Transition to Democracy in Chile." In Gunther and Mughan, *Democracy and the Media*, 165–94.

Tomaselli, Ruth, Keyan Tomaselli, and Johan Muller. "A Conceptual Framework for Media Analysis." In *Narrating the Crisis: Hegemony and the South African Press*, edited by Keyan Tomaselli, Ruth Tomaselli, and Johan Muller, 5–21. Johannesburg: Richard Lyon, 1987.

Tuan, Yi-fu. *Space and Place: The Perspective of Experience.* Minneapolis: University of Minnesota Press, 1977.

Tuchman, Gaye. *Making News: A Study in the Construction of Reality.* London: The Free Press, 1978.

Turner, Victor. *Drama, Fields and Metaphors.* Ithaca, NY: Cornell University Press, 1974.

Uduigwome, Isaiah Ozolua. "The Role of the West African Pilot in the Nigerian Nationalist Struggle." MA thesis, University of Ibadan, 1987.

Van de Goor, Loc, Kumar Rupesinghe, and Paul Sciarone, eds. *Between Development and Destruction: An Enquiry into the Causes of Conflict in Postcolonial States.* London: Macmillan Press, 1996.

Van der Zweerde, Evert. "Friendship and the Political." *Critical Review of International Social and Political Philosophy* 10, no. 2 (2007): 147–65.

Van Dijk, Teun A. "Semantic Macro-Structures and Knowledge Frames in Discourse Comprehension." In *Cognitive Processes in Comprehension*, edited by Marcel Adams Just and Patricia A. Carpenter. Hillsdale, NJ: Erlbaum, 1977.

———. "Social Cognition, Social Power and Social Discourse." Introduction to the Symposium on Discourse and Social Psychology, International Conference on Social Psychology and Language, Bristol, England, July 20–24, 1987.

Van Lieu, Joshua, and John Paul Jones. "Discursive Limits to Agency." In *Marginalized Places and Populations: A Structurationist Agenda*, edited by D. Wilson and J. O. Huff, 149–64. Westport, CT. Praeger, 1994.

Van Teeffelen, Toine. "Metaphors and the Middle East: Crisis Discourse on Gaza." In *The Decolonization of Imagination: Culture, Knowledge and Power*, edited by Jan Neverdeen Piertese and Bhikhu Parekh. London: Zed Books Ltd, 1995.

Van Valin, Robert D., Jr. "Meaning and Interpretation." *Journal of Pragmatics* 4 (1980): 213–31.

Verdery, Katherine. *National Ideology under Socialism: Identity and Cultural Politics in Ceausescu's Romania.* Berkeley: University of California Press, 1991.

Vickers, Michael. *A Nation Betrayed: Nigeria and the Minorities Commission of 1957.* Trenton, NJ: Africa World Press, 2010.

Volosinov, V. N. *Marxism and the Philosophy of Language.* Translated by Ladislav Matejka and R. I. Titunik. Cambridge, MA: Harvard University Press, 1973.

Volosinov, V. N. "The Study of Ideologies and Philosophy of Language." In Bennett et al., *Culture, Ideology and Social Process,* 145–52.

Wagner-Pacifici, Robin and Barry Schwartz. "The Vietnam Veterans Memorial: Commemorating a Difficult Past," *American Journal of Sociology* 97, no. 2 (1991): 376–420.

Walker, Andrew. "What Is Boko Haram?" Special Report 308. United States Institute of Peace, June 2012.

Walker, R. B. J. "State Sovereignty and the Articulation of Political Space/Time." *Millennium: The Journal of International Studies* 20, no. 3 (1991): 445–61.

Walsh, W. H. *Philosophy of History: An Introduction.* New York: Harper Torchbooks, 1967.

Wardle, Claire, and Emily West. "The Press as Agents of Nationalism in the Queen's Golden Jubilee: How British Newspapers Celebrated a Media Event." *European Journal of Communication* 19, no. 2 (2004): 195–214.

Watenpaugh, Keith David. "Cleansing the Cosmopolitan City: Historicism, Journalism and the Arab Nation in the Post-Ottoman Eastern Mediterranean." *Social History* 30, no. 1 (2005): 1–24.

Watts, Michael. "Black Gold, White Heat: State Violence, Local Resistance, and the National Question in Nigeria." In Pile and Keith, *Geographies of Resistance,* 33–67.

Webster, Frank. *Theories of Information Society.* London: Routledge, 1996.

Welch, Claude E., Jr. "The Ogoni and Self-Determination: Increasing Violence in Nigeria." *Journal of Modern African Studies* 33, no. 4 (1995): 635–50.

White, Hyden. *The Content of the Form: Narrative Discourse and Historical Representation.* Baltimore, MD: Johns Hopkins University Press, 1987.

———. "The Value of Narrativity in the Representation of Reality." In Mitchell, *On Narrative,* 1–23.

Williams, Colin. "Social Mobilization and Nationalism in Multi-cultural Societies." *Ethnic and Racial Studies* 5, no. 3 (1982): 349–65.

Wittman, Donald. "Various Concepts of Power: Equivalence among Ostensibly Unrelated Approaches." *British Journal of Political Science* 6, no. 4 (1976): 449–62.

Young, Crawford. *The African Colonial State in Comparative Perspective.* New Haven, CT: Yale University Press, 1994.

Yumul, Arus, and Amut Özkirimli. "Reproducing the Nation: 'Banal Nationalism' in the Turkish Press." *Media, Culture & Society* 22 (2002): 787–804.

Yun, Ma Shu. "Ethnonationalism, Ethnic Nationalism, and Mini-nationalism: A Comparison of Connor, Smith and Snyder." *Ethnic and Racial Studies* 13, no. 4 (1990): 527–41.

Yuval-Davis, Nira. *Gender and Nation.* London: Sage Books, 1998.

Zachernuk, Philip S. *Colonial Subjects: An African Intelligentsia and Atlantic Ideas.* Charlottesville: University Press of Virginia, 2000.

Zhao, Dingxin. "State-Society Relations and the Discourses and Activities of the 1989 Beijing Student Movement." *American Journal of Sociology* 105, no. 6 (2000): 1592–1632.

Zubaida, Sami. "Nations: Old and New: Comments on Anthony D. Smith's 'The Myth of the Modern Nation and the Myths of Nations.'" *Ethnic and Racial Studies* 12, no. 3 (1989): 329–39.

Index

Page numbers in italics refer to figures and tables.

Abacha, Sani: Abiola attack against regime of, 172; Abiola takeover, request to allow, 178; Abiola's endorsement, initial of, 170; administration and regime supporters, 169, 171; calls for sacrifice and patriotism by, 165; collapse of regime, 150, 213; constitutional conference held under, 284; coup by, 174; death of, 191; imprisonment, assassination, and exile under, 191–92; Interim National Government, role in, 149; newspaper attitudes concerning, 166; newspaper support for, 167; Ogoni crisis during regime of, 274, 275, 276–77; in power, 169; in presidential election, 1993 aftermath, 175, 179–80, 181, 182–83, 186; problems faced by, 177; regime impact, 193

Abdullazeez, Yakubu, 162

Abiola, Moshood: Abacha praised by, 174; Abacha regime attacked by, 172; death of, 191, 198; generals commended by, 165; in hiding, 182; imprisonment of, 181, 183–84, 185; limitations of, 171; mandate of, 166, 169, 170, 174–75, 191; newspaper owned by, 241; Nigeria near disaster according to, 171; Obasanjo opposed to interests

of, 192; as party flag bearer, 159; presidency, repercussions, perceived in event of, 164; presidential election annulment, reaction to, 150, 164; presidential election victory, 1993, *148*, 149, 161, 162, 167, 174, 178; presidential election victory reclaiming attempt, 177, 178–79, 180, 182–83; press support for, 178–79; running mate, 169–70

Abubukar, Abdulsalami, 191

Abubukar, Ahmadu, 201–2

Abubukar, Balarabe, 183

Abuja, capital move to, 84, 85–86, 100

Abu-Lughod, Lila, 21, 29, 296n92

Aburi Accord, 113, 220

Accra-Lagos union, proposed, 95, 307n67

action, knowledge relationship to, 33

action concepts, 31–32

Action Group (AG): central and regional government dealings with, 114; crisis, 111; ethno-regional organization around, 47; formation of, 58, 60; independence target date, position on, 69, 100; Lagos status, position on, 95, 98, 101; newspaper coverage of, 59, 60, 61, 65, 66, 79–80; newspapers

Action Group (AG)—*(cont'd)*
   as mouthpiece for, 109, 110;
   Nigerian nationhood, position
   on, 4–5; northern region,
   turning to, 79; regional interests
   represented by, 59; rivalry with
   National Council of Nigeria
   and the Cameroons (NCNC),
   55, 63–65; self-government
   campaign, involvement in,
   68–71, 74
actors and agency, deleting, 139
Adamawa, imperialism in, 56
Adelabu, Adekoge, 144
Affairs of West Africa (Morel), 56
affiliation, 88
Africa: nation as imagined in, 19;
   white colonial regimes in, 239,
   326n53
African Concord magazine, 241
African National Congress (ANC),
   10
African politics, long-term, print
   media role in, 7
Afrikaners, 239, 261, 326n53,
   329n10
Agbaje, Adigun, 23, 24, 233, 265
Agu, Emma, 165, 316n72
Aguda, Akintola, 171, 250
Ajasin, Adekunle, 180
Ajayi, Ade J. F., 246
Ake, Claude, 170
Akilu, Haliru, 238
Akintola, Samuel Ladoke:
   AG delegation led by, 48;
   assassination of, 111, 114–15;
   Azikiwe, Nnamdi, relations with,
   49–50; newspaper support for,
   69; as NNDP cofounder, 110
Akintoye (King of Lagos), 90
Alakija, Oluwole, 94–95
All People's Party (APP), 191
Alliance for Democracy (AD), 191

All-Nigeria Constitutional
   Conference, 141, 142
amalgamation of protectorates
   (Nigeria): aftermath of, 173;
   history of events since, 219;
   implementing, 12; "mistake
   of 1914," 72, 195, 196, 202,
   213, 217, 284; national unity
   efforts since, 214; Nigerian
   union basis questioned since,
   222; opposition to, 14, 72; press
   during, 265; press narratives on,
   5; theory *versus* reality, 13
amelioration, 267
Amnesty International, 264
analytical philosophy, 31
Anderson, Benedict, 7, 19, 232–33
Annan, Kofi, 191
anticolonial struggle, 92, 171
antiestablishment press, 265
Anyaoku, Emeka, 191
apartheid, 10, 21–22, 239, 326n53
Arewa Republic, 218, 219
army chiefs, proposed meeting of,
   141
arts, 51
Asia, 19, 239, 326n53
Askanist Movement, 75
Askew, Kelly, 22–23
Association for Better Nigeria
   (ABN), 160
Audu, Bala Dan, 153
Auta, Ibrahim, 274
authoritarian era nation-building,
   188
autonomous individual, liberal
   democracy emphasis on, 21
Awolowo, Obafemi: central and
   regional government dealings
   with, 114; at constitutional
   conference, 128; defenders of,
   61; "ethnic boosting" criticized
   by, 93–94; fight for soul of NYM,

58; imprisonment of, 111, 119; Lagos status, views on, 83, 95, 98, 99, 100, 101; newspaper criticism of, 56, 60, 61, 63; newspaper owned by, 49, 109; newspapers as mouthpiece for, 109, 110; "Nigeria" idea contested by, 13, 16; Obasanjo opposed to interests of, 192; as opposition leader, 110; release of, 122–23, 126; secession, talk of possible, 212; as self-government supporter, 69, 70; trial involving, 155; unitary government supported by, 124; as Yoruba leader, 16, 128

Ayok, Juri Babang, 236

Azikiwe, Nnamdi ("Zik"): Akintola, Samuel Ladoke, relations with, 49–50; background, 92–93; constitutional talks, participation in, 78; eastern secession, warning against, 140, 313n143; election defeat, newspaper commentary following, 64–65; emergence and ascendancy of, 93; fight for soul of NYM, 58; as Ibo leader, 62, 66, 94–95; on Ibo nation and Nigerian unity, 15; Lagos ownership, position on, 102; Lagos status, position on, 95, 100; as nationalist leader, 92–93; newspaper as mouthpiece for, 109, 110; newspaper criticism of, 61, 63, 64, 67–68, 78; newspaper owned by, 24, 49, 93; newspaper support of, 60, 78; NYM collapse blamed on, 63; as president, 110, 111; press pioneers cited by, 19; on self-government, 7, 48; tax policies of, 58; unification, position on, 116; unitary to

federalism support switch made by, 123–24; Yoruba-Igbo tension, role in, 62

Babangida, Ibrahim: Abacha, Sani compared to, 183; ascent to power, 149; capitol moved during regime of, 84, 305n4; election, 1993 annulled by, 149–50, 167, 173, 191; exit from power, 165, 181, 193; press coverage of, 159–60, 162–63, 168; prodemocracy forces, response to, 155; regime, narratives, of, 169; regime impact, 193; transition to civil rule under, 149–50, 154, 155; Zango-Kataf crisis trials under, 238–39

Badey, Albert, 271

Balewa, Sir Abubakar Tafawa: administration aftermath, 114; assassination of, 111, 131, 138, 313n134; collapse of regime, 213; *Nigerian Citizen* as mouthpiece of, 109; on Nigerian unity, supposed, 16; as prime minister, 110, 115; southern counterparts battled by, 200

Bali, Domkat, 157–58

Bamaiyi, Ishaya, 193

banal nationalism, 7

Banal Nationalism (Billig), 11

Barnett, Cliff, 146

Barthes, Roland, 290

Bauchi, 56

Bello, Sir Ahmadu: death of, 111, 131; legacy of, 249; on mistake of 1914, 195, 214, 284; newspaper as mouthpiece of, 110; newspaper criticism of, 72, 73; newspaper founded by, 110; newspaper praise of, 167, 169;

Bello, Sir Ahmadu—*(cont'd)*
Nigerian Citizen as mouthpiece of,
109; Nigerian self-government,
caution concerning, 3–4,
47–48; Sharia-inspired crusade
compared to that of, 208;
southern counterparts battled
by, 201
Bennett, W. Lance, 16, 17, 18, 68,
193
Bhabha, Homi, 26, 289
Biafra, Republic of, 113, 145, 158,
202, 210, 212, 216, 221, 270
Billig, Michael, 11–12
binaries, construction of simplistic,
107
Bini (Benins), 66, 67, 90, 102
black people of the world, spiritual
haven for, 81–82
Bogdanour, Vernon, 261
Boko Haram, 285–86
Bolger, Jim, 277
Bormann, Ernest G., 17, 18
Boro, Isaac Adaka, 259
Bosnia, 173
boundaries, qualities of, 90,
306n32
Boyce, Brendan, 10, 146
British colonial government,
69–70, 90, 119
British Mirror Group, 49
British parliamentary Human
Rights Group, 264
Buhari, Muhammadu, 286
Buhari, Muhammed, 218
Burton, Sir Richard, 91

Calhoun, Craig C., 228
CAN (Christian Association of
Nigeria), 152
Candido, 182
capital city, nationalizing, 28
"capitalist" (term), 58

capitol: Nigeria without, 98, 99;
requirements for, 99–100; shift
in, 84, 85–86
Carruthers, Susan, 108, 140, 143
case studies, 27, 28
Castells, Manuel, 205
Catholic Herald, 153
cattle rearing, 51
Central African countries, 108
Central State, 66
centrality of territory, 83, 84, 86
characters, 241–42
Chatterjee, Partha, 19
Chick, John D., 23, 24
Chipkin, Ivor, 10, 146, 147
Christianity, 203
Christians: Hausa attacks on, 237–
38; Islamic hegemony imposed
on, 234; Islamization feared by,
206; in Kaduna, 205; Kataf, 158,
315n41; Muslims, clash with,
205, 209, 238
Chukwumerije, Uche, 155
cities, nature of, 91–92
citizenry-based conceptualization of
territoriality, 232
civic institutions, 21
civic nation, 188
civil justice, 206
civil law, 206
civil society, 228
civilians, psychological mobilization
for, 108
class, 39, 259
class relations, 40–41
Clifford, Sir Hugh, 84–86, 195
Coleman, James, 93
"collapse thesis," 189
collective action, 6, 35–36
collective fine, proposed for
northern region mass killings,
144
collective identity, 6, 12, 116, 205

colonial boundaries, 9

colonial era: fault lines created in, 290; issues defining, 28; minority ethnic groups during, 265–66; and postcolonial era compared, 24

colonial Nigeria, capitol of, 84

colonial rule, campaign to end, 3

colonial states, 9

colonialism (British colonialism), 4, 12, 19, 53, 54

Colville, Gilbert, 51

commerce, 12

Commission of Inquiry into the Fears of Minorities and the Means of Allaying Them, 258

Committee for National Understanding (CUU), 151

common interests and values, 89, 104

common value system, 8

commonalities, presenting opposing, 7–8

Commonwealth Summit, 277–78

communicative discourses (term), 147

Communist Party, 39

"communist-minded" (term), 54

communities of discourse (term), 228, 280

community, loyalty to symbolic, 187

Condit, Celeste M., 17, 18, 66, 266

confederation, call for, 215, 217

conflict, narratives of, 68, 107

Connor, Walker, 187, 188, 288

consciousness, origin of, 33

consensus, construction of, 87, 104

consent, 87, 104

constitution, 118, 195, 200, 205

constitutional conference, 1960s, 128–29

constitutional conference, 1994: calls for, 154, 157, 158, 166, 192, 198; national survival requiring more than, 173; outcome of, 178; potential outcome of, 175–77. *See also* Sovereign National Conference

constitutional conference, 2014, 283–84, 285

Constitutional Conference Election, 176

constitutional talks, 1953, 76–80, 101

content-function interaction, 17

cosmopolitanism, 205

Cottle, Simon, 107

countercoup, 1966, 120–21, 122, 215

counterhegemony, 86, 89

counternarratives, 18, 29, 289–90

country, nation *versus*, 194

coup, 1966, 113–14, 122, 123, 131

coup, 1990, 193–94

Cox, Kevin R., 230

Creoles, 92

criminal justice, 206

crisis, narration demanded by, 254, 268

Crowder, Michael, 90

Cudjoe Commission of Inquiry, 235

cultural factors, 11

cultural groups, 21

cultural validation, 109

culturo-historical diversity, 21

Dahl, Robert, 25

Daily Champion: Abacha regime, commentary on, 180; Babangida, Maryam praised by, 169; constitutional conference, commentary on, 176, 177; Interim National Government supported by, 165; narrative, analyzing, 150; newspapers, other criticized by, 186; Nigerian

Daily Champion—*(cont'd)*
nation extinction fears seen
as warmongering by, 166;
Obasanjo, commentary on, 180;
presidential election, 1993 and
aftermath, commentary on, 161,
162, 177, 179, 182
"daily plebiscite," 7
Daily Service (newspaper): in
case studies, 27; comforting
fantasies spun by, 68; on
eve of independence, 49;
founding of, 61; Lagos status,
position on, 95, 99, 100, 101,
102–3; as mouthpiece, 109;
nationhood advocated by, 82;
NCNC criticized by, 64; on
NCNC-AG alliance, 77; Nigerian
independence, position on,
103; NYP crisis covered by, 63;
ownership narrative of, 83–84;
on political figures, 63, 67–68,
78; on regionalism, 62; self-
government advocated by, 76;
self-government campaign
impact on narrative of, 69,
70–71, 72, 74–75; Yoruba-Igbo
relations, commentary on, 61
Daily Times (newspaper): in
case studies, 27; on eve of
independence, 49; nationhood
advocated by, 82; on Nigerian
independence, 54; Nigerian
nationhood advocated by,
5, 12
Dambazau, Malam Lawan, 172
Dare, Olatunji, 162
Davies, H. O., 61, 81–82, 83
Dawson, Andrew, 241
de Tracy, Destutt, 36, 37
Dear, Michael, 235
Degenaar, Johan, 8–9, 188
degradation, 267

democracy: concept of, 161;
creation of, 188; essentialization
of, 147; national democratic
life, dangers to, 190; nation-
building, reconciling with, 146;
press commentary on, 160, 161;
press/media role in, 223, 224;
questions of, 189; requirements
for, 162; struggle for, 10;
transition to, 170; and wrath of
ages, 202–4
democratic crisis, narratives on,
189
democratic culture, challenge of
creating, 9, 188
democratic discourse, 149
democratic era nation-building,
188
democratic freedom, 147
democratic pluralism, 21
democratic press, 223
democratic rule, restoration of,
194–95
democratic society, 146
democratization, 147, 159
democratization agenda, 147
dependence, spaces of, 230
depth hermeneutics, 31, 32
Derrida, Jacques, 26
devastation/despoliation theme,
269
dialectic discourse, goal of, 266
dialogue, 224
Dick, Nottingham, 259
Dienstag, Joshua, 17, 287
differentiation, 158
discursive territoriality, 227–28,
257
dissent, 87, 104
Diya, Oladipo, 165, 186
dog (term), 164
domain, 32
dominance, 87

dominant groups, 8
dominant-marginal relations, 280
domination: defined, 41; fears of, 117–18; hegemony and, 87; narratives on, 158; in postcolonial states, 10–11; press and, 13, 117–18; resistance to, 40; social and political consciousness in context of, 17; struggle for or against, 282; symbolic construction of, 139; types of, 40
domination, relations of: analysis of, 41, 299n47; collective identity and, 116; establishing, 65; euphemization and, 134; expression and counterexpression of, 29; identifying, 28; ideology and, 39–40; individuals and groups embedded in, characterization of, 54; Marxism and, 33–34; meaning intersection with, 41, 97; meaning mobilization in service of power in context of, 71; national unity and nation-building in context of, 33; parameters of, 28; press and, 29; theory of, 20
"dominion" (term), 54
Donnan, Hastings, 230
Doornbos, Martin, 8
Dosunmu (King of Lagos), 90
double hermeneutics (defined), 32
Dröge, Franz, 33–34
duties, 232
Dutinma, Mohammed Sani, 215

eastern region: criticism of, 69, 127, 129; in First Republic foiled coup, 111–12; Lagos status, position on, 77, 96; Lagos ties of, 102; leadership, 15, 62, 63, 68, 118, 120, 122, 135–36; military intervention proposed for, 140; minority agitations in, 142; newspapers as mouthpiece for, 109, 110, 113, 194; Nigerian crisis and, 136, 140; Nigerian independence backed by, 71; northern region killings, response to, 131; northerners in, 132, 137; political party representation, 47; secession, proposed of, 139–40, 141
easterners in northern region, killing of, 130, 132, 135, 138, 139
economic crisis, 175
Edebwin, D. V., 102, 307n96
Edelman, Murray, 16, 17, 18, 68, 193
editorials, nationalism issues covered in, 27–28
Edmondson, Laura, 22
Edney, J. J., 232
educated elites, 91
education, 50, *60*
Egba, 91
Egbe Omo Oduduwa (Society for Oduduwa descendants), 58, 60, 63, 94, 95, 100
Egypt, 21, 29, 296n92
Ejoor, David, 112, 130
Ekeh, Peter, 222, 324n120
Ekwueme, Alex, 192
elaboration, 87–88
elections, 147, 188
elementary sequence, categories of, 267–68
Eley, Geoffrey, 228
Emerson, Rupert, 9, 18–19, 80–81
emirs, 198
Empire Day, 54

Enaharo, Anthony: background, 3; imprisonment of, 155, 180; Movement for National Reformation (MNR) led by, 154; nation self-government advocated by, 157; pro-independence leanings of, 4; pro-independence motion submitted by, 3, 47, 69; pro-SNC element reorganization move of, 221; release of, 122

engagement, spaces of, 230

entitlement, 266–67

Eriksen, Thomas H., 239

ethnic and ethno-regional crises, 9

ethnic diversity, 21, 187

ethnic division and disaffection, 157

ethnic domination, 40

"ethnic group" (term), 120

ethnic groups: colonialism impact on, 12; democratic freedom tied to interests of, 147; democratic rule restoration impact on, 197; disaffection by, organizing, 187; disunity between, 135; dominance, fear of outside, 16, 295n73; national identity, forging out of, 9, 188; nations as, 287; recognition and representation of, struggle for, 21; *versus* state, loyalty to, 187; state creation based on, 142; struggles between, 29, 65–67; territoriality, struggle over, 29; against Yoruba, 199, 200

ethnic interests, 147, 149

ethnic minorities, 262

ethnic nation, 287–88

ethnic nationalism, drift toward, 159

ethnic nationalities: divisions, 284; narratives of, 12, 295n60;

relations among, 6; salience of, 15; self-determination among, 9; space and power, appropriation of, 86; treatment of, 157; twin evils, call for united front against, 196

ethnic pluralism, 222

ethnic problems, management of, 259

"ethnic question," 11

ethnic wars, 86

ethnicism, denunciation of, 164

ethnicity, 7, 8, 187

ethno nations: accommodation of, 258; in African postcolony, 19; knowledge role in life of, 36; newspapers representing, 143; place in Nigerian federation, 173; reinvention, post-colonial of, 19; self-government of, 157; in service of Nigerian nation, 81

ethno-linguistic nations, 25

ethnonationalism, literature on, 21

ethnonationalist space, 86

ethno-regional blocs, 47

ethno-regional domination, 40

ethno-regional groups: colonialism impact on, 12; democratic freedom tied to interests of, 147; disaffection by, organizing, 187; hegemony and, 28; nations as, 287; newspapers as mouthpiece for, 109; space appropriation by, 83; strategies and tactics of, self-government campaign impact on, 68; struggles between, 29

ethno-regional interests, 147, 149

ethno-regional passions, 223

ethno-religious conflict, 29, 223

ethno-religious identities, 38

ethno-religious passions, 223

ethno-spatial hegemony, 96–103

ethno-spatial politics, 83–84

euphemization, 123, 134, 311n66
ex-June Twelvers, 170
exploitation/appropriation theme, 269
"extremism" (term), 55
"extremists" (term), 54

factual knowledge, 33, 34
Fadipe, Joseph, 152
Fairclough, Norman, 25–26
Fajuyi, Adekunle, 111
Falae, Olu, 192
Fay, Brian, 31–32
federal form of government, 116–17, 124–26
federal government, 110, 113, 205
Federal Military Government (FMG), 238–39
federal *versus* unitary system, 117, 118, 119, 124–26, 141–42
federalism, 154, 275
First Republic collapse, 108, 110–13, 114, 134
Fisher, Walter R., 17
Fodio, Shehu Usman Dan, 208, 209, 234, 249
Fontana, Beneditto, 96
form-function interaction, 17
Foucault, Michel, 26, 255
Fourth Republic, 29, 190, 194, 206, 284
fractionalization, 217
fragmentation, 52–53, 65
Fraser, Nancy, 228
Fredrick, C. J., 9
Freedman, Des, 107
freedom, 10, 11, 147
Fulani: as cattle herders, 51; characterization of, 56–57; Hausa conquered by, 234; imperialists, so-called, 74; jihad, 200, 209; as separate ethnic group, 13, 222, 295n62,

324n120; status of, 239, 261, 326n53, 329n10; territory lost to, 50
future, past in, 286–88

Gambari, Sulu, 209
Gee, James P., 289
genre, 242
Ghanaian nation narrative, 81
Gibbons, Michael, 30, 31
Giddens, Anthony, 32, 228
Gigiano, G., 187
globalization, 205
Goldie, Sir George, 13
government location, 85, 86
Gowon, Yakubu: appeal for end to killings in north, 132, 137–38; balance of power under, 127; as Christian, 152; eastern problem military solution requested of, 140; at end of civil war, 216; federal system of government, move toward, 125; government takeover by, 111–12, 121; inaugural address by, 127; national conference held by, 126; newspaper message addressed to, 127–28; northern region leanings of, 123; political prisoners released by, 122; twelve states created by, 124, 311n71; unity cited as not existing by, 133, 215
Gramsci, Antonio, 23, 24, 87, 88, 228, 233
grand narrative: character of, 29; common nationhood myth of, 27; definition and overview of, 5; hegemony and counterhegemony within and beyond, 104; illusions of, 281; nation as, 18; nature and character of, 19–20; Nigerian

grand narrative—*(cont'd)*
  nation as, 12, 289; power and
  domination within, 6; and prose
  of power, 288–91; twilights of,
  178–87
grand nation: against Abacha
  regime, 177; aspiring to be,
  287; attempts to represent, 188;
  construction of, 189; fragments
  of, 49–57; with grand narrative,
  19; knowledge role in life
  of, 36; narratives, evident in,
  287; nationalist press making
  possible, 80; North encouraged
  to join, 55, 57; press role in, 6,
  25; struggle for soul of, 192
Green Peace, 264
group consciousness, 17–18
group power, 18
groups: competing political
  narratives of, 293n11; forms of
  thought within, 35–36; heritage
  of, 35; knowledge role in life of,
  36
Guardian, The: Abacha regime,
  commentary on, 181; analysis
  of, 192; on constitution, 200;
  on constitutional conference,
  175–76, 177, 212; Interim
  National Government
  (ING), commentary on, 166;
  Kafanchan clash addressed by,
  196; narrative, analyzing, 150;
  Obasanjo criticized by, 203;
  on Ogoni crisis, 262, 274–75;
  Otta meeting covered by,
  156; ownership of, 262; past,
  glorification by, 222; on political
  marginalization, 203; politician
  arrests opposed by, 180;
  presidential election, 1993 and
  aftermath, commentaries on,
  155, 160, 161, 170, 185, 186;

on religious conflict, 209–10;
  on restructuring, 216; on Sharia
  law, 207–8
guilt, collective *versus* personal, 144
Gumi, Sheikh Abubakar, 152

Habermas, Jurgen, 30, 32–33, 188,
  228
Hammack, Phillip L., 6
Hanne, Michael, 5, 293n11
Haruna, Mohammed, 285
Hassan, Lt. Col., 112
"hate media," 108
Hausa: historic overview of, 234;
  Kataf-Hausa clashes, 229, *251*;
  long residence, territoriality
  claim based on, 232; Muslims
  predominant among, 158,
  315n41; as separate ethnic
  group, 13, 222, 295n62,
  324n120; status of, 239–40;
  troops, 141
Hausa language, adoption of, 234
Hausa-Fulani: alliances, anticipated
  of, 157; divide and rule by,
  196; domination, perceived
  by, 151, 155, 159; economic
  underdevelopment, minority
  accusations of, 234–35;
  exploitation and appropriation
  associated with, 269; formation
  of, 234; hegemony, perceived
  by, 178, 275; international press
  criticism of, 276–77; jihadists,
  208–9; in Kaduna, 205; middle-
  belt, loss of, 219; military regime
  seen as representative of, 154;
  minority relations with, 234;
  narratives and counternarratives
  concerning, 221–22; newspapers
  supportive of, 262; Nigerian
  crisis, involvement in, 136,
  137; oligarchy, 212; as political

construct, 222, 324n120;
political elite, 282; region
dominated by, 15; rest of north
versus, 197, 199; resurgence
against, 152; soldiers, 196; status
of, 12; territory amalgamation
without consent of, 13
heartland (term), 272
Hegel, G. W. F., 33
hegemonic normative knowledge,
34
hegemony: battle for, 98; concept
of, 87; condition of, 87–88;
framework of, 24; intellectual
exercise of, 89; narratives on,
158; regional and ethnic, 195–
96; space central to, 90; spatial
struggle for, 83; struggle for and
against, 28; theory of, 23; unity
and, 97; web of, 228
Helle, Has Jurgen, 33
Hendricks, William O., 267
Hick's Report, 58–59
history, end of, 189, 197, 286
history-making, 107
Hitler, Adolf, 66, 67
Horwitz, Donald, 263
hospitals, *60*
Hotline magazine, 163–64
House of Dosunmu, 92
human rights groups, 154
human survival, resources for, 227
humanities, 17
Hyden, Goran, 147

Ibadan, 91, 102, 144
Ibadan conference, 1950, 71
Ibo (Igbo): attacks on, call for
retaliating against, 215–16; coup
lead by, 131; criticism of, 203–4;
defense of, 63; domination,
feared of, 66, 117, 126–27, 133;
education, 93; exodus from

western region, 137; flight from
north, 129, 134; gifts of, 168;
hardships faced by, 214; Hausa
attacks on, 237–38; Hausa-
Fulani alliance, anticipated
with, 157; hegemonic and
counterhegemonic moves by,
104, 216; interests, protecting,
118; killings by, 138, 313n134;
in Lagos, 98; Lagos status,
views on, 95, 102; leadership
and political influence of,
93, 135; massacre of, 132,
134, 135, 139, 165; nation,
commentary on, 15; nationalist
movement, involvement
in, 92; newspaper publicity
enjoyed by, 93; newspapers as
mouthpiece of, 194; Nigerian
crisis, involvement in, 136, 137;
Nigerian unity, faith in, 215;
plight of, 165; pogrom against,
112; political influence of,
94; region dominated by, 15;
secession attempt by, 216; status
of, 12; taxation of, 58; territory
amalgamation without consent
of, 13; unification, position on,
116
Ibo State Union, 94
Ibru, Alex, 262
Idemili, Samuel Okafor, 24
identification, constructing symbols
of, 116
identity: components of African,
146; formation of, 255;
metaphors, competing of, 5,
293n11; narrative of, 149;
redefinition of, 146
identity politics, 147
identity-based nation, 146
ideological soldiers, 140, 145
ideological validation, 109

ideology: concept and definition of, 25, 26, 28; Marxian analysis of, 34; mode and strategy of, 116; modes of operation of, 28, 41–43; press interpretation of, 8; as social cement, 287; sociology of knowledge and, 34–39; symbolic conception of, 39–41; term usage, 36, 37
Ideology and Modern Culture (Thompson), 25
Igboland, metaphor for, 221
Igbo-Yoruba relations, 61–62, 94–95, 212
Ige, Bola, 218
Ikara, 237
Ikoli, Ernest, 61
Ilorin, 50, 59
Ilorin-Kabba province, 142
"imagined community" (term), 11
imperialism, 53–54, 56, 70
imprisonment, 123, 311n66
indigeneity, principle of, 235
intellectual and moral leadership, 87
intellectuals, 87–88, 89
interests, 28, 87
Interim National Government (ING), 149, 165, 166–67, 191, 218, 324n109
internal colonialism, 264
interpretive social science, 31–32
interpretive theory, 30–34
Ironsi (Aguiyi-Ironsi), J. T. U.: assassination of, 111, 120, 121, 122; government takeover by, 111; Ibo domination feared under, 126–27; newspaper support for, 110, 114, 117, 118, 119, 120, 121; political prisoner release alleged supported by, 122–23; unification decree enacted by, 113, 115–16; unitary

system of government imposed by, 126
Islam, 21, 204–5
Islam jihad, nineteenth-century, 208
Islamic emirs, 198
Islamic State (ISIS), 286
Islamization, 206
Ives, Sarah, 21
Iwanyanwu, Emmanuel, 162
Iwe-Iroyin, 265
Iyiam, Tony, 193

Jacobs, Ronald N., 228, 241–42, 268
Jakande, Lateef, 142
Johnson, John Payne, 16, 295–96n73
Johnson, Major, 112
Jonathan, Goodluck, 282, 283–84, 285, 332n8
Jones, J. P., 227
Joseph, Richard, 149
journalists, modern public sphere character determined by, 109
June 12, 1993 election. *See* presidential election, 1993
justice, 19, 235

Kabba, 50
Kaduna (Nigeria): capitol move, proposed to, 85–86, 101; ethnic minority groups in, 234; Ibo in, 214; riots in, 209–10; Sharia law, attempt to introduce in, 205, 209; telephone line linking other cities to, 4, 52; Zango-Kataf crisis spread to, 237, 238
"Kaduna Mafia," 167–68, 169, 173–74
Kafanchan command clashes, 198
Kaita, Malam Isa, 75–765
Kangura (newspaper), 108

Kano, pogrom in, 138–39
Kano, riots in, 48
Kataf: Christians predominant among, 158, 315n41; homeland, attachment to, 235; minority status of, 240; original ownership, territoriality claim based on, 232; Zango-Kataf crisis, 234–42
Kataf leaders, trial of, 274
Kataf-Hausa crisis, 229, 251
Katsina, Hassan Usman, 134, 141, 193–94
Kenya, 108
Kingibe, Babagana, 169–70
knowledge, 33–34, 34–39, 298n25
Kobani, Edwin, 271
Kosoko (King of Lagos), 90
Kotangora, Sani, 163–64, 192
Kutigi, Idris, 285

labor, divine division of, 168
labor, mediation borne by, 33, 34
Lafia Native Authority, 130
Lagos: African educated elite of, 14; annexation of, 90–91; anti-imperialist, anticolonial sentiment in, 54; British impressions of, 91, 306n37; as center of unity, 97; centrality and primacy of, 83; development of, 102; Ibo in, 62, 118; Ibo influence in, 94; Ibo leaving, 137; merger of, 59, 95, 96, 97, 100, 142; northern legislators jeered at in, 73; ownership of, 95, 96, 97, 101, 102, 104, 307n96; politics of, 95; press, 14, 85; riots in, 209–10; self-determination, 142; social order in, 89; as space of struggle, 90–96; status of, 49, 76, 77–78,

84, 91, 93, 95, 96–103, 142; Yoruba claims to, 86, 141
Lagos constitution talks, 131
Lagos Town Council, 96, 98, 99
Lagos Youth Movement, 93
Lagos-Accra union, proposed, 95, 307n67
Lagos-Ibadan press, 153, 240, 242
Laitin, David, 89
language, political life relationship to, 30–31
Language, Semantics and Ideology (Pêcheux), 290
Last, Murray, 285
Law, Alex, 7
leadership, conditions for, 87
Lefebvre, Henri, 230, 231
legitimation, experts in, 87–88, 104
Lekwot, Zamani, 238, 239, 243, 248, 251, 252, 253, 254, 274
Leslie, Michael, 147
Levine, Daniel, 205
liberal democracy, 21
"lifeworld," components of, 228
limited liability company, 152, 315n22
literacy, 50
London, 97
London Conference on the Nigerian (Independence) Constitution, 258
London Rainforest Action Group, 264
long residence, territoriality based on, 232
Lucaites, John L., 17, 18, 66, 266
Lugard, Lord Frederick John Dealtry: amalgamation move made by, 72; disunity in time of, 4; Fulani, attitude toward, 56–57; minorities, legacy impact on, 196; national disunity since time of, 74; Nigerian nation formation, role in, 12, 13–14

Lyttleton, Mr., 101, 103
Lyttleton Constitution, 99

Macaulay, Herbert, 91, 92
MacPherson Constitution, 58, 62, 77, 98–99
Madueke, Ojo, 170–71
Madunagwu, Edwin, 162
majority-minority relations, 29
Mandani, Mahmood, 95
mandate (term), 174
Mandela, Nelson, 277
Mannheim, Karl, 34, 35–36, 37, 38, 39, 40
marginal (term), 261
marginal ethnic groups, 259, 261
marginal identities, 178, 261–62, 279–80
marginal narratives, 267
marginal voices, politics of, 266–68
marginality, press and, 264–66
Martin, Wallace, 231
Marx, Karl, 37, 38, 40, 41
Marxism, 33–34, 39, 87
mass media, 11
"massacre" (term), 138–39
McEachern, Charmaine, 10, 22, 286
meaningful totality, 281
meanings: mobilization of, 24, 25, 27, 289, 290; network of, 28
media: discursive nature of messages in, 25–26; nation, nationalism or nation-building intersection with, 7; national development role of, 29, 296n92; political space created by, 147; power construction in, 26; role in democracy, 224
media diversity, 147
media narratives, 22, 107
media organizations, conflicts between, 143

media-conflict interface, 107–8, 112–13
media-democracy interface, 222–23
media-nation interface, 7
mediated knowledge, 33
mediation, 33
"mediatized conflict," 107
metacode, theory of narrative, 266
metaphors, 54
metonymy, 197
middle, call to embrace, 170
Middle-Belt, 75, 151–52, 167, 178, 184, 194, 200–201, 212, 217, 219, 220–21, 287
militarization, 108
military, 172, 176, 196
military force, unity maintained by, 8
millennial existence, 205
Miller, David, 231
Mink, Louis O., 193
minorities: agitation by ethnic, 262; democratic rule restoration impact on, 197; ethnic nations, 259; mention of, call for stop to, 125; narratives about, 29; plight of, 176; restiveness of groups, 259; rise of consciousness of, 263; treatment of, 157
minority (term), 261
mobilization, press as instrument of, 108
"moderation" (term), 54, 55
Mohammed, Adamu A., 202
Mohammed, Aliu, 238
Mohammed, Murtala, 84, 305n4
Month and a Day, A (Saro-Wiwa), 258
Morel, Edmund Dene, 56
Morning Post: Awolowo release covered by, 123; military takeover impact on, 113–14; as mouthpiece, 110, 113; national

unity appeal by, 134–35; newspapers, other criticized by, 145; Nigerian nation emergence, hope for, 135; on northern region mass killings, 130; system of government, reversal on, 125–26; on unification, 116, 119, 120
"Moscow Purge," 65
Moss, P., 227
Mourning Day, 1966, 131–32
Movement for National Reformation (MNR), 154–55
Movement for the Survival of Ogoni People (MOSOP), 258, 264, 271, 277, 278
multiethnic states, 5, 19–20, 28
multinational oil company, 29
multiple narratives and counternarratives, 18
multiple nations, competing narratives of, 6
music, 22
Muslims: Christians, clash with, 205, 209, 238; Hausa, 158, 315n41; political power of, 151, 152; terms considered pejorative by, 164

NADECO (National Democratic Coalition), 178, 180–81
Najmabadi, Afsaneh, 207
Napoleon Bonaparte, 37, 40
narrative discourse, 255
narrative frames, *260*
narrative lie, 18
narrative metacode, theory of, 266
narrative of precedence (defined), 144
narrative theory, 24
narratives: clash of competing, 281; of conflict, 107; counternarratives invited by, 18;

democratization agenda, role in, 147; dialectical function of, 269, 280; as elaboration type, 88; end of, 286–87; function of, 286; human viewpoint diversity reflected in, 17, 18; legitimacy of existing, 19; marginal voices, politics of, 266–68; meaningful totality construction, role in, 281; of nation media, 22; nation relationship to, 18, 27; national life, role in, 289; political entity, understanding, role in, 6; power, mobilizing through, 103; as research focus, 17; rhetorical function of, 280; role in politics, 17; sociology of knowledge role in understanding, 35, 298n26; space qualities transferred into, 89–90; unification as narrative, 116
Narratives of Nation Media (McEachern), 22
nation: as battleground for meaning, 25; boundaries and character of, 9; concept, deconstructing, 8–9, 18, 19, 33, 188, 287; *versus* country, 194; defined, 9, 18–19, 80–81, 294n39; democratic practice impact on, 146; elusiveness, 8; emotional apparatus of, 11, 173; formation, completion of, 9, 294n39; freedom and security of, importance of, 19; idea of, 28; identification with as human need, 19; identity-based *versus* democratic society, 146; images of, constructing, 21; media intersection with, 7; narrative relationship to, 18, 27; nations, other within main, 16, 19, 188; postcolonial, 8–12, 18–20; state

nation—*(cont'd)*
　　and, coincidence between, 81;
　　state as expression of, 9; war,
　　mobilization for, 142–43
Nation and Narration (Bhabha, ed.),
　　26
Nation Betrayed, A (Vickers), 258
national conference, 1990s. *See*
　　constitutional conference, 1994;
　　Sovereign National Conference,
　　1994
national conference, 2015, 286
national consciousness, 21
national consensus, struggle for,
　　282–86
National Council of Nigeria and
　　the Cameroons (NCNC) (*later*
　　National Council of Nigerian
　　Citizens): ethno-regional
　　organization around, 47; Ibo
　　domination attempts, accusation
　　of, 66; independence target
　　date, position on, 100; internal
　　forces, divisive, 65; Lagos
　　status, position on, 95, 98, 99,
　　101, 102; military system of
　　government supported by, 62; as
　　nationalist party, 58; newspaper
　　as mouthpiece for, 109, 110;
　　newspaper coverage of, 59,
　　79–80; Nigerian nationhood,
　　position on, 4–5; northern
　　region, turning to, 79; regional
　　interests represented by, 59;
　　regionalization, views on, 62;
　　rivalry with Action Group (AG),
　　55, 63–65; self-government
　　campaign, involvement in,
　　68–71, 74; unification, position
　　on, 116
National Democratic Coalition
　　(NADECO), 178, 180–81
national democratic life, 190

national development, press role
　　in, 29, 296n92
national identity, 22, 188
national narratives, 27
national political reform
　　conference, 2005, 284
National Question: addressing,
　　193; choices to be made, 194;
　　national conference to tackle,
　　176, 180, 284; secularism debate
　　linked with, 205
National Republican Conviction
　　(NRC), 149
national unity: challenges of,
　　108; credit for, 135–36;
　　culturo-historical and ethnic
　　diversity, reconciling with, 21;
　　parameters of, 33; press role in,
　　6; requirements for, 129
nationalism: circumstances
　　giving rise to, 10; as endemic
　　condition, 11; Euro-American
　　experience with, 19; issues of,
　　9–10; literature on, 21; media
　　intersection with, 7, 21. *See also*
　　Nigerian nationalism
nationalist ideology, 19
nationalist struggle, 86, 263
nationalist terminology, 8–9
nationalities, union of countries,
　　question, 193
nation-building: in the arts, 22–23;
　　challenges in multiethnic
　　states, 5, 28; conceptions,
　　differing and definition of, 187;
　　democracy, reconciling with,
　　146; *versus* democracy creation,
　　188; end of, 130; ethnic nation
　　accommodation and, 259; media
　　and, 7, 21–25; nation-destroying
　　versus, 188; parameters of, 33;
　　press role in, 153; questions of,
　　189

nation-destroying, 169, 182, 187, 188, 189

nationhood: achieving, 5; construction, deconstruction or reconstruction of, 24; crisis of, 115–22; issues of, 9–10; media role in making, 291; myth of common, 27; narratives of, 29, 115–16; Nigerian, 16, 19, 24, 82; notion of, 26; postcolonial crisis of, 7; print media narratives concerning, 12; ruptures within discourse on, 29; single or multiple, 6; unfinished nature of, 11–12

nations: colonialism impact on, 12; competing political narratives of, 5, 293n11; world divided into, 19

nation-state: becoming, process of, 147; as colonial creation, 19; defined, 9, 294n39; status, identity role in, 11

nation-states: attempts to build, 9–10; communication spaces, radio broadcasting role in constructing, 22; dismemberment of, 159; future of, re-examining, 195

Nazis, 67

NCNC-AG alliance, 68–71, 74, 76, 77–80, 103

neo-Gramscian perspective, 23, 24

NEPU (Northern Elements Progressive Union), 75

New Nigerian: on Abiola, 183; analysis of, 192; Azikiwe loss covered by, 123–24; Babangita regime defended by, 159–60; coup, 1966, reaction to, 115, 117, 131–32; domination, narrative on, 126–27; east circulation, ban on, 140; eastern region minority agitations promoted by, 142; federal form of government supported by, 124–25; founding of, 241; narrative, analyzing, 150; national-building and destroying, 153; newspapers, other criticized by, 143–44, 145, 186; on northern region mass killings, 133–34, 135; as northern region mouthpiece, 110, 113, 129, 143; on Ogoni crisis, 262, 277–79; Otta meeting, commentary on, 155–56; political prisoner release reported by, 122–23; presidential election, 1993 and aftermath, commentary on, 160–62, 179, 182, 184; press role in nationhood crisis noted by, 143; sectional advantage allegedly advocated by, 129; on Sharia law, 208, 209; unity, statements supporting, 121–22; Yoruba role, position on, 137; on Zango-Kataf crisis, 240, 243, 244, 247, 252

New York, 97

news media, 11

newspaper narratives (Nigeria): collective identity struggle, role in, 6; divisiveness in, 141; First Republic collapse and, 108; on independence, 48–49; political independence role of, 3; self-government campaign impact on, 68–76; unification and fragmentation, attempts in, 52–53

newspaper press. *See* press

newspapers: battles between, 143–44; as legitimation experts, 104; national development role of, 29, 296n92; proprietors, 109

Newswatch, 260, 262, 268–69, 272, 276

Ngbati press, 240

Nicolson, I. F., 13

Niger delta region, 262, 264, 268

Niger Delta Republic, 259

Nigeria: allegiance, transferring, 188; decolonization period in, 263; defined, 146; disintegration, potential of, 157, 173, 175, 177, 179, 185, 186–87, 191, 202, 213–14, 215, 218, 283; as "geographical expression," 13, 16; idea of, 13; intellectual and material developments of, 20; invention of, 5; "nation" as synonym for, 173; national space, competing claims within, 190; nations within, 16–17, 188; plot to split, 147, *148*; reinvention of, 189, 195, 196; restructuring, 180, 284, 285; secession (*see* secession); self-rule, 263; separatist movements, 66, 74–75, 211; survival as nation, 195, 196, 211, 212; three regions, creation of, 15; transition to civil rule, 149–50, 154, 155; twenty-year plan for, 119, 310n47

Nigeria, Federal Republic of, ideological soldiers for, 145

Nigeria, military government, post-1979, 155, 156–57, 179, 184

Nigeria, military years (1966–1979): case studies of, 29; literature on, 23; military government, press bias against, 144; military government, press support for, 113–15, 117–20, 122; press, impact on, 118–19; unitary government under, 124–25

Nigerian Citizen (newspaper): in case studies, 27; on education and literacy, 50; on eve of independence, 49; on Fulani, 51; Lagos status covered by, 77; on moderation and extremism, 54–55; as mouthpiece, 109; nationalism advocated by, 4, 52–53; NPC characterization by, 75, 303n110; power struggle narratives, 49–50; pro-imperialist views of, 53–54; region building advocated by, 81

Nigerian civil war (Nigeria-Biafra War): debates on eve of, 29; June 12 crisis compared to, 150; narratives preceding, 216; on Nigeria's fate trajectory, 171; outbreak of, 113; prelude to, 108, 145; press role in, 108, 145; purpose of, 219–20; retrospective analysis of, 185; war waging questioned, 202; Zango-Kataf crisis compared to, 254

Nigerian crisis, 1966, 113–15, 143

Nigerian cultural and political identity, 12

Nigerian independence: approach to, 109; aspirations for, 59, 82; movement toward, divisions coinciding with, 15, 100–101; nationalism in time of, 24; negotiation for, 13; newspaper coverage of, 4, 54–55; northern region unprepared for, 53–54; period of, 23; self-rule prior to, 263; target date, controversy over, 3–4, 5, 47–48, 49, 69, 103

Nigerian narrative, genealogy of, 12–18

Nigerian nation: death predicted for, 163, 166; description of,

195; emergence, challenges to, 196; emergence, hope for, 114, 118, 135; ethno nations in service of, 81; as grand narrative, 289; grand narrative concerning, 12; idea and nature of, 29; idea in press, 24, 115, 123, 128; narration of without crises, 291; origin of, 12; united nation, call for, 135

Nigerian National Alliance (NNA), 110

Nigerian National Democratic Party (NNDP), 92, 110

Nigerian nationalism: articulating idea of, 23–24; leadership of anticolonial, 92; movement, 92; newspaper promotion of, 120–21; Nigerian Youth Movement (NYM) role in, 58, 301n40

Nigerian nationhood, 16, 19, 24, 82

Nigerian Press, The (Agbaje), 23

Nigerian Tribune: on army chief proposed meeting, 141; Balewa-led government, position on, 115; in case studies, 27; on colonialism and imperialism, 4, 53; comforting fantasies spun by, 68; on constitutional conference, 128–29; on eastern region's position on crisis, 140–41; on ethnic rivalries, 65–66; on eve of independence, 49; form of government, reversal on, 126; "imperialism" term use by, 54; military government, position on, 113, 119; as mouthpiece, 109, 110, 113; on northern region mass killings, 130, 132–33, 136; on Ogoni crisis, 262,

275; on political figures, 65; on regions, 55–56; on religion, 153; self-government advocated by, 76; on self-government talks, 51–52; on taxation and revenue allocation, 58–59; on unification, 118–19

Nigerian union, 149, 189, 211, 222, 287

Nigerian unity: achievement not yet reached, 13, 128, 133; advocacy of, 16, 295–96n73; as British invention, 16; challenges to, 4; imperialism as obstacle to, 53; newspaper support for, 74–75; path to, 81–82; struggle for, 14–15, 23, 24; symbolization of, 71–72

Nigerian Youth Movement (NYM): crisis and collapse of, 58, 61–62, 63, 93; leadership of, 60; organ of, 49, 61

non-Muslim communities, 198

normative knowledge, 33, 34

Northern Elements Progressive Union (NEPU), 75

Northern Muslims, political power of, 151, 152, 218

Northern Nigerian Federation, 217–18

northern "oligarchy," 184, 193, 198–99

Northern People's Congress (NPC): alliance with NNDP, 110; defense of, 75; ethno-regional organization around, 47; formation of, 58, 75, 303n110; independence target date, position on, 69, 100; Lagos status, position on, 101; newspapers as mouthpiece of, 109, 110, 143; political parties, other work with, 78, 79 northern region (Nigeria): alignment against, 69–70; "clique" in, 171; coup, 1966, position on, 117; coup, danger of, 197–98; defense of, 139; divided nature of, 184; domination, pre-Ironsi, 127; factionalizing of, 219–20; federal form of government supported by, 124; fuel crisis in, 153; grand nation, invitation to join, 55, 57; Lagos status, position on, 77, 96; leadership, 75–76; mandate from narrative of, 173–74; mass killings in, 129, 132–34, 135, 136–39, 144, 165; military controlled by, 196; nationalism in, 74; newspaper characterization of, 51–52, 54–56, 57, 71–76; newspapers as mouthpiece of, 109, 110, 113, 129; Nigerian crisis, involvement in, 136; political parties turning to, 79; political supremacy of, 174; power acquisition by, 199; press, 75; sacrifices made by, 214; secession, potential of, 48, 74–75; and southern regions compared, 53–54; split threatened by, 4; unification in, 217; unity, defending, 199; unity and fractionalization in, 200–201

northerners: gifts of, 168; killing, alleged of, 137; Nigerian unity favored by, 172; reputation of, 138; rule restricted to, 173; tax proposed for, 144

Nwafor-Orizu, 111

Nyamnjoh, Francis, 21

Nyiam, Col., 194, 196

Nzeogwu, Chukwuma Kaduna, 111, 117, 123, 133, 310n37

Nzeribe, Arthur, 160

Oba, 65, 66, 102

Obasanjo, Olusegun: ascendancy of, 197; as Christian ruler, 152, 203; confederation, call for criticized by, 215; death, consequences in event of, 202; decision to sack government of, 198; Lagos riots, response to, 210; newspaper criticism of, 180; Otta meeting convened by, 155–56; political reform conference held under, 284; praise for, 203, 204; presidency of, 218–19; in presidential election, 1999, 192; release of, 191; religious threat to administration of, 208; staff of, 201–2; transition committee, 194; as Yoruba president, 199

objectivity, drive toward, 34, 298n25

Odugbemi, Sina, 162, 170

Ofeimun, Odia, 91–92, 190

Ogoni: leadership of, 258; mass action and confrontation by, 259; narratives of experiences of, 268–79; nation, allegiance to, 188; overview of, 257, 263–64; political slavery of, 259; self-determination, struggle for, 157, 261

Oguloma citizens, 144

oil-producing areas, minorities in, 260, 262, 264, 268–69

oil-producing community, 259

Ojike, Mbonu, 98

Ojukwu, Emeka Odumegwu, 111–12, 113, 118, 120, 122–23, 125, 131, 133, 135–36, 139–40, 143, 158, 210

Okadigbo, Benedict, 243, 246, 250, 252, 253
Okonkwor, Raphael Chude, 23–24
Okrika people, collective fine paid to, 144
Olawoyin, Josiah Sunday, 142
Olorun-Nimbe, A. B. I., 65, 66
Olukotun, Ayo, 23
Omoruyi, Omo, 150
Omu, Fred, 20, 23, 24
"One Zambia, One Nation" (slogan), 22
Onoh, Christian, 152
Oodu'a People's Congress (OPC), 199, 209–10
Ooni of Ife, 69
Opadokun, Ayo, 151
Orase, Samuel, 271
Orase, Theophilus, 271
Organization of African Unity (*later* African Union), 9
organized violence, planning required for, 108
original ownership, territoriality based on, 232
Orkar coup, abortive, 193, 196
Osaghae, Eghosa, 239, 259
other: collective identity *versus,* 116; expurgation of, 178, 196, 199
otherness, narratives of, 68
Otta meeting, 155–56
"our" survival, resources needed for, 227, 257
"ours" (term), 90
Owonaro, Sam, 259
Oyekan, Oba Adeyinka, 142
Oyo Empire, 200
Oyovbaire, Sam, 190

Paasi, Anssi, 90, 306n32
Pakistan: as metaphor for separation, 58, 301n42;

"Pakistanists" (term), 117;
"Pakistanized" (term), 119
pan-Nigerian movement, 94
Papastergiadis, Nikos, 16
paper soldiers, 108, 113–15, 119–20, 143
past: in future, 286–88; future framed in context of, 194; glorification of collective, 222; recreating of, 192; remembering, 283
Path to Nigerian Freedom (Perham), 13
peace, 19
Pêcheux, Michel, 290
Pelecki, Andrew, on importance of narratives, 6
Penrose, Jan, 89–90, 98, 103, 229, 230, 231–32
People's Democratic Party (PDP), 191, 282, 283
Perham, Margery, 13
persuasion, 87
philosophy, 34, 298n25
pig (term), 164
Plato, 17
plot, 241
"pogrom" (term), 138–39
political activities, suspension, proposed of, 114
political consciousness, 17, 18
political control, 230
political crisis, 1953, 3–4, 47–48
political developments, 20
political inquiry, positivist approach to, 30
political leaders, newspapers as mouthpiece for, 109
political life, 30–31
political marginalization, 203
"political minions" (term), 60, 61
political narratives, 287

political parties: ethno-regional
  blocs and, 47; newspaper
  commentaries on, 62, 63–65;
  newspapers as mouthpiece for,
  109; self-government campaign,
  involvement of, 68–71; struggle
  between, 59–61
political pluralism, 147
political power, 19
political prisoners, release of,
  122–23
political reality, 107
political region, nation as, 287
political truths, 107
political victories, press role in, 109
political-religious crises, medial
  role in, 205–6
politics: language role in, 288–89;
  narratives' role in, 17; nature of,
  151; polemics, introducing into,
  145; space and, 86
Port-Harcourt, 101
Post Express: analysis of, 192;
  confederation call analyzed
  by, 215; on constitution, 200;
  Enahoro, Anthony, commentary
  on, 221; hegemony concerns
  of, 194; Ibo hardships pointed
  out by, 214; Nigeria's survival as
  nation heralded by, 195, 196; on
  political marginalization, 203;
  on religious conflict, 209; on
  restructuring, 216–17; secession
  considered unlikely by, 212; on
  Sharia law, 211; on sovereign
  national conference, 211, 214;
  unity challenges cited by, 198
postauthoritarian press,
  expectations of, 223
postcolonial entities, challenges to,
  9–10
postcolonial era, 24, 27, 290
postcolonial nation, 8–12, 18–20

postcolonial states: "nation"
  concept in, 19; nation-building
  and interethnic relations
  in, 28; nationhood crisis in,
  7; nationhood notion in,
  26; nature and role of, 8;
  sanctification and sacralization
  of, 9; unity lacking in, 11
postcolony, ethnic nations in, 19
post-election 1993 crisis. *See*
  presidential election, 1993
postindependent Nigeria, inclusion
  and exclusion in, 29
power: concept defined, 228;
  establishing and sustaining, 40;
  ideology as meaning in service
  of, 24; meaning in service of,
  25–27, 28, 29, 30, 41, 42, *42*,
  43, 48–49, 71, 288, 289, 290,
  291; mobilizing, 103; narratives
  of, 149, 203; negotiation of, 28;
  network of, 28; press and, 13;
  prose of, 288–91; reification
  of, 237; relations and word
  meanings, 79–80; section
  monopoly of, 176; in social
  relations, 228; space and, 228–
  29; struggles, narratives, 49–50;
  and territoriality, 229–33
power blocs, 158
Power of Knowledge, 168
preindependence era, 222
presidency, fight for, 153–54
president, installation of first
  elected from south, 194
presidential election, 1993:
  aftermath, press coverage of,
  160–66, 187; annulment of,
  149–50, 162–67, 184, 187,
  189, 191; civic nation and, 188;
  crisis following, 150–51, 191;
  hopes stemming from, 147;
  June 12 question, resolving,

177; narratives concerning, 166–73, 177–78, 188; results of, 149; victory, struggle to reclaim, 178–87
presidential election, 2015, 282–83
press: amalgamation coverage and commentary by, 14; conflict, role in, 113; democracy, role in, 223; domination relations and, 29; ethno-linguistic nations in, 25; ethno-spatial hegemony construction and, 96–103; evolution of, 23, 109; grand nation in, 25; literature on, 23–25; marginalized groups, advocacy for, 264; meaning mobilized in service of power by, 43; minorities, preoccupation with, 268; nation, narratives on, 19; national development role of, 20; nationalist *versus* reactionary sections of, 80; nation-building role of, 23; nationhood crisis as reflected and contested in, 20; Nigerian cultural and political identity, role in forging, 12; peace, potential for restoring, 143; political contestations, role in, 41; power, securing and resisting by, 104; pre-civil war role of, 108; sectional nature of, 190; and territoriality discourse, 242–54; territoriality struggle and, 228–29; war preparation role of, 142–43
Press and Politics in Nigeria, 1880–1937 (Omu), 23
press narratives, 5–6, 224
Prest, Arthur, 63, 69
print media, 5–6, 7–8, 23
problem solving, newspaper and magazine failure to promote, 224

prodemocracy movement, 154, 155, 178, 183
proestablishment press, 265
pro-Hausa press, 245, 252
pro-June 12 press, 162, 166, 178
pro-June 12 supporters, 170–71, 184
pro-Kataf press, 243, 245, 248, 249–51
prominorities press, 269–70
Provisional Ruling Council (PRC), 206
pseudo-nation (term defined), 9, 294n39
pseudo-nations, crises, fallout in, 9–10
psychological mobilization as war-waging precursor, 108
public life, symbolic form role in, 41
public limited company (term defined), 152, 315n22
public officials, accountability, media role in, 147
public spheres, 228

quasi-amelioration, 268
quasi-degradation, 268
"Quislings" (term), 221

radical press, 23
radio broadcasting, 22, 23
Radio Cotonou, 137
Radio Nigeria, 193
Radio Television Libre des Milles Collines (RTLM), 108
Rapport, Nigel, 241
"reactionary" (term), 79
"real north" (term), 74, 75
regional domination, 40
regional rivalries, 54–59
regionalism, 259
regionalization, 62–63

religion, 7, 21, 164, 259
religious conflict, 204–11
religious crises, 158, 205–6,
    315n41
religious interests, 147
religious-political rivalries, 9
Renan, Ernest, 7, 82, 222
*Repressive State and Resurgent
    Media under Nigeria's Military
    Dictatorship, 1988-1998*
    (Olukotun), 23
Republic of Nigeria (term), 116
resources, 235, 264
responsibility, collective *versus*
    personal, 144
restructuring, politics of, 211–22
revenue allocation, 58–59
rhetorical function, 266
rhetorical narrative, 66, 266
Ribadu, Muhammadu, 201
Ricoeur, Paul, 30, 32, 249
rights, 232
ruling regimes, 110
Rwandan genocide, 108

Sacks, Robert D., 231, 232, 236,
    256
Said, Edward, 83, 88, 255
Saleh, Dahiru, 160
Sammani, Muhammad, 221
Saro-Wiwa, Ken, 157, 258, 259,
    262, 264, 270, 271–72, 273,
    274, 275, 276, 278
Scammell, Margaret, 222–23
Schlesinger, Phillip, 7, 223
schools, *60*
science, 34, 298n25
"science of ideas" (term), 36
scientific knowledge, basis for, 36
secession: actual, 113; advocacy
    of, 172; move toward, 135;
    potential, 48, 74–75, 125, 139–
    40, 150, 178, 211–12

Second Republic (1979-1983), 23,
    206
sectarian groups, 21
sectarian identity, 222
secularism, 205, 209, 211
selective details, 68
self-determination, 187, 211, 263
self-government, 51–52, 68–76, 82
Semetko, Holli A., 222–23
Senghor, Leopold Sedar, 9
separatist movements, 66, 74–75,
    211
Sewell, William H., Jr., 268
sexual domination, 40
Shagari, Shehu, 218
Sharia legal code: attempts to
    introduce, 205, 206, 285;
    conflict over, 205; debate
    on, 194, 206; newspaper
    commentary on, 206–11, 217;
    storm over, 206–7
Shaw, Thomas, 51
Shell Petroleum Development
    Company, 269, 270, 272
Shonekan, Ernest, 149, 150, 165,
    174, 179, 191, 218, 316n72,
    324n109
singularities, presenting opposing,
    7–8
Sklar, Richard, 61–62
slave trade, 12, 272
Smith, Anthony, 12
social amenities, *60*
social antagonism, 34
social consciousness, 17, 18
social contract, 8
Social Democratic Party (SDP), 149
social formation, interests and
    values of, 89
social groups, 89, 104
social inquiry, 30, 32–33
social life, 31
social order, 89

social power, 19
social reality, 41, 279–80
social relations, 228
social sciences, 17, 30, 31, 39
"socialist" (term), 58
society, 88, 241, 327n60
Sokoto, 56
Sokoto caliphate, 50
south (region of Nigeria):
    mouthpiece of, 151; newspaper
    characterization of, 57; power
    shift to, 194, 198–99; press, 75,
    304n114; unity in, 217
South Africa, 10, 21–22, 239, 277,
    326n53
South-East, 214
southern compeer, expurgation of,
    57–68
southern domination, fears of, 117
southern minorities, secession
    threatened by, 178
southern Nigeria, 52
southern press, 155, 159, 238, 240
southern regions, struggle between,
    52, 57, 59
southerners, 56, 172
Sovereign National Conference,
    1994: calls for, 159, 170–71,
    176, 203, 212; elements
    supporting, 221; goals and
    purpose of, 180, 197, 211;
    opposition to, 214; press
    coverage of, 154; Yoruba
    autonomy via, 199
Sovereign National Conference,
    2014, 284
Soviet Union, 65
Sowemimo, Sobo, 172
Soyinka, Wole, 186, 202, 277
space: characteristics of, 227,
    230–31; defined, 89–90;
    emotional power of, 229–30;
    latent powers of, 89–90, 101;

material dimension of, 229,
    230; narratives, relation to,
    229; narratives about, 103;
    negotiation of, 228–29; and
    politics, 86; of struggle, 234–42
spatial politics, territoriality as
    dimension of, 227
spatiality (defined), 237
"spirit of June 12," 180
Spitulnik, Debra, 22
state: corporeal density of, 8; loyalty
    to, 187; and nation, coincidence
    between, 81; restructuring, 195,
    196–97, 211–22
state structures, 20
state-nation (concept), 9, 188
Storey Commission of Inquiry, 99
storyability, 266, 267
*Structural Transformation of the Public
    Sphere, The* (Habermas), 228
Suberu, Rotimi, 262
Sule, Maitama, 168, 218
Sweet, James, 146
symbolic construction, 41
symbolic convergence theory,
    17–18
symbols, traditional, 38
synecdoche, 197

Tamarkin, M., 9, 188
Tanzania, 22–23
taxes and taxation, 58, 130, 144
Taylor, Charles, 31, 232, 237
telephone line, 4, 52–53
TELL magazine: Abacha
    regime, commentary on,
    177, 179, 181, 182–83;
    Abiola supported by, 184–85;
    analysis of, 192; Babangida,
    commentary on, 155, 159,
    163–64; on constitution, 200; on
    constitutional conference, 154,
    158, 166, 173–74, 211,

TELL magazine—*(cont'd)*
212; on democratic rule
restoration, 195; democratic
rule restoration, narrative upon,
194–99, 200; founding and early
years, 240–41; Hausa-Fulani
domination bid criticized by,
219; on Ibo leaders, 203–4;
on Lagos riots, 210; military
command, commentary on,
165; military criticized by, 172;
minority revolt, commentary
on, 178; on NADECO, 181;
narratives, analyzing, 150, 151;
New Nigerian critical of, 160;
Nigeria disintegration feared
by, 157, 171, 202; northern
factionalizing by, 219–20;
northern region changes
and diversity noted by, 194;
Obasanjo, commentaries on,
156; on Obasanjo presidency,
218–19; on Ogoni crisis,
262, 270–71, 272, 275–76;
presidential election, 1993 and
aftermath, commentary on,
162–63, 168–69, 172, 174–75,
178, 180; on religion, 152; on
restructuring, 216; secession
fears voiced by, 211; on Sharia
law, 206–7, 208; on southern
president, 213; twin evils cited
by, 195–96; on Zango-Kataf
crisis, 240, 243–44, 247–48
tellability, 266, 267
territorial crisis, 254–55
territoriality: defined, 90; discourse
and press, 242–54; power and,
229–33; sociospatial dialectic
in, 256; struggle over, 228–29;
symbolic manifestation of, 227
territory, 229, 230, 240
terrorist groups, 285–86

text, release from isolation, 88
theater, 22
"theirs" (term), 90
"them" (term), 90
TheNEWS: Abacha regime,
commentary on, 175, 179,
181; Abiola supported by, 179,
183–84, 185; Babangida regime
coverage by, 159–60; Babangida
regime crackdown predicted by,
163; constitutional conference,
commentary on, 173, 175;
ethnic minorities, treatment of,
157; founding of, 241; Interim
National Government (ING),
commentary on, 166; interviews
given by, 171; on "Kaduna
Mafia," 167–68; minorities,
revolt of covered by, 178;
narrative, analyzing, 150; *New
Nigerian* critical of, 160; Nigerian
disintegration feared by, 177,
186; on Ogoni crisis, 262,
271–72, 274, 276; presidential
election, 1993, commentary
concerning, 147, *148*, 155,
171, 172, 174, 180, 181–82;
Sovereign National Conference,
prospective covered in, 170; on
Zango-Kataf crisis, 240, 243,
246, 250, *251*, 252–53, 254
Third Republic, 29, 152, 190, 206
Thomas, Bode, 69, 70
Thompson, John B.: depth
hermeneutics explained
by, 32; on domination and
power, 42, 43, 65; on enemy
construction or identification,
54; ideology concept as recast
by, 25, 26, 36, 37, 39–40, 41;
passivization described by, 139;
power relations, strategies for
legitimizing, 75; traditional

symbols and values, persistence of pointed out by, 38; on unification, 97, 116
thought, 35–36, 299n27
Thussu, Daya Kishan, 107
Tilde, Aliyu, 200
time-space relations, 241, 327n60
Tofa, Alhaji Bashir, 149, 159, 161
Townsend, Henry, 14, 265
transition-to-democracy programs, 259
tribalism: accusations of, 58, 61, 63, 118; concept of, 95; denunciation of, 116, 126, 164; minimizing, 120; tribal bitterness, 145
"tribe" (term), 120, 199
truth, discovery, revelation, and presentation of, 266, 269
Turner, Victor, 268
Tutsi (Rwanda), 239, 261, 326n53, 329n10
twelve states, creation of, 124, 311n71

ultimatum (term), 181
Umar, Abubakar, 202
UN Committee for the Elimination of Racial Discrimination (CERD), 264
unfreedom, 10–11
unification, 52–53, 97, 115–22, 196
Unification Decree No. 34, May 24, 1966, 111, 113, 115–16, 120
Union of the Federated States of Nigeria (UFSN), 155
Union of the Federation of Nigeria (UFN), 155
unitary system: *versus* federal system, 117, 118, 119, 124–26, 141–42; support for, 117, 119; unification through, 116
United Nations, 274

United Progressive Grand Alliance (UGPA), 111
unity, 97, 116, 122
unity in diversity, principle of, 196
Unrepresented Nations and Peoples Organization, 264
Urhobos, 65
"us" (term), 90, 227–28
US State Department, 286

value knowledge, 33–34
values, traditional, 38
van Dijk, Teun A., 25
verstehen (explanation), 31–32
Vickers, Michael, 258
violence and national consensus, 282–86
Volosinov, V. N., 7, 228

Wachukwu, Jaja, 67
Walsh, W. H., 193
warmongering, 166
war-news relationship, 143
wartime, media behavior in, 108
Weekly Trust: analysis of, 192; Enahoro, Anthony, commentary on, 221; on Ibo attack retaliation, 215–16; on Kaduna riots, 210; leaders attacked by, 218; on national convention, 212; on Nigerian civil war, 219–20; on north development and potential, 217–18; north fragmentation, attempt to prevent, 201, 220; on restructuring, 212–13, 214–15, 216; on Sharia law, 207, 209; Yoruba criticized by, 199–200
West African Pilot (newspaper): Awolowo release covered by, 123; Balewa-led government, position on, 115; in case studies, 27; on colonialism, 55;

West African Pilot—(cont'd)
   comforting fantasies spun by,
   68; in countercoup aftermath,
   120–21; emergence of, 93;
   ethnic biases of, 93–94; on
   ethnic groups, 65–67; on eve of
   independence, 49; federalism
   support abandoned by, 141–42;
   Ghanaian nation narrative of,
   81; grand nation advocated by,
   80; Lagos status, position on,
   95, 96–97, 98–99, 101–2, 103,
   141, 142; as mouthpiece, 109,
   113; name turned into verb,
   59; on national unity, 130–31,
   135–36; nationalism advocated
   by, 4, 24, 122, 129; nationhood
   advocated by, 82; on NCNC-AG
   alliance, 77–78; newspapers,
   other criticized by, 145; Nigerian
   independence, position on,
   103; on northern region mass
   killings, 138, 143–44; ownership
   narrative of, 83–84; on political
   figures, 63, 65, 78; on political
   parties, 59–61, 64; regional
   alliance shift of, 79; regional
   biases of, 56, 57; regionalization
   opposed by, 62–63; self-
   government campaign impact
   on narrative of, 69–73, 75–76;
   on unification, 116–18, 119;
   unitary system of government
   supported by, 125; Yoruba
   domination attempt perceived
   by, 65–67
Western other, counterhegemonic
   perspective against, 278–79
western region: Balewa-led
   government impact on, 115;
   coup, 1966, position on, 117;
   crisis in, 1962, 185; danger
   to, 61; east-west rivalry, 57,
   96; economic conditions, 59;
   ethnic groups in, 65, 66, 81,
   102; exodus from, 137; Lagos
   and, 77, 95, 96, 97–99, 100,
   101, 102–3; leadership, 16, 68;
   newspapers as mouthpiece for,
   4, 110, 113; Nigerian crisis,
   involvement in, 136; Nigerian
   independence backed by, 71;
   northern soldiers stationed in,
   136; political party affiliations,
   47, 49, 65, 69; protection of,
   136; violence in, 111
white colonial regimes, 239,
   326n53
Williams, Adebayo, 168, 171,
   172–73
Wilson, Thomas M., 230
Wiwa, Owens, 270–71
Wolch, Jennifer, 235
women, empowerment of, 169
word meanings, power relations
   and, 79–80
World Conference of Indigenous
   Peoples, 264
World War I, 143

Yahaya, A. D., 284
Yakassai, Tanko, 151, 152–53, 270,
   271
Yar'Adua, Umaru Musa, 192
Yerima, Sani Ahmed, 206, 207, 208
Yoruba: achievements of, 94;
   appeasing, 192; autonomy
   sought by, 199; defense
   of, 68; domination by,
   152–53; education, 93;
   future, determining own,
   141; gifts of, 168; Hausa-
   Fulani alliance, anticipated
   with, 157; hegemonic and
   counterhegemonic moves by,
   104; interests of, 153; isolating

and expurgating as other, 199–200; in Kaduna, 238; in Lagos, 90, 102; Lagos claimed by, 86, 100, 101, 102; Lagos influence of, 93; leadership of, 16, 128; nation, fiction of, 200; as nationalist movement leaders, 92; newspaper portrayal of, 136, 137; newspaper publicity enjoyed by, 93; Obasanjo, views on, 192; political elite, 282, 283; president, prospective, attitudes concerning, 164; region dominated by, 15; secession, potential by, 212; status of, 12; terminology referring to, 61, 65–66, 67; territory amalgamation without consent

of, 13; territory lost from, 50; troops, 141
Yoruba Empire, 200
"Yoruba lackeys" (term), 221
Yoruba-Igbo relations, 61–62, 94–95, 212
Yorubaland, metaphor for, 221
Young, Lagos colonial governor, 91, 306n37
Yusuf, Jolly Tanko, 152, 168

Zambia, 22
Zamfara, 206–7, 211
Zango-Kataf crisis, 157–58, 234–42, 255–56
Zaria, 237
Zweerde, Van Der, 287, 333n23